CW00392599

NEW INT
BIBLICAL (

Old Testament Editors,
Robert L. Hubbard Jr.
Robert K. Johnston

JOB

Old Testament Series

NEW INTERNATIONAL BIBLICAL COMMENTARY

JOB

GERALD H. WILSON

Based on the New International Version

Job
New International Biblical Commentary
© 2007 by Hendrickson Publishers, Inc.
P. O. Box 3473
Peabody, Massachusetts 01961-3473

First published jointly, 2007, in the United States by Hendrickson
Publishers and in the United Kingdom by the Paternoster Press.

Paternoster is an imprint of Authentic Media,
9 Holdom Avenue, Bletchley, Milton Keynes, MK1 1QR, UK
1820 Jet Stream Drive, Colorado Springs, CO 80921, USA
OM Authentic Media, Medchal Road, Jeedimetla Village,
Secunderabad 500 055, A.P., India
www.authenticmedia.co.uk
Authentic Media is a division of IBS-STL UK, a company limited by
guarantee (registered charity no. 270162).

Printed in the United States of America

First printing — May 2007

Library of Congress Cataloging-in-Publication Data

Wilson, Gerald Henry.
    Job / Gerald H. Wilson.
        p. cm. — (Old Testament series new international
biblical commentary ; 10)
    "Based on the New International Version."
    Includes bibliographical references and indexes.
    ISBN 978-1-56563-219-6 (alk. paper)
    1. Bible. O.T. Job—Commentaries. I. Title.
BS1415.53.W55 2007
223'.1077—dc22
                           2007001634

ISBN 978-1-56563-219-6 (U.S. softcover)

**British Library Cataloguing in Publication Data
A catalogue record for this book is available
from the British Library.**

ISBN 978-0-85364-731-7 (U.K. softcover)

Table of Contents

Foreword
New International Biblical Commentary

As an ancient document, the Old Testament often seems something quite foreign to modern men and women. Opening its pages may feel, to the modern reader, like traversing a kind of literary time warp into a whole other world. In that world sisters and brothers marry, long hair mysteriously makes men superhuman, and temple altars daily smell of savory burning flesh and sweet incense. There, desert bushes burn but leave no ashes, water gushes from rocks, and cities fall because people march around them. A different world, indeed!

Even God, the Old Testament's main character, seems a stranger compared to his more familiar New Testament counterpart. Sometimes the divine is portrayed as a loving father and faithful friend, someone who rescues people from their greatest dangers or generously rewards them for heroic deeds. At other times, however, God resembles more a cruel despot, one furious at human failures, raving against enemies, and bloodthirsty for revenge. Thus, skittish about the Old Testament's diverse portrayal of God, some readers carefully select which portions of the text to study, or they avoid the Old Testament altogether.

The purpose of this commentary series is to help readers navigate this strange and sometimes forbidding literary and spiritual terrain. Its goal is to break down the barriers between the ancient and modern worlds so that the power and meaning of these biblical texts become transparent to contemporary readers. How is this to be done? And what sets this series apart from others currently on the market?

This commentary series will bypass several popular approaches to biblical interpretation. It will not follow a *precritical* approach that interprets the text without reference to recent scholarly conversations. Such a commentary contents itself with offering little more than a paraphrase of the text with occasional supplements from archaeology, word studies, and classical theology. It mistakenly believes that there have been few insights into the Bible since Calvin or Luther. Nor will this series pursue an *anticritical* approach whose preoccupation is to defend the Bible against its detractors, especially scholarly ones. Such a commentary has little space left to move beyond showing why the Bible's critics are wrong to explaining what the biblical text means. The result is a paucity of vibrant biblical theology. Again, this series finds inadequate a *critical* approach that seeks to understand the text apart from belief in the meaning it conveys. Though modern readers have been taught to be discerning, they do not want to live in the "desert of criticism" either.

Instead, as its editors, we have sought to align this series with what has been labeled *believing criticism*. This approach marries probing, reflective interpretation of the text to loyal biblical devotion and warm Christian affection. Our contributors tackle the task of interpretation using the full range of critical methodologies and practices. Yet they do so as people of faith who hold the text in the highest regard. The commentators in this series use criticism to bring the message of the biblical texts vividly to life so the minds of modern readers may be illumined and their faith deepened.

The authors in this series combine a firm commitment to modern scholarship with a similar commitment to the Bible's full authority for Christians. They bring to the task the highest technical skills, warm theological commitment, and rich insight from their various communities. In so doing, they hope to enrich the life of the academy as well as the life of the church.

Part of the richness of this commentary series derives from its authors' breadth of experience and ecclesial background. As editors, we have consciously brought together a diverse group of scholars in terms of age, gender, denominational affiliation, and race. We make no claim that they represent the full expression of the people of God, but they do bring fresh, broad perspectives to the interpretive task. But though this series has sought out diversity among its contributors, they also reflect a commitment to a common center. These commentators write as "believing critics"—scholars who desire to speak for church and academy, for academy and church. As editors, we offer this series in devotion to God and for the enrichment of God's people.

ROBERT L. HUBBARD JR.
ROBERT K. JOHNSTON
Editors

Abbreviations

ANESTP	*The Ancient Near East: Supplementary Texts and Pictures Relating to the Old Testament.* Edited by J. B. Pritchard. Princeton: Princeton University Press, 1969
ANET	*Ancient Near Eastern Texts Relating to the Old Testament.* Edited by J. B. Pritchard. 3d ed. Princeton: Princeton University Press, 1969
BDB	Brown, F., S. R. Driver, and C. A. Briggs. *A Hebrew and English Lexicon of the Old Testament.* Repr. Peabody, Mass: Hendrickson, 2004
c.	century
ch(s).	chapter(s)
esp.	especially
ET	English translation
Gk.	Greek
HALOT	Koehler, L., W. Baumgartner, and J. J. Stamm. *The Hebrew and Aramaic Lexicon of the Old Testament.* Translated and edited under the supervision of M. E. J. Richardson. 4 vols. Leiden: Brill, 1994–1999
Heb.	Hebrew
ISBE	*International Standard Bible Encyclopedia.* Edited by G. W. Bromiley, et al. 4 vols. Grand Rapids: Eerdmans, 1979–1988
KJV	King James Version
lit.	literally
LXX	Septuagint
MT	Masoretic Text
NAB	New American Bible
NASB	New American Standard Bible
NIV	New International Version

NJB	New Jerusalem Bible
NKJV	New King James Version
NLT	New Living Translation
NRSV	New Revised Standard Version
NT	New Testament
OT	Old Testament
p(p).	page(s)
pl.	plural
REB	Revised English Bible
RSV	Revised Standard Version
sg.	singular
Syr.	Syrian
UT	C. H. Gordon. *Ugaritic Textbook.* 3 vols. Analecta Orientalia 38. Rome: Biblical Institute Press, 1998
v(v).	verse(s)
VT	*Vetus Testamentum*
YLT	Young's Literal Translation
ZAW	*Zeitschrift für die alttestamentliche Wissenschaft*

Introduction

Title

While the book of Job takes its name from its central character, there is no reason to assume that Job is the author of this work, since the text refers to him in the third person (except in the conversations quoted in the dialogues). As he is hardly known outside this book, we do not know much about who Job is. A single New Testament reference to Job (Jas. 5:11) describes his "perseverance," but adds little to our understanding. Two references in Ezekiel (14:14, 20) connect Job with two other ancient men of great renown and righteousness: Noah and Dan'el.[1] This connection highlights the righteous character of these three men and fits well with the emphasis in the first few chapters on Job's righteousness. What we know about the central character of this book, therefore, comes principally from details we find in the book itself: he is a righteous, faithful, wealthy Uzzite who is the father of many children and who enjoys great prominence among the non-Israelite "men of the East" (Job 1:1–5).

Dating

The dating of the book of Job is a complex issue about which there is little scholarly consensus. Scholars have fixed the date of the book variously from the patriarchal period (drawing on the picture of Job as a patriarchal clansman in ch. 1) to the postexilic period. While the association of Job with Noah and Dan'el in Ezekiel might seem to affirm an early date for the book, there is no reason to preclude the possibility of a much later literary expansion of an earlier tradition. Some point to the large number of Aramaisms in Job as evidence of a late origin in the Persian period. Others, who find evidence of Aramaic expressions much earlier in the history of the OT, discount Persian influence. Some also attribute the picture of *the* Satan in the prologue to the influence of Zoroastrian dualism. While there are scholars who ascribe certain related ideas and themes to a dependence on Second Isaiah, others understand Isaiah to be familiar with an earlier Job.[2]

The core message of the book, that it is necessary to endure faithfully in the face of extreme loss and suffering, is particularly apt to address the questions of the dislocated Diaspora community. This emphasis suggests, in my opinion, a late, rather than early, date for the final form of the book. Hartley and others resist an exilic date, suggesting that an author in that period would certainly have made plain the connections to the exile (Hartley, *Job*, pp. 17–20). They also would have expected an exilic author to acknowledge Israel's sin as the cause of exilic suffering—a circumstance that does not fit well with Job's claim of innocent suffering. It is difficult to second-guess the author of any book and conclude what one would *certainly* include. It may well be that the author so inhabited the presumed non-Israelite identity of Job and his friends that he did not mention the exile and left it to more subtle expression. As regards the acknowledgment of Israel's sin, it is clear from the shaping of the Psalter that there were those in Israel at certain times (perhaps as late as 300–200 B.C.) who did not unequivocally associate the exile with judgment for sin. Indeed Psalm 89, which concludes the earlier segment of the canonical collection (Pss. 2–89),[3] expresses no awareness of sin but takes God to task for his failure to keep his covenant promises to David and his descendants. This early Psalter collection represents a view that was in vogue in Israel sometime not long before 200 B.C. By this time, the subsequent generations of the Diaspora community who had not participated in the sinful excesses of the collapsing monarchy were desperately seeking to understand how to hang on to a God who seemed to have abandoned them among the nations. To such a community, Job's message would seem to resonate with particular power.

Any discussion of the dating of Job needs to take into consideration that the structure of the book implies different stages. It is quite probable that the narrative in the prose prologue-epilogue is much earlier than the poetic dialogue, monologue, wisdom poem, and theophany. Certainly the combination of these elements in the present canonical configuration represents a later movement to speak to a different context. There is no conclusive evidence to command assent to any particular date(s). A date for the final form in the exilic or postexilic period seems most appropriate. Regardless of the actual date of composition, the resonance of the primary message and themes of the book with the situation of the Diaspora community would have insured its preservation, transmission, and ultimate canonization.

The Wisdom Context

The book of Job falls squarely into that genre of biblical writing known as Wisdom literature. A brief discussion of the nature of biblical wisdom and the literature it produced is necessary in order to situate the book of Job within its appropriate context. Most generally, the biblical word for wisdom (Heb. *khokmah*) refers to the special abilities or characteristics of certain individuals. In this sense wisdom is what we might call "know-how"—practical skills and talents in areas as diverse as metal work, painting, agriculture, political scheming, and the like.

More specifically, biblical wisdom is a way of looking at life that seeks skill and mastery through reflection on observation and experience. Those who dedicate themselves to the life-long pursuit of such understanding are known as *sages* (Heb. *khakamim*). These sages collected their own insights, along with those of others, and handed down this instruction to future generations in an attempt to create a growing understanding and mastery of life. One of the primary means of transmitting knowledge from sage to sage (or age to age) was through proverbial aphorisms like those collected in Proverbs 10–31. These brief sayings encapsulate sagely observations on life in memorable form to be learned and followed by generations of students.

The underlying conviction of these proverbial statements and the worldview that produced them is this: those who seriously pursue wisdom will find it and thus gain mastery in life that will lead to blessing, satisfaction, and even prosperity. Those who resist the teaching of wisdom, on the other hand, are willful fools who will meet trouble and destruction. The following adage reflects this worldview, known as "retributive wisdom" or *retribution:* The wise prospers, while the fool perishes. (The biblical observation that one reaps what one sows also falls into the same category.)

While retributive wisdom carries an almost naïvely positive expectation, other forms of wisdom add balance to the equation. According to observation and experience, the hallmarks of the wisdom enterprise, wise and righteous persons do not always prosper, and the foolish and wicked often seem to avoid suffering and judgment. As a result, biblical wisdom also produced more pessimistic compositions that question the basic assumptions of retribution thinking—especially the belief that humans can discover and master wisdom through their own powers of observation and will subsequently experience blessing and prosperity.

The hard-eyed observations of "pessimistic wisdom" compare and contrast the assumptions of retribution in more expansive literary forms, including the extended discourses of Ecclesiastes and the dialogue/debate at the heart of Job. These discussions expose the weaknesses of retributive thinking and explore alternative worldviews that acknowledge the prosperity of the wicked, the oppression of the poor, and the suffering of the innocent. They also raise questions regarding the sovereignty and justice of God, who permits such circumstances to exist. In the end, however, these questioning forms of wisdom do not seek to undermine faith in God. Rather, they offer their own testimony to a continuing reliance on God and acknowledge the pain and confusion that inhabit the real world of the observant sage. Both Ecclesiastes and Job, after their devastating critiques of naïve retributive thinking, counsel readers that the only way forward is to remain in a deep relationship of absolute dependence on God (what Israel calls "fear of God"), acknowledging his sovereign freedom and admitting, along with Job, that knowing this God transcends (but does not remove!) the questions and doubts that diligent sages uncover in their searching.

In the biblical canon, pessimistic, questioning wisdom is allowed to stand in continuing tension with retributive wisdom. Neither form of wisdom subdues and vanquishes the other, but together both occupy the opposing extremities of orthodox faith. The book of Proverbs stands alongside Ecclesiastes and Job. The proverbs testify to the observed truths that commend the life of wisdom and righteous reliance on God over against the bankruptcy of wicked dependence on self-centered power and control. Questioning wisdom, however, cautions us against assuming a simple cause-and-effect relationship between our righteousness and the experience of prosperity. The righteous suffer, but this does not mean that they will not finally experience divine blessing, even if they experience extreme suffering like Job.

The book of Job reflects this pessimistic, questioning form of wisdom. Job reveals the failure of naïve assumptions of retribution as adequate explanations of the world. Job's own experience, as confirmed by the evaluation of God himself, demonstrates that the innocent righteous *do* suffer in the real world, and that God—whose sovereignty Job never questions—allows such suffering and injustice to go on in this world without clearly judging its perpetrators. Yet, the ultimate purpose of the book of Job is not to reject the validity of retribution or even to raise questions regarding the justice of God. The book finally counsels that maintaining a faithful relationship with God is the only adequate refuge in a world where suffering and injustice remain unavoidable realities.

The Text of the Book

The book of Job is by far one of the most difficult Hebrew texts in the OT. The textual notes that grace the pages of most honest translations of Job contain a multitude of references to obscure, difficult, unknown, and unintelligible Hebrew words and phrases. The difficulties do not undermine our confidence in the message of the book as a whole, but they do render precise interpretation of many passages difficult, if not impossible. While any given translation may obscure the issues by rendering opaque Hebrew into clear English, comparing different translations will often reveal where these problems lie—the extreme variations are due to the difficult Hebrew text behind them.

The difficulty of the text ought to recommend caution and humility in our interpretation of this book. Rather than understanding the text based on the meaning of words, often the interpreter draws conclusions concerning the meanings of obscure words and phrases from the larger framework of the surrounding text and the book as a whole. This may sometimes be the only way forward, but the danger is that it allows the interpreter's view to rule unchecked and to align meaning with predetermined understanding—thus the need for caution and humility.

The ancient versions of the book of Job, while occasionally useful, are often of little help in clarifying obscure words and details of the Hebrew text. Interestingly, the Greek translation (LXX) is considerably shorter than the Hebrew text (by about 400 lines!). Most scholars have concluded that the Greek is a shortened version of the Hebrew, rather than an older version of the text that was later expanded.[4] Often the LXX omits difficult or repetitious texts and on occasion appears theologically motivated in its alterations. The Aramaic Targum to Job generally follows the Hebrew text closely and expands at points with historical and theological explanations. The oldest such Targum, the fragmentary 11QtgJob from Qumran, is usually dated to the second-century B.C. This early paraphrase largely follows the Hebrew text. Other versions, including the Syrian Peshitta (fifth-century) and the Latin Vulgate (fourth-century) are translations from the Hebrew and occasionally offer insights to the original Hebrew. But, for the most part, the Masoretic Hebrew text, carefully preserved by generations of scribes, remains our primary witness to the text of Job.

The Structure of the Book

A few words are necessary about the structure of the book of Job and its various literary components, which have been the subject of considerable discussion throughout the history of interpretation. Some scholars have identified certain components as late intrusions into the original book that should be removed altogether. Others suggest considerable reordering of materials in order to bring the book in line with their understanding of its nature and purpose.

Prose prologue and epilogue. The major division of the book is between prose narrative and poetic discourse. The first two chapters and the final eleven verses of the final chapter (42:7–17) are prose narrative—enveloping the central poetic sections. The prose sections present a cohesive narrative about the loss and restoration of Job's family and possessions that (were the poetic center excised) would provide an effective cautionary tale encouraging righteous readers to endure suffering faithfully as a test of God, certain that their faithfulness will be rewarded by restoration. This morality narrative may well represent an early traditional story about Job that circulated independently from the poetic elements that now occupy the core of the book. As they now stand, however, the sections of the prose narrative function as prologue and epilogue to the poetic materials and serve a different purpose within the context of the whole canonical form of the book.

Poetic dialogue. The poetic discourse divides into several distinct sections, some of which may have existed independently before being brought together. The first of these elements is the extended poetic dialogue between Job and his three friends that begins with Job's desperate complaint in chapter 3 and continues through chapter 31 (with the exception of ch. 28, which will be considered separately below). Following Job's opening lament, these chapters of dialogue are organized into three cycles of debate between Job and his friends (chs. 4–14; 15–21; 22–31), in which each of Job's friends speaks in turn, followed immediately by a response from Job. The friends speak always in the same order—Eliphaz, Bildad, and then Zophar—except that in the third cycle of speeches, Bildad's speech is truncated (only 6 verses), Zophar does not appear at all, and Job's response to Bildad is considerably longer (6 chapters). Job's final speech concludes with a postscript (31:40c) indicating that, "The words of Job are ended." This signifies the completion of the dialogue cycle and Job's argument so that the reader does not anticipate further input from either the friends or Job.

A wisdom poem. In the middle of Job's extended last speech appears a beautiful poem in praise of the unsearchable nature of divine wisdom. The poem (ch. 28) is a skillfully constructed composition that contrasts the successful human search for hidden riches in inaccessible regions of the earth with the inability of human wisdom to search out and acquire true wisdom. All the industrious efforts of humans cannot find true wisdom, since the way to it is known only to God himself, who created it. As a result, humans are entirely dependent on divine revelation for any access to wisdom. The poem calls us, therefore, to adopt the "fear of God," which is the only sure path to wisdom. In its present position, the poem forms part of Job's discourse and provides a transition between his final response to his friends (chs. 26–27) and his conclusion, in which he expresses his desire for vindication and meeting with God (chs. 29–31). Most interpreters consider this poem an originally independent composition that was subsequently inserted into the Joban literary complex.

The poetic Elihu monologues. Immediately following Job's final speech (chs. 26–31) and its concluding postscript, six chapters of monologues from a previously unknown speaker, Elihu, appear rather unexpectedly. A prose introduction to these speeches (32:1–5) explains why Elihu has been invisible to this point—his humility and reticence to speak out in a meeting of older and more experienced sages. There are several striking elements to note concerning Elihu, however. First, Elihu is nowhere mentioned in the dialogue cycle, nor does notice of him appear in any other part of the book—even when the *three* friends are mentioned in the divine rebuke in 42:7–9. Second, Elihu's speeches break with the pattern established in the dialogue cycle in that there is no response from Job (nor is one anticipated after the postscript to his words in 31:40c). Elihu is also the only speaker, other than God and the narrator, to mention Job by name—and he does so a remarkable ten times in these six chapters. Finally, while Elihu employs the same type of formulas to introduce his speech as those found in the dialogue cycle, he uses them *inappropriately* on at least two occasions.[5]

The Elihu speeches begin with attempts to legitimate the words of this young sage (32:1–33:7), proceed to attack the claims of Job (33:7–35:16), and conclude with efforts to justify God and condemn Job (36:1–37:24). The speeches clearly show great familiarity with the dialogue cycles, presenting certain interpretations of arguments advanced by Job in response to the friends and seeking to counter them.

The theophanic appearance of God. After the monologues of Elihu end rather abruptly in 37:24, God suddenly appears on the scene, speaking out of a whirlwind in full theophanic glory. God's address ignores Elihu's contributions completely. The five chapters of divine speech (38–42) take the form of a rather bombastic interrogation of Job regarding his ability to understand the divine plan for creation or to exercise any modicum of control over it. There are two separate examinations of Job (38–39 and 40–41), and each concludes with an opportunity for Job to respond (40:1–5; 42:1–6). Both sections consist largely of a catalogue of the wonders of the physical creation and the marvelous wild creatures that inhabit it. Without the two sections containing Job's responses, these five chapters could represent an independent wisdom composition in praise of the wonderful works of God in his creation.

Questions Raised by the Structure of the Book

The complex structure of Job and the distinctive characteristics of its various structural components have raised questions among interpreters regarding both the literary unity of the canonical book and its intended meaning. What follows here is a consideration of the major questions and some of the possible interpretive responses.

Prose prologue and epilogue. The primary question concerning this "prose envelope" is whether it represents an originally independent unity. Without the poetic section separating them, these two prose elements provide a satisfying moral narrative about the need for enduring faith in the face of the test of extreme suffering. As a combined narrative, the prologue and epilogue speak rather hopefully to the suffering community of the postexilic Diaspora, admonishing them to continue to hold fast to their ancestral faith, even when it appears to hold no benefit. This narrative presents the view that Israel's tribulations are a test of her faithfulness. As Job holds on to his faith even to death and is ultimately rewarded by divine blessing that exceeds his former prosperity, so the text admonishes Diaspora Israel to remain faithful. It seems reasonable to assume that this complete narrative circulated independently at an earlier date and was later adapted as the external framework for the canonical book of Job. In our discussion of the significance of the canonical form below, we will return to the question of how the earlier narrative as prologue and epilogue functions in the final form of the book.

The poetic dialogue. If the external prose frame of the canonical Job once functioned independently, can the same be said of the poetic dialogue between Job and his three friends? The dialogue is certainly a cohesive composition with a clear structure and thematic development. As a freestanding literary work, the dialogue reflects critically on the weakness of the naïve retribution theology presented by the three friends. The critique is based primarily on Job's experience of innocent suffering and also on extensive observation of the ongoing prosperity of the wicked, who openly reject God and actively oppress the poor. All of the friends' attempts to apply reverse retributive thinking in order to convict Job of sin on the basis of his suffering ring hollow. And, in the end, the arguments of the friends dwindle into silence, thereby effectively defeating the proponents of retribution.

Some interpreters redistribute the lengthy final speech of Job in order to fill out the truncated speech of Bildad, and to supply the missing contribution of Zophar. This completes the three cycles of debate in a more balanced fashion and undermines any apparent victory won by Job's anti-retribution critique. Such a format in an original and independent dialogue would have explored the tensions between a theoretical retribution theology and the experience of innocent suffering in the real world. We will consider the effect of placing the unbalanced dialogue within the larger framework of the final form in the next section.

Since non-biblical texts evidencing a similar critique of retribution theology are known among the broader wisdom traditions of the ancient Near East,[6] it might seem proper to assume an intended audience from an earlier, even monarchical, date. But even if its origin is early, the dialogue provides a later alternative to the predominant Deuteronomic stream of thought that played such a significant role in shaping canonical scripture. This validation of innocent suffering, and the undermining of a strictly retributive worldview, resonates with the experience of the later generations of the Diaspora community, who were seeking to live faithfully in the midst of escalating pressures to compromise ancestral traditions through cultural assimilation in the foreign lands where they lived. Thus the adaptation of an earlier exploratory dialogue to speak to a later Diaspora context is not surprising.

The poetic Elihu monologues. The exceptional characteristics of the Elihu chapters strongly suggest that these monologues are a later addition to the poetic core of the book. However, the obvious dependence on the poetic dialogues makes it unlikely that this section ever functioned independently. The Elihu monologues were probably written in response to the dialogues and appended to provide a modified interpretation of them. The issue that arises, then, is whether the Elihu speeches should be removed in order to recover the original meaning of the book.

If these chapters were omitted, the theophanic appearance of God in chapters 38–41 would immediately follow Job's concluding demands for an audience with God (chs. 29–31). This would give a whole new tenor to the interaction between God and Job—God would be responding almost in haste to Job's demands rather than delaying significantly to speak according to his own timing. We will consider below the effect of inserting the Elihu speeches in their present position.

The wisdom poem. Most interpreters consider the poem which comprises chapter 28 to be an independent wisdom poem that was later inserted in its present position. The poem serves here, however, as part of Job's final expression of his claims. Some scholars would remove the poem from its canonical position and either omit it altogether or relocate it as part of the speech of another. Clines, for example, places chapter 28 as the conclusion of the Elihu monologue. Since there is no textual evidence for such a move, the interpreter justifies this proposal by evaluating the poem's fit (or lack thereof) with the expression of Job (and other speakers) in the rest of the book. Other interpreters leave chapter 28 in its canonical position and seek to explain its literary function in the canonical composite.

The poetic theophany. The theophany of God in chapters 38–41 may represent an adaptation of an earlier independent composition. These chapters refer to God with the Tetragrammaton (*yhwh*)—the peculiarly Israelite name for God. This shift clearly sets the section apart from the earlier dialogues and Elihu speeches where the deity is called *'eloah*—a form of the generic designation "God" with special associations with the region of Edom.[7] The Tetragrammaton links the theophany with the prose prologue/epilogue which also uses the name *yhwh*. We will consider this link further in our discussion below on the final form of the book.

Without connecting links to the Joban story, chapters 38–41 offer a cohesive reflection on the sovereignty of God over his creation. Such a text could be the result of independent wisdom reflection on the relation of God to his creation. However, there is nothing to indicate that this section was not composed specifically to occupy its present position in the book of Job.

Purpose of the Book and Final Form

Although the book of Job contains many distinctive components, some of which may have circulated earlier as independent compositions, there is an intentional editorial unity with a cohesive purpose and message in the canonical form of the book. How do these diverse elements work together in the final canonical form of the book of Job? We begin with the meaning of the final form, followed by a more thorough consideration of the related issues with details of the evidence.

First, in its original, independent state, the poetic dialogue wrestles with the incomprehensibility of human suffering in relation to a retributive worldview. The outcome of the debate is inconclusive—especially if one redistributes the extended final speech of Job to create a balanced and complete third cycle (see the discussion of "The poetic dialogue" above). While the testimony of Job may be more persuasive in this reconstruction, there is no definitive rejection of the theology of retribution. When, however, the prose prologue is separated from the longer morality narrative—with its understanding of suffering as a divine test that the innocent must endure—and is placed before the poetic dialogue, the character of both segments changes decidedly. As prologue, the opening narrative removes from discussion several issues that figure prominently in the debate section. No longer can the reader wonder about the character of Job—whether he has sinned or is innocent—as both the narrator and God unequivocally describe him as one "blameless and upright; feared God and shunned evil" (1:1; compare 1:8). In addition, the prologue leaves the reader in no doubt regarding the reason for Job's suffering; it is a divinely sanctioned test of his willingness to endure faithfully without payment. With these issues settled from the outset, the dialogue can no longer be about the *reason* for innocent suffering—we *know* why Job is suffering. Nor can the debate actively pursue the question whether retributive theology is an adequate understanding of the world. We know that Job is innocent and yet suffers extremely; a strict interpretation of retribution is not able to illuminate his circumstance or that of any innocent sufferer.

The reader of the final form, then, must look for another issue to drive the dialogue. *The* Satan raises this question in his discussions with God: Is it possible to hold on to faith in God without receiving benefit? The upshot of the double tests Job endures in the first two chapters is to show that, indeed, it is possible for a human like Job to continue to live in fear of God even when he loses everything and stands on the brink of death without hope of restoration. Since Job's faithfulness appears to answer *the* Satan's question in chapters 2 and 3, what is left for the dialogue to accomplish? The dialogue states the issue in its most extreme form: Is it possible to endure, holding on to God, even if one dies *without being acknowledged as righteous?* As the dialogue progresses, the friends increasingly move to consider Job's suffering as the deserved divine punishment for some sin. The reader knows from the prologue that this cannot be the case, since both God and the narrator affirm Job's blameless character.

As the friends become increasingly suspicious, Job's concern shifts from maintaining his own integrity before them to seeking some public vindication by God. The wisdom poem of chapter 28 marks the transition. As Job's speech, it declares the inability of human endeavor to ferret out divine wisdom and points instead to the adoption of a relationship of absolute dependence on God. From here to the end of Job's speeches he emphasizes more and more his desire for vindication. He has given up on convincing his friends, it seems, and expects to die without them having acknowledged his righteousness. He is willing to accept this, but he wants to have his day in court, knowing that God will have to publicly admit: "He is a righteous man!" This is the import of Job's final plea in chapter 31, and his words end without any resolution of this question.

At this point Elihu intervenes, rejecting the idea of Job's righteous character and affirming that his suffering is God's statement of Job's guilt. God will not respond to Job's summons, Elihu claims, because God has already rendered definitive judgment on Job's sin through the suffering he is experiencing. The Elihu speeches have the additional literary effect of delaying God's appearance. This delay heightens the dramatic tension of the story, leaving the first-time reader to wonder whether God will arrive or not. Of course, in subsequent readings we know that God will come and thus read Elihu's speeches with that insight in mind. From the prologue we know that Elihu is wrong about Job's guilt, and from the theophany we know he is also wrong about God's judgment on Job. Elihu's final words in chapter 37 ironically rely on theophanic storm imagery to proclaim the awesome majesty of God to whom Job must submit. These words unwittingly prepare for the actual appearance of God in chapter 38.

The appearance of God in the whirlwind puts the lie to Elihu's claims that Job's suffering is God's final judgment against his sin. The introductory formula to God's initial speech mentions Job as the object of these words. The earlier introductory formulas in the dialogue and Elihu sections never mention the recipient, since the pattern of give and take is clear from the context. Here after Elihu's speeches, however, it is necessary to indicate that God is addressing Job and not Elihu. We know, therefore, that, at least in the final form, the Elihu speeches are part of the growing composition (even if the book does not refer to them at any other point).

In his speeches, God ignores Elihu and does not take sides in the argument with the three friends. Instead God examines Job and his understanding of God's sovereign control of creation. Some read the rather harsh and sarcastic language of the divine monologues as a rejection of Job and a rebuke of his arguments. This interpretation, however, conflicts with God's later affirmation of Job's words in 42:7–8. How, then, ought one to understand God's bombastic hammering of Job? The overwhelming appearance of God seems an intentional move on the part of the author to represent the absolute otherness of the sovereign creator God, who is beyond all human knowing. How else is it possible to describe a God who is so removed from human experience and unknowable and yet who condescends to come in response to Job's desire for meeting? God's appearance overwhelms Job. He is made small before God not because he is sinful or in the wrong, but because *all humans* recede to insignificance in the presence of

God (e.g., Ps. 8). The very presence of God threatens humans with catastrophe, and yet God makes a way for humans to stand in his presence without destruction (e.g., Exod. 33:18–23).

Thus, Job fades away before the presence of God not because he is sinful, but because he can do no other in the face of holy God. Job's first response to God's examination (40:1–5) is in effect a *non*-response. Overwhelmed by direct experience of God himself, Job's words fail. This initial response functions as a moment of relief in the divine attack and creates dramatic tension for the second wave of divine testing. There is no resolution here, only a delay that points the reader to the final response of Job (42:1–5) for resolution.

And how does God appear in these chapters? The God of Job 38–42 is mysterious, distant (and yet near!), fearsomely other than humans. He is the powerful creator and sustainer of the universe who is still in control. The inability of humans to exercise any control over nature or the wild animals highlights the absolute sovereignty of God over all things. As Job is forced to acknowledge his own lack of understanding and power, he is forced to submit to the wisdom and power of God. We see the mystery of God in his essential otherness, but also in the reality that holy God permits evil to exist in this world even in the face of righteousness. Humans are unable to fully understand what God is about in this world and so God is able to act freely, limited only by his essential holy character. We have the sense that in this divine encounter Job learns (as does the psalmist) that God is "not a God who takes pleasure in evil; with you the wicked cannot dwell" (Ps. 5:4). Because God is at once holy and free, he cannot be called to account by humans, because they have insufficient understanding to judge (Job 42:1–3). God cannot be coerced into action, nor is he obligated to respond to human demands and pleas.

The divine appearance in overwhelming power essentially ignores Job's questions and demands. God never explains the reason for innocent suffering. The reader knows Job suffers as a test, but Job never learns this. He is forced to continue (as are we!) with mystery. Neither does God seek to justify his actions or clarify his purposes. God simply appears and places Job (and the friends—and you and me) in a position of powerless surrender to the free grace of God at work in the world. There is no hope of restoration here, nor is there any offer of personal vindication for Job. There is no marvelous "Ah ha!" experience of understanding. Job still suffers, his friends still consider him a sinner, and he is still unable to understand why he suffers and why God permits evil to plague the world.

Job does not receive answers or understanding in this encounter, but rather God himself! Despite the suffering and mystery, the powerless inability to control oneself or one's world, God is still worth holding onto in a relationship of absolute dependence (which is the fear of God). Job's experience, then, pushes *the* Satan's question to the limit. Job has lost all of his possessions, wealth, family, health, and friends. He stands at the brink of extinction with no one to believe in his righteousness. And yet Job is willing to submit to this God who has come to him in overwhelming power and freedom. We need to remember that when Job submits in 42:1–6 he has no inkling of what is to come in the epilogue. He has no hint of God's coming affirmation (42:7–8) or of the abundant restoration of all he has lost (42:10–15). He submits not because he recognizes his sin, but because he cannot but recognize that God is the ultimate foundation of all existence and worthy in himself of continued relationship.

When Job does at last submit (42:1–6), there is no clear indication he is admitting sin. Instead, his motivation is a new and direct understanding of God as a result of the theophany: "My ears had heard of you but now my eyes have seen you" (42:5). This new understanding of God leads Job to regret his former brash insinuations about God. And so Job changes his opinion about God, his understanding of the deity, rather than repenting of a named sin (42:6), and with this new understanding Job also lays down his need for personal vindication. This new experience of God— overwhelming as it is—is enough. Job is willing to lose everything, to suffer, and to die, even without any hope of justification. But he is *not* willing to give up on the God who has come to him in power and grace. Job's submission decisively answers the question of *the* Satan and wraps up the core message of the book.

How, then, are we to understand the epilogue that follows this conclusion? God first rebukes the three friends and affirms Job (42:7–8). God thereby affirms Job's speeches as relating truth about God in the world. We must therefore view the friends' words about God—and the naïve retributive theology that governs their thinking—as false. So deep is their failure that they must make sin offerings and seek (in the greatest irony!) intercession from the one they had sought to condemn as a sinner.

In the second part of the epilogue—*after* Job's decision to submit and lay down his quest for vindication—God restores

Job's fortunes. Expectation of restoration in no way motivates Job's change. Neither is there any indication that God intends the restoration as a response to the faithfulness of Job. Such a connection is unlikely, since it would seriously undermine the critique of retribution that occupied such an important place in the dialogue section. In addition, according to God's freedom (as established in the theophany section) God can choose to restore or not to restore Job's fortunes. So, rather than a retributive response to Job's faithfulness, the restoration is a free and gracious gift of God.

Finally, we need to remember that Job's loss and suffering have been, from the very beginning, a *test*. Once Job completes the test, having held faithfully onto God in the face of utter loss, the restoration of the epilogue amounts to a "resetting of the clock"—God is free to return Job to his pre-test circumstances, should God choose to do so. And "free" is the operative word here, since God is under no obligation to restore Job. This restoration was certainly a part of the originally independent prose narrative, with its exhortation to remain faithful in the face of extreme suffering. In that context the restoration might have been understood as a divine reward for faithful living. But in the canonical form of the whole book of Job the issues shift and become more complex, and we must read them accordingly.

Notes

---

1. While Noah is the righteous man God chose to survive the flood, Dan'el is most likely *not* the OT personality Daniel. Scholars more commonly identify Dan'el with the righteous man from the Ugaritic narrative of Aqhat. The name in the book of Daniel is spelled differently (*daniyʾel*) than the Dan'el mentioned in Ezekiel (*daniʾel*).

2. See the discussions in J. Hartley, *Job*, pp. 17–20, and M. H. Pope, *Job*, pp. xxx–xxxvii, for more complete information.

3. See G. H. Wilson, pp. 229–46.

4. See the discussion in Hartley, *Job*, pp. 3–4, and Pope, *Job*, pp. xxxix–xli, for further details.

5. See the discussion in §§112, 114, below.

6. See "Sumerian Job" and "Pessimistic Dialogue between Master and Servant" in Pritchard, pp. 437–38 and 589–91.

7. See the discussion in Additional Notes §157, below.

§1 Introducing Job (Job 1:1–5)

1:1 / The first chapter serves as a prose prologue to the dialogue sections that form the core of the book. The focus from the very first word is on the main character. Hebrew word order (lit., "a man there was in the land of Uz") intentionally emphasizes the **man,** Job. This word order signals that the reader should pay particularly close attention here to the introduction of this man and his circumstances, for he will play an important role in what follows.

Because the OT elsewhere associates Uz with Edom, the words **in the land of Uz** do more than locate Job geographically; they associate his story and the book's wisdom with *non-Israelite* wisdom. It should not surprise us that Israel included foreign wisdom texts in its Scriptures. Wisdom is a peculiarly universal take on life that frequently seems to stand outside the particular religious belief system of the sage. Since wisdom analyzes the observations and experiences of life rather than the special revelations of God that make up the beliefs and expectations of the Torah and Israel's covenant faith, wisdom observations could pass without prejudice across national boundaries in the ancient Near East. Israel is aware of foreign wisdom (Gen. 41; Jer. 49:7; Dan. 1–2) and appreciates it (1 Kgs. 4:30; Ezek. 28:12).

Although Job's story and words are non-Israelite in origin, his experience and concerns are universal and so have appealed to those of many nationalities and faiths throughout the centuries. In the Wisdom literature of ancient Israel, this material speaks to Israel's particular concerns—especially during the period of the exilic Diaspora. The biblical text clearly has resisted any temptation to cloak Job in the guise of Israelite respectability, and has allowed him, rather, to stand as an example of a wise man by referring to him as "the greatest man among all the people of the East." This suggests that his narrative is intended, from the outset, to have significance beyond the narrow national confines of Israel—however broadly conceived—and is understood to speak to the deepest issues of the human condition.

Whose name was Job. The similarity of Job's name (*ʾiyob*) to the Hebrew word for "enemy; opponent" (*ʾoyeb*) has led some to suggest a symbolic interpretation of the name. In this view, which undermines the historicity of the book's central character, Job is the literarily conceived "opponent" who confronts God. There are examples of the name in various forms in early ancient Near Eastern texts, however, so a symbolic understanding of the name is not *necessary*. It is perfectly reasonable to conclude that the name of this individual was Job. This ought not to obscure the fact, however, that the narrative at different points exploits the name and its meaning to emphasize the hostility between Job and his God. In 13:24, for example, Job considers God an "enemy" (*ʾoyeb*) and treats him as an "opponent" (*tsar*) in 16:9 and 19:11.

The resumptive phrase **this man was** repeats the opening words with only slight variation and reestablishes that we are to focus on this man, Job—and not his location or his name. Three descriptive phrases then emphasize Job's integrity, which, as we will see, dominates the rest of the book's discussion and argument. First, Job is **blameless and upright.** The Hebrew for "blameless" (*tam*) describes not sinless perfection, but a person who is "whole" and "complete" and who has taken pains to maintain right relationships with God and others. In Psalm 19:13, the psalmist equates "blamelessness" with avoiding "great transgression." Israelite faith assumed the sinful nature of humans, and the sacrificial system provided a way to break down the barrier between sinners and a holy God. The "blameless" person was the one who took measures to restore and maintain right relation with God. The Hebrew term translated "upright" (*yashar*) has the sense of "straightness" or "directness." Job is not twisted, crooked, or convoluted in his dealings with God and humans. Rather, he is straightforward and direct in deed and speech. These two words occur repeatedly throughout the book—both together and separately—to emphasize and reemphasize the integrity of Job that is at the core of the book's discussion and message.

As well as being able to maintain right relationship with God and straight dealings with fellow humans, Job also **feared God.** This invisible, inward relationship to God is at the core of Israelite faith and practice. According to the sages, the "fear of the LORD" is the starting point of true knowledge (Prov. 1:7a), and true wisdom leads one to "fear God and keep his commandments"—the essential duty of all humanity (Eccl. 12:13). Fear of Yahweh is more than simple terror (see, e.g., Exod. 20:20), or even reverent awe at the "otherness" of the deity. It is the appropriate humility with which humans recognize and accept their absolute dependence on God for life, forgiveness, restoration, and salvation. Abraham is said to "fear Yahweh" when he is willing to sacrifice his only son, Isaac, trusting that God will still fulfill his promise of descendants (Gen. 22). That Job "feared God" indicates far more than that he paid scrupulous attention to religious piety and was straight in his dealings with others. The foundation of Job's outer piety is complete trust and reliance on God. The events that follow will put this inward attitude to the test.

Because of Job's trust in God, he **shunned evil**. Relying on God and being firmly established on the "way" of obedience, Job was able to avoid those tempting side-paths that lead to sin and disorientation. Job, then, is like the "blessed" one in Psalm 1:1 who will not walk, stand, or take up residence with those persons who characterize the God-forsaking life of evil (the "wicked," "sinners," and "mockers").

1:2–3 / Job is not only righteous, but he is wealthy as well. He has **seven sons and three daughters**. Seven, made up of four (the points of the compass and thus the earth) and three (indicating divinity or the heavens), is the number of completeness, of all heaven and earth. Job, then, is blessed with a perfect complement of sons and daughters.

His wealth is no less complete, consisting of massive herds including **seven thousand sheep** and **three thousand camels**. Together Job's herds add up to ten thousand, as do his yokes of **oxen** (500) and **donkeys** (500). Job also commands the services of a **large number of servants**. The numbers do not lie! This man was so blessed that the narrator sums up his stature with unrivaled superlatives: **He was the greatest man among all the people of the East.**

1:4–5 / A single example of his almost compulsive caution and scrupulous attention to religious detail illustrates Job's piety. Job's sons and daughters engage in a continuing round of feasting, to which Job responds with concern and religious care. The word for **feasts**, *mishte*, comes from the root *shatah*, "drink." Together with the emphasis on the sisters being invited **to eat and drink** with their brothers (see also 1:13; 18), the implication is that drinking was the most prominent feature of these gatherings.

While these are probably joyous celebrations of sibling unity there is certainly nothing religious about them, and it is striking that there is no mention of the brothers inviting Job and his wife. Had Job been present at the feasts, he would not have had to wonder whether his children had offended God in their inebriation. After each feast, Job **would send** (another indication he was not himself present) **and have them purified,** performing ritual actions to bring them into a state of holiness fit for service to God. The **burnt offering** he offered on behalf of each child was an ʿolah, or "fully burned" offering, used most often to atone for sin and restore right relationship (see, e.g., Num. 29:36; also Job 42:8).

Job performed this sacrificial ritual **early in the morning** as a sign of his seriousness and diligence, not allowing anything to intrude to inhibit his purpose. He was concerned for the spiritual welfare of his children, who may have **sinned and cursed God** during their festivities. The sin of cursing God, of course, plays an important role in the book of Job and becomes the crux of the test proposed by the Satan later in this same chapter: will a suffering Job curse God to his face as the Satan suggests (1:11; 2:5)? Here Job takes great care to respond with effective sacrificial precautions to even a hint of a possible curse (**in their hearts**). Verse 5 concludes with the assurance that such scrupulousness characterized Job's **regular custom.**

Additional Notes §1

1:1 / The Hebrew word order in Esther (2:5) gives similar weight to the central character, Mordecai. Lit.: "a man, a Jew, there was in Susa the capital." See also Nathan's rebuke of David (2 Sam. 12:1). Lit.: "Two men there were in a single city."

The **land of Uz** occurs elsewhere only in Jer. 25:20, in a list of foreign dignitaries ("the kings of Uz"), and in Lam. 4:21, which links it with the land of Edom. Uz is a personal name in genealogies in Gen. 10:23; 22:21; 36:28; 1 Chr. 1:17, 42. Two of these passages, Gen. 36:28 and 1 Chr. 1:42, relate Uz to Edom (in lists of descendants of the Horite kings of Seir/Edom). The final two chapters of Proverbs bear introductory superscriptions (30:1; 31:1) attributing the material to non-Israelite sages—Agur and Lemuel. Both of these superscriptions use the term massaʾ, which often describes a prophetic "oracle." However, since "king" Lemuel is unknown among the kings of Israel and Judah some have concluded that the term massaʾ here is a place name, and Lemuel is "king of Massaʾ,"

a foreigner. If this is the case, then Agur by analogy is most likely a foreigner as well. The NIV follows the prophetic, rather than geographic, interpretation. The literary relationship between Prov. 22:17–24:22 and the Egyptian wisdom text of Amenemopet also demonstrates that the editors of the Wisdom literature were not afraid to adapt such texts to their own beliefs and purposes. For an ET of the Amenemopet text, see "The Instruction of Amen-em-Opet," in *ANET*, pp. 421–25.

Other, less persuasive suggestions for a symbolic rendering of the name **Job** include: "the penitent one" (compare the Arabic ʾwb, "return, repent"), foreshadowing Job's dramatic shift toward the end of the book; and "Where is my [divine] father?" (ʾayya-ʾabum), a possible reference to Job's fierce determination to call God out of hiding and into public confrontation. See the discussion in Hartley, *Job*, p. 66.

Blameless and upright occur together only three times in Job (and nowhere outside this book), always describing Job (1:1; 1:8; 2:3). The Hebrew *tam* appears at Job 1:1, 8; 2:3; 8:20; 9:20, 21, 22—almost half of its total occurrences in Scripture. All but 8:20 either confirm or protest the integrity of Job (similarly, see also the adjectival form *tamim* in 12:4).

Proverbs 1:7 employs the more particular phrase "fear of Yahweh," where the distinctive name of Israel's covenant God appears. On the other hand, Ecclesiastes uses the more generic designation ʾelohim, "God." The reference in Eccl. 12:13 to "keep his commandments" makes it clear, however, that it is Yahweh who is intended in both instances.

1:3 / **People of the East** suggests again that Job is not an Israelite. The "East" (Heb. *qedem*) is for Israel a description of what lies "before" (*qedem*) one when facing the rising sun. By extension, the term also describes the lands on the "other side" (to the east) of the Jordan to the borders of Mesopotamia.

§2 In the Presence of Yahweh (Job 1:6–12)

1:6 / Having established the character of Job on the basis of social reputation (1:1), evidence of divine blessing (1:2–3), and demonstrable piety (1:4–5), the narrative takes a darker turn to reveal hidden circumstances affecting Job. **One day** is not just *any day* or a day selected at random, but actually *the* day in Hebrew. It probably indicates a particular day set in advance for a formal gathering when, unknown to Job or any other human, a meeting takes place in which the children of God **came to present themselves before the LORD** in order to report on their activities. The NIV's translation of *bene haʾelohim* as **angels** (generally Heb. *malʾak*) is unusual. These are better understood as the "children of God," or divine beings who carry out the will and purposes of Yahweh, the God of Israel.

1:7 / Among these divine functionaries is found **Satan**, who is not distinguished from the other "children" as an intruder or interloper. The NIV has chosen (probably for theological reasons) to translate the Hebrew *hassatan* as the name Satan rather than as the title that the presence of the definite article (*ha*) suggests—"*the* Accuser." Although we can perhaps see in this text the seeds of Satan—the rebellious angel later described as the spiritual enemy of God—*the* Satan here appears merely as one of the functionaries of Yahweh whose role seems to be **roaming through the earth** in order to test the reality of human faith in God. *The* Satan takes his place among the children of God and is able to act only within the restriction Yahweh places on him.

1:8 / According to this understanding of Satan, the testing of Job cannot be seen as the result of a battle between the hostile will of Satan and God in which the innocent human Job is trapped and battered. Rather, it is clear that Yahweh is always in control and that the test proceeds with his knowledge and permission. In fact, Yahweh initiates the discussion when he trots Job out as the epitome of human righteousness, using the terms from verse 1 to characterize Job: **blameless and upright, a man who fears God and shuns evil.**

God's description of Job in these terms has two effects. On the one hand it confirms the public acclamation of Job's righteousness with which the book begins. And this confirmation is incontrovertible in that it comes from the highest, most reliable source possible: the mouth of God himself. The reader is aware of this divine affirmation, but Job is not. Thus the reader is able, throughout the book, to return to the solid ground of Job's innocence in the face of Job's increasingly radical rhetoric and his friends' determination to convict him of sin.

On the other hand, the fact that God affirms Job's righteousness directly to *the* Satan, *the Accuser,* the very one responsible for testing the validity of human protestations of faith, has the effect of issuing a challenge that almost cannot go unaccepted. What is an Accuser expected to do, but to *accuse* and propose the most strenuous test of faith possible. That is exactly what *the* Satan does.

1:9 / *The satan* responds to God's strong affirmation of Job's outstanding character by proposing a test of Job's apparently impeccable faith. Job's piety is suspect, says *the* Satan, because God has always given him protection and abundant blessing. Job does not **fear God for nothing** but because he "gets the goods." The phrase rendered "fear God" is the Hebrew *yareʾ ʾelohim*—the foundational attitude of humility and utter dependence on God that defines true faith in Israel's understanding. "For nothing" is the Hebrew *khinnam,* meaning "for no compensation; without cause." There *is* a cause-and-effect relation, *the* Satan suggests, between human righteousness and divine blessing, but it is the opposite of the relationship that the common theology of retribution presupposes. It is not that those who are righteous receive the blessing of security and prosperity, but that those who are secure and prosperous have every good reason to demonstrate their piety in order to maintain their comfortable state. This seems to suggest that we can never measure *true piety* by wealth, prosperity, or security, but *only* by poverty, suffering, and want. Unless Job (or *any* professed believer) is proven to serve God "for nothing," there is no certainty that his righteousness is grounded in the fear of God alone.

1:10 / Job is pious, says *the* Satan, because he receives blessing from God. God protects all Job has by putting a protective

hedge of thorny bushes around his possessions and family. It is
still possible to see such thorny hedges topping the walls of
sheepfolds in Israel and the West Bank. The thorns protect the
sheep and goats by discouraging their escape and by hindering
the entry of predators. A cynical observer could see Job's cautious
sacrifices (v. 5) as just such a hedge to insure that no thoughtless
impropriety on the part of his inebriated children would undermine Job's continuing prosperity and blessing.

1:11 / Having raised the question of the reality of Job's
righteousness, *the* Satan proposes the only kind of test that can
prove the case. This is not a wager, since neither party will gain
anything. In fact, the test in no way benefits either God or Job—
who both know and affirm Job's righteousness—nor does it benefit *the* Satan, who passes immediately from the scene at the end of
2:7. Rather, the test is solely for the *reader*, who alone is left wondering if it is possible to "fear God for nothing." If God will **stretch
out** his **hand and strike everything he has,** the truth will be
known. Three passages outside of Job employ the same Hebrew
verb, *shlkh*, to describe God stretching out his hand. In Exodus
3:20 and 9:15, God declares his intent to "stretch out" his hand and
strike the Egyptians with plagues to secure the release of his
people. In Psalm 138:7, the psalmist expresses confidence that
God will "stretch out" his hand to turn aside the anger of the
psalmist's foes. In all of these cases this verb describes God's
power unleashed against his enemies and the enemies of his
people. What *the* Satan suggests is that God take up a hostile position against the one who is his "servant" and treat Job instead as
an enemy. (For a discussion of curse here see Additional Notes §3,
on v. 21, below.)

1:12 / One might take God's reply to *the* Satan—the man
is in your hands—as a passive expression of divine permission
which protects God from participation in the suffering of Job by
allowing *the* Satan to do the dirty work. But verse 11 has already
made it clear that *the* Satan is only implementing the power of
God who will, by permitting the agency of *the* Satan, "stretch out"
his hand to strike Job's family and possessions. God's response is
the equivalent of saying "Let the test begin!" And *the* Satan departs **from the presence of the LORD** to carry out the will and purpose of God.

Additional Notes §2

1:7 / We also see *the* Satan's role in testing human faith in 1 Chr. 21:1 (see also 2 Sam. 24:1), where he appears to be inciting David to take a census of fighting men (an action for which God punishes Israel later in the chapter).

1:10 / Based on the agrarian function of the literal thorny hedge, it is probably no coincidence that the rabbis came to call such careful distancing of oneself from any possibility of error, as Job demonstrates in v. 5, "putting a hedge around the law" (*seyag lattorah;* see Mishnah *Pirke Avot* 1:1; 3:14; *Bavli Yebamoth* 90b = *Sanhedrin* 46a).

§3 The First Test: Loss and Destruction (Job 1:13–22)

1:13–19 / The test commences with the rapid-fire destruction of all that Job has experienced as divine blessing up to this point. The destruction proceeds in reverse order to the introduction of Job's possessions, in a sort of *chiastic* literary structure (in which elements are stated in one line and then reversed in the second). First **the Sabeans,** raiders from the southern reaches of the Arabian Peninsula, carry off **oxen** and **donkeys** and kill **servants.** The **fire of God** then destroys **sheep** and **servants,** and **Chaldeans** carry off **camels** and kill more **servants.** There is artful variation here in splitting the destruction of the sheep and camels into two independent episodes. Finally, Job's children die when the house where they were feasting collapses in a **mighty wind.** The repeated transitions between reports, **while he was still speaking,** emphasize the rapidity with which these disastrous events occur. The constellation of events leaves no possibility of happenstance and clearly indicates the presence of God's hand in the destruction.

1:20–22 / Job's response to these horrific losses is immediate and completely in character with his proclaimed righteousness. He **tore his robe and shaved his head** as public signs of mourning. He then **fell to the ground** not as another sign of his agony of grief, but **in worship** (the usual translation of the Hebrew verb *shkhh,* which in the Hitpael stem, as here, regularly means "to prostrate oneself before God in worship").

Job's spoken response is of the utmost significance at this juncture, because the reader, having been alerted by *the* Satan's prediction in 1:11, is waiting to learn whether Job will "curse God." Instead, Job's words in the face of devastating loss mirror his piety. First, he renounces any claim on all that had been his (**Naked I came . . . naked I will depart**). Second, Job affirms the freedom of Yahweh to give and take as he chooses (**The LORD**

gave and the LORD **has taken away).** Job concludes with exactly the opposite response to that predicted by *the* Satan: **may the name of the** LORD **be** *blessed.* The NIV's translation here **(be praised)** obscures the essential tension between *the* Satan's prediction and Job's actual response. In both cases the Hebrew verb used is *brk,* "bless." In verses 5 and 11, the biblical editor's hesitation to use either of the normal words for "curse" (Heb. *ʾrr,* or *qll*) to describe human action toward God has led to the substitution of the verb *brk,* "bless," as a circumlocution. While *the* Satan says, "he will *bless* God," he means "he will *curse* God" (see also, e.g., Ps. 10:3). Here in verse 21, *the* Satan's anticipation that Job will "curse" God is confounded when Job instead "blesses" him. Of course, in light of the euphemistic use of "bless" to mean "curse" (1:5, 11), Job's statement here must be read carefully in context for the reader to determine Job's true intent. The decisive clues are found in the worshipful stance of verse 20 and in the concluding summary of verse 22: **In all this, Job did not sin by charging God with wrongdoing.** If blessing meant cursing here, the narrative would end at verse 21.

This concluding exoneration of Job, innocent of any "sin," brings us full circle back to the righteous character of Job affirmed at the beginning, questioned and tested in the middle, and reaffirmed at the end of chapter 1. Lest the reader assume the narrative is complete and the question decided, the initial phrase in 1:22, "in all this," stops just short of *completely* vindicating Job and leaves the door open for further development of the dominant theme: Is it possible to "fear God for nothing"? The final phrase of the chapter, "charging God with wrongdoing," is obscure on account of the uncertain word *tiplah,* translated "wrongdoing." Most emendations that scholars have suggested are unpersuasive, and Pope is certainly correct when he concludes that "reproach" or "blame" is the most likely sense in this context (Pope, *Job,* p. 17).

Additional Notes §3

1:15 / Because of the great distance between Uz/Edom and the kingdom of Saba, or Sheba, whence the **Sabeans** came, some have questioned the accuracy of this detail, and others have suggested an alternative identity for this group. See the discussion in Pope, *Job,* p. 13, and Hartley, *Job,* p. 76.

1:17 / In the OT, the **Chaldeans** are most often identified with the Neo-Babylonian Empire founded by Nabopolassar in the 7th c. B.C. The earliest mention of Chaldeans outside the OT is in the 9th c. B.C., when they were a semi-nomadic group living to the west of the Tigris River. Job's narrative fits the earlier semi-nomadic period better than the later.

1:20 / Tearing the clothes was a common sign of grief and mourning (2 Sam. 1:11). Cutting the hair or shaving (Heb. *gzz*, "shear sheep; cut hair") the head (or forehead) was a mourning practice among the Canaanites and other Near Eastern peoples (Isa. 22:12; Jer. 7:29; Mic. 1:16), but Israelite law prohibited it (Lev. 19:27–28; Deut. 14:1). Job's practice is consistent with his presumed non-Israelite status.

1:21 / With Job's reference to coming naked **from my mother's womb** the author is laying a comparative groundwork for the later curse on the day of his birth (3:1). Note Job's patient acceptance here in contrast to his impatient complaint in chapter 3.

The NIV consistently translates the Heb. *brk*, "bless," as "praise" whenever it is directed by humans to God. It seems the NIV translators are theologically uncomfortable with the idea that humans can offer any blessing that will add to the completeness of God. Apparently the OT writers had no such difficulty, since they often talk about their desire and intention to return to God the blessing they have received. There is certainly something significantly different between desiring to "praise" God and wanting to "bless" him. The one wishes to verbalize reasons for which God is praiseworthy, while the other actually desires to *give* rather than just describe.

1:22 / Proposed emendations for *tiplah,* **wrongdoing,** include ʿ*awlah,* "wickedness," *nebalah,* "folly," and *tepillah,* "protest." Drawing on the similarity of the Heb. construction here between *natan tiplah,* "give blame/reproach" and the more positive *natan kabod,* "give glory" (1 Sam. 6:5; Jer. 13:16; Prov. 26:8), Pope also suggests *tiplah* may be "very nearly an antonym to 'glory'" (Pope, *Job,* p. 17).

§4 Return to the Presence of Yahweh (Job 2:1–6)

2:1–3 / With only a few variations—and only *one* of real significance—these verses exactly repeat 1:6–8. Repetition and variation are part of the literary toolbox of ancient narrators and storytellers and may owe much to the oral tradition of telling and retelling these stories over the centuries. The similarity of language carries the hearer into the second conversation between *the* Satan and God and leads us to ponder what is to come. Will *the* Satan acknowledge the integrity of Job's righteousness? How will God respond to the battered innocent sufferer now that his righteousness has been tried and proven? The variations introduce unexpected complications and suggest that final resolution still remains in the future.

The first significant variation comes toward the end of 2:3, when God, having recalled his **blameless and upright** servant to the attention of *the* Satan as in their first encounter, continues his commendation of Job with the additional words: **And he still maintains his integrity.** God already knows the outcome of the test and evaluates Job's response to the previous loss positively without any input from *the* Satan. God goes on to describe the initial test of Job as one **without any reason,** using the same term (*khinnam*) that *the* Satan had used to question the sincerity of Job's righteousness ("for nothing," 1:9). God's words here confirm that the test *has never been for God's sake.* God knows the righteous character of his servant, Job, and has no need to test it. The test is *always for the sake of the reader,* for whom alone the possibility of disinterested faith in God has any meaning.

God says that *the* Satan **incited** God to **ruin** Job for no reason. Some take "incited" (Heb. *swt*) to mean "entice," "seduce," or "mislead," indicating that *the* Satan is responsible for misleading God to attack Job wrongly. This leaves us with an unnecessarily weak picture of a God who can be deceived into acting inappropriately. Clines (*Job 1–20,* p. 43) is right, in my opinion, to understand *swt* in the more positive sense of "urge" or "attempt to persuade." Otherwise these words undermine the key issue of the book, since Job's conflict is with God and *not the* Satan. *The* Satan poses the question regarding the validity of Job's righteousness, God carries out the test in its most extreme terms in order to leave no doubt, and now God invites *the* Satan to agree that the proof is persuasive.

2:4–6 / Such agreement, however, is not forthcoming since *the* Satan, the Accuser, remains true to his role and calls for the most stringent of tests of Job's integrity—personal physical suffering and the threat of death. In this second major variation from the earlier meeting, *the* Satan at first couches his reply in rather obscure proverbial terms: **Skin for skin!** The following line sufficiently clarifies the basic meaning of this phrase: **A man will give all he has for his own life.** The test has been insufficient to prove the case since Job may be willing to sustain the loss of family and possessions if only he can protect his life. To truly test his integrity and righteousness, God must once again **stretch out** his **hand** and personally afflict Job's **flesh and bones.** Unless there is a real threat of death, says *the* Satan, the true nature of Job's integrity will always remain suspect. God's response is to authorize this further (and final?) test, stopping just short of Job's death. Here again it is clear that God is the power behind the test (and suffering!) of Job, and that *the* Satan carries out the will and purpose of God.

Additional Notes §4

2:4 / **Skin for skin!** Scholars have suggested a number of competing interpretations, none of which wins the day. For the details consult the discussions in the commentaries by Hartley, *Job,* pp. 80–81; Pope, *Job,* pp. 20–21; and Clines, *Job 1–20,* pp. 43–45.

§5 The Second Test: Personal Suffering
(Job 2:7–10)

2:7–8 / **So Satan . . . afflicted Job.** Although *the* Satan appears to be the active party here, it is obvious from the preceding passage that he acts only with the permission of, and within the limits set by, God. The struggle is *not* between Job and *the* Satan, but between Job and God. The **painful sores** which afflict Job are not immediately identifiable, but the Hebrew term here (*shekhin*) also appears in the Exodus account (as one of the divinely instituted plagues against the Egyptians in Exod. 9:9–11), and in Deuteronomy (as part of the curse for failure to keep the covenant commandments in Deut. 28:27–28). Job's misery is complete as he is afflicted **from the soles of his feet to the top of his head.** His position **among the ashes** is one of mourning as well as social isolation. Because of his terrible disease and loathsome appearance, Job is relegated to the ash heap, outside the inhabited areas, to the place where the destitute resided on the fringes of society (and where the poor and ill still reside in refuse dumps in many cities around the world).

2:9–10a / In his agony Job receives some wifely advice. Job's wife has often been accused of serving as the devil's tool. Her advice that Job should, **"Curse God and die!,"** could appear to be an attempt to urge Job to fulfill *the* Satan's prediction. But the question that prefaces this, **"Are you still holding on to your integrity?"** so nearly duplicates God's earlier affirmation of Job's tenacious faith (2:3) that her advice simply states the crux of the issue in its most severe form. Will Job choose integrity and fear of God? Or will he end his pain by cursing God? The interchange between Job and his wife introduces the cycle of speech and reply that will make up the core of the book's dialogue section.

Job's reply to his wife seems to acknowledge that her intent is less than evil—and is perhaps even motivated by her desire to see her husband's pain and degradation ended. He does not call his wife **a foolish woman** but simply dismisses her speech as **like** that of "a foolish woman" (*nebalah*). The term *nebalah* does not indicate lack of intelligence but describes "moral obtuseness and blindness to religious truth" (Gordis, *Job*, pp. 21–22). Job goes on to instruct his wife in an attempt to sway her to adopt his firmly-held conviction that true piety demands holding firmly on to God whether one experiences **good** or **trouble.** Piety is not a form of barter, Job explains, but an irreversible commitment.

2:10b / The second test concludes in much the same way as the first with a positive evaluation of Job's response. **In all this**—a reference to the test of suffering and to Job's verbal responses—**Job did not sin.** His integrity remains intact following the most severe test—the threat of social rejection and death. One ought not to make too much of the specificity of the evaluation that Job did not sin **in what he said** (*bispatayw*, "with his lips"). This does not imply that Job may have sinned in action if not in words. The statement does, however, leave an unanswered question regarding Job's thoughts which have yet to be spoken, and in this way the phrase prepares the reader for the outpouring of Job's inner reflection and pain in the dialogue to come.

§6 Silent Comfort: Job's Three Friends
(Job 2:11–13)

2:11 / The appearance of Job's three friends *after* the apparently successful completion of the double test marks a new departure in the narrative. Having witnessed the second exoneration of Job's righteousness, the reader anticipates some resolution to his suffering. The immediate question that arises is what role these friends will play in that resolution. There is an element of surprise for the reader as the answer to that question unfolds.

The three friends support the Edomite connections already established in the story. One of Esau's sons, listed among his Edomite descendants in Genesis 36:10–11, is also called **Eliphaz**. This Eliphaz's designation as **the Temanite** indicates that he lived in Teman, an Edomite city south of the Dead Sea. **Zophar** and **Bildad** have less obvious affiliations with Edom (through various linguistic and genealogical connections, see the extended discussion in Clines, *Job 1–20*, pp. 57–59). Perhaps it is because Jeremiah 49:7 and Obadiah 8 attribute great wisdom to Edom that the text establishes the Edomite association here. These three skilled sages are equipped, therefore, for the intense dialogue and debate that is to come.

After the **three friends** learn of Job's plight they travel considerable distances to reach his side **together,** a sign of their deep concern. It would have taken a considerable time for word to reach the friends and then for them to make long-distance arrangements to meet. The purpose of the friends' visit is to **sympathize with him and comfort him.** The Hebrew verb for "sympathize" is *nud*, which denotes shaking the head or body back and forth as an indication of taking on the pain or grief of another. The Hebrew for "comfort" is *nkhm*, which normally means (in the Piel stem as here) to comfort *with words*—in contrast to the silent waiting that ultimately characterizes the friends' vigil.

2:12–13 / The friends finally **saw** Job **from a distance,** but his disfigurement was so great as a result of his diseased suffering that **they could hardly recognize him.** Much as Job's later intention to confront God boldly face to face is completely undone by the actual vision of God when he comes (42:1–6), so here the friends' good intentions to "sympathize" and "comfort" evaporate when they actually encounter the sufferer in his tattered flesh. No intelligible words escape their mouths, no wise or comforting words can they muster as they are instead reduced to inarticulate wails, tears, and the external rituals of grief and mourning—**they tore their robes and sprinkled dust on their heads**—to express their distress. This reaction perhaps prefigures the friends' role in the coming debate. Their inability here to gather words to respond to the physical suffering of their friend foreshadows their future failure to reply to his verbal expressions of agony.

Sitting **on the ground** is a common stance for mourning the dead (see also, e.g., Lam. 2:10; Isa. 3:26; 47:1). The friends sit down **with him** as a sign of their identification with his suffering that approaches death. Clines, *Job 1–20*, makes much of the fact that these actions are part of mourning *for the dead* and thinks that the friends' treatment of Job as *already dead* is an isolating and ultimately frustrating experience for the sufferer rather than a comfort. Most commentators, however, see these acts as a form of solidarity with Job's extreme suffering. The period of **seven days and seven nights** is an emphatic strengthening of the standard time of mourning (seven days; see Gen. 50:10; 1 Sam. 31:13; also Sir. 22:12; Jdt. 16:24). Among Jews the period of mourning after the funeral is known as *Shiva*, from *shevaʿ*, "seven." The nature of the mourning here is extreme and exhaustive, in response to the extreme and exhaustive nature of Job's suffering. The extended silence—**no one said a word to him**—mirrors the traditional Jewish practice of the guests remaining silent until the primary mourner speaks. "Comforters are not permitted to say a word until the mourner opens [the conversation]" (*Talmud Bavli, Mo'ed Qatan, 28b*). The fact that this silence lasted the entire "seven days and seven nights" also suggests the inability of the friends to find words to meet Job's suffering, **because they saw how great** it was. Further, the silence indicates that the dialogue that will follow is *not* a response to Job's suffering, but rather to his spoken protest against his treatment by God. At this point the stage is set for the heart of the book, and the dialogue/debate begins.

§7 Job's Protest out of Pain: Opening Curse (Job 3:1–10)

At last, Job himself breaks the protracted silence with an explosive speech. This passionate monologue, which stretches from 3:3–26, is divided into two sections: an opening curse (3:3–10); and a questioning lament (3:11–26).

3:1–2 / An introduction that summarizes the coming monologue prefaces Job's speech: **After this, Job opened his mouth and cursed the day of his birth.** These words connect the prose prologue of the first two chapters ("after this"), with the ardent curse that follows ("cursed the day of his birth"). Although the concluding postscript at the end of chapter 31 ("The words of Job are ended") matches this introduction, the latter seems inadequate to introduce the whole collection of dialogues and seems best suited as an introduction to chapter 3 alone.

Verse 2 begins with the redundant (in this context) standard introduction to the individual speeches in the dialogue. Literally, this would be translated "and Job replied and said." This indication of a "reply" need not mean that some previous statement, to which Job's speech is a response, has been lost. It is more likely that the phrase simply marks the beginning of this first speech, as throughout all the remaining speeches of the dialogue cycles.

3:3 / Job's opening curse begins with a balanced poetic phrase. He parallels the perishing of **the day** of his birth with the hoped-for destruction of **the night** in which conception occurred (NIV **"A boy is born!"**—the verb *harah*, however, always means "conceive" and never "give birth"). This verse foreshadows the focus on "that day" (vv. 4–5) and then "that night" (vv. 6–9) in the verses that follow. References to "that day" or "that night" introduce each of these two sections. The Hebrew *jussive*, a form of the verb that indicates the wish or will of the speaker, frames all the verses of this curse (vv. 3–10). The translation reflects the force of the jussive by the repeated use of the word **may.**

3:4–5 / Job's curse on **that day** expresses a desire that the light which is characteristic of the daytime be totally over-whelmed by **darkness** and **deep shadow** so that **no light shine upon it.** Job's hopes for this day are obviously symbolic of his wish never to have been born into such a painful life, since it is not pos-sible to change or obliterate a past event. Job's anger at having been born to suffer lashes out at "That day" by desiring that **God** should **not care about it**—the Hebrew *drsh* means "to have suffi-cient concern to look into a matter" or "to check on someone's well-being." Such a lack of divine concern reflects Job's personal experience at this point of pain, and so he projects his own experi-ence on the hated "day of his birth." In contrast to God's studied indifference, Job hopes that "darkness and deep shadow" will be more interested in "That day" and will **claim it.** This is a rather negative use of the verb *gʾl,* often used to describe divine "re-demption." Rather than pray that God redeem him, Job desires that "darkness" will buy back the day of his birth for its exclusive use. Job concludes his curse on "That day" with the summative hope that it will be shrouded in perpetual **cloud** and that an eclipse of the sun bring startling terror.

3:6–7 / Job pronounces an equally scathing curse on **that night,** wanting to blot his birthday from the calendar—perhaps so that its yearly celebration would not bring continued reminders of his painful existence. Returning to the metaphor of birth, Job calls down joyless barrenness on "That night." If the "night" was **bar-ren** and unable to conceive (as Job wishes his mother had been?), it could not later give birth to the "day" in which Job was born to suffer.

3:8–10 / In these three verses, Job returns to the more in-clusive view of day as comprised of both night and day. He calls on the skill and power of **those who curse days**—possibly profes-sional practitioners like Balaam in Numbers 22–24—to direct their curses on **that day.** Their cursing is related to their ability to **rouse Leviathan,** the sea monster associated with the threat of destruc-tive chaos.

While the reference to Leviathan may stop short of a quest for undoing the order of all creation (Clines, *Job 1–20,* p. 87), it does conjure images of creation. Job hopes for the **morning stars** to **become dark** and depicts the day as waiting **in vain** for the coming of **daylight** or **the first rays of dawn.** Although this is not the undoing of *all* creation, it is certainly the undoing of the creation *of this particular day.*

The section concludes with the reason (introduced by the Hebrew particle *ki,* "for") for Job's destructive urges against his day of birth. "That day" deserves cursing, says Job, because it failed to **shut the doors of the womb** to prevent his birth. Nor did it prevent him from experiencing **trouble.** Since God is the one who opens and closes the womb (see, e.g., Gen. 16:2; 20:18; 29:31; 30:22; 1 Sam. 1:5, 6), it might seem that Job misdirects his accusation against the day. The preceding verses, however, cast some light on the matter. Job wants the chaotic Leviathan to be unleashed (v. 9), apparently, in order to stop the orderly progress of time associated with the regulation of night and day at creation. The day's crime, in Job's estimation, is that night progressed to day, allowing his birth to occur, rather than having stopped, freezing the moment in time *before* he could escape the womb.

The "trouble" (Heb. *ʿamal*) Job desires to escape is the kind of stress and struggle associated with physical labor and effort, or the extreme hardship of slavery. This does not describe Job's internal, psychological turmoil (however real that may be!). Rather, it is Job's term for the burden of life that weighs him down from the outside. Job repeatedly employs this word to refer to his plight (e.g., 3:20; 4:8; 5:6, 7; 7:3; 11:16; 15:35; 16:2; 20:22).

Additional Notes §7

3:1–26 / There are still debates concerning the division of the text of chapter 3. Habel (*Job,* pp. 98–99, 102–6, accepts the two-fold division. Clines, *Job 1–20,* pp. 75–77, and others suggest three segments (vv. 3–10, 11–19, 20–26) or some variation on this schema (so Terrien, 3:903). These divisions are really not at odds with the structure I suggest, but simply divide the second segment thematically. Hartley (following M. Fishbane, "Jeremiah iv:23–26 and Job iii:3–13: A Recovered Use of the Creation Pattern," *VT* 21 [1971], pp. 151–67) accepts a two strophe structure that divides after v. 13 (vv. 3–13, 14–26). Despite the evidence cited by Hartley, *Job,* pp. 88–89, the division after 3:13 seems arbitrary, especially in light of the continuation of the thought of 3:13 by the presence of *ʿim,* "with," at the beginning of 3:14. Fortunately, strophic structure seems to have little effect on the interpretation of the chapter as a whole.

3:1 / The phrase **opened his mouth** recalls the concluding remarks of the first and second tests (1:22; 2:10), as well as the episode of the friend's silent visit (1:13).

3:2 / **He said:** Heb. *wayyaʿan ʾiyyob wayyoʾmar.* See the introductions in 4:1; 6:1; 8:1; 9:1; 11:1; 12:1; 15:1; 16:1; 18:1; 19:1; 20:1; 21:1; 22:1; 23:1; 25:1; 26:1. The long, final speech of Job in 26–31 is further marked by two extending continuation markers (*wayyosep ʾiyyob seʾet meshalo wayyoʾmar,* lit. "Job continued to lift up his *mashal* [proverb] and said") in 27:1 and 29:1. Both Gordis, *Job,* p. 32, and Clines, *Job 1–20,* p. 69, deny the need for any speech preceding this one. Gordis suggests an alternate meaning of the root ("break into speech, intone, chant") while Clines (*Job 1–20* following BDB) notes other biblical passages where the "reply" is to an occasion or circumstance rather than to a previous speech.

3:3–10 / **May . . .** While many of these jussive forms are identical with the imperfect verb, which expresses incomplete action in past, present, or future, a few of these verbs (such as *yehi* in 3:4 and 3:7) are unambiguously jussive by form as well as context. This strengthens our confidence that the rest of these verbs are to be rendered similarly in this context.

3:5 / There has been considerable discussion on the meaning of the Heb. *tsalmawet,* **deep shadow.** The general consensus is that it is a combination of "shadow" (*tsel*) and "death" (*mawet*), literally "shadow of death." In this case *mawet* is understood to function as a superlative, emphasizing the ultimate nature of the "shadow" that precedes "greatest darkness." The same word in Ps. 23:4 (traditionally "shadow of death") and Isa 9:2, therefore, may refer to the deep shadow at the bottom of desert ravines where the sun infrequently shines. The term occurs ten times in the OT, seven of which are found in Job; five times in the words of Job himself (10:22; 12:22; 16:16; 24:17 twice), once in the mouth of Elihu (34:22) and once in the divine monologue (38:17).

The final phrase of v. 5, **may blackness overwhelm its light,** is difficult and subject to various treatment. Pope, *Job,* p. 29, and Clines, *Job 1–20,* p. 70, argue persuasively that *kimrire yom* refers to an eclipse of the sun that brings darkness during the day.

3:8 / **That day:** because of the appearance of the chaotic sea monster Leviathan in the parallel line, some have suggested emending the two occurrences of the word *yom* ("day") in this verse to *yam* ("sea"). See the discussions in Clines, *Job 1–20,* p. 71; Pope, *Job,* p. 30; and Hartley, *Job,* p. 94. Since the verse seems a return to the more inclusive view of **day and night,** it seems best to follow the existing text. The hope here may be that **Leviathan** unleashed will "swallow the day-night of his birth" (NIV *Study Bible,* p. 737, n.). See also Hartley, *Job,* p. 94, n.; Pope, *Job,* p. 70.

§8 Job's Protest out of Pain: Questioning Lament (Job 3:11–26)

Job moves here from curse to lament. The translation indicates the shift from the repetition of "May" in verses 3–10 to repeated questions ("Why . . .") in verses 11–26. Job does not really anticipate answers to these questions. Instead, he asks them in order to express his frustration at being locked in a painful life of suffering. Job laments that he did not perish at birth (having failed, by cursing, to turn back the clock to prevent conception and birth altogether) and expresses his passionate longing for the kind of peace and rest that he envisions the dead to experience. That imagined peace of the dead contrasts sharply with Job's description of his ongoing experience of life as "turmoil," weariness, "misery"—with no rest or quietness. The lament is divided into two major sections introduced by the plaintive Hebrew interrogative *lammah*, "Why?" (3:11–19, 20–23), and concludes with a final statement of cause (as in the curse) marked by an initial Hebrew *ki*, "for."

The first segment of the lament is further divided into two descriptions of the supposed peaceful rest of the dead (3:11–15, 16–19). Each of these subsections begins with Job's lament that he did not perish at birth (3:11–12, 16) and goes on to describe the relative ease of the dead (vv. 13–15, 17–19).

3:11–12 / Job begins with a lament that he survived the birth process. If conception and birth could not be avoided altogether (vv. 3–10), why did Job not at least **perish** as he **came from the womb?** The reference to **knees to receive me** describes the ministrations of the midwife prepared to catch the child as it came from the birth canal (with the mother most likely in a squatting position). The lack of "knees to receive" or **breasts** to feed may be an oblique reference to infanticide, in which the child was not fed or cared for after birth but exposed to the elements and left to die. Job suggests that it might have been kinder in the long run to have allowed him to die, than to nurture him to endure an adulthood fraught with frightful suffering.

3:13–15 / Death at birth, in Job's estimation, would have brought **peace** and **rest.** Despite the fact that elsewhere in Job the abode of the dead is a place to be feared and avoided, here its terrors pale in comparison with a life of suffering. The point is not that death is so wonderful, but that life has become intolerable! Although in Ecclesiastes, for example, life may be troublesome, laborious, contradictory, and ultimately meaningless, it does *not* become completely intolerable as it does in Job (Eccl. 2:17–18; 3:19–21; 9:4–5). In his descriptions of the dead, Job follows the common view of *Sheol* as the great leveler of society. No one escapes by virtue of wealth, status, wisdom, strength, or righteousness. In this first picture it is the powerful and wealthy who find rest in death. They are **kings and counselors . . . rulers who had gold, who filled their houses with silver.** While they have now lost all in death, says Job, they still are to be envied by those who live and continue to suffer.

3:16–19 / Better still, Job avers, never to have been born at all, but to have been miscarried or **never** see **the light of day.** The Hebrew *nepel* most likely refers to the miscarriage of a child who is not yet viable (see also Eccl. 6:3). Job would have experienced the rest and peace he longs for if he had been **hidden** like those in the abode of the dead. In this picture of the dead, it is largely the poor and powerless who are in view (although v. 19a does mention **the great** as well as **the small**). Even the **wicked** know peace here and the **weary are at rest. Captives** as well as the **slave** avoid the abuses of their taskmasters and **enjoy their ease.**

3:20–22 / Another **why** introduces the second half of the lament at the beginning of verse 20. While the first lament reflected Job's individual plight, this section generalizes the experience of misery, using a series of plural participles referring to **those who . . .** (*ʿamel,* v. 20a; *lemare,* v. 20b; *hamekhakkim,* v. 21a; *hassemekhim,* v. 22a). Job thus adds weight to his complaint by pointing to the fact that it is more than an isolated personal event. It is, instead, the common experience of many sufferers. It is remarkable that he makes no mention here of *innocent suffering.* The implication is that life is inappropriately bitter for all those who live it. So bitter is life that many are seeking release through **death,** and **rejoice when they reach the grave.**

3:23 / Verse 23 marks an important shift of focus in the second section of the lament. The NIV has taken the opening words of verse 20, "Why is light given . . ." as introducing verse 23 as well, so the first word here (*legeber*, "to a man") continues on in the same vein as before: **Why is life given to a man . . . ?** While "a man" here is still a generalization, it is now *singular*, in contrast to the plural used in the preceding verses. This has the effect of subtly shifting the argument back from universal experience to the specific experience of Job. The shift back to Job continues in the remainder of this verse—**whose way is hidden**—and particularly in the concluding words: **whom God has hedged in.** This obvious play on *the* Satan's comment to God during their earlier meeting (1:10) takes an ironic twist in the mouth of Job. For *the* Satan, God's "hedging" is a protective act, caring for and preserving Job. For Job, who wishes only to die and escape from his suffering, God's "hedging in" constitutes an outrageous divine intrusion that not only prevents Job's death, but also prolongs his suffering.

That one's **way is hidden** means that one has lost the ability to know how to proceed effectively on one's life journey (*derek*, "way") to God. The "way" is not simply one's destiny. It also describes the daily, practical application of fearing God in order to understand how to act rightly in each circumstance and so to relate rightly to God and fellow human beings.

3:24–26 / Chapter 3 ends with a concluding statement of cause introduced by the Hebrew *ki*, "for." In this final statement, Job once again reverts to personal discourse about his specific circumstances, employing the first-person pronouns "me," "my," and "I." We see that his general, more universal comments in the preceding verses have come from personal experience rather than general speculation.

Why does Job desire to depart this life? Why does death appear more attractive than living? Because, he says, life is marked only by **sighing** and **groans.** These guttural utterances of pain or depression are more common, he says, than the basic necessities of life: **food** and **water.** Rather than responding to Job's hunger by providing food, God supplies "sighing" instead.

What Job **feared** and **dreaded** has happened. It is not completely clear whether this means that Job's scrupulous attention to religious detail in the past was motivated in part by the fear that some trouble would come upon his family and himself, or (as seems more likely to me) that the suffering of his trials has left him anticipating the worst as inevitable. The former view would seem to undercut the affirmation of Job's disinterested righteousness that was at issue in the test.

Regardless, the conclusion is clear. Job has descended—through no fault of his own as far as he (or the reader!) can see—from great blessing to utter despair and constant suffering. For him there is **no peace, no quietness . . . no rest, but only turmoil.** It is noteworthy that Job does not mention, or even apparently long for, the more material trappings of blessedness—wealth, health, family, or reputation. What Job seeks is a more spiritual wholeness that is able to face the vagaries of life with a calm assurance and restful peace. Job mourns this loss more than that of his flocks, wealth, and even his children. With all these "things" stripped away, Job is left to struggle at the naked core of life with the primary issue that energizes the debate, and indeed the whole book. Is a God who would allow such things to happen worth holding on to in faith? Or, to state things in a slightly different way: Is it possible to continue to believe in a good God in a world where righteousness no longer has any apparent reward?

Additional Notes §8

3:11 / In the parallel lines in this verse, Job uses the synonyms *rekhem* and *beten* for **birth** and **the womb,** and juxtaposes *mut,* **die,** with the less common *gwꜥ*, "expire, breathe one's last" (NIV **perish**).

3:23 / **God** first appears here in the poetic portion of the book. In the prose prologue, God was identified as "the LORD" (*yahweh*), or by the more usual generic designation, *ʾelohim,* "God." Here, however, Job uses (as is usual in the poetic section) the less common designation, *ʾeloah,* "God."

Although the verbs employed in 1:10 and here in v. 23 for **hedged in** differ slightly in their Hebrew spelling, most commentators understand both to be from the same root and to share the same root meaning: "hedge in (with thorns)." See Clines, *Job 1–20,* p. 101. The confusion over the similar-sounding Hebrew letters *samek* and *sin* is not uncommon.

§9 Trust in Your Piety (Job 4:1–6)

Here what is commonly known as the "first dialogue cycle" begins, taking the reader through Job 14:22.

Having been unable to find words to respond to the extremity of Job's physical suffering earlier, the friends are much less reticent in replying to Job's angry monologue. Job's words, and not his situation, spark the dialogue and debate. The first to speak is Eliphaz, who appears to be the eldest and is given pride of place as well as space (regarding Eliphaz's seniority see Pope, *Job*, p. 35). He speaks first in all three rotations and is allowed twice as much space as each of the other two friends. Eliphaz, whose name means something like "my God (is) pure gold," begins a bit hesitantly, as if concerned how Job will respond, but he builds rather quickly to an assured presentation of his views. His major assertion in this chapter seems to be that because *all* humans are less than righteous before God (4:17), Job ought to trust that God will respond mercifully to Job's consistent demonstration of diligent piety.

His first point seems to be that because *all* humans are less than righteous before God (4:17), *all* deserve divine judgment. Even the angels are subject to error and judgment. Therefore, how can any human hope to avoid sin? As a result, Job's suffering must be deserved, and his only hope is to accept God's discipline (5:17). He must throw himself upon the mercy of God, trusting that God will respond graciously in light of Job's consistent demonstration of diligent piety. Eliphaz returns to similar arguments in his second speech, reiterating the universal sinfulness of humanity. His criticism of Job becomes harsher as he assumes that Job's claim of innocence is deceitful. He warns Job strongly that the only way to escape the coming judgment of God is to confess his sin. In his concluding speech, Eliphaz claims that God is unaffected by human behavior, whether wicked or righteous. As a result, God remains an unbiased judge of human deeds whose decisions are always true and final.

4:1–2 / Eliphaz begins with a cautious rhetorical question that reveals his evaluation of Job's initial monologue as being overwrought and **impatient.** His restraint (**If someone ventures a word**) suggests he knows that what he is about to say will irritate, rather than comfort, Job. Nevertheless, Eliphaz feels constrained to reply: **But who can keep from speaking?** The dream experience of 4:12–17 will clarify the reason for this sense of compulsion.

4:3–4 / Eliphaz begins by commending Job's wisdom, by which he has consistently helped and **instructed many** others in need. We do not know exactly what troubles Job addressed in his wisdom, as Eliphaz describes them in more general metaphorical terms of physical ailments: **feeble hands; those who stumbled; faltering knees.** Each line that follows the generalization "instructed many" gives more specifics. Job's assistance to others is described as instruction (a key wisdom office) through which he has **strengthened** (Piel *khzq*, "make strong"), **supported** (Hiphil *qwm*, "cause to stand"), and **strengthened** (Piel *ʾmts*, "make strong/brave") those in need.

4:5–6 / When Eliphaz turns his attention to Job's turmoil he reveals a sharper edge beneath this apparent commendation. Job's wisdom is of no avail in his own suffering. He is far from "strengthened," "supported," or encouraged. Instead, he is **discouraged** and **dismayed.** Eliphaz turns Job's anxieties into the basis for a subtle assault on his **piety** (*yirʾatka*, "your fear," refers to the foundational "fear of God" affirmed of Job in 1:1, 8; 2:3) and **blameless ways** (the NIV translation of *tom*, "completeness," a near synonym of *tam* in 1:1, 8; 2:3). If Job is so certain of his piety and blameless character, Eliphaz seems to say, why is he so anxious under suffering, when he ought to be full of **confidence** and **hope?** Rather than attempting to comfort Job by encouraging him to trust in God's merciful response to his righteous character, Eliphaz seems, by these words (and those that immediately follow), to admonish Job to acknowledge the presence of some sin— however minor or unintentional—to account for the divinely instigated punishment he is experiencing.

§10 Aphoristic Support (Job 4:7–11)

4:7 / Following the customary methodology of a sage, Eliphaz now brings together a series of aphorisms based on observation to support his claims (4:7, 8–9, 10–11). The first of these provides a thematic introduction to the whole collection and calls for a reaffirmation of the idea of retribution. In this way of thinking the **innocent** never **perish**, nor are the **upright** ever **destroyed.** Eliphaz's restatement of retribution recognizes the possibility of righteous suffering that stops short of complete destruction or death. Proverbs also recognizes that the wise and righteous can experience poverty, oppression, and injustice (see esp. the "better . . . than . . ." statements such as Prov. 15:16; 16:8, 16; 19:1; 22:1). Clearly in Job's case the suffering has stopped short of death, although the friends' mourning and their speeches betray their conclusion that he is not long for this world without some form of repentance. The use of the question format prevents Job from ignoring Eliphaz's claims and presses him to acknowledge both their truth and their implications for his own situation.

4:8–9 / The second aphorism is a variation on the classic observation "you reap what you sow" (Gal. 6:7 [KJV]; see also 2 Cor. 9:6). Eliphaz's observation is that **evil** (ʾawen) and **trouble** (ʿamal) come only to those who **plow** and **sow** them (see Prov. 11:18; 22:8). The sideways implication is, of course, that Job's own "trouble" (3:10) is not so innocent, but the result of some sin Job is unwilling to acknowledge or admit.

4:10–11 / The final two aphorisms add fearsome warning to the preceding admonitions—"those who sow trouble" will experience what the "innocent" and "upright" never will—divine destruction by **the blast of his anger.** If **the teeth of the great lions are broken,** all their powerful roaring and growling (probably an allusion to the angry words of Job's initial monologue) is of no avail. Unable to secure and hold their **prey** without the use of their fangs, they perish and leave their **cubs scattered** and defenseless.

Additional Notes §10

4:7 / The **innocent** (*naqi*) are not *sinless,* but have been declared blameless in specific circumstances—esp. in cases of violent bloodletting. The verb *ʾbd,* translated **perish,** describes the ultimate end of the wicked in Ps. 1:6. **Destroyed** (*kkhd*) implies making something disappear by effacing it. In the alternation of verbs of destruction here and in 4:9, *kkhd* is paralleled in 4:9b with *klh,* "come to an end; disappear; be destroyed." Both imply complete destruction.

§11 Dream a Little Dream (Job 4:12–21)

4:12–16 / Chapter 4 concludes with an extended account of a dream, which is resonant of dreams found in the prophetic and apocalyptic literature (see, e.g., Dan. 2:19, 45; 7:2, 7, 13; Zech. 1:8). This dream adds weight to Eliphaz's speech since it offers divine confirmation for his message. The dream is **disquieting** to Eliphaz because in it he felt a spiritual presence that caused **fear and trembling** and shaking; even Eliphaz's **hair . . . stood on end.** These physical symptoms affirm the supernatural nature of the event. An unidentifiable **spirit,** or **form,** appears and speaks in **a hushed voice.**

4:17–19 / The two rhetorical questions in verse 17 summarize the spirit's message: **Can a mortal be more righteous than God? Can a man be more pure than his Maker?** The obvious answer to both questions, according to Eliphaz is "No!" This negative comparison of humans and God advances the argument that since no innocent person ever perishes, those threatened with divine destruction must have sinned in some way. *No* human is free of sin, and thus *all* are deserving of divine judgment and punishment such as Job experiences.

The "voice" goes on to compare the **angels**—whom God **charges . . . with error,** despite their elevated nature—with humans **who live in houses of clay.** The description here indicates the even more fragile, transient, and therefore sinful, character of human beings. The Psalms in particular often compare human frailty, fragility, and transience to the firm and trustworthy eternality of God himself. While there the purpose of human weakness is to drive humans to trust more fully in their maker for deliverance and security, here human frailty is simply an explanation of the experience of divine punishment—and thus a means of justifying God (theodicy).

4:20–21 / The dream report concludes with several additional images of human frailty. Humans are quickly **broken to**

pieces (like a defective toy that expires on the day it is received). Particularly poignant is the description of humans as **unnoticed** with the result that **they perish forever.** The sense seems to be that no one really sees the destruction, although the masculine singular form of the participle (*mesim*) could imply that it is *God* who is failing to notice Job. This would create a significant tension with God's statement to *the* Satan in chapters 1 and 2: "Have you considered (*hasamta libbeka*) my servant Job?" This play on *sim,* "consider, notice," must be intentional, and it also reflects Job's later complaint that God seems to take little notice of his suffering servant. On the other hand, Job also complains that God's attention to him is hurtful as God watches him in order to block his every move like a wary master chess opponent, or to cause Job hurt (see 7:20; 13:27; 19:8; 23:6; 33:11).

The last image of the dream in verse 21 is that of a **tent** completely destroyed when **the cords** (perhaps better "tent pegs") are **pulled up.** Having had a tent almost blown away on the edges of a tornado, I find this picture very illustrative of destruction and dispersal of a life. **Wisdom** (*khokmah*) is an important word in Job and this is its first appearance in the book. As the book employs the term throughout, it means something like "gaining understanding of the purpose of life and how to attain it." The untimely destruction of the human beings in verse 21 prevents their ever gaining such understanding. It is important to remember, however, that these are not the grossly wicked who turn their backs intentionally on God in 4:8–11, but those frail humans who are infected with sin simply because they are created from "the dust" and "live in houses of clay." These people, Eliphaz claims, must expect divinely instituted suffering too—just like their more intentionally sinful counterparts.

Additional Notes §11

4:20 / Hartley, *Job,* p. 110, n. 11, discusses the difficult Hebrew construction (*mibbeli mesim*) on which the NIV bases its translation **unnoticed.** He suggests reading *mesim* as a participle of *sim* and understands a following ellipsis of *leb,* "heart." He reads the whole as "without setting their heart," or "unaware," meaning that destruction comes upon them before they are even aware. The difficulty with Hartley's suggestion is that the verb *sim* would have to occur in the Hiphil stem, which it does not. Clines, *Job 1–20*, p. 113, accepts the ellipsis and explains the Hiphil participle as a back formation from *yasim* (which, although Qal, is identical in form with the Hiphil), or perhaps a noun meaning "attention." He translates the phrase "without anyone (else) setting it to heart," which supports the NIV translation. Others, following a suggestion by M. Dahood, read *mibbli-m shem* ("Northwest Semitic Philology and Job," in *The Bible in Current Catholic Thought* [ed. John L. McKenzie; New York: Herder & Herder, 1962], pp. 55–74) with the meaning "without a name," or "nameless." See the discussion in Pope, *Job,* p. 38, and Clines, *Job 1–20*, p. 113.

§12 Born to Trouble (Job 5:1–7)

5:1 / Eliphaz now addresses Job directly again. The Hebrew word forms make this clear: **call** (2d masculine singular imperative) at the very beginning of verse 1; **will you turn** (2d masculine singular imperfect) at the end of this verse; and **answer you** (which marks the return of 2d masculine singular suffixes).

Eliphaz assumes that Job will ultimately change his petition—from asking for death (in order to escape suffering) to a plea for divine deliverance from his pain in this life. Eliphaz has expressed his view that *all* humans are sinful and deserve divine punishment like that Job is experiencing, and so he admonishes Job that no relief is forthcoming. Not even **the holy ones** (a reference to the *bene ʾelohim* of chs. 1 and 2) could intercede in this case. The suggestion of intermediation here is the first introduction of an important motif that continues through the rest of the book (e.g., 16:20; 22:30).

5:2–5 / Eliphaz buttresses his opening statement with more aphoristic statements regarding the dangerous foolishness of **resentment.** While the proverb here seems originally to have concerned resentment and **envy** directed towards other humans, Eliphaz employs the saying here to caution Job against adopting such attitudes against the punishment that comes from God. Resentment kills, he warns, and so does envy. The **fool** (*ʾewil,* see also v. 3) and the **simple** (*poteh*) make their first and only appearance here in Job. Both words occur much more frequently in the rest of biblical Wisdom literature (the "fool" appears twenty-eight times in the OT, nineteen of them in Proverbs). The "fool" is the one who is innately incapable of wise understanding, and therefore resistant to instruction. The "simple" are untutored youths who *may* learn wisdom with proper diligence and training. The former are mostly beyond hope, while the latter teeter on the brink of either wisdom or foolishness, depending on the decisions they make. The term "simple" is from the Hebrew verb *pth,* "entice; deceive;

seduce," and describes those who are vulnerable because of their naïve openness to deception and seduction. The use of both terms here suggests that Eliphaz is accusing Job of acting more like an untutored, naïve youth or a recalcitrant fool than the respected sage he is known to be.

Eliphaz continues with an observation of the destiny of the "fool." This kind of observation, introduced by the verb *ra'iti,* "I saw," is characteristic of the Wisdom literature, particularly Ecclesiastes, where understanding is most often the result of observation and analysis of life circumstances and events (see Prov. 7:7; 24:3; Eccl. 2:13; 3:16, 22; 4:4, 15; 8:9, 10, 17). Although the "fool" may *seem* to be **taking root,** the appearance is misleading, because **suddenly his house was cursed.** This last line of verse 3 and the first of verse 4 (**His children are far from safety**) are not-so-subtle reminders to Job of his own situation and suggest that his circumstances are ultimately the result of his *foolishness.* Eliphaz does not expand on the parallel much further but goes on to describe the fate of the aphoristic children, **crushed in court.**

Like Job, the fool will also lose **his harvest** to **the hungry** who take it **from among thorns.** There is a possible double meaning behind this difficult phrase. On the one hand, the thorns may represent the sad state into which the fool's field and harvest have fallen. On the other hand, the thorns offer an ironic reflection on the "hedge of thorns" with which farmers protected their fields, and which *the* Satan uses metaphorically to describe God's protection of Job (1:10). In neither case, however, has the "hedge" proven very effective!

5:6–7 / This aphoristic section concludes with an additional proverbial summary. The proverb in verse 6 implies that **hardship** (*'awen*), unlike weeds, **does not spring from the soil** without premeditation, nor does **trouble** (*'amal*) **sprout from the ground.** The kind of "trouble" Job experiences (see the discussion of *'amal* in 3:8–10 in §7), suggests Eliphaz, is no accident, but the consequence of human sin. The final proverb in verse 7 drives this insinuation home, declaring a human affinity to **trouble** that parallels the innate tendency of **sparks** to **fly upward** in the wind. This conclusion links back to the previous summary statement of 4:17, which denies any hope of sinless human existence. To err is human, Eliphaz demurs, and trouble is the inevitable result of errant human nature.

Additional Notes §12

5:5 / On **from among thorns** see the clear discussion of the difficult Heb. and the many alternative translations in Clines, *Job 1–20*, p. 141.

§13 Trust in a Merciful God (Job 5:8–16)

5:8 / The only hope for Job now, according to Eliphaz, is to acknowledge his innate sinfulness and its destructive consequences. Imaginatively (but rather naïvely, perhaps) placing himself in Job's position, Eliphaz describes a course of action in which humans should **appeal to God** and **lay** [their] **cause before him.** Ironically, with one qualification, this is exactly what Job comes to desire in his demand to confront God (13:6, 15–19; 31:35–37). That one qualification, however, decisively establishes the distinction between Eliphaz and Job. Job rejects Eliphaz's foundational assumption of the innate sinfulness of humans as a justification for divine punishment. Job wishes to appeal to God, to be sure, but not for gracious mercy overlooking his sin. Rather, Job looks to God to vindicate his integrity: "Till I die, I will not deny my integrity. I will maintain my righteousness and never let go of it; my conscience will not reproach me as long as I live. . . . Let God weigh me in honest scales and he will know that I am blameless [*tummati*]" (27:5–6; 31:6).

5:9–16 / In contrast, Eliphaz sees Job's only hope in the power of God to overturn human expectation. God is a wonder-worker whose miraculous deeds of divine providence and grace are able to **water** the whole earth, and turn **daytime** into **darkness** and **noon** into **night** for the wicked. In this section Eliphaz describes a series of reversals in which God's unfathomable power and purposes turn worldly perspectives on their ears. The **lowly** are set **on high, those who mourn** are **lifted to safety** (v. 11); the **plans of the crafty** and the **wise** come to nothing (vv. 12–13); the **needy** are delivered **from the clutches of the powerful** (v. 15); and even **the poor have hope** (v. 16). God's purpose in all of these wonderful acts is to provide hope and to shut the **mouth** of **injustice** once and for all.

Additional Notes §13

5:11–16 /   The parallels with the Beatitudes in the Sermon on the Mount (Matt. 5:3–10), while far from exact, are certainly interesting. In both texts, God's will and purposes turn worldly expectations upside down.

§14 Blessings of Divine Correction (Job 5:17–27)

5:17 / At the end of his first speech, Eliphaz equates Job's suffering with divine discipline and encourages Job not to resist it. Since God's purposes are both unfathomable (5:9) and undeniably good (5:16), anyone (and especially Job) ought to trust this wonder-working God, accept correction, and not **despise** his **discipline.** Eliphaz drives his encouragement home with a proverb featuring the common wisdom generalization, **blessed is the man** (*ʾashre ʾenosh*) **whom God corrects.** He then quickly turns to directly address Job personally, employing the second masculine singular in the second half of the verse: *ʾal timʾas,* "[you] **do not despise.**" Eliphaz continues this direct address throughout the rest of the chapter, leaving no doubt that he not only desires to provide more universal instruction (as in 5:8–16), but that he also intends his speech to influence the behavior of his friend, Job.

5:18–19 / Job should accept God's discipline because, although painful, it leads ultimately to restoration. Eliphaz promises divine *healing* and *protection.* All that stands in the way of retribution, he seems to say, is Job's unwillingness to admit his wrong and yield to God's disciplinary punishment. If Job would submit, then God's protection would firmly surround him as it did before his suffering began. **From six calamities he will rescue you; in seven no harm will befall you.** Numerical admonitions such as this are a common feature of wisdom teaching (see, e.g., Prov. 30:18–31). The calamities that the following verses list do not seem to fill out the number six or seven, but appear rather to describe a broad protective net cast over all of Job's relationships and activities.

5:20–21 / God will protect a submissive Job physically **in famine** and **in battle.** His reputation will be safe from slander from **the lash of the tongue.** The approach of **destruction** will produce no fear.

5:22–23 / By referring to the beginning and ending calamities in the preceding two verses, **famine** (v. 20a) and **destruction** (v. 21b), Eliphaz links these two sections. The first section is a general promise of security (vv. 20–21) and the second promises the restoration of creation harmony (vv. 22–23). The result is a continuing argument for Job's submission to God. In this second set of verses, the harmonious pre-fall creation serves as a model. Like the original humans, Job will **need not fear the beasts** who **will be at peace** with Job as with the first humans. Nor will he experience the toilsome relationship with the fallen and cursed earth, since he instead **will have a covenant with the stones of the field** so that they do not impede his tilling and keeping of the earth. This rather radical use of images of creation harmony communicates the most emphatic promise of Job's future restoration imaginable.

5:24–26 / The final set of promises focuses most directly on the circumstances of Job's personal experience of suffering and loss. These verses stress three reversals in Job's circumstances that encourage his submission to God's discipline. Eliphaz promises Job the reversal of the devastating losses that the tests in Job 1 and 2 recount: **property** (v. 24; 1:13–17), **children** (v. 25; 1:18–19), and his personal physical well-being (v. 26; 2:7–8). The fact that both passages recount the losses and reversals in the same order confirms the link between these accounts. Job's **tent** will remain **secure** and he will not lose any of his property. His children **will be many,** and so he will have abundant **descendants.** And, in stark contrast to Job's weakened body ravaged by disease and wracked with pain, his submissive being will **come to the grave in full vigor . . . in season,** rather than before its time.

5:27 / The speech concludes with an affirmation of the truth of Eliphaz's viewpoint that draws on the joint experience of all three friends: *We* **have examined this, and it is true** (emphasis added). So they call Job to **hear** this word—an idiom that has more the sense of "heed" or "obey" rather than simply "listen." Eliphaz makes it clear that he needs to acquiesce in the following admonition that Job **apply** his teaching to himself.

Additional Notes §14

5:17 / The **man:** the Heb. ʾ*enosh*, "human," a synonym for the more common ʾ*adam*, "human being," emphasizes the vulnerable weakness and frailty of human beings. See Ps. 8:4, "what is man [ʾ*enosh*] that you are mindful of him, the son of man [*ben* ʾ*adam*] that you care for him?" And also Ps. 94:12: "Blessed is the man [ʾ*ashre haggeber*] you discipline, O LORD, the man you teach from your law."

In the second half of v. 17 the divine name *shadday* appears for the first time in Job. This name occurs thirty-one times in the book of Job and only seventeen times in the rest of the OT. The name is found in Exod. 6:2–3 as the patriarchal designation of God before the revelation (in the exodus) of his more personal name, Yahweh. The traditional translation is "the Almighty," based on the LXX translation *pantokrator*, "all-powerful one." Nevertheless, most scholars today, following the lead of Albright, pp. 173–93, accept "the mountain one" as the probable meaning, related to the Akkadian word *shadu*, "mountain," and linking God with his formative appearances in mountain regions (such as Sinai, Horeb, Moriah). The common association of deities with mountains offers general confirmation of such an idea. The use of the term in Job may be intended to emphasize the association of Job with the Israelite patriarchs, for whom this designation of God was more common.

5:22–23 / This passage apparently brings together the descriptions of the relations between humans and beasts in Gen. 1:25–30; 2:19; 3:1, 14; and 9:2. In the first of these passages, God creates the "beasts of the earth" (*khayyat ha*ʾ*arets*), the same term used in Job 5:22b, and places them in a peaceful (vegetarian!) relationship with the first humans (Gen. 1:25–30). The Gen. 2 account of the creation of animals (corresponding to Gen. 1) employs instead the term "beasts of the field" (*khayyat hassadeh*, also here in v. 23b) to describe an equally harmonious relationship between humans and beasts. The third set of passages describes *the* serpent as the shrewdest representative of the "beasts of the earth" (*khayyat ha*ʾ*arets*, Gen. 3:1), and as one of the "beasts of the field" (*khayyat hassadeh*, Gen. 3:14) in the subsequent curse. Following the flood in Gen. 6–8, God recommissions humanity to fill and exercise authority over the earth, but the post-flood relationship between humans and "beasts of the earth" (*khayyat ha*ʾ*arets*, Gen. 9) is one of *fear* and carnivorous competition rather than harmony.

5:24 / On the one hand the **tent** reference reflects the nomadic, patriarchal setting. On the other hand, the "tent" in Job is sometimes a metaphor for the vulnerability of human life that is constantly under threat. See 4:21; 11:14; 18:6, 14, 15; 19:12; 20:26; 22:23. Of these, 4:21 and 18:6 clearly use the tent as a metaphor for life.

§15 Impatience Justified (Job 6:1–13)

The first chapter of Job's response to Eliphaz divides into three parts. Initially (vv. 1–13), he defends the sense of growing impatience with his circumstance that Eliphaz has attacked (4:1–6). Job then turns to a counterattack on the fickleness of some friendship (vv. 14–23). He concludes chapter 6 with a pointed demand to know where sin resides within him that is commensurate with the punishment he bears (vv. 24–30).

6:1–4 / Job's **impetuous words** are the consequence of unbearable **anguish** and **misery**. Using the metaphor of the market scale, he claims his suffering is beyond measure—exceeding even the imponderable mass of all the **sand of the seas**. The cause of Job's suffering is the *enmity of God* (*shadday*), which he experiences as an archer's attack with poisoned **arrows** that pierce his **spirit** (*ruakh*), rather than just the body. Like an army arrayed in ranks and prepared to overrun the enemy, **God's terrors** stand ready against Job.

6:5–7 / Job can muster aphorisms to support his arguments with the best of the sages! He follows his opening defense with two proverbs affirming complaint as a natural response to deprivation and suffering. In reverse mode, Job reminds Eliphaz that it is only natural for hungry animals (**wild donkey** and domesticated **ox**) to **bray** or **bellow** in their discontent. Most commentators understand the food Job describes in the second proverb as disgusting and repulsive, and thus Job's refusal of it is only natural. This interpretation associates the objectionable food with Job's suffering or the advice of his friends, both of which he finds unpalatable. On the other hand, the verse may be saying that those who are gravely ill often reject even bland food without appreciation.

6:8–10 / Job's desperation is extreme as he expresses, for the first time in these verses, the preference for complete divine destruction over continuing in his suffering state. Job's **request** and **hope** is that God will finish the job he began. Death is better than the pain he experiences. It is one of the ironies of the book that the very restraint God institutes in his exchange with *the* Satan, as evidence of divine *mercy*—"you must spare his life" (2:6)—Job now sees as the most agonizing prolongation of his unrelenting suffering. Mercy in this state of pain is *not* continued life, but release from pain in death. To modern readers, with our ability to keep the weakened and suffering human body alive almost indefinitely, Job's anticipation of the release of death may not seem more understandable than shocking. There is a truth in the tension between *length of life* and *quality of life* that we need to consider carefully. Job does not contemplate suicide—even assisted by a physician—but desires divine action to end his suffering. This is perhaps akin to Job preparing a statement precluding the use of "heroic measures" to prolong his life.

Job does not just desire death, but death *with honor!* Clines, *Job 1–20*, p. 174, refers to the prisoner under interrogation and torture who fears the moment when strength and courage may fail and the prisoner will break. Death offers Job the **consolation** his friends have thus far failed to bring; Job would prefer to die at the hand of God with his integrity intact, not having **denied the words of the Holy One.** This last phrase seems to be another way to state the general piety and blamelessness of Job rather than a reference to any *specific* divine word Job has kept. Job's integrity plays an increasingly important role as the dialogue progresses. Here it is no longer simply the means of establishing Job's innocence in the face of his suffering; it has become Job's "bottom line." He is willing to suffer and even to die, as long as his tombstone reads: "This was a righteous man!"

6:11–13 / The final verses of this opening section of chapter 6 return to Job's defense of his impetuous speech. Here Job's failure to **be patient** links directly to his **hope**—or rather lack thereof. His **strength** to endure patiently is grounded, Job says, in the continuing ability to hope. Hope, he claims, grows out of a sense that even in the worst of circumstances one still has the **power to help** oneself—to change one's lot. One would have to become an inanimate substance with no sense or at least impervious to feeling—**flesh** would have to become **stone** or **bronze** to endure patiently in Job's situation. Reduced to poverty, pain, and despair, Job can see no **prospects** of change. In a moving insight

into the link between poverty and despair Job notes that the
power for change—and with it hope—was taken away when his
success was **driven** from him.

Additional Notes §15

6:4 / For the image of **arrows** as the instrument of divine punishment see Pss. 38:2; 120:4.

6:6 / The vocabulary here makes interpretation difficult. Clines,
Job 1–20, p. 158, offers a good review of the options, most of which attempt to identify some vegetable or plant food (*khallamut*) that generates
an excess of "slime" (*rir*) or "gelatinous" material to be eaten. In the development of Job's argument here, the point seems to be that while hungry
animals complain when not fed, people who are dreadfully ill (as Job is)
may even complain ungratefully when offered food to sustain them. The
perception of the food as "slimy" or objectionable has more to do with
the sick person's queasy stomach than with the food itself. If Job's suffering were removed, he suggests, he might be more agreeable to the medi-
cine offered.

6:14 / Job turns now to castigate his friends for their failure of true friendship. In a rather shocking statement, he claims that true **friends** would remain loyal even if their companion went so far as to forsake **the fear of the Almighty.** It is Job's fear of God (1:9) that has been at issue in the test of suffering, and now Job hints that his will to fear may be eroding. Intense suffering often diminishes our ability to understand and believe. When the pursuit of survival exhausts our energies, we have little left to sustain our faith. This is when we most need believing friends who resist the temptation to criticize our struggling faith, and instead come alongside us to give testimony of the continuing faithfulness of God that we have such difficulty seeing through our pain. This is precisely what Job's friends fail to do. They are so focused on what they consider to be Job's failure, that they trivialize his pain and confusion and condemn, rather than comfort him.

6:15–20 / Job compares his friends (**brothers**) to the **intermittent streams** that flow through the wadis of the rugged countryside of the Near East during times of abundant water. These normally dry stream beds can **overflow** with water in the early spring as the result of **thawing ice** and **melting snow.** But in the hot summer months the running waters **cease to flow** and the streams dry up. Job's friends are like such unreliable streams that **vanish from their channels** just when they are most needed, and with disastrous results. **Caravans** of traders stake their hopes and very lives on these less-than-trustworthy sources of life-giving water. Many **perish** when they turn aside from their trade route in a desperate attempt to find water elsewhere in the desert. It is not just the harsh and arid desert that claims these lives, however. A false sense of **hope** leads them to destruction as they search in vain for a water source they have used before, that they *know* should be there, but now is not. They are ultimately **disappointed** and perish. In the same way, Job's friends are not only unreliable sources of comfort, but misleading mirages that threaten to draw a desperate Job away from the true trade route—the path of Yahweh—to his destruction. The friends' counsel is, in Job's view, not only insensitive to his suffering, but ultimately a threat to his saving relationship with God!

6:21 / Like these unreliable streams that lead trusting travelers to their destruction, Job's friends have also **proved to be of no help.** Job explains this failure as stemming from two fearful responses the companions have made to Job's circumstances. First, harking back to the description in 2:12–13 of the friends' first glimpse of Job's pain-ridden body, Job claims they saw **something dreadful** and were **afraid.** Rather than being driven in compassion to comfort and uphold Job, they recoil in fear and disgust. Rather than hearing his complaint with a sympathetic ear, they have sought thus far to dismantle his integrity in an attempt to retreat to the comforting world where retribution is a punishment for the guilty, and the righteous (themselves included!) can rely on blessing. Their words, Job claims here, are self-focused and self-concerned rather than true words of compassionate comfort.

There is certainly a lesson for us to learn here about comforting those in the midst of dreadful pain and suffering. Sometimes their blunt, even rageful, expressions of anguished questioning of God can so discomfit us that we strike back with pious words of almost naïve trusting. It is as if we think our words can offset their anguish and restore our own sense of balance. As Job shows us here, however, such words at these times of suffering most often demonstrate to the sufferer that we have not heard them and have not really felt along with them the pain that threatens to engulf them. I have sometimes found it is better to read into such a setting the harsh, almost despairing words of Psalm 88, where God is the enemy and the speaker has all but given up hope. At least this helps sufferers to see that others have walked this path of pain before them, have thought similar thoughts of anger and abandonment, and yet are still engaged in dark and painful conversations with God. Often understanding is more important than comfort.

6:22–23 / The friends' fear, according to Job, is that their comforting may cost them more than they are willing to give. Job responds with a series of questions that deny he ever expected the friends to, "**Give something on my behalf,**" or "**pay a ransom . . . from your wealth.**" While it seems clear that he does not envision an actual exchange of money, just what kind of "ransom" the friends may fear to give up is left vague. Comforting those struggling with deep pain and loss can be an exhausting process for the comforter. It may be that the friends fear the depletion of their emotional and psychological resources.

The preceding verses, however, give us a clue that there may be another cost the friends are seeking to avoid. When Job claims in verse 21 that his friends **see something dreadful and are afraid,** is he speaking only of his own dreadful appearance? Or do his suffering and impatient response raise another specter of dread? Is it the threat that the friends' carefully constructed world of cause and effect might fail, that their retributive explanations of what has happened to Job are perhaps inadequate, that strikes terror into the friends' hearts and, at first, renders them dumb? Their failure to come compassionately to Job's aid—to seek to rescue him **from the hand of the enemy**—makes them, in the end, the **ruthless** ones (v. 23b), who would "barter away" their friend (6:27b) rather than admit that their "safe" world might be built on a crumbling foundation!

Additional Notes §16

6:15–17 / For use of the image of water flowing (or not flowing!) in these desert streams as a metaphor of divine blessing or judgment, see Isa. 32:2; 35:6; 43:19, 20; 44:3; Joel 1:20; Nah. 1:4; 1 Kgs. 17; Pss. 74:15; 78:16, 20; 126:4.

§17 Show Me! (Job 6:24–30)

6:24–27 / The final section of chapter 6 begins with Job's demand that his friends show him just **where** he has **been wrong**—how he has sinned and how that sin is commensurate with the suffering he experiences. When he remarks **how painful are honest words,** it may be that Job is comparing his own words with those of the friends. Although his words are "painful" they are at least "honest." The deceitful, self-serving character of the speech of Eliphaz, however, leaves Job unmoved and renders his **arguments** unpersuasive.

Job questions even the sensitivity of his friends. In their haste **to correct** what they see as an attack on the very fabric of their lives (the comforting structures of retribution), they treat Job's **despairing** words not as harsh truth that needs to be heard and validated, but **as wind** (empty and aimless ravings) that must be discounted. Job's final accusation seems a bit harsh, but it reveals what Job sees as the friends' ultimate submission to their ideology. The idea of retribution is so important to them that they are willing to sacrifice almost anything to maintain it. They are even willing to **cast lots** and gamble away the helpless orphan and **barter away** their **friend** in order to preserve their secure worldview.

6:28–30 / Job's "show me" attitude continues into the final verses of this chapter. In a statement that recalls the friends' horror when they first see the suffering Job and are unable to recognize him, Job demands to be seen and acknowledged as a living human being whose suffering and words deserve a compassionate response. **But now . . . look at me,** he cries, implying that the friends are having a difficult time maintaining eye contact, just as we are tempted to look away from those we meet who have suffered horrible disfigurement. This failure to *see* Job enables them to keep their tenuous hold on their carefully ordered world that would collapse if they ever acknowledged the truth of Job's claims.

With the words, **would I lie to your face?**, Job calls the friends' avoidance and retributive ponderings what they really are at their core: a declaration that Job's claims of integrity just *cannot* stand up in the face of the evidence of divine punishment, namely his horrible suffering and loss. If they were to look deeply into his eyes, the verse seems to imply, they would have to acknowledge his essential integrity from which his words gain validity. For this reason Job's very **integrity is at stake**, a point that increasingly dominates the dialogues. If Job *is* a man of integrity (as the reader knows from the very mouth of God himself), then his claims are not the result of **malice** or **wickedness**. The conflict is in full swing by this point in the dialogue. Job's friends are willing to sacrifice his integrity in order to preserve their carefully ordered worldview at any cost. On the other hand, Job's knowledge of his own integrity and righteousness forces him to dismantle any perception of the world filtered through faith in retribution that has so manifestly failed in his own experience.

Additional Notes §17

6:27 / The **fatherless** (*yatom*) orphans are among those classes of defenseless persons (including widows and aliens) who have no one to represent them in society, and are thus left at the mercies of the powerful. It is clear from the many exhortations to defend these helpless ones that exploitation of these groups—or, at the very least, the tendency to ignore their needs altogether—was very often a reality in Israel (e.g., Exod. 22:21; Deut. 24:17, 19–21; 27:19). For the author of Job, the oppression of the "fatherless" is a sign of utter spiritual bankruptcy (see esp. 22:9). In particular, Job levels such accusations against his friends and society as a whole (24:9–11; 29:12–13; 31:16–17, 21), and on one occasion Eliphaz suggests that Job's suffering is the consequence of his own cavalier treatment of widows and the fatherless (22:9).

§18 Hard Service (Job 7:1–5)

7:1–2 / Job likens his suffering to the **hard** labor endured by a **slave** or **hired man.** The comparison begins with a general description of the difficult lot of humans, considered in their frailty (ʾ*enosh,* see Additional Notes on 5:17, above). The **service** Job refers to is the Hebrew *tsabaʾ,* a term that often describes military service or warfare. The two categories of laborers—**hired man** (*sakir*) and **slave** (ʿ*ebed,* better "servant")—emphasize hard work rather than warfare. The pictures of the servant laboring in the heat of the day while **longing for the evening shadows,** and of the hired worker enduring hard labor with eyes firmly fixed on payday, are well drawn.

7:3–5 / Turning the general analogy to his specific circumstances, Job slips into first-person references. If the servant and hired man of verses 1 and 2 have "hard service," Job exceeds them all. They wait for the evening shade or the paycheck at the end of the work day, while Job has endured **months of futility** with no conclusion in sight. His **nights of misery** drag restlessly on, while thoughts that the whole experience must be repeated again in the morning plague him. Along with his pain and hopelessness, Job must also endure a failing body **clothed with worms and scabs,** covered with **broken and festering** skin.

Additional Notes §18

7:1 / **Service** (*tsabaʾ*): see also Num. 1:3; 31:14; Deut. 24:5; Josh. 22:12, 23; 1 Sam. 28:1. On at least one other occasion (Isa. 40:2) it also describes compulsory labor to retire a debt—in this case Israel's exilic captivity is compulsory service to pay for her sin. This same term in the plural (*tsebaʾot*) is often used to describe the militant hosts of heaven prepared for battle, as in the frequent divine epithet *yhwh tseba'ot,* "the Lord of hosts."

7:2 / The Heb. for NIV's **waiting eagerly** is from the verb *qwh,* and has the sense of waiting tensely on the edge of one's seat.

§19 The Fragility of Life (Job 7:6–10)

7:6–7 / Job's first-person reflections continue, but his focus shifts from the "hard service" of his suffering to a growing awareness of the fragility of his life. Speeding along even more quickly than a darting **weaver's shuttle,** the days of Job's life rush **without hope** to a rapid end. The intimation of a rapidly approaching end prepares the reader for the focus on death in the latter part of this chapter. Life is so fragile that, in Job's condition, death cannot be far away. Job says that **life is but a breath,** insubstantial at best and soon dissipated. Job's words here—"a breath (is) my life" (*ruakh khayyay*)—are a cynical play on the animation of the first human in Genesis 2:7. There God breathes into the nostrils of the yet inert human the "breath of life" (*nishmat khayyim*) in order to create a "living being" (*nepesh khayyah*). Elsewhere in Job, the animating "breath" (*nishmah*) that gives life is often associated almost interchangeably with *ruakh*. "The Spirit (*ruakh*) of God has made me; the breath (*nishmah*) of the Almighty gives me life" (33:4). Conversely, "If it were his intention and he withdrew his spirit (*ruakh*) and breath (*nishmah*)" (34:14). Job intends his words to remind God that his life is a tenuous and yet *divinely given* "breath," and that his prolonged suffering is therefore the result of God's unwillingness to withdraw that breath.

7:8–10 / There is an additional wordplay in the transition from verse 7b to 8a. As Job's "eyes will never see happiness again," so the **eye** of the one who **now sees** him (referring, at one and the same time, to God and to the friends) **will see** [Job] **no longer.** While they are looking at him, he will simply disappear. Job's imagined disappearance leads to a more general rumination on the departure of the dead from life, **as a cloud vanishes and is gone** (v. 9a). Here, however, the emphasis is no longer on the ephemeral nature of life and its fragile transience, but on the *permanence* of death. Once one is dead and in **the grave,** one simply **does not return.** There is little inkling in these words of even a glimpse of resurrection hope that some have seen elsewhere in Job (see, e.g., below on 19:23–27). Death is final for Job. It will mean the end of suffering, but it also means the end of any hope for redress of injustice. Unless Job speaks out now, unless he is able to secure from God a public admission of Job's righteousness, Job's integrity will remain in question among those left behind. He will go down to his grave with a sullied character. For this reason (note "Therefore" at the beginning of v. 11), Job cannot remain patiently waiting but must speak out before rapidly approaching death silences his complaint forever.

Additional Notes §19

7:6 / When Job says he is **without hope** he employs a term (*tiqwah*) based on the same root (*qwh*) as the verb in 7:2 that implies expectant anticipation or tense waiting. For Job, who expects only more pain until death releases him, all anticipation of the future is gone. Hope dissipates in the face of the numbing sameness of each day.

7:7–8 / The wordplay is more complex than a translation can illustrate: *loʾ tashub ʿeni lirʾot tob* (v. 7b) parallels *loʾ teshureni ʿen roʾi* (v. 8a). The balance of the similar negated verbs, the repetition of forms of *ʿen*, "eye/eyes," and the verb *rʾh*, "see," link these two lines firmly together.

§20 The Temptation of Death (Job 7:11–16)

7:11 / In the press of impending death, Job's almost frantic words pour out **in the anguish of . . . spirit** and **in the bitterness of . . . soul.** He **will not keep silent,** but must **complain** while there is still time. Job establishes a negative tone here as he responds in "bitterness" to the hostility he senses from God.

7:12 / Calling on creation imagery, Job compares the restriction and limitation he experiences with the boundaries God imposed on the chaotic waters at the very beginning. In forming the earth and firmament, God said to the surging primeval seas, "This far you may come and no farther; here is where your proud waves halt" (Job 38:8–11; see also Prov. 8:27–29; Jer. 5:22). Job questions whether he has exhibited such a rebellious spirit that God should **put [him] under guard** like the chaotic **sea** or **the monster of the deep** (Heb. *tannin,* "sea dragon; serpent"; see also Gen. 1:21; Ps. 148:7). Such sea creatures, here Tannin and elsewhere Leviathan (Job 3:8; 41:1–34) and Rahab (26:12; Isa. 51:9; see also the discussion on 9:13 in §27 below), also represents the chaotic power of the seas which YHWH is understood to have subdued in creation order (Ps. 74:13–14). Mesopotamian myth identifies the primeval seas with the god Mumu-Tiamat, in particular, who rises up and then is vanquished by the god Marduk, who then divides her body to create the protective environment in which the ordered world is made possible (see "The Creation Epic," *ANET,* pp. 60–72; *ANESTP,* pp. 501–03). Some biblical texts seem to reflect a similar idea of conflict between God and the sea serpent, Leviathan (see, e.g., Isa. 27:1). In other passages Leviathan appears to be a sea creature (the whale?) that humans might be expected to encounter on the sea (41:1–2; Ps. 104:26).

7:13–15 / God is not satisfied with keeping watch over Job. He goes so far as to plague his sleep with frightening **dreams** and terrifying **visions,** so that even sleep offers Job no respite from his suffering. This incessant attack, restriction that prevents escape, and the invasion even of the solace of sleep, all lead Job to consider the tempting final solution of **death.** This does not appear to be a real desire for death by suicide, but it is an extreme expression of Job's desire to escape the pain of his deteriorating **body** that almost makes death by **strangling** a preferable alternative. Job's *real* hope is not to escape in death, but to live without his continuing pain and suffering.

7:16 / Without hope for escape in this life, however, Job can only **despise** [his] **life** and plead that he would **not live forever.** In despair his challenge rings out to God: "**Let me alone!**" God's harsh scrutiny has left him to conclude that his **days have no meaning.**

§21 Enough of Divine "Care"! (Job 7:17–21)

7:17–19 / The picture of God placing a "guard," or senti-nel, over Job (v. 12), introduced the idea of divine scrutiny that dominates the rest of chapter seven. In an ironic and cynical play on the awed reverie of Psalm 8, Job questions whether divine oversight is protective care and grace, or, as Job styles it here, inva-sive examination with an intent to punish even minor infractions severely. God is, in Job's words, the "watcher of men" (v. 20), who never allows humans (and Job in particular) a moment's rest, ex-amining him **every morning** and testing his **every moment.** God never seems to **look away . . . even for an instant.**

7:20–21 / The chapter concludes with two questions that characterize Job's continuing confusion. On the one hand, he wishes to know **why** he has become God's **target.** Knowing no sin within himself that could explain his suffering, Job can only conclude that he has **become a burden** to God, who has now de-termined to remove him from existence in the harshest manner possible. On the other hand, Job wonders why God is unwilling to **forgive** any **sins** of which Job may be unaware. Job does not admit any guilt, but he directs the question at the character of God him-self. If God is a God of grace, where is that grace in relation to Job? Job is no gross sinner in rebellion against God. He is a pious man who has always taken scrupulous care to go above and beyond the expectations of faith. How is it, then, that God finds Job so of-fensive that God can extend no grace or mercy in his case? The chapter concludes with the note that the need for action is urgent because, unless divine redress is immediately forthcoming, Job is not long for this world.

§22 Does God Pervert Justice? (Job 8:1–7)

8:1–2 / The second friend, Bildad, begins without the slightest indication of compassion for Job's suffering. He immediately condemns Job's speech, calling it **a blustering wind.** His goal from the first is to defend the traditional wisdom understanding of retribution. Unlike Eliphaz before him, Bildad seems willing to acknowledge Job's essential righteousness and encourages patience in waiting for God's ultimate vindication.

8:3 / Bildad's counterattack proper begins with parallel rhetorical questions upholding God's essential justice: **Does God pervert justice? Does the Almighty pervert what is right?** The anticipated negative response to these questions establishes the foundation of unquestioned divine justice from which the rest of Bildad's argument proceeds. If God is cleared of injustice, then Job's loss and suffering must be understood in this light.

8:4–7 / Bildad sees the destruction of Job's children and Job's own suffering as a contrasting set of examples for divine judgment and divine grace. A series of initial "ifs" (Heb. ʾim, sometimes, as in verse 4, translated by the NIV as **"when"**) binds his argument into a cohesive unit.

Bildad seems convinced that the destruction of Job's children was the result of their sin. Although he poses his example as an undecided hypothetical (**When [if] your children sinned against him . . .**), the destruction that God unleashed is apparently decisive for Bildad (**he gave them over to the penalty of their sin**). Job's children got what they deserved, he says, as do all those who sin against God.

In Job's case, however, Bildad appears less certain. Here, as at the end of the chapter (vv. 20–21), the hypothetical case Bildad sets out for Job seems to assume his innocence. Accordingly, all that stands in the way of Job's ultimate restoration is an unwillingness to **look to** and **plead with** God. The first of these terms is not the more usual verb for seeking a divine word of direction (Heb.

drsh). Instead, we find here a less common verb (Heb. *shkhr*), which describes *intent watching* for something, as when a beleaguered military watchman anxiously scans the horizon desperately hoping to see reinforcements to fight the surrounding enemy. The second term (Heb. *khnn*) describes an act of pleading for mercy and compassion. Contrary to the suggestion in the NIV *Study Bible* notes for this verse, there is no implication that Job needs to "admit his sinfulness." In fact, the remainder of Bildad's first speech emphasizes *lack of understanding* rather than *sin* as Job's difficulty.

The third hypothetical "if" (**if you are pure and upright**) raises the question of Job's personal righteousness. As we have seen in the prologue, God himself has proclaimed Job to be righteous. The "hypothetical," therefore, has already been decided. For the traditional view that Bildad represents, however, the jury is still out, and the matter must be investigated further. In his discourse Eliphaz initially had assumed some innate and unavoidable human flaw as the explanation for Job's pain, but now Bildad cautiously opens the hypothetical door to question the reality of Job's claim to sinlessness.

Bildad alters the qualifying phrase from the prologue (*tam weyashar*) by replacing the initial adjective with the less common *zak,* meaning "clear; pure." The word most often describes the purity of oil or incense that is "unadulterated" with impurities. A verb (*zkh*) of the same root describes the care exercised in keeping something pure, or cleaning oneself. The word also has the more ethically motivated sense of occupying a position of moral standing in the community.

He will rouse himself. On the basis of retribution, Bildad assumes that righteous behavior will lead to divine support and reward. The Bible often employs the image of God *rousing himself* to heighten expectation of a change from divine absence to divine presence. If righteousness indeed marks Job's life, then unlike his children he can anticipate divine grace and restoration (**restore you to your rightful place;** the verb translated "restore" here is the Piel of the verb *shlm*). Bildad's anticipation of restoration for Job seems genuine and he returns to this idea at the end of this chapter (vv. 20–22) as a way of driving home his concluding point. But his conviction does leave open and unanswered the continuing question: "Why is Job suffering *now*?" Bildad's comments, although well-meaning, have raised the possibility that, rather than some mysterious divine purpose, the cause might well be some unrevealed and unconfessed sin of Job.

In another clear indication of the author's knowledge of the prose framework of the book, Bildad's expectation of restoration (**so prosperous will your future be**) prefigures the multiplication of Job's family and possessions in the final chapter (42:10–17).

Additional Notes §22

8:2 / The Heb. for **blustering wind** is *ruakh kabbir,* "great/ mighty wind," which emphasizes *strength* rather than *character.* The NIV choice of "blustering" emphasizes the *negative* character of Job's words rather than the sheer quantity.

8:4 / It seems clear from this reference to the destruction of Job's **children** that the author of the dialogue section was aware of the prose prologue—in which Job's loss is recorded—and builds upon it here.

§23 Trust Ancient Tradition (Job 8:8–10)

8:8 / Bildad now draws on the ancient traditions of **former generations** and **their fathers** to support his arguments. Such attention to the results of the investigations (Heb. *kheqer*) of one's predecessors is the foundation of the wisdom enterprise. The experiences and observations of generations of sages, gathered over the ages, were thought to provide ever greater understanding of the divine ordering of the world and the appropriate way to relate to it. Bildad calls Job to *affirm* the traditional teaching of wisdom (which, in Bildad's view, affirms retribution). The Hebrew verb *konen* means "to establish firmly," as in the foundation of a building. Bildad is encouraging Job not simply to **find out** about the teachings of past sages, but also to "buy into" the prevailing ideology instead of picking away at its flaws.

8:9 / Job should join ancient tradition and rely on it because individual sages—even single generations of sages—have but limited experience to observe and understand life's intricacies. As Bildad cautions Job, **we were born only yesterday,** and as a result we **know nothing.** The insubstantial and ephemeral nature of human life (**our days on earth are but a shadow**) prevents individual sages from hoping to gain clear insight into the workings of the world.

The tension Bildad describes, between those who would preserve tradition and those who would throw it off, is very real and seen in almost every generation. The tension seems particularly clear today among the young college students I teach. In a recent online discussion group on the Psalms and worship, the prevailing sentiment was that tradition stultifies the free activity of the Spirit. Only when pushed did the students grudgingly admit that there might be essential traditions of the faith passed down from the beginning that ought not to be allowed to slip away.

But Bildad's point is not only one about tradition or radical revisionism. He is also talking about the ability of *one* to speak words of truth that challenge, shake, and ultimately change the treasured traditions of the *many*. There is strength and comfort in unity, and Diaspora Judaism employed communal solidarity to great effect in resisting the pressures to assimilate to the majority, foreign cultures among which they lived. Jesus ran headlong into the resistance of such community tradition to his simple, direct, and yet radically challenging vision of the kingdom of God broken loose among the simple people of Israel. The Protestant Reformation was another occasion when the insights of the few met resistance from the established wisdom of "former generations."

8:10 / **Will they not instruct you and tell you?** Bildad comes down on the side of community and tradition. The new word of the *one* finds its place within the context of the established tradition of the community. He cautions Job not to push the boundaries of faith beyond the breaking point, but to allow his questions to be resolved within the confines of traditional **understanding.**

The book of Job honors the quest of the one against the many. Throughout, it respects Job's struggle to know and understand, and the end of the book particularly vindicates this (42:7–9). This affirmation leaves us with the clear message that the insight of *one* (a Job, a Jesus, a Martin Luther) can have legitimacy and that traditional understanding ought always to remain open to change wrought by new and valid insight. It is interesting, however, that canonically this has *not* meant that Job *replaced* the more traditional insights of Proverbs, but that *both* stand alongside each other in the final form of the OT.

§24 Weeds in the Garden (Job 8:11–19)

As does Eliphaz in his first speech (4:7–11), Bildad supports his argument with aphoristic observations from traditional wisdom. Having just encouraged Job to accept the guidance of the ancestors and their words in verses 8–10, here he quotes a few of their sayings to make his point. The Hebrew is pretty rough going at times, with lots of uncommon words and unusual constructions. Bildad draws three observations from nature regarding the fragility of life. He begins (vv. 11–12) and ends (vv. 16–19) with plant imagery illustrating how easy it is for robust, seemingly healthy plants to lose their strength, wither, and disappear. In between, a central aphorism drives the main point home—like the intricate weavings of the spider's web, life is fragile and easily torn.

8:11–12 / The **papyrus** plant (*gomeʾ*) needs abundant **water.** These tall reeds were common in marshy areas of the ancient Near East, and particularly in the delta region of Egypt, where their abundance facilitated the production of inexpensive writing paper from the pulpy residue of their stems. Although this plant is robust and important, Bildad observes, it depends on water for its life. Without sufficient moisture the tall reeds are stunted and the whole plant withers to a useless mass. The second half of the verse is parallel and extends this observation to include other categories of the reed family (*ʾakhu*) that are similarly dependent on an ample supply of water for growth. Bildad concludes that without water even well rooted and **uncut** reeds **wither more quickly than grass.**

8:13 / The withering reeds are, of course, a metaphor for the dependence of human life on God. Without connection to God, seemingly robust humans also wither into insignificance. While NIV's **destiny** seems to imply an unchangeable fate decreed by God (and therefore outside the control of humans), the Hebrew describes instead a "way" or "path of conduct in life" that humans travel as the result of their continuing choices. While this kind of destiny *is* the inevitable consequence of a lifetime of human choices, it *can* change if the direction of a person's life and decision-making also changes. That is, of course, the primary reason for wisdom instruction such as Bildad's metaphor—to encourage decisive change, and thus to alter the "course" or "destiny" of a life. Those who will wither from robust life to insignificance, Bildad concludes, are those **who forget God.** Forgetfulness of this kind is more than simple failure of memory. Rather, it is a *willful putting God out of the mind,* a decision to exclude God and his gracious acts from memory, and so from any influence in one's life. The most fearful prospect for the faithful Israelite is to be *forgotten by God*—that God will actively decide to put his people out of mind in a final act of rejection and dismissal (see esp. Jer. 23:39, but also Deut. 4:31; Pss. 10:12; 13:1; 44:24; 74:19; Lam. 5:20; Isa. 44:21; 49:15). For Israel, memory is the primary means of making God present and effective in their individual and communal lives. Consider how many times Israel is called in Deuteronomy *not to forget* God (e.g., Deut. 4:23; 6:12; 8:11, 19; 25:19; see also Isa. 51:13), and to *remember* all of God's mighty acts on their behalf (e.g., Deut. 5:15; 7:18; 8:2; 8:18; 9:7, etc.) as an incentive for committed obedience to his commandments (Num. 15:39–40). God instructs them to tell and retell these events to their children through the ages in order to encourage their continued remembrance of, and dependence on, their covenant relationship with God (Deut. 5:1; 6:3–12).

Bildad calls those "who forget God," who thrust him out of mind in order to pursue their own course in the world, **the godless** (from the Heb. *khnp,* "to be defiled, corrupted, polluted"). Like the plants that wither, those who write God out of their lives will see their **hope** perish.

8:14–15 / Shifting from the plant world to living creatures, Bildad introduces a second aphorism drawn from observing spiders and their intricate webs. The "hope of the godless" in verse 13 will perish because it **trusts** in something too **fragile** to uphold it. We never learn the source of the godless person's trust—whether self, or wealth, or power, or a stable world—but *whatever* it may be, it is no more able to support the weight of human expectations than the beautiful but fragile **spider's web** can support the weight of the human who **leans** against it. The Hebrew term for "lean" implies a purposeful use of someone or

something for support—as when the elderly lean on their canes or
the arms of those who assist them. This kind of leaning *assumes*
support will come. Thus the rather unreasonable expectation that
a "spider's web" would offer adequate support for a human reveals the foolishness of the godless, who expect to be able to stand
on their own in life without God. The spider's house collapses as
he leans on it and, even though he **clings to it** (or grabs hold of it?),
he cannot draw himself upright again.

8:16–19 / Bildad returns to the world of plants for this
final aphorism. In this case, the scene is a well-watered garden.
The noun translated **well-watered plant** occurs only here, so
we do not know the precise nature of this plant. From my own
endeavors with gardening, I am inclined to see a particularly tenacious and spreading *weed* that draws water intended for the garden plants to feed the rapid growth of its tendrils. The description
of the plant looking **for a place among the stones** (lit., "a house of
stones") seems more appropriate for a weed than a carefully
tended plant. Also, the fact that it is **torn from its spot** supports
the idea that this is a destructive weed rather than a productive plant.

Such an identification makes the parallel between *weed* and
godless even more striking. The weed—whose rapid spread and
abundant growth mirror the seeming prosperity and robust health
of the godless—will be torn out and forgotten so that even the place
it formerly occupied **disowns it** and claims, "**I never saw you.**" This
is, of course, the ultimate act of willful forgetfulness that is turned
back from God on those who forget him.

A concluding statement emphasizes the futility of the life
that refuses to acknowledge and depend on God. Like the plants
without water or stripped from the nurturing soil, the life of the
wicked ultimately **withers away,** leaving room for **other plants** to
grow in its place.

Additional Notes §24

8:11 / The Heb. *bitsa* refers to a marsh or "swamp" as the necessary environment for a healthy papyrus plant. The second half of the
verse, which describes the "reed" as without water (*beli mayim*), makes
this emphasis on water clear.

8:12 / The Heb. for **grass** (*khatsir*) can also be translated as "reeds," and in particular as "cattails" (Holladay, *Concise Hebrew*, p. 113). But the emphasis here seems to be on the less resilient "grasses" that might ordinarily be expected to wither more quickly than uncut papyrus reeds (see 1 Kgs. 18:5; 2 Kgs. 19:26).

8:14 / There is perhaps an intentional wordplay in the first half of this verse. The terms NIV translates as, "**what he trusts in**," is the Heb. *kesel*, which can also be rendered "stupidity; foolishness," and the one who displays such characteristics is a "fool" (Heb. *kesil*). This kind of confidence is *foolish*. This same term appears in Ps. 49:13, where the NRSV translation "foolhardy" captures the kind of unreasoned trust that the term is intended to relay here. The verb translated "to be **fragile**" (Heb. *qwt?*) is not otherwise known with this meaning. Elsewhere it is translated "feel a disgust for," which is not appropriate in this context. Translators supply the meaning "be fragile" from the demands of the context and the association with the spider's web.

8:15 / It seems more likely that all the verbs in this verse refer to the action of the godless. He "will lean" on the spider's house, but he "will not stand." He "will grab hold" of it, but he "will not rise up."

8:16 / NIV has derived the meaning **well-watered plant** for the Heb. noun *ratob*, which occurs only here, from the verbal root *rtb*, which also occurs only once (in 24:8), and is usually translated "be(come) wet" (Holladay, *Concise Hebrew*, p. 338). Other translation possibilities include "thrive" (NRSV; NASB) and "green" (KJV). Holladay (p. 338) offers "full of sap (as a plant)."

8:19 / The Heb. here is also difficult and variously translated. The phrase NIV translates **its life withers away** (*mesus darko*) means, literally, "rejoicing his way." Other translations offer variations on this possibility: "this is the joy of his way" (NASB); "these are their happy ways" (NRSV). On the one hand, this interpretation of the passage might be more cynical, suggesting that when such "weeds" are pulled up, they are quickly replaced by others. On the other hand, it may stress that the "weeds" proceed merrily to their end completely unaware of their fate—and replaceability.

§25 Retribution Will Work (Job 8:20–22)

8:20–22 / Following this collection of aphoristic support, Bildad ends his speech by returning to the affirmation of retribution with which he began. With the unambiguous assertion that **surely God does not reject a blameless man**—employing the same term (Heb. *tam*) used to affirm Job in chapters 1 and 2—Bildad opens a cautious door to confirming Job's character. Bildad's statement answers positively the question he himself raised in verse 3: "Does God pervert justice? Does the Almighty pervert what is right?" Although delayed, Bildad is confident that retribution *will* ultimately work. A righteous Job can consequently anticipate the ultimate resolution of his suffering in **laughter** and **shouts of joy**. Equally, those who oppose a righteous Job must also suffer the consequences of their hostility. Since God does not **strengthen the hands of evildoers**, Job's opponents **will be clothed in shame**—in *public* disgrace—and in the end will be obliterated, since their **tents** (an allusion to their lives as temporary dwelling places) **will be no more.**

While Bildad's speech affirms retribution, he accepts the delay of its effective enactment to allow for suffering such as Job's. Righteous sufferers have two options: to continue to "look to God" in faith and to "plead" with him for deliverance (v. 5). While Bildad does not explain the suffering of a righteous Job, clearly he understands the deaths of his children as retribution against "their sin" (v. 4). The result is that although Bildad maintains a rather tenuous acceptance of Job's claims of innocence throughout the speech, his commitment to retribution casts a lengthening shadow over the question of whether the innocent can suffer as he has.

§26 How Can a Mortal Be Righteous before God? (Job 9:1–4)

Job's response to Bildad's speech moves the discussion in a new direction. Up to this point in the book Job has largely been addressing the extremity of his suffering and raising the agonizing question as to how a *righteous person* can be allowed to suffer so horrendously. Now, however, in response to Bildad's suggestion that the resolution of Job's suffering lies in his willingness to "look to God and plead with the Almighty" (8:5), Job begins to consider the possibility of such a confrontation with the divine and its prospects for redress of his situation. To say the least, Job is pessimistic.

9:1–2 / Job begins by acknowledging that Bildad's assertions are **true**. What is it about Bildad's comments that Job affirms here? The most likely antecedent seems to be the *closest*. Bildad's speech concludes with two related statements: that "God does not reject a blameless man," and that Job, as a result, will yet experience "laughter" and "joy" (8:20–21). If this is indeed the truth that Job affirms, then the problem Job considers is *not* whether retribution works (he seems to accept its operation here), but whether God *knows* that Job is righteous! The effect of the heavenly scene (chs. 1 and 2), then, is to draw a stark division between the reader (who is privy to the secret meeting between *the* Satan and God) and the human characters of the dialogue (Job and his friends, who are kept in the dark). Job remains ignorant of the information that the reader has: God *knows* and has *already affirmed* the righteousness of Job.

In this light, Job's question in the second half of this verse takes on a different nuance: **But how can a mortal be righteous before God?** This is not some pessimistic dismissal of the possibility of human righteousness. What Job is asking is not so much how one can *be* righteous (as if God is so holy that any human by comparison is decidedly *un*righteous). Rather the verb *tsdq* means to "be *declared* righteous" or "(publicly) vindicated." To be righteous in this sense is not simply to be free of sin or guilt, but to be *publicly declared and recognized* as having fulfilled the demands of the circumstance under consideration. It is not just the matter of righteousness that is at stake here (Job *knows* he is righteous), but righteousness *before* God. Can one gain an admission of righteousness *in the presence of God?*

It is probably no accident that Job uses the verbal root *tsdq* here rather than the root *tmm,* that elsewhere describes his blameless character (1:1, 8; 2:3). The point is not so much the inward reality of Job's complete and integrated person, but the public recognition of it—by God. What Job begins to consider here is whether or not it is possible to receive what he wants so very badly in the face of his friends' mounting critique: divine confirmation of the essentially blameless character Job knows to be true within himself.

Is it possible to be so sure of our own righteousness before God? Often our pattern is to follow the surface reading of Job's opening comment here and to affirm the general pessimism that Eliphaz expressed in 4:17–21: humans are by nature sinful and thus ultimately deserving of any suffering that comes upon them. This sort of "worm theology" ("O, miserable worm that I am ...!") sides with Job's friends (a dangerous place to be, as we will ultimately discover!) against the final message of the book as a whole. Job does not deny that all humans are sinners in need of the gracious mercy and redemption of God. But... , and this is a very important *but* ... , all suffering is *not* the deserved consequence of our sin. There is suffering that comes on us unexplained and undeserved, and we must name this kind of suffering (whether our own or that of others) clearly for what it is—a pernicious evil out of sync with God's original creation intention for his world and its inhabitants.

So, if it is possible to suffer undeservedly, then it is also possible to recognize, acknowledge, and articulate our righteous stance in the face of such suffering. Not to do so would, in effect, deny the existence of evil in our world and attribute *all suffering*— whether deserved or not—to our God and creator. Further, we would also encourage others to join us as "worms" who must accept that somehow we *deserve* any pain and agony we suffer simply because we had the misfortune to be born human. We all know people like this. However well intended, this view is ultimately a travesty and trivializes the valiant and courageous suffering of myriads of the faithful throughout the ages. Such an attitude also prevents us from being able to hear the true message of Job.

9:3–4 / What Job desires more than anything else is for God to publicly declare him righteous. However, as convinced as he is of his own innocence in this matter, he is pessimistic about his chances of gaining public recognition from God. Any sort of **dispute** with God begins on a decidedly unequal basis. Job fears he would never be able to get a "word in edgewise" with God (**he could not answer him one time out of a thousand**). God's understanding is so **profound**, and his words so divinely abundant and astute, that Job would be unable to prevail in any argument.

Job does not present God in a very positive light here. God appears to be a particularly skilled and arrogant attorney-at-law, who employs his mastery of language and his knowledge of the legal loopholes to bludgeon his opponent into silence—and defeat. Job hesitates to open an argument with God from which he has little hope of escaping **unscathed.** Indeed, in some ways Job's words here prefigure the ultimate appearance of God in chapters 38–42, where God's questions so overwhelm Job that he remains virtually silent in the face of the divine onslaught (see esp. 40:1–5; 42:1–6).

Additional Notes §26

9:4 / The Heb. behind the expression "**come out unscathed**," is the verb *shlm,* which suggests "wholeness, completeness, health."

§27 Intimidation by Divine Power (Job 9:5–13)

Job's pessimism continues to color his evaluation of divine power. God's strength is not a comforting presence to which the afflicted can appeal in hope. God is instead an intimidating source of fear and uncertainty. Job further anticipates the divine theophany in chapters 38–42 when he describes the divine appearance as having the frightful force of hurricane winds that drive humans to their knees.

9:5–9 / Job says that God's power breaks in unexpectedly—**he moves mountains without their knowing it**—and with fearsome manifestations—**he shakes the earth . . . and makes its pillars tremble.** The imagery in these verses is quite consistent with the ravages of a powerful sea storm or hurricane. The **sun . . . does not shine** and even the **light of the stars** is obscured. Even in the midst of all this turmoil, however, God remains in control. He is the creator of **the heavens** and **the Maker of . . . the constellations of the south.** The tumultuous seas hold no fear for him since he **treads on the waves.**

God's anticipated presence is not only powerful but grounded in divine **anger** (see also v. 13). The source of this anger is less than clear in these verses, but it may be related to God's action in creation to limit the chaotic forces of the cosmos. Alternatively the anger may have to do with the threat of uncreation associated with the great flood (Gen. 6–9). The main point is that God's power revealed in creation conflict is irresistible—especially to any mortal who would wish to confront God in court.

9:10 / God's presence is intimidating not only because it is powerful, threatening to undo the stable foundations of the word, but also because it **cannot be fathomed** (Heb. *kheqer* is less concerned with intellectual contemplation than with hunting or searching out answers). Bildad has just exhorted Job (8:8) to pay close attention to what the ancestors had "learned" (Heb. *kheqer*), but Job counters here that no human has the ability to comprehend God's wonderful deeds. Rather than being beyond *knowing*, God's mighty acts cannot be *found*—they elude any who would search them out. The artful poem in chapter 28 will explore this same territory in even greater detail, with similar negative results. Humans are unable to find divine wisdom. Only God knows the way to it (28:12–28). God's deeds are powerful and humans are unable even to figure out what God is doing in the world (which is also the major point of Eccl., see esp. Eccl. 8:16–17).

9:11 / Words reminiscent of the comparison between the wind and the work of God in Ecclesiastes illustrate this lack of perception. "As you do not know the path of the wind, or how the body is formed in a mother's womb, so you cannot understand the work of God, the Maker of all things" (Eccl. 11:5). Similarly, Job is unable to see God when he goes by or even to perceive him, making any sort of contact, confrontation, or even conversation impossible.

The translation "**when he passes . . . goes by**" actually masks a revealing wordplay. The first phrase in Hebrew is *yaʿabor ʿalay*, which can mean "cross over, pass through." On many occasions, however, the verb *ʿbr* has the more pointed and negative meaning "transgress against." The picture is of one who passes over the agreed boundaries of relationship. When used in this sense, the verb most often describes Israel's transgression of her covenant obligations. In the light of this usage, we could read Job's statements about God as cloaking a hidden accusation that God has transgressed his covenant relationship with Job. A comparison with Isaiah 24:5 further clarifies this reading: "The earth is defiled by its people; they have disobeyed the laws, violated the statutes and broken the everlasting covenant." The verbs "disobeyed" (*ʿbr*; NRSV "transgressed") and "violated" (*khlp*) are the same two verbs Job uses in verse 11 to describe God's "passing by." In his suffering and in his inability to contact God Job feels his covenant relationship with God has been roughly violated and transgressed.

9:12 / God is a law unto himself, says Job. He defines the standard of righteousness and justice. **If he snatches away** (a clear reference to the losses Job sustained in chs. 1 and 2), no mortal can hope to **stop him.** God is too powerful, comes invisibly and unexpectedly upon the unsuspecting, and cannot be located or hauled into court for redress. In a phrase that recalls the opening of this section (v. 3), Job admits the futility of questioning God, of asking him: **What are you doing?**

9:13 / This section concludes as it began, with the **anger** of God. Here Job describes it as so overpowering that even **the cohorts of Rahab cowered at his feet.** The reference to "Rahab" alludes to the chaotic primeval waters that Yahweh subdued in creation. In Mesopotamian creation accounts, these waters are ancient chaotic gods whose struggle with the younger gods of order ends in the death of the ancient gods and the creation of the earth (see the discussion on 7:12 in §20, above). In the OT the name appears only a few times in reference to a sea monster subdued by Yahweh: "By his power he churned up the sea; by his wisdom he cut Rahab to pieces" (26:12). Similarly, "Awake, awake! Clothe yourself with strength, O arm of the LORD; awake, as in days gone by, as in generations of old. Was it not you who cut Rahab to pieces, who pierced that monster through?" (Isa. 51:9).

Additional Notes §27

9:5–9 / The description of God's action in the universe assumes an ancient Near Eastern cosmology rather than a modern scientific worldview. According to the ancients, the "earth" (Heb. *²erets*) was a flat, round plate suspended on the primeval waters. Over the earth arced the "firmament" (Heb. *raqia*ᶜ) like an inverted bowl. Together, earth and firmament formed a sealed environment in which the chaotic waters were held at bay and life in all its forms could develop and thrive. The earth was understood to rest on **pillars** that extended down into the waters under the earth and provided stability. This description assumes God's power over the creation and does not question his ability to shake the foundational stability of the earth. As in the flood account (Gen. 6–9), the intrusion of the chaotic waters into the tenuous environment of the human world threatens to undo creation, so here God is seen to bring the world to the brink of destruction by his power.

9:11 / See also Eccl. 8:8: "No man has power over the wind to contain it; so no one has power over the day of his death." Hab. 1:11, "Then they sweep past like the wind and go on," uses the same two Heb. verbs: **passes**/"go on" (Heb. ᶜ*br*) and **goes by**/"sweep past" (Heb. *khlp*). Most instances where the verb ᶜ*br* means "transgress against" involve Israel's transgression of the covenant (*berit*), although a few involve violation of the *torah*: Deut. 26:13; Josh. 7:11, 15 (*berit*); Judg. 2:20 (*berit*); 2 Kgs. 18:12 (*berit*); Isa. 24:5 (*torah*); Jer. 34:18 (*berit*); Dan. 9:11 (*torah*). In 1 Sam. 15:24, Saul admits to having transgressed the "command" (Heb. *pi*, "mouth") of Yahweh and the words of Samuel.

9:12 / The Heb. verb *khtp* appears only here. The noun from this root (*khetep*) appears only once as well, in Prov. 23:28, to describe a "robber" lying in wait for a victim. Holladay (*Concise Hebrew,* p. 120) suggests that the verb means "carry off" by disease.

9:13 / Less certain references to **Rahab** include Ps. 87:4; Isa. 30:7. The rest of the occurrences of Rahab in the OT and NT refer to the Canaanite prostitute from Jericho who figures prominently in the narratives surrounding the fall of Jericho and who becomes the ancestor of David (Josh. 2:1, 3; 6:17, 23, 25; Matt. 1:5; Heb. 11:31; Jas. 2:25).

§28 Loss of Confidence in Divine Justice (Job 9:14–24)

9:14 / **How then can I dispute with him?** How can Job hope to present a case in the face of the power and freedom that God represents? **How can I find words . . . ?** What argument can anyone muster to confront an opponent whose nature and deeds define the very nature of righteousness and who is, therefore, essentially beyond questioning?

9:15–16 / Job's frustration is also grounded in the realization that in any setting in which God could be brought to the dock, God stands not only as the accused, but also as **Judge.** The tables would soon turn so that it would be Job who would be forced to defend his innocence and to throw himself on the **mercy** of the court. Although God is too powerful to be captured and brought forcibly into court, Job contemplates the futility of hope even should such a confrontation ever take place. Even if brought face to face with God in a legal proceeding, Job despairs of securing a just **hearing.**

9:17–18 / Job's past experience of God leads him to expect more of the same. Because of God's irresistible power, he would **overwhelm** any opponent foolhardy enough to summon him into court. As in the opening verses of this chapter, again it is the **storm** that comes to Job's mind as the illustration of divine power unleashed in destructive fury. Should he confront God in court, Job's **wounds** would **multiply** even beyond his current state of misery. God's attack would be **for no reason**—a translation of the Heb. *khinnam* ("for no profit; reason") that *the* Satan employed earlier to question the sincerity of Job's service to God: "Does Job fear God for nothing [*khinnam*]?" (1:9). Ironically, as Job's faithful service to God returns no profit, so God's attack on Job is equally profitless.

The intensity of the attack would leave Job unable to respond. Face to face with God, Job says he would be unable **to regain my breath**—an expectation that proves true when God finally comes on the scene in chapters 38–42 (see esp. 40:3–5). In a sense, then, the delay of God's appearing allows Job to do what he will not be able to accomplish in God's overwhelming presence: to press his case unhindered by the crushing power and wisdom of God. As we will see later, when God *does* come, Job's complaint is effectively at an end, his mouth is shut. Now, however, without any such restraint he is able to express himself, his questions, and his doubts in the harshest and most articulate terms. Literarily, at least, the delay of God is very important, since it allows the free discussion among Job and his friends of these dark and difficult issues—and, of course, the reader overhears it all. (Compare this view of the delay of the coming of God in Job with the similar passage in 2 Pet. 3:1–13.)

This is also, of course, one of the chief characteristics of human life now, and at any time. We are free (and indeed encouraged by narratives like Job and Ecclesiastes) to ponder the imponderables, to seek answers where there are none, to acknowledge the myriad of ways our lives do not measure up to the promise of God's creation. By doing so we exercise an inalienable right built into the very fabric of our beings by the creator God who made us. By doing so we come to understand that this world as it currently exists cannot provide our spiritual hope and consummation. By doing so we align ourselves ultimately with the will and purpose of God, who intends for us and his cosmos so much more than this world we now know could ever hope to offer or contain. This is, of course, why there must be "a new heaven and a new earth" (2 Pet. 3:13; Rev. 21:1).

9:19–20 / These verses offer an effective summary of Job's reply up to this point. As far as **strength** goes, God is too **mighty** to be coerced into a courtroom dispute by a human plaintiff. Even if one (like Job) has a just case, God remains both judge and jury, setting the very standards of **justice**.

Even if I were innocent . . . blameless. Job is not admitting to some guilt here. He is speaking of a hypothetical courtroom confrontation and couches his language in appropriate terms. Should that confrontation ever occur, he is convinced that his innocence would provide no protection in this imagined conflict with God. Having bemoaned the ineffectiveness of human language to call

God to account, Job now despairs that, in God's overwhelming presence, even his own **mouth** will fail him and become the star witness for the prosecution!

9:21 / Job reaffirms his blamelessness using the same word (Heb. *tam*) with which the narrative began in 1:1. The word *tam* here also links back to the hypothetical blamelessness at the end of the preceding verse. Job couches both statements in identical language (*tam ʾani*, vv. 20, 21). Job's absolute claim in verse 21, therefore, clarifies any doubt that verse 20 may have raised.

I have no concern for myself. This phrase is difficult and has given rise to various interpretations. These range from the simple "I do not know myself" (NRSV), to the indecisive "I am no longer sure [of my blamelessness]" (NJB; see NAB "I myself cannot know it"), to the self-deprecating "I have no concern for myself." Coupled with the following parallel phrase, **I despise my own life,** the verse suggests that Job has reached a point of resignation, accepting the inevitability of suffering and eventual death. In this context, then, it seems Job is shifting the argument away from *personal* concern for redress to larger issues of more general principle. In "despising" his life here, Job sets the stage for his final submission in 42:6, where he uses this same self-deprecating phrase again: *ʾem ʾas,* "I despise [myself]."

9:22–24 / When Job says, **"It is all the same,"** he means that in his resignation he is able to acknowledge that his experience teaches that God treats **the blameless and the wicked** alike. His thesis statement lays out his contention in negative terms: God **destroys both** (the blameless and the wicked). Again, the term *tam* links this statement back to the hypothetical law case of verse 20 as well as to Job's clear protestation of innocence in verse 21. But now the context lends Job's claim a more universal and less personal application. Experience has led Job to draw a broad conclusion about God's treatment of humans. His conclusion contradicts standard retributive theology and sides closely with the understanding of Ecclesiastes (see Eccl. 8:14–15).

Two examples confirm Job's claim. The first describes a sudden death as the result of a **scourge.** The term (Heb. *shot*) can mean either a "whip" used for exacting punishment or an unexpected "flood." In the first alternative, the irony is that the **innocent,** while being subjected to punishment intended for the wicked, has unjustly died as a result. The other translation of *shot* (REB) suggests that a sudden flash flood has taken the life of the innocent. In either case, Job depicts God as "mocking" or "laughing" at the **despair** of this innocent. In the second example, Job envisions **judges**—called to consider a case of **land** fraud—who wear **blindfolds** which prevent their rendering a just verdict. Contrary to our traditional western image of a goddess of justice who is blindfolded in order to be able to rule without prejudice, Job's blindfolds render the magistrates incapable of seeing the truth of the matter. As God **mocks** the innocent, so also God impairs the vision of the judges and allows injustice to result.

Job asserted in verses 4 and 14 that dispute with God is impossible because of his overwhelming wisdom and power. Now Job has come to question whether God truly champions the cause of the innocent, or enforces justice in the world.

Additional Notes §28

9:21 / *I have no concern for myself.* See the discussion in Clines, *Job 1–20,* p. 237, who opts for the translation, "I do not care about myself," by comparison to the parallel phrase, "I despise my own life" (9:21c). Gordis, *Job,* pp. 96, 107, suggests, "I am beside myself [with misery]," on the basis of the similar idiomatic expression in Song 6:12. The same phrase (*loʾ ʾedaʿ,* "I do not know") appears in Job 42:3 to describe "things too wonderful for *me to know*" (emphasis added). The parallel phrase in 9:21c (*ʾemʾas*) also appears again in Job 42:6. The appearance of both terms in such close proximity may suggest that *loʾ ʾedaʿ* here in v. 21 should be understood as a statement of Job's mystification: "I just don't understand [why I am blameless and yet suffering]."

9:23 / The **innocent** here is a *plural* noun, and therefore more likely related to the destruction of a "flood" than that of a "whip." Others take the **scourge** more metaphorically (e.g., NRSV, "disaster"; NJB, "sudden deadly scourge").

Mocks: the same verb for this mocking laughter (*lʿg*) describes God's response to the futile plotting of the nations in Ps. 2:4. In Job 11:3, Zophar uses the same verb to criticize Job's speech as mockery.

§29 The Futility of Innocence (Job 9:25–31)

9:25–26 / Job feels his **days** swiftly ebbing away. The verbs pile up in this picture of his life: it recedes swiftly (*qll*, "be swifter; recede") into the distance before Job's eyes; his days **fly away** (*brkh*, "flee") before him like a **runner** (*rts*, "run") straining toward the finish tape but without any **joy** of victory. Other images of speed lend further urgency here. Job's swiftly fleeing days are like speedy **boats of papyrus** sailing along the Nile, or like predatory **eagles** that fold their wings and plummet from the sky to capture their **prey**. This last image echoes once again with the destruction and death that await Job just around the corner.

9:27–29 / God is powerful and unlikely to establish Job's innocence even if Job could bring him into court. Life is fleeting and likely to remain painful. Even if he were to change his attitude, to **forget** his **complaint** and adopt outwardly the signs of happy resignation, Job is certain his suffering would only continue. His only hope is for God to consider him **innocent,** but his conclusion that **I am already found guilty** almost convinces him that any struggle is in vain.

9:30–31 / The problem as Job sees it is not his sin or innocence, but God's treatment of him. Even a thorough cleansing would not suffice because God has already determined Job's guilt. God would just **plunge** him swiftly **into a slime pit** so that his suffering and gross physical ailments would only become worse. Even his garments would **detest** being close to his body.

Additional Notes §29

9:27 / **I will change my expression, and smile:** This sentiment echoes Ecclesiastes' exhortation to, "Go, eat your food with gladness, and drink your wine with a joyful heart, for it is now that God favors what you do. . . . Enjoy life with your wife, whom you love, all the days of this meaningless life that God has given you under the sun—all your meaningless days. For this is your lot in life and in your toilsome labor under the sun" (Eccl. 9:7, 9; see 5:18–20). Job seems to resist the way of resignation that Ecclesiastes adopts.

9:31 / A Heb. word for **slime** is not present in the text but is interpretively derived from the action of the verb *tbl*, "dip." The "pit" (*shakhat*, a frequent euphemism for *Sheol*) must contain something into which Job envisions himself being dipped, thus NIV's "slime."

§30 The Lack of Divine Parity Undermines Justice (Job 9:32–35)

9:32–33 / Job's frustration is a consequence of the lack of parity that exists between God and his creatures. **He is not a man like me.** Since God is not a human that can be hauled into court to answer for his actions, God's *otherness* undermines any hope Job might have of securing justice. As a result, Job conceives for the first time a vague idea of **someone to arbitrate** the dispute between two such unequal partners. This arbiter would have to be someone who could **lay his hand upon** both parties. The term for "arbitrate" (*mokiakh*) in the Prophets and Wisdom literature describes one who "rebukes" those who speak wrongly or who "mediates" in a court setting (Isa. 29:21; Ezek. 3:26; Amos 5:10; Prov. 9:7; 25:12; 28:23). The second use probably derives from the first, since the "mediator" or "arbiter" is committed to the truth and would necessarily "rebuke" those who brought false testimony in court. The term occurs twice more in Job: in the opening speech of Elihu (32:12), who accuses Job's friends of failing to rebuke him (NIV "proved Job wrong"), and then in God's questioning Job (40:2: "Let him who *accuses* God answer him"). This arbiter would stand **between us**—between Job and God—to protect the powerless from being overwhelmed by the powerful and to ensure justice.

9:34–35a / Job envisions that this arbiter would **remove God's rod from me.** Because of the arbiter's presence, God would be unable to intimidate Job with his "rod" and **his terror.** Depending on its context, the "rod" (Heb. *shebet*) is variously translated as "scepter," "(shepherd's) rod," "club (for battle)," or "rod (for discipline)." Whether Job understands this "rod" as a means of discipline or hostile attack is not clear but, coupled with the parallel "terror," the latter seems more likely. The fear of divine attack and its consequences prevents Job from speaking his mind. An arbiter would ensure an open exchange of accusations and evidence without fear of reprisal. In such a circumstance, Job says, **I would speak up without fear of him.**

9:35b / There is some controversy about how to understand the last half of this verse. The Hebrew is difficult, literally meaning something like, "because not so I with myself." NIV (**but as it now stands with me**) has taken the initial phrase to mean "my circumstances are not like those just described." The sense would be that Job is *not* separated from God by an arbiter, he *does* fear divine terror, and thus he is unable to speak openly. This interpretation is awkward in that Job immediately does what he says he cannot: he determines to speak out freely in the following verses (10:1–2). In light of this context, the translation that appeals most to me is: "But it is not so with me with myself." The sense here is that Job has ceased to fear the consequences of divine power and wrath. As he comes to admit in 10:1, "I loathe my very life." In other words, death holds no fear. He has seen the worst life has to offer, so he has no more to lose.

Job has moved clearly in this chapter to identify God as hostile and punitive in his relationship with him. We may have difficulty dealing with such brutally honest language that views God as the enemy. We may want to absolve God of any wrongdoing, and so we often employ twisted logic and thinking to explain away what Job finds obvious. God is in control. Although Job is righteous, he is suffering terribly. Therefore, it must be that God allows Job to suffer unjustly. Since Job accepts the correctness of the traditional view of retribution, he assumes that the righteous *should* prosper and God *ought* to uphold this basic covenant expectation. Since this is not happening in Job's case, he can only assume that God for some unknowable reason has taken a hostile stance against him. Job still believes, however, that if God could be brought into court and Job's testimony could be heard in the absence of intimidation, that justice would necessarily prevail.

Additional Notes §30

9:33 / The phrase **lay his hand upon** occurs only twice outside Job. It seems to describe the act of "closing the eyes" of a deceased person in Gen. 46:4 and implies joining forces with another in Exod. 23:1: "Do not help [lay your hand upon] a wicked man by being a malicious witness." Perhaps in Job the implication is that the arbiter would not take sides, but would instead join forces *equally* with both parties.

9:34 / **Rod:** for the meaning "scepter," see Gen. 49:10; Isa. 14:5; Ezek. 19:11, 14; 21:10, 13. For the meaning "(shepherd's) rod," see Lev. 27:32; Ezek. 20:37. For the meaning "(disciplinary) rod," see Exod. 21:20; 2 Sam. 7:14; Isa. 9:4; 10:5, 15, 24; 11:4. For the meaning "(battle) club," see Num. 24:17; Judg. 5:14; 2 Sam. 23:21; Isa. 14:29. Isa. 28:27 seems to refer to a "rod" used for agricultural purposes.

9:35b / For further discussions of the various interpretations of this verse see Clines, *Job 1–20*, pp. 220–21; Rowley, *Job*, pp. 99–100; Pope, *Job*, pp. 76–77.

§31 Determination to Press On (Job 10:1–2)

10:1 / Having reached rock bottom, Job throws caution to the wind and determines to make his case openly, strongly, and without consideration for future consequences. Since his **life** is loathsome, he has little to lose. By giving **free rein** to his **complaint** he may win a hearing, or at least be freed from suffering by divine judgment. "Complaint" would be better rendered "concern" or "consuming interest." What drives Job at this point is not so much a complaint as the desire to be publicly declared righteous by God. The notion of complaint tends to focus on Job's suffering and the injustice of it. The narrative (as revealed through the test motif in the prologue) is not so concerned with suffering as it is with whether the faithful should endure even if they are not acknowledged for their faithfulness. We will return to this point below.

Job's words pour forth from **the bitterness of** his **soul.** "Soul" is from the Hebrew *nepesh,* which describes the animated being that constitutes a living human being. This is not just some vague spiritual angst that motivates Job, but the deepest interest and concern of his living self in all its physical limitation and pain. To speak to one's *nepesh* is to deliberate deeply at the very center of oneself. When this deepest self is consumed by bitterness, the person's whole worldview is affected.

10:2 / **I will say to God.** Like a debater preparing for a match, Job imagines the best way to present his case to God and rehearses his speech, as he shifts to directly address God. Using legal terminology, Job assumes from the pain he is enduring that a judge's decision has been made in his absence. God has already condemned (Heb. *rshᶜ,* "declare wicked") Job without even revealing the evidence on which the decision was based. **Do not condemn me,** Job cries, at least **tell me what charges you have against me.** Literally, he says, "Reveal to me concerning what you bring a covenant dispute (Heb. *ryb*) against me."

Additional Notes §31

10:1 / **Loathe:** In 8:14, the verb *qwt* appears in a context that suggests the meaning "be fragile." If this usage also reflects that nuance, then Job might be saying "my life is fragile."

The verb for **free rein** is ʿ*zb,* "abandon; let go of." While this could mean that Job is going to *stop* complaining, it is clear by what follows that is not the case.

NIV's **complaint** is interpretive for the noun *shikh,* "what concerns/interests one."

§32 The Non-carnate God (Job 10:3–7)

10:3 / References to the "hand(s)" of God frame this short section of chapter 10, beginning with **the work of your hands.** The tension here, between God's creative care and his wrath, carries over into the next section ("Your *hands* shaped me," v. 8, emphasis added). In a near parody of the divine questioning of Job in chapters 38–42, Job directs his deepest concern to God in the form of a series of pointed questions. These questions are intended to encourage sympathy toward Job's plight and to force God to acknowledge the implications of Job's suffering for divine justice. Job's questions build on the essential otherness of God established in 9:32 with the statement, "He is not a man like me." As a result of this defining difference between God and humans, Job's questioning (like that later questioning of Job by God) takes on a more rhetorical function in which God is forced to reply in the way Job anticipates.

Does it please you to oppress me? This first question is perhaps the only one of the series that desires an answer. Surely his intense and continuing suffering has Job questioning the very character of God. Unlike the psalmist who declares in Psalm 5:4, "You are not a God who takes pleasure in evil; with you the wicked cannot dwell," Job wonders whether the power to make Job suffer is a source of divine delight (lit., "Is it good for you?"). The verb "oppress" has the sense of "burden, wrong" or even "exploit." The object "me" is not expressed in the Hebrew, so both "oppress" and the parallel verb **spurn** appear to refer to "the work of your hands." Job is, of course, the particular "work" at issue here. Job also uses the verb translated "spurn" (Heb. *m^es*) in 9:21c to describe how he "despises" or "rejects" his own life. That he has himself reached such a point of personal rejection does not mean it is comforting to think that God has come to the same estimation. Job *wants* to know here whether all hope is lost. If indeed God has rejected him and takes pleasure in making him suffer, then death is preferable.

In contrast to his rejection of the righteous Job, God smiles **on the schemes of the wicked.** The verb translated "smile" is the Hebrew *ypᶜ,* that normally describes the shining forth of the divine radiance like the sun. God "shines" in this way when he appears in theophany (e.g., Deut. 33:2; Ps. 50:2); when he comes to guide Israel (e.g., Ps. 80:1); and when he appears to avenge his enemies (e.g., Ps. 94:1). Job employs this particular verb for "shining" three other times (in 3:4; 10:22; and 37:15)—referring to light other than the light of God's own presence and face. Here, though, it is the light of God's own approving presence that Job has in mind— the same approving presence he himself desires so completely, but fails to experience.

10:4 / Job's truly rhetorical questions begin with an all-out assault on God's ability to know and understand what humans experience in life. God is so *other,* so *removed* from human life, that he can have no awareness of what suffering his treatment of his creatures causes. **Do you have eyes of flesh?** Since God is not a human like Job (9:32), he cannot see with the eyes of a mortal. "Flesh" (Heb. *basar*) does not so much emphasize physical eyes as it does the ability to see as humans see. For the narrator of Ecclesiastes, sight is the primary means by which he observes and experiences the vanity of human life, its painful contradictions and frustrations (e.g., Eccl. 1:14; 2:11, 13, 24; 3:10, 16, 22; 4:1, 4, 7, 15; 5:13; 6:1; 7:15; 8:9, 10, 17; 9:11, 13; 10:5, 7). As the parallel phrase, **Do you see as a mortal sees?** suggests, for God to see with "eyes of flesh" is for him to know through experience what human existence, with all its limitations, is really like. This second phrase relates to the first as a result clause: "Do you have eyes of flesh, *so that* you might see as a man sees?" The noun translated "mortal" here is the Hebrew *ʾenosh,* which emphasizes the weakness of humans and their limitations. It is the same noun Eliphaz uses in 4:17 to indicate the impossibility of weak humans ever being righteous before God. Since God is not a human (an *ʾenosh*) like Job, he *cannot,* Job suggests, truly know and identify with the lives of his creatures.

10:5 / Job continues this comparison by contrasting the length of human and divine life. Since God has no limitation on his **days** or the **years** he amasses, how can he understand the irreplaceable loss entailed in Job's prolonged suffering? For God, "days" and "years," indeed time itself, offers no limitation and is thus meaningless. Job intends to establish the vast distance between God and humans and the barriers these differences present to divine understanding.

10:6–7 / God has entirely too much time on his hands, says Job. To while away the eons of divine life, God spends his days and years probing into the **faults** and **sin** of his creatures. The terms for **search** and **probe** are not the more intensive verbs of trying, testing, and analyzing human behavior known from psalms such as 139:23: "Search [*khqr,* 'dig deep; hunt diligently into'] me, O God, and know my heart; test [*bkhn,* 'examine'] me and know my anxious thoughts." These are the more common verbs of looking, seeking, probing (*bqsh,* "seek; look for" and *drsh,* "care about; consider; question"). Job even questions whether God really expects to find anything in his probing (**you know that I am not guilty**). Although Job has not been privy to the divine affirmation of his blamelessness in the heavenly conversation with *the* Satan, he accepts that God is all-knowing and aware of his lack of offense. God has all the leisure to probe Job because he need not worry that there is anyone able to **rescue** him from God's **hand.** With the reference to God's "hand," the section has come full circle to where it began in verse 3. The creature, who is the work of God's hands, is now in the hand of God, or at his mercy. With "no one can rescue me from your hand," Job employs a common idiom to emphasize the hopelessness of his plight. Often this phrase, "no one can rescue," is a dire warning of destruction. It appears to have its roots in the circumstances of helpless prey dragged off by lions to their dens (Isa. 5:29; Hos. 5:14; Mic. 5:7; Pss. 7:3; 50:22). There is little hope that anyone could snatch the prey from the teeth and claws of the lion that has captured it. God stalks Job "like a lion" in 10:16.

On several occasions the complete phrase "no one can rescue"—including "from your/my hand"—describes the inevitability of divine judgment. In Deuteronomy 32:39, God claims the power of life and death over his covenant people. "See now that I myself am He! There is no god besides me. I put to death and I bring to life, I have wounded and I will heal, and no one can deliver out of my hand." Similarly, in Isaiah 43:13, God proclaims: "Yes, and from ancient days I am he. No one can deliver out of my hand. When I act, who can reverse it?" Job taps into this common usage to emphasize his vulnerability and his lack of any hope for deliverance.

Additional Notes §32

10:3 / The Heb. for **oppress** is ⁿshq (Holladay, *Concise Hebrew*, p. 286). It is interesting to note that the similar root ⁿsq, that would appear to be identical in the consonantal text, means "quarrel."

While the verb employed in the traditional blessing in Num. 6:25 ("The LORD bless you and keep you; the LORD make his face *shine* [Heb. ⁿwr] upon you . . .") is different than the verb for **smile** here in Job, the expectation of divine approval coupled with divine radiance is the same.

10:7 / **No one** (who) **can rescue** is the Hiphil participle from *ntsl*, "snatch away; deliver."

§33 Divine Care Overshadowed by Pain (Job 10:8–17)

Job often employs ironic contrasts and wordplay to communicate the contradictions of human life. This passage demonstrates both of these techniques well. Beginning with a description of divine care at Job's birth—the birth that he wishes had never occurred (3:1–11)—Job shows how the destructive attention unleashed on Job's present overshadows and undermines this act of divine intricacy and "hands-on" involvement.

10:8 / **Your hands shaped me and made me.** In light of the suffering Job is currently enduring at the hands of God, this statement is less an awe-filled expression of gratitude than an acerbic indictment of the creator. The same "hands" that mercilessly crush Job (vv. 3–7) are the creative hands that also "shaped" and "made" Job. The verb "shaped" sometimes describes the formation of plastic objects, including idols. In an ironic wordplay Job has chosen this verb (*ʿtsb*) that can also mean "grieve; offend" (Holladay, *Concise Hebrew*, pp. 279–80). By shaping Job at birth and then abandoning him to suffer unjustly, God has committed a grave offense against his creature. Against this picture of involved, careful shaping, Job's following question—**Will you now turn and destroy me?**—comes almost as a shock. Would the potter take his most delicate and intricate creation and smash it into fragments like a defective pot? The contradiction is strong and intentional: What is God doing? His present actions in relation to Job run contrary to all expectation.

10:9 / **Remember,** Job says. The act of remembrance plays an immensely important role in Israel's life of faith. The verbal root *zkr*, "remember" (and all of its related nouns) appears more than 350 times throughout the OT. In addition, the Hebrews had other ways to express the concept "remember" (such as "bring to mind" or "keep in your heart"). In Israel, remembering meant more than simply recalling a set of facts or feelings. A call to "remember" is also a call to "act" on the basis of what is remembered. God calls Israel, for example, to remember the commandments and to teach them to subsequent generations *so that* they would obey them (Deut. 4:10).

Forgetfulness is tragic because it represents not simply absentmindedness, but willful rejection of what ought always to be brought to mind. When Israel forgot God, it rebelled against him. When God forgot Israel, it was as if it had ceased to be his people (Jer. 23:39; Lam. 5:20; Pss. 13:1; 4:24). Job calls God to "remember" his involvement in creating Job in order to call God back from judgment to his original care. It is not clear whether Job expects this restoration of God's care to take place, or whether his intention is simply to mark the contradiction in clearest terms. In the *literary* context, however, it is the contradiction that is most important for the reader to comprehend. Job's experience (and ours) is often at odds with all we know and profess about the character of God. His power, his care for his creation and creatures, his absolute hostility to evil in all its forms and guises, do not always square with the undeserved suffering that falls from the blue on the righteous and unrighteous alike.

The background of **you molded me like clay . . . turn me to dust again** is clearly the creation of the original human from "the dust (*ʿapar*) of the ground" in Genesis 2. Humans are "dust" (*ʿapar*) and will ultimately return to "dust" (*ʿapar*) in death (Gen. 2:7; 3:19). Job draws on this well-known narrative when he questions whether the creator God will indeed consign his creation to the dust once more. As creation was an act of *election* in which God chose his human creations for relationship, so returning this creature to the "dust" constitutes an act of *un*creation and rejection of relationship.

A related passage in Isaiah 64:8 has further influenced Job's thinking: "Yet, O LORD, you are our Father. We are the clay, you are the potter; we are all the work of your hand." In the first half of Job 10:9, Job uses the word "clay" (*khomer*) to indicate the medium of human creation rather than "dust" (*ʿapar*) as in Genesis 2:7. The Genesis account uses the verb *ytsr*, "shape (as a potter shapes clay)," implying that the *ʿapar* is pliable like clay. Job's verb is the more general *ʿsh*, "make." In Isaiah 64:7, however, the substance God the potter (*yotser*) molds is "clay" (*khomer*). Note how the Isaiah passage also refers at the end to Israel as "the work of [God's] hand." In light of Job's use of the similar phrase "the work of your hands" to describe himself in verse 3, it seems likely that Job has this important passage in mind as well. While Job uses the Hebrew *yegia* *kappekah*, "labor of your palm," Isaiah's phrase is *ma* *ase yadka*, "work of your hand"—but the meaning is very close (see 14:15, where the phrase *ma* *ase yadeka* appears).

Isaiah 64:8 is part of a plea for deliverance that extends from Isaiah 64:1–12. The plea begins by invoking God's action in theophanic terms: "Oh, that you would rend the heavens and come down. . . . For when you did awesome things that we did not expect, you came down, and the mountains trembled before you" (Isa. 64:1, 3). The similarity to the theophany in Job 9:5–11 is clear. The plea acknowledges the power of God to save "those who . . . remember your ways" (Isa. 64:5). The people making this plea are suffering because of divine judgment for their sins (64:5–7). Several phrases here resonate with the situation of Job: "All of us have become like one who is unclean, and all our righteous acts are like filthy rags; we all shrivel up like a leaf" (64:6). Similarly, "You have hidden your face from us and made us waste away" (64:7). Into the midst of this desperation comes the remembered foundation of hope: "Yet, O LORD, you are our Father. We are the clay, you are the potter; we are all the work of your hand" (64:8). Having remembered the source of their hope, the people renew their plea: "Do not be angry beyond measure, O LORD" (64:9a)—a sentiment that has much in common with that expressed in Job 7:20–21.

10:10–12 / Job stresses the creative care of God in these two verses containing alternative metaphors for the birthing process. The images are striking, and they may demonstrate some understanding of the process of development and growth of a child within the womb. The precise connections of the individual images with birth processes are not always clear, although the general sense is obvious. God oversees and supervises the mysterious growth and development of the child from conception to birth, insuring that the body is formed and jointed appropriately.

You gave me life. Life is not simply an accident of human reproduction, but the gift of divine creation. From the moment of conception and birth Job has experienced the **kindness** (*khesed*, "loyal covenant love") that characterizes God's enduring relationship with his people. God's **providence** (Heb. *pequddah*, "administrative guidance") has overseen Job's path. The **spirit** (Heb. *ruakh*) that God protectively guards is the animating life force granted to every human since God breathed the breath of life into the first human being (Gen. 2:7). This life force turns the inanimate body into a *nepesh khayyah* ("living being"). As long as the "spirit" remains, humans live. When the spirit is withdrawn, it returns to its source in God and the human dies (Gen. 6:3; Pss. 39:5; 104:29; Eccl. 3:19; Isa. 2:22; 42:5; Ezek. 37:5). The fact that God **watched over** (*shmr*) Job's spirit is here a good thing—a sign of God's protective care. Elsewhere, however, Job employs this same verb (*shmr*) to describe God's intense scrutiny of Job in order to harshly punish any sin, however small (e.g., 7:20–21).

10:13–15 / What Job considers to be God's hidden motives, however, contradict all this evidence of divine care, loyalty, and protective providence. God's true purposes are far less simple and obvious; they were **concealed** in his **heart** even from the beginning of Job's life. Even as God's hands carefully molded his creature and oversaw his path in life, it was in his **mind** to scrutinize his behavior and bring harsh punishment for any infraction.

If I sinned . . . If I am guilty demonstrate more of Job's hypothetical conjectures which do not intend to confess his sin (see the discussion on 9:19–21 in §28), but rather emphasize how God stands almost eagerly anticipating an opportunity to punish Job's **offense**. In **you would be watching me** he employs the same verb (*shmr*, "keep, watch, guard") which referred in the previous verses to God's protective care. Here, however, God is carefully watching for any hint of sin. Behind Job's plaint here—that God **would not let** his offense **go unpunished** for any sinfulness on his part—is a legal declaration of innocence (lit., "make/declare me innocent"), which is here negated. God would not declare Job innocent had he actually sinned (in contrast to God's statement of Job's blamelessness in the heavenly courtroom scene in the prologue). With "If I am guilty," Job imagines the consequences of being declared guilty in God's courtroom and is only able to cry out **woe to me!** The Hebrew interjection *ʾallay*, expressing deepest misery, occurs only here and in Micah 7:1.

While Job does not deny the correctness of divine punishment for sin, he refers to the concept here in a backhanded way to stress the *inappropriateness* of his own *innocent* suffering. If deserved punishment is the cause of "woe," Job's innocent suffering is doubly painful since it is undeserved. Although he is "innocent," Job experiences the **shame** of public approbation (shame is not an inner feeling but the public embarrassment of public condemnation) and feels **drowned in . . . affliction.**

10:16–17 / Any of Job's attempts to resist public condemnation and to exhibit a sense of confidence in his own innocence are met by increased suffering. A new list of confounding **witnesses** for the prosecution crush any hope for a declaration of innocence. It is as if God stalks Job **like a lion** and brings his **awesome power** crashing down on Job like a hapless shipwreck survivor repeatedly smashed by **wave upon wave.**

Additional Notes §33

10:10 / The **milk** represents male semen, which in this view is "poured" into the womb, coagulates into **cheese** (an embryo?), and ultimately develops **bones, sinews, flesh,** and **skin.** Related descriptions are found in Ps. 139:13–16; Eccl. 11:5; Ezek. 37:4–8; 2 Macc. 7:22–23; Wis. 7:1–2.

§34 The Approach of Death (Job 10:18–22)

10:18–19 / At rock bottom again, Job wonders why God would expend such intricate care in shaping and forming Job for birth only to subject his life to such pain and terror. Job would rather have **died before any eye saw** him. Although he wishes he had **never come into being,** to have gone **straight from the womb to the grave** would have been the next best thing!

10:20–22 / Once again, as in 3:13–15, Job anticipates the approach of death: **Are not my few days almost over?**, and he desires **a moment's joy** before passing into the inalterable darkness and oblivion that is death. The words he uses to describe *Sheol,* the abode of the dead, are common in imagery of the ancient Near East. *Sheol* is **the place of no return** (lit., "I will go and I will not return"), **the land of gloom and deep shadow.** A continuing string of related expressions emphasize the darkness: **deepest night,** "deep shadow," **even the light is like darkness.** In addition to being a place of continual darkness from which there is no return, this passage implies that *Sheol* is also a place of **disorder,** or chaos—the opposite of God's creation intention and, perhaps, an indication of the absence of his ordering presence.

Additional Notes §34

10:21 / **Deep shadow** is the Heb. *tsalmawet,* lit. "shadow of death"—a way of expressing a superlative, "darkest shadow." See the discussion on 3:4–5 in §7.

See the related description of the abode of the dead from "The Descent of Ishtar to the Nether World" (Pritchard, *ANET,* pp. 106–9): "To the Land of no Return . . . to the dark house . . . to the house which none leave who have entered it, to the road from which there is no way back, to the house wherein the entrants are bereft of li[ght], (where) they see no light, residing in darkness. . . ."

§35 Zophar (Job 11:1)

11:1 / The last of Job's three friends makes his debut with rather breathtaking harshness. **Zophar** rejects Job's claim to righteousness and even undermines his integrity by classifying Job's claims as idle mockery which cannot go uncontested. The key to Zophar's viewpoint is found in 11:6, where he clearly states that Job's suffering is the result of his sin and is even less severe than deserved. While Zophar does hold out hope for Job, it has little to do with a confrontation with God. Such a collision would in Zophar's mind lead only to Job's condemnation. Job's hope, such as it is, can be found only in confession, repentance, and appeal to divine mercy. Submission would lead to restoration, security, and renewed confidence. But, before he offers even that hope, Zophar has much to say in opposition to Job.

§36 Call to Refute Job (Job 11:2–6)

11:2 / Zophar's attack focuses at first on the multitude of Job's **words** that are **unanswered**. Job is a **talker** whose words should be discounted. In classic wisdom teaching, the sage is the one who speaks *few* words, choosing them carefully and using them to good effect. The hot-headed fool speaks voluminously without thinking, and he often gets into trouble as a result: "When *words* are many, sin is not absent, but he who holds his tongue is wise" (Prov. 10:19). Similarly, "A man of knowledge uses *words* with restraint, and a man of understanding is even-tempered" (Prov. 17:27). And again, "Do not be quick with your mouth, do not be hasty in your heart to utter anything before God. God is in heaven and you are on earth, so let your *words* be few" (Eccl. 5:2; see also Prov. 12:18; Eccl. 5:3, 7; 6:11; 10:14). Zophar seems to imply that the very multitude of Job's words renders his wisdom—and thus his integrity—suspect. He feels it is necessary to respond to Job, or otherwise all his words will be **vindicated.** According to Proverbs 26:5, a sage should, "Answer a fool according to his folly, or he will be wise in his own eyes" (and in the eyes of others. This conclusion will return with unexpected effect at the end of the third dialogue cycle when Zophar is unable to continue the debate. Thus his own silence will appear tantamount to vindication of Job's viewpoint.) Zophar's call to refute Job's words is a public declaration that he considers Job a fool, and not wise.

11:3 / Zophar continues to undermine Job's speech. His volume of words is suspect, and one wonders whether he is just a glib talker. His speech is **idle talk** (Heb. *bad*, "empty/idle talk; chatter") not worthy of a hearing. Even more negatively, Zophar accuses Job of mockery (Heb. *lᶜg*, a sort of stammering ridicule of others; Job employed this verb himself in 9:23 when he claimed that God "mocks the despair of the innocent"). Zophar fears that, without a firm **rebuke,** Job's many words will **reduce men to silence,** and it will seem like he has won. This is, in fact, exactly what happens at the end of the third cycle of dialogue. Bildad's third (and last) speech is severely truncated, while Zophar (ironically, in view of his comments here) fails to speak at all. The effect is to suggest that Job's friends are unable to counter his argument—a conclusion buttressed by the opening comments regarding Elihu in 32:4–5, and by Elihu's own comments in 32:10–22.

11:4 / You say to God. Zophar now confronts Job's more specific claims. With sarcastic exaggeration, Zophar summarizes Job's speech as claiming a **flawless** set of **beliefs** on which he unimpeachably grounds his arguments. Job is also claiming to be **pure** or unadulterated to anyone who, like Zophar and the other friends, takes the trouble to scrutinize him carefully. This kind of "purity" is accomplished by "sorting" or "sifting out" the bad so that only the good remains (from the verb *brr,* meaning "sort, sift"). Zophar rather scathingly assumes that such claims in the mouth of the suffering Job are patently dishonest.

11:5 / Zophar's desire that God would appear to respond to Job's complaint—**Oh, how I wish that God would speak**—will ultimately mirror Job's desire for God himself to hear his case. Up to this point in the narrative, however, the prospect of confronting God has filled Job with dread and a sense of futility (see esp. 9:1–4, 14–16, 32–35). This exasperated exclamation from the lips of Zophar, however, marks a turning point in the book. From here on, Job begins increasingly to contemplate the possibility—however fearful—of carrying his case directly to God. Zophar assumes that God's speech would certainly be **against** Job, and would set his distorted representations straight. If Job's comments in chapter 9 are any indication, he would probably agree that any hope for vindication by God is tenuous at best. On the other hand, Zophar's sarcastic explosion has planted a seed in Job's heart that takes root and blossoms as he becomes gradually determined to state his case in the presence of God, and is ultimately persuaded that God would be forced to uphold his claims (see 13:3, 15–16; 19:23–27; 23:2–6; 24:1; 30:20–21; 31:35–37). It is particularly interesting that, in his final expression of desire to be heard and vindicated (31:35), Job employs the same explosive idiom (*mi yitten li . . . shomea* ^{c} *li,* "Who will give to me . . . someone who listens to me") found on the lips of Zophar here in verse 5. What Zophar expresses in snide sarcasm, Job will express in deepest sincerity (and agony): the desire to be heard by God!

11:6 / If God were to confront Job as Zophar wishes, he would reveal to Job **secrets of wisdom** that he could not otherwise know. This is, of course, a way of denigrating the "flawless beliefs" Job is relying so heavily upon. Since **true wisdom has two sides**—perhaps meaning there is one side available to human observation and experience as well as another side known only to God—Zophar asserts that Job has some surprises coming when God reveals the true reasons behind Job's suffering.

One of these surprises that Zophar anticipates Job will encounter in a confrontation with God, is the fact that God has already **forgotten some of** his **sin,** so that Job's suffering, in all its intensity, will be discovered to be less than he actually deserves.

Additional Notes §36

11:2 / The Heb. for **talker** is *ʾish sepatayim,* "a man of two lips." Clines, *Job 1–20,* p. 254, suggests the phrase may mean "a glib talker."

The Heb. for **vindicated** is from *tsdq,* "be declared right/innocent" (or having fulfilled the expectations of the judge's ruling of *mishpat,* "justice"). See the discussions on 9:1–2 in §26 with regard to *tsdq* and the discussion on 13:17–18 in §44 with regard to *mishpat.*

11:4 / The Heb. for **flawless,** *zak,* describes oil in Exod. 27:20 and frankincense in Exod. 30:34 that are of the best quality, "clear" or "pure" enough to be used in the ritual practices of the tabernacle.

Job's **beliefs** are lit. "things I have received" (Heb. *leqakh,* "receive, accept"), probably referring to the wisdom teaching that has formed Job's education and understanding.

11:5 / *How I wish* **that God would speak** (emphasis added), Zophar exclaims with the Heb. idiom *mi yitten,* lit. "Who will give." This idiom expresses the strong desire that someone would take the action suggested in the verb attached to this phrase (in this case *dabber,* "to speak"; see the discussion on 14:4 in §47 with regard to *mi yitten*). Here Zophar identifies God (Heb. *ʾeloah*) as the speaker he hopes can rebut Job.

In the Heb. this verse begins with the adversative adverb *weʾulam,* "but on the other hand; to the contrary." NIV translates the preposition *ʿim* as **against** instead of the more usual "with." The context does imply that God's speech would undermine Job's claims. See the comments in Hartley, *Job,* p. 195.

11:6 / The word translated **secrets** here is the pl. of Heb. *taʿalummah,* derived from the verb *ʿlm,* "hide; cover over." These "secrets" are things which God has hidden from human view—they are unavailable to general wisdom observation and experience and can only be received through revelation.

The **two sides** (*kiplayim*) of wisdom appear here in the dual, indicating a pair (such as *raglayim*, "two feet," *ʾoznayim*, "two ears," *ʿenayim*, "two eyes," etc.). There is much debate about the meaning in this context. Clines, *Job 1–20*, p. 254, has a concise and helpful discussion of the options.

The NIV translation of the verb *yasheh* (Hiphil of *nshh*, normally "cause someone to forget"), **forgotten**, seems to assume an underlying Qal imperfect (*yisheh*, "he forgets") rather than the Hiphil form presented in the Heb. text. The point is not that God forgets Job's sin, or causes Job to forget it, but that memory of Job's sin has been removed from those who stand in judgment over him. It is only *part* of Job's sin that is forgotten, as the partitive use of the preposition *min* indicates.

§37 The Limitless Mysteries of God (Job 11:7–10)

11:7–9 / For Zophar—as for most of us—God has depths and heights that are ultimately unreachable by human wisdom. He asks Job a rhetorical question, something like, "Do you think you can actually find the definitive research into the nature and person of God that explains everything?" The Hebrew for **mysteries** (*kheqer*) describes the end product of a probing search process, whether physical exploration or within the human mind. Zophar questions whether any human (including Job) has the necessary access to the deepest recesses of God that would allow such a search to be carried to completion. Nor are humans capable of exploring the ultimate **limits** (*taklit*) of God. This is, in fact, what works like Job and Ecclesiastes are trying to do: to explore the uncharted hinterlands of faith in YHWH where human pain and suffering run headlong into the sovereignty and gracious mercy of the creator. Verse 7 should probably be rendered something like: "Can you really search out the depths of God, even if you search him out to the farthest limits of his being?"

It is likely that these two terms in verse 7 (*kheqer* and *taklit*) represent the "depths" and "breadth" of God in almost spatial terms as a sort of *merismus* indicating the complete wholeness of God by relating the divergent parts of space which God fills. Verses 8–9 employ similar rhetorical devices to clarify and emphasize the reference to completeness. The unsearchable limits of God are **higher than the heavens . . . deeper than the depths of the grave . . . longer than the earth and wider than the sea.** As humans are incapable of exploring the farthest reaches of the physical world (**what can you do? . . . what can you know?**), any hope of ever searching the limits of God is utterly ludicrous.

11:10 / Not only is God ultimately unknowable in his plans and purposes, his free exercise of his power is irresistible. If God determines to lock Job **in prison** and to try him in **court,** there is no one who **can oppose him.** This is a backward glance at Job's own fears, eloquently expressed in 9:14–20, 32–35.

Additional Notes §37

11:7 / The verb *khqr,* related to the noun for **mysteries** (*kheqer*), describes the thorough investigation carried out by spies (2 Sam. 10:3; Judg. 18:2), the probing of a legal case (Job 29:16) or personal opinion (1 Sam. 20:12), as well as exploration of the foundations of the earth (Jer. 31:37), and the failure to penetrate a forest (Jer. 46:23). The noun can refer to prudent deliberations (Judg. 5:16) or wisdom teachings passed down from earlier sages (Job 8:8).

The term for **limits** is related to the verb *klh,* "finish, end, complete; consume," and suggests the farthest bounds and limits and the complete exhaustion of a commodity. See Ps. 139:22 (complete extremity of hatred); Job 28:3; Neh. 3:21.

§38 Warning and Hope (Job 11:11–20)

11:11–12 / Zophar turns from argumentative persuasion to admonition tempered with hope. In the classic "stick and carrot" approach, Zophar begins by warning Job of the negative consequences of his stubborn refusal to acknowledge his sin and submit to God. While Job may persuade some humans of his innocent suffering, God **recognizes deceitful men** when he sees them. Such human beings are by implication **evil** and will certainly fall under divine scrutiny and judgment. Zophar is clearly warning Job that his many words have the effect of drawing Job into this class of persons under the punitive attention of God. He should therefore exercise care to extricate himself from this association.

In an even more significant warning, Zophar refers to Job as **a witless man** for whom there is no hope of redemption. In a humorous proverb, the futility of hoping that such a person might **become wise** is matched by the unlikely possibility that **a wild donkey's colt** might be **born a man.** This proverb is a much-debated passage, and scholars have proposed a variety of different interpretations. Pope (*Job,* p. 86) suggests persuasively that the comparison is between a "witless man" gaining sense and a "wild donkey" (*pere⁾ ⁾adam*) being born "tame" (*ᶜayir*). This also retains the sense of improbability that is the crucial element in this verse. It does not seem that Zophar means to suggest that Job is beyond hope, since he spends the rest of this chapter trying to convince him to repent and be restored. Instead, this proverb cautions Job not to push the limits of divine patience lest he find himself to have departed finally from the path of wisdom and redemption.

11:13–14 / From warning to hope, Zophar now exhorts Job to give up his resistance, to acknowledge his sin, and to accept the ready forgiveness of God. The first step is to **devote** his **heart** to God, which involves both *preparation* and *firm commitment.* Again, since the "heart" is the center of moral reflection and decision, this is not *emotional* commitment. Such commitment would require Job to submit his searching wisdom questions to the "mysteries of God" that are beyond human pondering. Once he reverses his attitude according to Zophar's advice, Job will be ready to **stretch out** his **hands** to God, in a gesture of submission and supplication—like persons drowning at sea who stretch out their hands eagerly to those who would draw them into the safety of the lifeboat.

Such a moral submission necessitates that he **put away the sin.** The psalmist informs us that God is "not a God who takes pleasure in evil; with [him] the wicked cannot dwell" (Ps. 5:4). So the one who would dwell in the security of God must **allow no evil to dwell in** his **tent,** expressed literally as "keep it/to be far away" (Heb. *rkhq*). This transformation to devotion to God by avoiding evil reflects the standard entreaty of wisdom fervor: "Fear YHWH and turn from evil" (Prov. 3:7; Pss. 34:15; 37:27).

11:15–19 / In Zophar's opinion, this submission to the mysterious power and will of God would lead to restoration for Job. We see this clearly in the conditional structure of verses 13–19. The first two verses (vv. 13–14) begin with the conditional particle *ʾim* ("if . . . if . . ."), and verse 15 introduces the last five verses with the temporal particle *ʾaz* ("then . . ."), describing the result of fulfillment of the conditions.

Then, Zophar tells Job, **you will lift up your face without shame.** The Hebrew here (*mum*, "blemish; disfigurement") describes more a freedom from *blemish* than NIV's "shame." The allusion is probably to the growing physical disfigurement brought on by Job's descent into suffering and disease (2:7–8, 12). Freed from the visible consequences of his suffering, Job would be able to **stand firm and without fear.** The Hebrew for "stand firm" comes from *yatsaq,* pouring out an image made from molten metal. That which has been poured out (*mutsaq*) in this manner solidifies as it cools into a rigid product that can stand on its own.

Further, Zophar says, **you will surely forget your trouble.** Job's current struggles under the distress of constant pain and suffering will be no more worthy of memory, suggests Zophar, than **waters gone by** in a stream. The tone of life will change from **darkness** to light, as the enduring experience of Job's remaining lifetime (Heb. *kheled*) will be **brighter than noonday, and darkness will become like morning.**

You will be secure. With trouble and darkness forgotten in the past, Job would experience security throughout the rest of his life. A new sense of inner confidence would match the change in his outward circumstances. This inward change would be based on a renewed sense of **hope,** as well as freedom from external attack. Job would be able to **look about** for his former attackers and yet take **rest in safety** when he sees no one. The next verse restates this promise, that Job will be able to **lie down, with no one to make him afraid.**

The final restoration is the return of those who will **court** Job's **favor.** Clearly in his pre-suffering heyday as "the greatest man among all the people of the East" (1:3), Job had been much sought out for his wisdom and generosity (4:3–4; 29:2–25). But his suffering brought all that to an end as those who had been eager to approach him now hang back in fear of making contact (30:1, 9–12). Zophar envisions a possible future day when a repentant Job will once again hold audience with those who seek his support. Those in influential positions in Christian service who have fallen through their own sinful failings can testify to the truth of this kind of avoidance by former friends and associates. It is one of the great mercies of God when former leaders, brought low by the consequences of their own sin, can be restored to significant service through a process of repentance, humility, and accountability. God has a way of using those who have been so humbled by enabling them to use the understanding gained through their experiences to reach out effectively to others who suffer in similar ways.

11:20 / Zophar's final words are a cautious warning that although restoration such as he envisions is possible for those who repent and submit to God, there is no such **hope** for those who refuse. The tension between the "hope" (v. 18) that encourages Job to lie down in "safety" and the lack of "hope" here that is but a **dying gasp** for those who refuse to submit to God, is surely intentional. The only **escape** for the evil is the death rattle with which they will depart this life.

Additional Notes §38

11:11 / The **men** here are *metim* (from a Near Eastern root, *mt*, for "male," known in Ugaritic and Egyptian). The complete phrase, *mete* *shaw*ᵓ, has more the meaning of "worthless men" and appears also in Ps. 26:4.

11:12 / A **witless man** is Heb. ᵓ*ish nabub* (a passive participle from *nbb*, "hollow out"), perhaps a morally empty man who is beyond hope of redemption. See the extended discussion in Clines, *Job 1–20*, p. 254.

The verb for **become wise** is Heb. *lbb*, related to the noun *leb/lebab*, "heart." Because the *heart* is the center of moral reflection and decision-making, the verb means to "be intelligent" or "capable of moral reflection and decision."

11:17 / The use of the verb *qum*, "rise up; arise; stand" in this context likens the change in Job's life to the shining of the sun in its noontime brilliance as well as to its death-defeating breech of darkness at dawn. Literally, the statement reads something like: "The rest of your life will rise up even more than noontime, and darkness (will become) as morning."

11:18 / An ironic wordplay may be hidden in the Heb. for **look about**. Two Heb. verbs share the same root consonants (*khpr*) but have very distinct meanings. One would be translated "be ashamed" (a subtle reference to the state the renewed Job is leaving), while the other means "search about; look for." The latter is most likely the nuance at work in our passage.

§39 Job's Equal Wisdom (Job 12:1–3)

12:1 / Undeterred by Zophar's stringent warnings, **Job** answers Zophar's harshness with equal venom.

12:2 / **Doubtless.** Job begins his reply to Zophar with the same word with which he began his response to Bildad (ʾomnam, "surely, certainly, without a doubt," 9:2), but here the word drips with intentional sarcasm. Job *clearly* has his doubts about the wisdom of the three friends—especially after the rather unfeeling rebuke that Zophar has just pronounced. He directs his reply at all three friends and their cumulative attack.

The phrase **you are the people** seems awkward in English, but in Hebrew it has the sense of "everyone," or at least "everyone that counts!" The friends are acting, Job implies, as if they have attained a wisdom that exceeds that of all the sages in the world. As a result, in their arrogance, they assume that without them **wisdom will die** and cease to exist. This is certainly an extreme way of saying that any viewpoint besides one's own has no validity.

12:3 / But Job demands that the three friends assume the humility of the true sage, who acknowledges that he is only one among many sages: **I have a mind as well as you.** Job stands firmly on the ground of his own wisdom. Job's "mind" (again, a reference in Heb. to the "heart" as the source of reflection and decision-making) is as adept at sorting out the observational and experiential data of wisdom as his friends. He is not **inferior** to them. In fact, Job says almost maliciously, **who does not know all these things?** Zophar's exalted insights are not so unique or elevated, but represent the common understanding of the universal community of sages. What a put down!

But—and it is a point that could easily slide by unnoticed—it is worth noting that Job's words take no issue with what the friends have been saying. "Who does not know all these things?" As far as the traditional understanding of the operation of retribution, Job is in complete agreement. He has no wish to alter the foundations of wisdom teaching. Job's problem (the *character* Job, if not the author/editor of the book) is not with the principle of retribution, but with the friends' misguided attempts to turn his circumstance of suffering into an indictment of sin and unrighteousness. *This* Job knows to be invalid; he knows his own blamelessness as doubtlessly as he has (tongue firmly planted in cheek) declared the worthy and unexcelled wisdom of the friends. It is because he *knows* his righteousness is unimpeachable that Job increasingly wishes to come together with God in a legal setting. God will have to acknowledge and affirm Job's integrity, and justice will be served. If Job did not affirm the *principle* of retribution, he would have little reason to seek an audience with God.

Additional Notes §39

12:3 / **I have a mind as well as you:** In a similar move, the epilogue in Eccl. 12:9–14 begins by affirming Qohelet as a sage (*khakam*) who writes truth. Then he places Qohelet (and his words) within the larger context of the "words of the sages" (*khakamim*). Qohelet is not the only sage whose words must be heard. Job's three friends are dangerously near to being "wise in their own eyes," a condition that Prov. 3:7 describes as being the negation of the appropriate stance of faith: "fear the Lord and turn from evil." The Heb. for **inferior** is interesting: *lo' nopel 'anoki mikkem*, "I am not falling from you." The use of the participle suggests an ongoing and continuous state of parity.

These are particularly difficult verses, and interpreters have made numerous attempts at emendation. Job's overall point seems to be that it is easy for the friends (and others like them) who have not experienced Job's suffering to assume it is deserved punishment from God. As a result, while they are engaged in ferreting out the supposed sin of an innocent man, those truly deserving of judgment go unnoticed and unpunished. This is, of course, an accusation Job has previously directed to God himself (7:17–21; 10:3–6).

12:4 / Job emphasizes the ludicrous nature of his position as **a laughingstock.** A man who is **righteous** (*tsaddiq,* "declared innocent") **and blameless** (*tamim* [sg.], "whole, intact; blameless; a person of integrity"), one who formerly had **called on God** with confidence he would be **answered,** is now subject to the ridicule of his friends. The tension in the last phrase of verse 4 (lit., "a righteous, blameless laughingstock!") is almost palpable.

12:5 / The meaning of the initial word (Heb. *lappid,* "torch") is debated, with some opting for the meaning "torch" and others understanding a form of the word *pid,* "ruin; destruction." The latter option, used by the NIV (**misfortune**), makes more sense in context than the former. The stilted rendering would thus be: "For destruction (there is) contempt to take notice by the one **at ease,** it is the appropriate **fate of those whose feet are slipping.**" The sense of the verse, therefore, is that the one who experiences no trouble himself disdains even to take notice of the sufferings of others, assuming they are the just due of sin.

12:6 / While those who are without suffering are wasting their time justifying the suffering of the innocent, the real destructive elements of society—**the marauders**—are left in peace and **those who provoke God** remain **secure.** The last phrase of this verse is clear in its literal sense ("who brings God in his hand"), but it is difficult to connect this singular statement to the plural groups mentioned in the first half of the verse. The precise meaning of the phrase—what it means to "bring God in his hand"—is debated. Some suggest it refers to those who think their own hand wields the power of God—in other words, they are in control of their lives. Perhaps the picture is of the pagan who carries his idol in his hand wherever he might choose to go (a meaning indicated by the NIV's, **those who carry their god in their hands**). The use of the designation ʾ*eloah*—Job's normal term for the one creator God—would imply that these comfortable persons assume they can bend God to their will as easily as they influence pagan idols.

Additional Notes §40

12:4–6 / Some commentators eliminate these verses as a later intrusion that interrupts the flow of Job's speech from vv. 3 to 7. There is some difficulty with these verses, as evidenced by the LXX which omits vv. 4a–b and offers a very different version of vv. 4c–5. See the comments in Pope, *Job*, p. 90, and Rowley, *Job*, pp. 112–13.

12:4 / There is nothing to definitively indicate that the friends have laughed at Job, it does seem they all refuse to take his claims of righteousness seriously.

The Heb. word order draws out and emphasizes the incongruity of **a mere laughingstock, though righteous and blameless.** The noun "laughingstock" appears first and is then followed in quick succession by the two adjectives "righteous" and "blameless" (Heb. *sekhoq tsaddiq tamim*).

12:6 / **Marauders** is Heb. *shoddim* (a participle of the verb *shdd*, "lay waste; devastate"). The verb here (Heb. *shlh*, NIV **undisturbed**) means "experience peace and quiet" (Jer. 12:1; Ps. 122:6; Job 3:26; Lam. 1:5), but it can also suggest a *false* sense of security, or *negligent* unconcern (2 Chr. 29:11; 2 Kgs. 4:28). The verb upon which the participle translated **those who provoke** is based is the Heb. *rgz* (in the Hiphil stem). The normal meaning is "cause to shake/quake; agitate."

§41 The Creation Gives Testimony (Job 12:7–10)

12:7–8 / As Job sees it, **the animals** and **the birds of the air** are more aware of the true nature of life than the humans he just described. The friends, with their assumption of superior wisdom, could even receive instruction from the rest of the animate and inanimate creation. To **ask the animals** or to **speak to the earth** is a way of encouraging sages to pursue the traditional forms of wisdom observation and investigation of the natural world. Many proverbs reflect the end result of this kind of *conversation* with the earth and its inhabitants (Prov. 30:15–31; Eccl. 1:1–11).

The animals and the physical world know what the friends and their associates seem to have missed. If consulted appropriately, **they will teach you.** The verbs here signify *instruction* (Heb. *yrh*, the verbal root from which the noun *torah*, "guideline; instruction; the Law" comes), *revelation* (Heb. *ngd*), and *testimony* (Heb. *spr*). These communications would ordinarily be undertaken in order to declare the mighty works of YHWH on behalf of his beleaguered covenant people (Ps. 78:4–6).

12:9 / The knowledge that the friends are missing, and to which the natural world is privy, however, is not the saving acts of God for his people, but the state of affairs Job is lamenting: that the innocent suffer, while the "marauders" go unpunished! "Just look around you," Job seems to be saying to the friends, "and you will have to acknowledge the truth of what I am saying." The rather sarcastic rhetorical question of verse 9—**Which of all these** [animals and physical creation] **does not know that the hand of the LORD has done this?**—is intended to undermine the very personal wisdom of which the friends think so highly. Surely the friends must be the only persons remaining in the world who have not understood. If they were nearly as wise as they claim, then the only explanation for their lack of understanding would be that they have willfully rejected the testimony proclaimed by the rest of creation.

12:10 / The animals know what Job is talking about—the risky and painful nature of life in the world—because they, like humans, realize that **the life of every creature and the breath of all mankind** is in God's hand. Thus, whatever happens must ultimately be traced back to the power and control of the creator. The world and its creatures do not suffer because God has somehow lost control. As the following verses (vv. 11–25) make abundantly clear, Job understands God to be firmly in control of all aspects of worldly power and wisdom.

Additional Notes §41

12:7–8 / Clines, *Job 1–20*, p. 293, understands that in these verses Job is placing words in the mouths of the friends—that Job is claiming the friends are treating him as a rank amateur who needs the most basic and obvious forms of instruction.

12:9 / This is the only place in the whole poetic dialogue section where the divine name **the LORD** (Heb. *yhwh*) occurs. Elsewhere, Job's common designation for the deity is *ʾeloah*, "God." The similarity between this phrase (**the hand of the LORD** has done this) and Isa. 41:20 has led some to suggest that Job has been influenced by Isaiah here. See the discussion in Pope, *Job*, p. 91, and Rowley, *Job*, p. 114.

§42 God's Power Confounds Human Wisdom (Job 12:11–25)

In these fifteen verses Job establishes common ground with his friends. He concedes, one might say, to their basic assumptions about the power and control of God in the world. For Job, however, this awareness of the power of God leads in a very different direction. The difference is Job's absolute conviction of his own innocence in the face of the overwhelming onslaught of suffering and loss. This tension casts doubts on the friends' continuing affirmations of the justice of God. The section is divided into two parts: a set of rhetorical questions (vv. 11–12) that introduce a hymn to the power of God in the world of human affairs (vv. 13–25).

12:11–12 / In a series of rhetorical questions, Job calls the friends (and, of course, the reader) to a discriminating use of wisdom faculties in the long-term observation of real life experience. The **ear** must be as discriminating in its reception of **words** as the **tongue** is as it **tastes food.** Not all food pleases the tongue, and some things taken into the mouth will be rejected as unfit or unworthy to eat. Similarly, Job implies, not all opinions, no matter how carefully constructed or authoritatively espoused, are worthy of acceptance. That is why, he suggests, discerning wisdom is the province of **the aged,** who through **long life** should gain the experience that guides **understanding.** In the hymn that follows, Job clearly affirms the view that God is the source of wisdom and that his power often confounds and subverts human attempts at power and understanding. Thus the friends ought to use their sagely abilities in a discerning fashion that would allow them to perceive how God's power often runs counter to expectations founded on the assumption of retribution.

12:13 / One cannot attribute **wisdom** (*khokmah*) and **understanding** (*tebunah*) to the gradual accretions of sagely old age, because these end results of the wisdom enterprise remain forever, uniquely and freely the gifts of God, to whom they belong. In addition to "wisdom" and "understanding," God possesses the **power** (*geburah*) with which to carry out the **counsel** (*etsah*, "counsel, plan") that puts this wisdom into effect in the world. If human wisdom is the ability to perceive and understand the order that God has established in his world, divine wisdom is the ability to bring that vision of God into being. This combination of divine "wisdom" and divine "power" creates an aspect of *mystery* that runs counter to the friends' claims to clearly understand the purposes of God behind what he displays in his acts.

12:14 / Unlike the powers and actions of human kings and despots, what God accomplishes cannot be frustrated or undone except by God himself. In words reminiscent of the experience of Israel during the exile, as well as of Job's earlier losses, Job says that what God **tears down cannot be rebuilt; the man he imprisons cannot be released.** When God brings punishment, it cannot be lightly overturned. Thus Job's only hope is to persuade God of his innocence so that God will modify his judgment. To do this he must gain a hearing—and so Job's part of the dialogue turns more and more frequently and persistently to this request.

12:15 / **If he holds back the waters.** Job returns to an image of the natural world to illustrate the absolute control of God over his creation. Note that Job mentions only the destructive consequences of God's power, as the lack of water brings **drought** and **if he lets them loose** the waters **devastate the land.**

12:16 / The NIV translation, **strength and victory,** obscures the connection between this verse and verse 13, which expresses similar sentiments in different language. The difficulty is the translation here of the Hebrew *tushiyyah* as "victory," although the more appropriate meaning (reflected in 5:12 and 11:6) is "effective counsel." In verse 13 Job began this hymn to the power of God with the statement, "To God belong wisdom [*khokmah*] and power [*geburah*]." Now he repeats the same ideas with different words and in reverse order: "To him belong strength [*oz*] and effective wisdom [*tushiyyah*]."

Because God is the master of both power and effective wisdom/counsel, both the **deceiver** (those who use deception to persuade others to their view) and the **deceived** (those who are so deceived) are under God's control and judgment. At different points in the dialogue both the friends and Job might level an accusation of deception at the other. The "deceiver" here is understood as one who *willfully* leads others (the "deceived") astray.

12:17 / Because God has power and authority over all wisdom, he is able to have his way with those whom the world considers powerful and wise. The next seven verses describe how God exercises his decisive power over various representatives of earthly authority and wisdom. Among the first to experience the judgment of God on their supposed wisdom are **counselors** and **judges.** Humans may recognize the former (Heb. *yoʿatsim,* "counselors") for their ability to give good guidance and direction because they "know the times" and thus the appropriate action for every occasion. God's evaluation of their wisdom is revealed, however, when he **leads** them **away stripped**—describing the abject shame of captives carried away into exile, their nakedness revealing their shame and powerlessness (as well as their failure to read and respond effectively to the "times"). As for the **judges** upon whose wisdom humanity relies to provide order in contexts of social conflict, God **makes fools** of them, overturning the supposed wisdom of their decisions.

12:18 / Kings have no easier time of it. While God's power assures that those he imprisons stay confined (v. 14b), the **shackles put on by kings** (evidence of their presumed power over their subjects and enemies) are easily removed by God. And the "kings" themselves are reduced to wearing a mere **loincloth** rather than their usual royal finery—possibly an indication that they, too, are being led away into captivity. This reminder of God's power to remove the shackles of slavery imposed by human kings would probably bring hope to those languishing in the Diaspora.

12:19 / Religious officiants are next to experience the disorienting display of the power of God. Using the same language as for the "counselors" in verse 17, Job says God **leads priests away stripped.** The **men long established** are clearly those of note and power in society—and perhaps there is an intentional reference to those (among the priests?) who depend on long hereditary pedigree for their position and authority. God **overthrows** them, although the meaning of the Hebrew *slp* is more "twist, distort; mislead."

12:20 / God removes the essential qualities of guidance from those on whom human society depends. God "removes the lip/language" of the **trusted advisers** (Heb. *mesir sapah leneʾe-*

manim), people relied on for words of sage advice. God likewise takes away **the discernment** of the **elders.** The Hebrew word for "discernment" (*ta'am*, "taste; perception") creates a play on the proverb in verse 11: "Does not the ear test words as the tongue tastes food?" As taste is the means of discerning the worth or edibility of food, so the long experience of the "elders" is thought to have given them discernment in life. Without the guidance of these trusted advisers, society is at a loss and chaotic.

12:21 / In a possible reference to military power and leadership, God **pours contempt on nobles.** The "nobles"—from the Hebrew *ndb*, "volunteer (for military service)"—are not always associated with military duty, but the appearance of the **mighty** (Heb. *'apiqim*), whose "belt" or "girdle" (*meziakh*) is lowered (*rippah*) so that they are unprepared or unequipped for battle—would suggest that the military establishment is under consideration here. The NIV's translation **disarms** seems to be the result of a militaristic interpretation of a rather obscure phrase.

12:22 / Verse 22 introduces a more general aspect as it moves the discussion from descriptions of divine confrontation with human wisdom and power to consider the light God controverts with **darkness** and **deep shadows.** The picture is an ominous one, with the **light** of human wisdom seeming to recede and fade before the spreading gloom unleashed by God. The claim that God **reveals the deep things of darkness** is, of course, deeply ironic. The reader is led to expect a profound revelation that will enlighten as to the mysterious purpose of God, but receives instead the opposite of light: utter darkness. The "deep shadows" which God **brings . . . into the light** are the Hebrew *tsalmawet*, "shadow of death" (Pss. 23:4; 107:14; Isa. 29:18), which always carries with it a sense of divine punishment and deepest threat to continued human existence.

12:23 / The remaining verses of chapter 12 focus on the collision between the power of God and the great nations and leaders of the earth. If verses 16–21 speak of the power of God over leaders at a more local level, verses 23–25 declare his sovereignty over those great nations (*goyim*) that have pretensions to world domination and control. These claims fade before the realities of God's sovereign power as creator. It is God who **makes nations great** and who **enlarges** them. He is also the one who **destroys** and **disperses them.**

12:24 / The destruction of nations entails the judgment of their leaders as well. The form this judgment takes is most appropriate, given the emphasis in this chapter on "wisdom" and "power." God **deprives the leaders of the earth of their reason.** The word "deprives" here is the same Hebrew word (*mesir*) used at the beginning of verse 20 to describe the silencing or removal of the "lips" (or *language*) of the "trusted advisers." It is the *heart* (Heb. *leb*, NIV "reason"), the center of moral reflection and decision-making, that God causes to turn aside (the lit. meaning of *mesir*). The "leaders" are the *ra ʾshe ʿam ha ʾarets*, the "heads of the peoples of the earth."

Deprived of their ability to make sound decisions, these leaders are **wandering** aimlessly through a **waste** (Heb. *tohu*), which reflects the chaos that existed at the beginning before God brought order to the *formless void* (Heb. *tohu wabohu*, Gen. 1:2). This "waste" is called **trackless** (lit., "no path"), a probable reference to wilderness areas so infrequently traveled by humans that no established paths had been worn into the soil. The word "path" (Heb. *derek*) in this expression often describes the moral life path that humans choose to follow. In wisdom circles there are generally understood to be only *two* such ways available to each individual: the way of wisdom or the way of folly; the way of righteousness or the way of wickedness; the way of life or the way of death. Here the lack of *any* way suggests that the possibility of choice has been removed and indicates that destruction is unavoidable.

12:25 / The chapter (and this discussion of God's power and wisdom) comes to an end with a dark picture of senseless leaders groping helplessly through utter **darkness—like drunkards.** To **grope** here is to find one's way by feel rather than sight. The verb translated, "**he makes them stagger,**" is the same verb used in verse 24 to describe the leaders being sent "wandering" by God. The message is clear: God exercises his wisdom and power to turn mighty leaders into blind, groping, drunks struggling to find their way where there is no way.

Additional Notes §42

12:12 / Hartley, *Job*, p. 213, takes the two phrases **the aged** and **long life** as epithets of God, a way of denying that the friends have the last say on wisdom: "Since God is the oldest by far, he certainly is the wisest." But see the comments of Pope, *Job*, p. 92, regarding the similar suggestion of W. Quintens, to whom this idea is apparently to be traced. Pope understands v. 12 as a rhetorical question anticipating a negative answer and undermining the friends' claims to wisdom and understanding.

12:14 / Jeremiah (1:10; also 45:4; 24:6; 31:28; 42:10) uses these same two verbs (*hrs*, "throw down; overthrow" and *bnh*, "build") in his opening prophecy combining judgment *and* hope. This passage understands God's purpose in "throwing down" the former structures of the kingdom as preparing the way in the future for "building" a new and redeemed structure for the faithful people of God. Job, on the other hand, understands that God's judgment can only be reversed by God himself.

12:15 / The verb for **holds back** (Heb. *ʿtsr*) describes the withholding of rain in divine punishment in Deut. 11:17; 1 Kgs. 8:35; 2 Chr. 6:26; 7:13. Elsewhere it describes, more positively, the restraint of a plague from complete destruction (Num. 16:48, 50; 25:8; 2 Sam. 24:25; 1 Chr. 21:22). In Ps. 107:33–37, for example, the word describes God employing his power over the waters of the earth in accord with the idea of retribution.

12:16 / Clines, *Job 1–20*, p. 299, understands this repetition from v. 13, **to him belong strength and victory,** to indicate the beginning of a new strophe (vv. 16–21) of the hymn. Further, he reads Job's statement **both deceived and deceiver are his,** as his cynical recognition that "God makes no evident distinction between the morally culpable and the blameless" (p. 299). This, then, is an extension of Job's argument in vv. 4–6 that marauders seem to get away without suffering consequences while the righteous experience public ridicule and shame.

12:17 / The use of a series of participles at the beginnings of vv. 17–20 and 22–24 creates a striking visual impression in the Heb. text. Four consecutive verses begin with the letter *mem* (*molik, musar, molik, mesir*) and then, after a single line break for v. 21 (*shopek*), an additional three *mems* (*megalleh, masgiʾ, mesir*). A similar set of *five* consecutive verses beginning with the same letter (in this case *he*) is found just below in 13:7–11.

The leading away of shackled, naked captives was a common practice in the ancient Near East, as depicted in numerous carved inscriptions and victorious reliefs. For just one example, consult the illustration in Pritchard, plate 7. Clines, *Job 1–20*, p. 300, gives an extensive list of such illustrations.

12:18 /   Clines, *Job 1–20*, p. 300, following Gordis, takes the term translated by NIV as **shackles** as some sort of belt or "regal garments" symbolic of the king's authority. This interpretation has the advantage of corresponding more exactly with the kings' reduction to **a loincloth** in the second half of the verse. Regardless, the meaning remains clear: the power of God overrules and diminishes the authority and status of kings.

12:22 /   Some commentators (e.g., Clines, *Job 1–20*, p. 297) consider that v. 22 introduces a third strophe of the hymn to divine power. According to this division, vv. 13 and 16 initiate earlier strophes with similar references to God's wisdom and power.

The Heb. for **deep things** (*ʿamuqot*) is a passive participle of the verb *ʿmq* and means "be deep or profound." Instead of profound enlightenment, however, humans experience profound confusion and lack of understanding.

The use of the Heb. word for death, *mawet*, here in **deep shadows**, may be an unusual way of indicating the superlative, and *tsalmawet* does mean "deepest darkness." But the association with the standard word for "death" continues to color the expression with anxious anticipation far beyond the meaning "really, really *dark!*" Over half of the occurrences of this word are found in Job. See the various uses of *tsalmawet* in Isa. 9:2; Jer. 2:6; 13:16; Amos 5:8; Pss. 23:4; 44:19; 107:10, 14; and Job 3:5; 10:21, 22; 12:22; 16:16; 24:17; 28:3; 34:22; 38:17. Also see the discussion on 3:4–5 in §7 and on 10:20–22 in §34.

12:23 /   The NIV translation **disperses** assumes that this verb (Heb. *nkhh*, "lead") is parallel to the negative term **destroys** (Heb. *ʾbd*) in the preceding line. Clines, *Job 1–20*, pp. 281, 303, suggests a chiastic arrangement to this verse with *nkhh* offering a positive divine action. His translation is "he disperses nations, and he leads them"—a rendering that is more in keeping with what we know of the nuances of this verb elsewhere.

§43 Worthless Physicians (Job 13:1–12)

Job returns to the discussion in the first person with words that recall the beginning of his speech in 12:1–3. Once again he claims an equal footing with the friends with a wisdom which is certainly "not inferior" (and Job would probably claim *superior*) to theirs. Having received abuse at the hands of the friends, Job accuses them of wickedness and partiality of judgment and begins with renewed vigor to seek an audience with God—Job's greatest fear and only hope.

13:1–2 / Job's descriptions of the exercise of divine power in chapter 12 were based on his own observations of life. With the words **my eyes have seen . . . my ears have heard and understood it,** Job foreshadows his ultimate submission to God in 42:5, where he says: "My ears had heard of you but now my eyes have seen you." Seeing God brings new knowledge that is superior to that gained from hearing only. The difference of interpretation that separates Job and his friends is not a matter of **inferior** information or intelligence. They all observe and **know** the same details. Their different stances, according to Job, are the result of the friends' refusal to follow their observations and reflections to their logical conclusions. If they are equally wise and have equal access to information, Job's only conclusion is that his friends are *willfully distorting reality* for their own purposes.

13:3 / Having found no satisfaction among the friends and having no hope at this point of persuading them, Job must turn to the only court of appeal left to him. He proclaims his **desire to speak to the Almighty and to argue** his **case with God.** The friends have driven him to confront God directly despite the deep misgivings he expressed in 9:14–20. Clines (*Job 1–20*, p. 305) suggests that Job has abandoned hope for divine vindication and is seeking "reconciliation rather than victory." When Job says he wants to "argue my case," he is using a legal idiom based on the Hebrew verb *ykkh*, which in the Hiphil stem (as here) can mean either "rebuke; correct; set straight," "support a particular position in a legal conflict," or "arbitrate/decide between disputants." This term first appears in the dialogue cycle from the mouth of Eliphaz, who declares in the midst of his first speech: "Blessed is the man whom God corrects" (5:17). The adversative particle *ʾulam* "but," with which verse 3 begins is emphatic in nature, stressing the contrast with what precedes. Job's desire to present his case before God grows out of his increasing frustration with the friends' lack of openness and understanding.

13:4 / The adversative particle *ʾulam* also introduces verse 4, indicating how emphatically contrary the friends' actions are to those of Job. Job seeks truth by approaching God. The friends, on the other hand, **smear** Job **with lies**. The term "smear" (Heb. *tpl*, "plaster over") describes plastering over a wall or other object in order to cover up what is underneath. In the next chapter, this same term describes God "covering" Job's "sin" (14:17). Here the implication is that the friends' "lies" are obscuring the reality of Job's innocence. Instead of friends who stand solidly behind Job, defending him to God, these three have all become **worthless physicians** who offer false testimony before God.

13:5 / Job wishes his friends were **altogether silent**. The construction is another emphatic one, meaning "completely silent." Job wants the friends' deceitful smear job to stop so that he can stand on his own merits. **For you, that would be wisdom** he says, rather sarcastically quoting Proverbs 17:28 ("Even a fool is thought wise if he keeps silent, and discerning if he holds his tongue") to good effect as he lashes out at his detractors as fools.

13:6 / Job calls his friends to listen (rather than speaking) to his **argument** and his **plea**. Both terms are legal ones, used in a court of law. The first is from the same verb (Heb. *ykkh*, "support a position in a law case") Job used in verse 3 to express his desire to set his facts before God. The second (Heb. *ribah*; pl. *ribot*) is related to the noun *rib*, "law suit," which in the Prophets often describes God's accusation against Israel for breach of its covenant obligations. Job seems to be implying that God's refusal to act according to expectations has severely affected his relationship with God.

13:7 / Job now embarks on an extended accusation of the friends' false testimony against him and describes how God's examination as judge will find the friends' arguments not only lacking, but also deceptive. The false physicians have more to fear, says Job, from the coming of God to hear Job's case than does Job himself.

Will you speak wickedly . . . deceitfully? Job's initial accusation is that the friends' words in the dialogue thus far twist the truth. On the one hand, they are speaking *ʿawlah*, "perversity; wickedness"—words that distract from the fulfillment of justice. On the other hand, their words are *remiyyah*, "deceitful"—that will lead those who examine Job (especially God!) to wrongful conclusions about his righteousness. He thereby implies a certain willful misleading in order to obscure the truth.

13:8 / The friends' twisting of the truth grows out of their determination to defend God at all costs. Rather than looking objectively at the events and experiences of life and allowing their wisdom to carry them to necessary conclusions, the friends have a need to prove God right that leads them to distort and misrepresent what they see and know. Job asks the friends, with rather ironic sarcasm, **will you show** God **partiality?** (lit., "will you lift up his face"). The idiom "lift up [someone's] face" has the sense of favoring or showing approval. At the end of Job, God responds to Job's intercessory prayer for the three friends by "lifting up [Job's] face" (42:8–9) as a sign of divine approval. In a sense, Job says here, the friends seek to **argue the case for God**—their primary concern is to justify God rather than to support Job, or even to seek the truth of the painful realities that confront the honest observation and experience of human existence.

13:9–10 / But God would not look kindly on such distortion of truth and frustration of justice, regardless of the friends' motivation. In a veiled threat, Job suggests that his own attempt to bring his case before God would have the unexpected effect of bringing the friends' opposing views under the scrutiny of God the judge. Such an examination (a thorough and searching probing into the depths, from *khqr*, "search, spy out, explore; examine thoroughly") could not **turn out well** for the friends (as it indeed does not in the epilogue, 42:7–8). In a clear allusion to 12:16 (using again the Heb. *tll*, "mock, deceive, trifle with"), where Job referred to God's power over both "deceived" and "deceiver," Job asks whether their distorting words would be as persuasive to God as they are to humans, who are more easily convinced. It seems that, despite his own inexplicable suffering at the hands of God, Job still believes that God establishes and upholds justice in the world. As a result he fully expects that God will **rebuke** (an emphatic form of the verb *ykkh*) the friends for hidden **partiality**. The reference to the friends' partiality being **secretly** expressed suggests that they are fully aware of how their words have distorted reality.

13:11–12 / In the presence of God's **splendor** the friends would experience only terror and **dread**. The Hebrew terms here pointedly avoid the value-laden phrase "fear of God" (Heb. *yir'at 'elohim*), employing instead words that express the negative. The word for **terrify** (Heb. *b't*, "fall upon; startle; terrify") normally refers to the attack of enemies. "Dread" is a translation of the Hebrew *pkhd*, "be in great dread." If Job's case were finally to come before God, the friends would find themselves charged with perjury and their **maxims** (the distorted wisdom traditions they have been using in their attempt to silence Job's critique) would be recognized for what they really are: **proverbs of ashes** (as worthless as ashes thrown on the heap where Job sits in his misery). Similarly, their **defenses** would be as useless as a **clay** pot (or shield) held up to deflect the blow of a sword or mace.

Additional Notes §43

13:3 / Besides Job, who makes the term *ykkh* one of his own, only Eliphaz employs this verb in the dialogue cycle (using it once in each of his three speeches: 5:17; 15:3; 22:4). Outside the dialogue cycle, Elihu uses the term once (32:12) and God uses it once in confrontation with Job (40:2). Job employs the verb on a number of occasions with the following nuances: "correct/rebuke," 6:26; 13:10; "argue/take a position," 6:25; 13:3, 15; 16:21; 19:5; "decide between parties," 9:33. Other than these occurrences of the Hiphil of *ykkh*, the verb appears in Job only once in the Hophal with the meaning "be admonished" (33:19).

13:4 / The Heb. translated **worthless** (*'elil*) sometimes describes pagan idols in a contemptuous manner, stressing their lack of existence or worthlessness.

13:5 / The Heb. construction for **if only you would be** is the interjection *mi yitten*, "who will give," expressing a strong desire unlikely to be fulfilled except by divine action. See the discussion on 14:4 in §47.

13:7 / The word *remiyyah* (here **deceitfully**) most often means "slackness, looseness," as in a bow that is not stretched tight, or the slack hand of a lazy person (Prov. 10:4; 12:24; 19:15; Jer. 48:10). Perhaps the connection is with the person who does not wish to pay much attention to the details of truth and thus allows improper conclusions to reign.

13:12 / The word for **defenses** is difficult and variously rendered. On the one hand, *gab* can be associated with the rounded "bosses" of shields (in 15:26, *gabbe maginnayw* is lit. "the bosses of his shield"). On the other hand, *gab* may relate to other Semitic words expressing verbal response or "answers." NIV's translation "defenses" could actually be taken in either way, as verbal or physical forms of defense.

§44 I Will Defend My Ways (Job 13:13–19)

Job now shifts from accusing the three friends to addressing his complaint to God. Verses 13–19 provide a transition between Job's address to the friends and his address to God. The friends still remain in view as *audience* while Job increasingly focuses on his anticipated confrontation with God.

13:13 / Job cuts off any response from the friends, commanding them to **keep silent**. Having just characterized their arguments as distorted and deceitful, he finds no merit in allowing them to comment further. The dialogue is not yet over; there is much more to come from the friends, but at this point Job is intent on articulating his need for a hearing with God. Job commands: **let me speak,** using a cohortative expressing self-encouragement or determination, with the pronoun (ʾani, "I") providing emphasis: "Let me speak *myself!*" His words are the only trustworthy witness remaining to present his case. Job is not certain what the result of any meeting with God would be: **then let come to me what may.** His need simply to address God is becoming more important than any assurance of a successful outcome.

13:14–15 / Job is ambivalent about this encounter he desires. On the one hand, he questions himself: **Why do I put myself in jeopardy and take my life in my hands?** The first phrase literally says, "why do I lift up my flesh in my teeth?," which is a difficult image to interpret. The second phrase is clearer and appears elsewhere (Judg. 12:3; 1 Sam. 19:5; 28:21; Ps. 119:109) with the sense of "risk my life." The clear meaning of the second implies that the earlier phrase should be understood along the same lines, demonstrating Job's determination to proceed even at the risk of his life (as in NIV).

Though he slay me. Verse 15 is perhaps one of the most familiar from the book of Job—and also one of the most hotly contested in recent days. The crucial question is how to read Job's response to the distinct possibility that his encounter with God might result in his death. He introduces this first phrase with the particle *hen*, which can be translated either "behold!" or "if." In the former case, Job would be expressing his resignation that God *will* terminate his existence. This seems somewhat unlikely since Job has already complained (see above, §8, on 3:23) that God unpleasantly *prolongs* his life without allowing him to die, despite his intense suffering. Death really seems to hold little fear for Job—only release! In this context it seems best to read *hen* as "if," and leave Job's death as a potential, but as yet undecided, possibility.

With **yet will I hope in him** we come to the most debated part of the verse. The various known Hebrew manuscripts offer competing versions of the original text. These alternatives are found in the consonantal text (called the *ketiv,* "what is written") and in the marginal Masoretic notes (called the *qere,* "what is read"). The consonantal text presents the particle *lo'* to negate the following verb (Heb. *ykhl,* "hope; wait expectantly for"), so that the translation would read "I will *not* hope." The marginal note, however, reads a prepositional phrase *lo* (meaning "to/for him"), to be translated "I *will* hope for him." NIV has chosen to follow the *qere,* while the majority of modern interpreters think the *ketiv* better reflects the context. Rather than expressing monumental faith, Job is instead indicating just how hopeless his circumstances really are. It is possible that this encounter with God will end in Job's death without any vindication. There really is no clear reason to hope for any positive outcome. *Nevertheless* (a better rendering of the adversative particle *'ak* than NIV's "surely") **I will surely defend my ways to his face.** In this setting Job has no hope of deliverance from death—he actually desires death as a release from his suffering—but he is determined to seek vindication, even though the attempt may result in his death. He has little, if anything, to lose.

13:16 / Indeed, this will turn out for my deliverance. Despite his resignation, Job's determination does admit one tiny seed of hope that *might* result in deliverance. Of course, if there were *absolutely* no hope, it is doubtful that even Job would persevere in his quest. The possibility is found in the fact that it is unlikely a **godless man would dare to come before** God. This is *bleak* hope in light of the terrifying nature of divine power Job explored in chapter 12, and even more so in light of his fearful words in 9:20 "Even if I were innocent, my mouth would condemn me; if I were blameless, it would pronounce me guilty."

13:17–18 / Again Job calls the friends (with an imperative in the plural) to **listen,** to pay attention to his speech. They are to observe that he has **prepared** his **case** carefully. The verb "prepare" (Heb. *ʿrk*) means "to arrange carefully; put in order" and can refer to the preparation of a meal (Isa. 21:5), to a sacrifice (Lev. 24:3), or to soldiers in battle array (Gen. 14:8; 1 Sam. 4:2; Jer. 6:23). "Case" (Heb. *mishpat*), is the legal definition of what should have occurred in a given circumstance brought to court. Job has carefully constructed his description of how his life meets the standards of *mishpat.*

I know I will be vindicated. This statement appears more confident than might be expected in light of Job's earlier resignation. The verb translated "vindicated" is the Hebrew *tsdq,* which can either mean to "be righteous" or "be *declared* righteous; be vindicated." In this context it seems more likely that Job continues to be convinced of his innocent righteousness while the public vindication of that righteousness remains in question.

13:19 / Despite his confidence, Job is willing to allow others to test his righteous character in court. **Can anyone bring charges against me?** The construction is a bit more confident and emphatic than it appears here. The Hebrew reads, literally, "Who is he who will contest with me?" Obviously Job is certain that there is *no one* capable of presenting evidence of his guilt. Therefore, he is willing to place his life in the balance. **I will be silent and die.** Clines, recalling that Job's death remains a matter outside his control, suggests that Job's vow here is to remain silent "until the day of his death (whenever that may be)" (*Job 1–20,* p. 315). This verse constitutes Job's call to God to respond, and it marks the shift to Job's direct address of God.

Additional Notes §44

13:14 / Hartley, *Job,* p. 221, takes the initial Heb. phrase here (*ʿal mah,* "for what reason, why?") as concluding v. 13, "for whatever reason." Clines, *Job 1–20,* p. 282, deletes the same phrase (*ʿal mah*) as dittography from the final *mah* in v. 13. Hartley takes the emended v. 14 as a question ("Shall I put my flesh between my teeth and take my life in my hands?"), while for Clines it becomes a statement of Job's determination to proceed come what may ("I will take my flesh in my teeth, and put my life in my hand").

13:15 / The NAB translation of **yet will I hope in him** suggests one other possibility: "I will wait for him." This follows the alternative meaning of the verb *ykhl*, "wait expectantly for." Here the verb indicates Job's determination to wait for God's coming rather than hope for deliverance.

§45 Desire for Fair Hearing (Job 13:20–22)

As he has previously noted (9:5–13), the greatest barrier to the kind of confrontation with God Job envisions is the painful potential for intimidation through divine power and increased suffering. Job's initial address to God seeks to establish the boundaries of open courtroom debate.

13:20–22 / **Only grant me these two things.** According to Job, two factors inhibit his will and ability to continue his case with God. First, God's **hand** presses Job harshly in the form of his suffering and pain. Second, Job anticipates that the **terrors** in the presence of God himself might render Job mute or at least ineffective in his complaint. If these two constraints can be removed, then Job will be able to speak openly and **will not hide from** God. It is unlikely that Job is demanding that all suffering be removed prior to any confrontation. He is already willing and able to speak out of the pain he is currently experiencing. But God's power to *increase* his pain even further has the potential to render Job incapable of proceeding. Job clearly refers here to the reservations he expressed in 9:32–35. There, however, Job had desired an umpire or mediator to prevent such intimidation. Now he turns that plea directly to God himself.

Then summon me. If God can assure these conditions, Job is confident he can stand and speak his case before God. The two halves of this verse describe the give and take of courtroom examination and cross-examination. **I will answer . . . you reply.** Job will respond to God's questioning, but he is also willing (almost eager, it seems) to subject God to a thorough examination: **or let me speak.** Ultimately it seems that *neither* of these scenarios is played out when God finally comes on the scene in chapters 38–42. Job never questions God when he appears and, although God does ask questions, Job has little to say in response.

The chapter concludes with a series of questions and accusations that may mark the beginning of Job's carefully "prepared case" (v. 18). It is likely that the section between 13:23 and 28 presents this case. Nowhere else in the remainder of the dialogue does Job examine God in this fashion.

13:23 / **How many wrongs and sins have I committed?** Job begins with a request for the specific charges for which he is being punished. This may be a standard legal opening (see Jer. 2:5 and Gen. 31:36 for similar statements) and seems to assume that the speaker expects to be completely exonerated. This is equivalent in modern terms to the defense attorney receiving the charges against the client so that he or she can build a case refuting each one. Job is not admitting guilt here; rather, he is demanding that God make his claims against Job a matter of public record: **Show me my offense and my sin.**

13:24 / Job's questions now take on a more accusatory tone. These are not rhetorical questions. They reveal Job's real desire to understand the cause behind his suffering. To **hide your face** implies more than that God is merely absent or distant in Job's experience. For God to hide his face in this manner is to express his judgment or anger and results in destruction for those so abandoned. "On that day I will become angry with them and forsake them; I will *hide* my *face* from them, and they will be destroyed. Many disasters and difficulties will come upon them, and on that day they will ask, 'Have not these disasters come upon us because our God is not with us?'" (Deut. 31:17; see also Deut. 32:20; Pss. 13:1; 27:9; 69:17; 88:14; 104:29; 143:7; Jer. 33:5; Mic. 3:4).

Why do you **consider me your enemy?** God is not just absent; he has taken up a position of hostility against Job. As we have seen, Job's name (Heb. ʾiyyob) is based on the Hebrew root ʾyb, meaning "be an enemy to" (see the discussion on 1:1 in §1). Some have suggested an intentional symbolism because the central human character of this work bears a name that means "enemy; opponent." Since Job is unaware of the heavenly counsel of chapters 1–2, he cannot know that God has already declared Job "my servant" (Heb. *ᶜabdi*) and affirmed his blameless and upright character (1:8; 2:3). On the basis of appearances, Job can only conclude that God is treating him as an enemy to be crushed and defeated.

13:25 / Job illustrates the extent of God's enmity with two preposterous examples. God's hostility toward Job is so extreme that it is almost as if he is chasing after a **windblown leaf** in order to **torment** it. Imagine a dry, withered leaf swept from its last hold on the branch of the winter tree. It is already dying, without mooring, and rushing to destruction, but God is not satisfied and seeks it out to inflict even more damage. Similarly, Job likens God's pursuit of him to chasing **after dry chaff** (a traditional term for that which is completely useless and worthless) to harm it. These images are surely intended to be extreme and sarcastically humorous, at God's expense.

13:26–28 / **For you write down bitter things against me.** The opening word "for" (Heb. *ki*) implies that God's written complaint reflects the extreme vindictiveness described in the preceding verse. The "bitter things" God enters into the record against Job are the result of God's need to inflict punishment beyond what Job deserves or is even reasonable. Like the "windblown leaf," Job is hurtling toward destruction. Like the "chaff," he is worthless and useless. And yet God is still seeking him out for additional pain and suffering. The written account of "bitter things" can hardly be the official accusations made in a court of law since Job is still seeking access to those. Hartley envisions a written contract with blessings and curses for obedience or disobedience (*Job,* p. 228). Clines, however, thinks of punishments exacted by a judge as penalties in a law case (*Job 1–20,* p. 320). The fact that Job refers to written statements suggests the official nature of legal documents. Job will later submit his own affidavit in support of his claims (19:23; 31:35).

In his reference to **the sins of my youth,** by "youth" (Heb. *neᶜurim*) Job most likely means the period of time between infancy and the early teen years. Since such "youth" have not yet reached the age of moral decision-making and culpability, for God to punish Job for such "sins" would be seen as unusual and extreme.

You fasten my feet in shackles. God adds to this extreme punishment his close supervision and limitation. Like one who is hampered by "shackles," Job feels unable to flee from God's painful attention. Further, God keeps close watch to prevent Job's escape. As was the custom for a particularly important prisoner, God is constantly on guard watching all the **paths** (or possible avenues of escape). The final evidence of God's close scrutiny limiting Job's movement, **putting marks on the soles of my feet,** is more difficult to assess because of the obscurity of the language. Literally, the Hebrew says something like, "concerning the root of my feet you scratch/incise for yourself." Various scholars have taken this to imply some marking of the soles of a prisoner's feet so that his tracks could be easily distinguished should he seek to escape. Others understand the reference as describing an impression or footprint left in the earth, meaning that God is carefully tracking Job wherever he may go (see Clines, *Job 1–20,* pp. 321–23; Hartley, *Job,* pp. 228–29 for further possibilities). The point, however, is still clear: God dogs Job's footsteps, allowing him no escape.

So man wastes away. Interpreters have variously understood the final verse of chapter 13 as either an aphoristic conclusion or summary of Job's bitter reflections, or as the beginning of the new set of complaints in chapter 14. Like the question in verse 25, this verse characterizes the one to whom God devotes so much negative attention as one who is weak, tenuous, worn out, and worthless. Perhaps the connection is the image of the long-term prisoner who wastes away in close confinement, losing strength and moldering **like something rotten.** Elsewhere the verb "wastes away" describes the physical decline of Sarah in her old age (Gen. 18:11).

Additional Notes §46

13:27 / The term for **shackles** (Heb. *sad*) is used only here and in the nearly identical phrase in 33:11. Often *sad* is translated "stocks." Although the precise meaning of the word is difficult to determine, some intentional binding of the feet as a form of detention is clearly intended.

13:28 / Pope, *Job,* pp. 97–98, moves v. 28 to follow 14:1–2. Clines, *Job 1–20,* pp. 323–24, sees the verse as the conclusion of the set of three verses (vv. 26–28) and parallel to the preceding three verses (vv. 23–25). Both sets of verses question why God would spend such energy on someone who is so fragile and useless.

§47 The Brevity of Human Life (Job 14:1–6)

The first part of chapter 14 considers the shortness of human life. The discussion consists of two, three-verse sections (vv. 1–3; vv. 4–6). Each segment begins with a description of human powerlessness and concludes with a direct address to God about his scrutiny and judgment.

14:1 / **Man born of woman.** Job has in mind *humanity* as a whole rather than any specific person. This human life, he says, is **of few days and full of trouble.** The word for "few" is the Hebrew *qtsr,* which describes something which has been "cut short" or "shortened"—brought to a premature end. The effect is to emphasize the restrictive nature of the shortness that interrupts the anticipated flow of life. By contrast, the **trouble** that accompanies this abbreviated life is complete. The word for "full" (Heb. *seba*ᶜ) stresses complete satisfaction or satiation—"full to the max," so to speak—so that no more could even be imagined!

14:2 / This brief life, full of trouble, is also a *fragile* life that **springs up like a flower and withers away.** Flowers (Heb. *tsits*) can symbolize great beauty as well as great fragility and transience. A second metaphor parallels the first. A human is also like a **shadow** that **does not endure.** This human shadow is said to "flee" or "seek to escape" (Heb. *brkh*), thus the translation **fleeting.** In this context, the verb for **endure** (Heb. ᶜ*md*) can also mean "take a stand; stand (still)." The picture is of a constantly moving shadow which has little substance and no lasting existence.

14:3 / Given the weak and insubstantial character of humans, Job questions why God would give such careful attention to them. Job's question begins with emphasis (Heb. ʾ*ap,* "indeed; even!")—literally, "even concerning this [such a weak human being] do you open your eyes?" Despite the obvious insignificance of humans, God nevertheless spends his time scrutinizing them in order to punish every infraction, no matter how small

(Job expresses a similar concern in 7:17–21). **Will you bring him ... for judgment?** The purpose of divine scrutiny and care, Job says (contrary to Ps. 8!), is to bring the human into judgment. The context is again a legal one, where both God and his human opponent are held up to the standard of "justice" (*mishpat*)—the declaration of what *ought to have occurred* in a situation. The preposition behind NIV's **before you** is better translated "with you," emphasizing that both God and humans are being measured against *mishpat*. This reminds me of our contemporary cadre of personal injury lawyers who are constantly on the lookout for persons who have been injured, and on whose behalf they can file suit in court.

14:4 / Who can bring what is pure from the impure? Using an idiom that occurs often in this book, Job expresses a future impossibility in order to point out the extremity of God's dealings with humans. The idiom (Heb. *mi yitten*, lit., "Who will give?") most often expresses a deep, heartfelt wish that is nevertheless considered impossible. The heartrending cry of David after learning of the death of his son, Absalom, is an apt example: "O my son Absalom! My son, my son Absalom! If only [lit. *mi yitten*, "who will give"] I had died instead of you—O Absalom, my son, my son!" (2 Sam. 18:33). Here, however, Job speaks the phrase in order to point out just how equally unlikely it is that any human could live a totally sinless life. What **is pure** (Heb. *tahor*) in relation to **the impure** (Heb. *tame'*) represents that which is *ritually clean* as prescribed by the law. It is obviously impossible to make a lamb that is by definition *unclean* into a *clean* lamb fit for sacrifice. Job wonders how God can expect weak and *unclean* humans to live up to standards of *cleanliness* that are beyond their abilities ever to reach (compare the statements of Eliphaz in 4:17 and of Job himself in 9:2).

14:5 / Man's days are determined. There is some question about whether this statement actually claims that God predetermines the extent of each specific human life. The verb *khrts* can mean "settle, determine," as in the judgment in a law case (e.g., 1 Kgs. 20:40). Since humanity as a whole is in view here, this may be a reference to the divine limitation of human life just prior to the flood (Gen. 6:3). The **number of ... months** are, literally, "with" God rather than **decreed** by God. The idea that God knows the days and months of a human life is very different from his having decreed or predetermined them in advance. It is certainly true that God has **set limits** to life that humans **cannot exceed,** but does this mean that the will of God presets the very day and hour of a person's death? It seems unlikely that is the case elsewhere in Scripture. See, for example, the case of King Hezekiah, whose death is prophesied by Isaiah but then is prolonged by fifteen years in response to his earnest plea (2 Kgs. 20:1–11). Job's point is clear regardless of whether these verses declare limits or precise determination. Humans are restricted to divinely prescribed limits and have no power to transgress the boundaries God has established. Human life is short and marked by powerlessness to control its progress or outcome.

14:6 / So look away from him. Since humans are by nature weak and powerless, subject to impurities that separate them from God, Job questions whether God's diligent punishment is fruitful for anyone concerned, since humans, even those responsive to God's discipline, are simply incapable of the kind of perfection of character and practice God seems to expect. It is better for humans, Job thinks, that God should **look away**—a reference to God relaxing his continual scrutiny—and **let him alone.** Freed from unending divine surveillance, humans would be able to live out the rest of their days with a modicum of comfort—although Job's characterization of the human as **a hired man** suggests some doubts as to the possibility of a positive relationship with God. The sentiment is like that of the returning Prodigal Son in Luke 15:11–32 who, having reached the end of his personal rope, plans to ask his father to take him on in the reduced capacity of servant so that he might at least have hope of survival. Whether or not Job has any hopes of restoration to a full relationship with God (as the Prodigal is restored to sonship) is uncertain.

Additional Notes §47

14:2 / Because of their beauty, **flowers** are part of the ornamentation of the temple (1 Kgs. 6:18, 29, 32, 35). 1 Pet. 1:24 quotes Isa. 40:6, while in Matt. 6:28–30 Jesus' reference to the "grasses [in other translations 'lilies'] of the field" may allude either to Ps. 103:15–16 or Isa. 40:6. Both of these passages refer to "grass" (Heb. *khatsir*) and "flower of the field" (*tsits hassadeh*) as metaphors for the brevity of human life. See also Isa. 28:1, 4; 40:6–8; Ps. 103:15–16.

14:4 / The expression *mi yitten* occurs 10 times in Job (6:8; 11:5; 13:5; 14:4, 13; 19:23; 23:3; 29:2; 31:31, 35). All but one of these (11:5, spoken by Zophar) are found in the mouth of Job! Outside the book of Job, the idiom is found an additional 13 times in the OT.

14:5 / **Man's days are determined.** Although some suggest the statement in Gen. 6:3 describes a period of delay between God's decree of judgment and the onset of the flood, it seems most likely to me to be a general limitation of the length of human life that begins to take effect with the gradual decrease in lifespans noted in the postdiluvian generations (Gen. 11:10–26). While this is a rough limit to human life, there have always been those who exceeded the limit as well as those cut short before reaching it.

14:6 / The verb **let alone** (Heb. *khdl*) is taken variously as "stop; desist" (meaning that God should stop punishing him); or "leave [someone] alone." The difference is negligible. Another verb with the same root consonants would give the meaning "become fat; have success." Those who suggest this latter verb take this verse to say that God should **look away** so that the person would be able to enjoy and experience success in life. This latter understanding has some connection with the views of Eccl. (Eccl. 2:24; 3:13; 5:18; 8:15; 9:7).

The same Gk. word for **hired man** (Gk. *misthotos*) appears in the LXX version of Job 14:6 and in Luke 15:19.

§48 Metaphors from Nature (Job 14:7–12)

14:7 / The following verses contrast the tenuous nature of human life and the looming threat of death with the more hopeful future of a tree. **At least there is hope for a tree.** Job's pessimism is clear—the implication of his metaphor is that there is *no similar hope* for humans. Even should a tree be **cut down** to the ground, there is hope that it will **sprout again** (Heb. *khlp*, lit. "exchange; replace; renew"). The **roots** or **stump** of the felled tree may yet sprout **new shoots** that become vital enough that they **will not fail.**

14:8–9 / Even should the stump languish in decay for a long time in the arid conditions of the Middle East without any sign of life, the supply of sufficient water may be enough to revitalize the moribund **stump** and **roots** to **bud and put forth new shoots like a plant.** These kinds of observations of the natural processes of the plants are typical of the wisdom methodology of the sages. They drew on observation and experience in all of life to provide analogies to understand the meaning of, and appropriate responses to, human existence. Should the author of Job have the condition of the exilic community in mind, these would be apt metaphors for encouraging hope. The "shoot" out of the truncated "stump of Jesse" became an important exilic metaphor for the ultimate restoration of the Davidic kingship (e.g., Isa. 11:1, 10).

14:10 / Job continues, however, with the counter example of human fragility and transience. Unlike the tree, with its hope of ultimate revitalization, when **man dies and is laid low** there is no hope of restoration. This is, of course, a very clear indication that Job (and the author of the book) has no clear belief in a future resurrection or even some kind of spiritual afterlife. The whole point of the contrast here is that once humans die, there is no hope of a future return. The verb translated "laid low" (Heb. *khlsh*) more likely means "be/become weak"—a reference to the loss of vitality when humans die in contrast to the tree's continuing potential for new life (Clines, *Job 1–20*, pp. 328–29). Verse 10 employs two words for "man," or human being: *geber* and *ʾadam*. The first term emphasizes the strength and power of living humans. Even such a vital human being cannot escape the limitations of death. When he **breathes his last,** people will look around and ask, "Where is he?" (a more literal translation of the Heb. behind NIV's **he . . . is no more**). The implication of these verses spoken out in the direction of God is to encourage God to act *now* while there is yet hope for life within Job, *before* his death removes any opportunity for restoration.

14:11 / Shifting metaphors, Job describes the evaporation of **water** from **the sea** and the drying up of a major river. The verse is reminiscent of Isaiah 19:5 ("The waters of the river will dry up, and the riverbed will be parched and dry"), a verse that depicts God's future judgment on the source of vitality and abundance for Egypt. The Isaiah parallel may suggest that the emphasis here is on the *improbability* of these occurrences. As improbable as it might be for the "sea" (or a large lake) to completely dry up, or for a river like the Nile to completely disappear, so the restoration of life to deceased humans is equally unlikely.

14:12 / Similarly, then, a human being **lies down and does not rise** for as long as the heavens exist. Clines (*Job 1–20*) denies any belief in an ultimate demise or destruction of the heavens and earth. The Hebrew phrase *bilti shamayim,* **till the heavens are no more,** also reflects the atmosphere of extreme improbability established in the preceding verse. As a result, the phrase indicates the continual existence of the heavens, against which the continuing disappearance of the deceased is measured. In what amounts to almost a direct denial of the possibility of resurrection, the last half of the verse speaks of humanity in its collective sense: they **will not awake or be roused from their sleep.**

Additional Notes §48

14:7 / **New shoots.** Heb. *yoneqet* is a feminine participle of the root *ynq,* "suckle; suck," which most often describes the action of the human infant taking in the mother's milk. As a description of new shoots from an older root it has a parallel in the English term "sucker."

14:9 / The **plant** (Heb. *nata^c*) refers to cultivated vegetation purposefully planted by a gardener and carefully watered and tended.

14:11 / The use of the Heb. *nahar*, "river," rather than *nahal*, "wadi, seasonal stream," suggests that Job has a more exceptional circumstance in mind than the occasional drying up of local streambeds that would refill during the rainy season.

The only significant difference between this verse and Isa. 91:5 is that Isaiah uses the initial verb *nsht*, "dry up," instead of Job's *ʾzl*.

It is possible here in v. 11 that the author has in mind the gradual decline of the Dead Sea, leaving behind the evidence of its decrease in the deposits of salt and its own increased salinity that are some of its characteristics today.

14:12 / Hartley, *Job*, p. 235, points out the link to Isa. 26:19 and Dan. 12:2, "clear resurrection passages," where similar verbs (Heb. *qum*, "arise," and *qits*, "awake") affirm the resurrection of the dead.

§49 Erosion of Hope (Job 14:13–22)

14:13 / Once again, Job uses the idiomatic expression, "who will give" (Heb. *mi yitten*), to indicate the utter impossibility of hope (see the discussion on 14:4 in §47). **If only you could** . . . is actually an admission that such deliverance will *never* occur. Job is twisting the normal ways of thinking about **the grave** (which is actually a reference to *Sheol,* the abode of the dead). As we saw above (on 10:20–22), *Sheol* is the place of no return, where all go upon death, regardless of their character in this life. Job takes this dreaded end of human life—an end without hope of restoration—and turns it into a place of refuge from the **anger** of God! The remaining wishes he expresses in this verse are equally impossible. His desire that God could **set** . . . **a time** (Heb. *khoq,* i.e., provide a limit to Job's stay in *Sheol*) falters with the realization that *Sheol* is the place from which *none return.* So too, then, this dashes his hope that God will **remember** the dead. For Job, even death seems a desired hiding place from the power of God's anger.

14:14 / The impossibility of what he desires comes home to Job as he cries out in response to his own foolish hopes: **If a man dies, will he live again?** In this context the question is rhetorical and he expects a negative response. Job has already covered this territory in verses 10–12 (note the similar terminology: *geber yamut* in vv. 10, 14). Dead men do not rise, awake, or rouse from their sleep (v. 12). Job will continue to **wait** for the arrival of his **renewal,** but this restoration must come in this life because there is no return from death. Life, as Job characterizes it, is **service** (Heb. *tsaba*ʾ), a reference to the hard labor of a hired hand or a servant. Job uses the same word in 7:1, where he also describes humans as "like a hired man" (Heb. *sakir,* see also 14:6).

On the other hand, Job may be suggesting another impossible scenario in which one who is suffering as he is might wait expectantly for restoration or renewal. *If* the dead man might live again, then it might be possible to wait out the long days of service in *Sheol* in expectation of being restored both to life and to God's favor (see Clines, *Job 1–20*, pp. 330–32; Hartley, *Job*, pp. 236–37). In this case, the implication is that since there is no hope of the dead rising to new life, there is equally no reason to wait expectantly for restoration and renewal.

14:15 / In the midst of his "impossible dream," Job envisions a restoration of reciprocal relationship with God. Although the language here is similar to that in the earlier courtroom contexts of *summons and response* (9:15–16; 13:22), the legal aspects recede in this passage where God **will call** seeking Job's **answer**, but in a context of longing (**you** [God] **will long**). The verb "long" (Heb. *ksp*) has the sense of "yearn, long for; be hungry," and indicates passionate concern and desire bordering on *need*. In 10:3, Job confronts God for "spurning" the work of his hand and oppressing Job. The change in divine attitude towards his creature described here makes all the difference, as the following verses reveal.

14:16–17 / Earlier Job described God keeping close watch on his paths, even marking the soles of his feet (or noting every footprint) so as to track his every step. In that instance (13:27), Job perceived that God's intent was to remark every sinful misstep for punishment. Here, as Job dreams of an impossible future with God, God **will count** Job's **steps** not to mete out punishment, but to forgive sin. Although watching over every step, God will **not keep track of my sin**. Instead Job's **offenses will be sealed up in a bag**. Elsewhere the idea of "bagging" (Heb. *tsrr*) sins describes a means of storing them up for a later accounting. While that is a negative image fraught with anxiety over future judgment and punishment, here Job's sins are "bagged up" in order to be done away with (sort of like setting out trash for the collector!). Job also uses a different image here to describe his sin as being "covered over," using a term (Heb. *tpl*) for "smear over" (this term describes "smearing" with lies in 13:4 and Ps. 119:69).

14:18–19 / Familiar, perhaps, with the effects of erosion on the crags and wadis in the Judean desert along the Jordan Rift Valley (a fault line that extends along the Jordan River valley, past the Dead Sea, and on into the Red Sea beyond Eilat), the author paints imagery of the wearing away of mountains and stream beds through the action of wind and water. The adversative adverb *ʾulam* (as in 13:3, 4) introduces this new set of images, indicating a new direction in the narrative. And thus Job's rather wistful, but improbable, vision of a new relationship in which God would overlook Job's sin (vv. 15–17) comes to an abrupt halt in these verses with the realization that nothing has yet changed. God is still the destroyer of **man's hope.**

Over time, wind and water weaken mountain crags and bluffs so that significant promontories collapse and fall. The words **as a mountain erodes** emphasize the *length* of time involved in the erosion process. The related phrase at the beginning of verse 19, **as water wears away stones,** reflects this focus on time as well. The erosion of mountains and the persistent and gradual wearing down of rock and stone are *long-term* processes. Certainly Job must have felt his own suffering involved the same sort of continual, grinding hostility from God, wearing him down until he would at last collapse and fail.

The "water" imagery in verse 19 perhaps indicates more immediate changes, as torrents can carve out trenches and carry away quantities of "stones" and **soil** overnight. Observing the tumbled rocks and fallen trees mixed together like pebbles and toothpicks at the mouths of coastal rivers in Oregon following an extremely wet winter, I have been amazed by the power of water unleashed in torrents down these streams that run from the mountains to the sea. Similarly, at times we may feel in our own lives the overwhelming power of circumstances tumbling us along against our will and carrying us away beyond our control. These are fearful times in which it may seem that all is lost and that God has indeed become the destroyer of hope.

We are not certain from Job's narrative just how long the process of his descent actually took. On the one hand, the rapid-fire description of Job's losses in chapter 1 suggests that God destroyed all of his family and possessions in a single day (1:13–22). On the other hand, Job's personal descent into illness, suffering, and pain near to death appears to be a more long-term process, and his words throughout the dialogue seem to confirm a long, drawn-out ordeal. Regardless of the actual time span, however, days may seem like years to those in extreme pain, and weeks of unrelenting pain may seem to last a lifetime. So, as wind and rain and flood and torrent wear down mountains, carry away rocks like pebbles, and wash away the soil, so God acts powerfully and over time to **destroy man's hope.**

14:20 / Job turns his reflections into a direct address to God, as the use of the second person "you" in this verse indicates. The term for **man** here is *ʾenosh,* a word that emphasizes the weak and transitory nature of humans, who do not endure (see Additional Notes on 5:17 in §14). If the mountains and rocks which are part of the creation of God crumble and fall, what hope do weak, insubstantial humans have for lasting existence? Job tells God, **you overpower** man (Job is still speaking here of the more general oppression of humans, mirroring his own case) **once for all,** meaning "forever" (the Heb. *lenetsakh* emphasizes the *enduring* nature of God's action).

The picture in **he is gone . . . you . . . send him away** is of the descent of the deceased into *Sheol.* Overpowered by God, the weak human cannot hang on but instead descends through death to the abode of the dead. The **change** of **countenance** is perhaps the settling of the face into motionlessness when life departs at the moment of death.

14:21 / *Sheol* is the place of no return, where there is no memory of life. Those who have departed to the grave no longer know what occurs in life with their **sons.** Whether they **are honored** or **brought low** is a matter of little consequence since the deceased person **does not know . . . does not see.**

14:22 / Description of any **pain** and mourning on the part of the dead is highly unusual in the OT, and so some commentators have assumed that this refers to the moments preceding death (e.g., Hartley, *Job,* p. 240). In light of Job's oft-expressed desire to escape his suffering in the oblivion of the grave, it seems unlikely that the continuing pain and mourning here describe the experience of the deceased. Job reflects here that death is not *all* gain since it means being cut off from one's family relationships and knowledge of those left behind. For Job, however, this is not an important issue, since he has already lost his children and any hope or fear of their future.

Additional Notes §49

14:15 / While the Heb. phrases used in 10:3 (*yegiaʿ kappeka*) and here (*maʿaseh yadeka*) are distinctive, the meanings are very close.

14:22 / Clines, *Job 1–20,* p. 336, calls mention of the dead's suffering in the OT "unparalleled." Pope, *Job,* p. 111, however, thinks pain is a continuing experience of the dead. This would undermine Job's desire to escape suffering in death.

§50 Sin Prompts Your Mouth (Job 15:1–6)

The "second dialogue cycle" begins here as we return to the argument of Eliphaz, from whom we last heard in chapters 4 and 5. There Eliphaz operated from the assumption that humans are "born to trouble" (5:7) and therefore "reap" what they "sow" (4:8). It is impossible for "a mortal to be righteous before God." Since even God's servants, the angels, are untrustworthy, "how much more" are humans subject to "error" (4:18–19). As a result, Job must deserve his suffering. His only hope is to accept God's discipline (5:17) and throw himself upon the mercy of God (5:8).

Eliphaz does not change his argument much in chapter 15, although he criticizes Job more harshly. The problem is still that humans are impure and as a result are unable to claim righteousness before God (15:14). Again Eliphaz says that God's "holy ones," who are even themselves unworthy of divine "trust," set a standard of righteousness to which humans cannot hope to attain (15:15), because humans are by nature "vile and corrupt" (15:16, 34–35). Eliphaz offers no real solution in this chapter to Job's situation, except by implication. He declares that Job's claim to innocence is "deceit" (15:35), and that therefore his suffering is actually the deserved result of his "sin" (15:5). Most of chapter 15 is a warning of coming judgment, implying that Job's only hope is to confess his sin.

15:1–3 / Eliphaz opens by harshly condemning Job's **empty notions** (lit., "vain, empty knowledge"), which he compares with the destructive effects of a **hot east wind**. The "east wind" can also be an image of empty striving and deceit (Hos. 12:1) and is thus parallel to "empty notions." By insisting that such vanity and deceit characterize Job's words, Eliphaz implies that Job is *not* one of the sages. Job's attempts to **argue** his case are **useless** and of **no value**. Although Eliphaz couches his condemnation in a set of rhetorical questions regarding the proper activity of a

wise man, the shift in verse 4 to directly address Job (**but you** . . .) makes it clear that he is confronting Job here.

15:4 / Not only are Job's words considered "empty," "useless," and of "no value," they also have a negative effect since they **undermine piety and hinder devotion.** It seems most likely that the hindrance to which Eliphaz refers is that people will experience a crisis of faith when they observe the suffering of Job and his belligerent reaction to it. The term "undermine" (Heb. *prr*) is even harsher than it may appear, since it has the sense of "break out; burst out; break; destroy" as well as "invalidate." The Hebrew word translated "hinder" is *grᶜ*, meaning "diminish; reduce." The elements of piety that Job breaks and diminishes are, literally, "fear" (Heb. *yirʾa*) and "occupation" (Heb. *sikha*). The former is the foundational relationship of dependence on God that characterizes the core of Israelite faith (see the discussion on 1:1 in §1 with regard to the "fear of God"). The latter term describes one's deepest deliberation and moral decision (thus NIV's "devotion" is most appropriate).

15:5–6 / Job is not wise (vv. 2–3); his words are detrimental to those who seek to live faithfully (v. 4); and as a result Eliphaz concludes that Job's words can only be the outpouring of his sinful character: **your sin prompts your mouth.** Job is seeking to twist the truth in order to deceive: **you adopt the tongue of the crafty.** Eliphaz implies Job's culpability in his very selection of words. "Adopt the tongue of the crafty" is from the Hebrew *bkhr*, meaning "choose; select; prefer." Job's words **testify against** him (lit., "declare you guilty"), therefore no additional evidence from Eliphaz is necessary (although Eliphaz is more than willing to provide more testimony of his own!). In a similar way, the Sanhedrin sought to lay the blame for the conviction of Jesus on his own words: "Then the high priest tore his clothes and said, 'He has spoken blasphemy! Why do we need any more witnesses? Look, now you have heard the blasphemy' " (Matt. 26:65; see also Luke 22:71).

Additional Notes §50

15:1 / The term **replied,** from the Heb. *ᶜnh,* "answer," in this context suggests that the various headings that introduce the parties of the dialogue/debate (3:2; 4:1; 6:1; 8:1; 9:1; 11:1; 12:1; 15:1; 16:1; 18:1; 19:1; 20:1; 21:1; 22:1; 23:1; 25:1; 26:1) have the sense of "enter/continue debate."

15:2 / The idiom of **empty notions** is different, but similar, to that of Ecclesiastes' "chasing after the wind" (2:11, Heb. *re'ut ruakh*, meaning "vain, empty striving"). Eliphaz's phrase is Heb. *da'at ruakh*, "vain, empty knowledge."

In Hos. 12:1 the **east wind** (Heb. *qadim;* MT v. 2) is an image of vain striving and deceit: "Ephraim feeds on the wind; he pursues the *east wind* all day and multiplies lies and violence." In the dream of Pharaoh interpreted by Joseph (Gen. 41), the east wind destroys the grain crops. For similar effects of the east wind see Ezek. 17:10; 19:12; Jonah 4:8; Hos. 13:15. In other contexts the east wind destroys ships (Ps. 48:7; Ezek. 27:6), brings locusts (Exod. 10:13), drives back the sea (Exod. 14:21), and drives out with a fierce blast (Isa. 27:8).

15:3 / The term **argue** is the Heb. *ykkh*, which describes setting forth one's case in court (see the discussion on 13:6 in §43).

15:5 / The verb *'lp*, NIV **prompt**, in the Piel means "teach." The image is of the small child learning to recite from memory the "aleph-bet"—the Heb. version of the alphabet—founded on the same verbal root. All words are formed on the basis of this foundation, so error at this point compounds itself throughout life.

In his first speech, Eliphaz had warned Job against following the path of the "crafty," who would experience the judgment of God (5:12–13). The **crafty** are the *'arumim*, from the noun *'arum*, that can mean "subtle; shrewd; clever; or crafty" with either positive or negative connotations. The term also describes the serpent in Gen. 3:1 as "more crafty [subtle] than any of the wild animals the LORD God had made."

With subtle sarcasm, Eliphaz questions the legitimacy of Job's wisdom. The wisdom enterprise acknowledges its debt to the sages of the past upon whom the core insights of the wisdom tradition depend. It was through the preservation, transmission, and refinement of these ancient insights that sages were able to come to an increasingly clear and complete understanding of an orderly world. Thus Bildad's first speech appeals to the learning of the "former generations" and the "fathers," compared to whom Job and the friends appear to be those "born only yesterday" who "know nothing" (8:8–9).

15:7–8 / When he asks Job, **are you the first man ever born?**, Eliphaz is denying the antiquity of Job's insights and questioning their validity. Eliphaz's subtle reference to the creation of Wisdom itself as "the first of [God's] works" (see Prov. 8:22–31) underlines his criticism. Proverbs 8:25b describes Wisdom with the same phrase that concludes verse 7: **brought forth before the hills.** Thus Eliphaz is asking Job whether he thinks he is the embodiment of Wisdom. Does he think his words have the authority to set aside all the deliberation of all the sages throughout the preceding ages? Verse 8 levels the same criticism: **Do you limit wisdom to yourself?** Wisdom was a cooperative, corporate enterprise marked by humility and mutual consensus rather than by brash independence and radical departures of individual thinking. Job's refusal to accept the long-held beliefs of the sages undermines the very fabric of the wisdom structures (which is what v. 4 refers to, rather than general piety and faith in God). In doing so, Job threatens to shatter the foundational security of the friends and the traditional sages.

Do you listen in on God's council? On the one hand, this phrase continues the general criticism of Job as one who sets up his own insights as the ultimate measure of true wisdom. Eliphaz accuses Job of thinking he has knowledge of the *very mind of God* in these matters. That is pretty ironic, since Job claims to be utterly at a loss to understand what God is doing in his case. Job does not claim to know what *is*, but he always confidently declares what he knows *cannot be!* The friends are unwilling to follow the logic of Job's observation and experience to its ultimate conclusion—the usual methodology of traditional wisdom—because it would shake the very foundation of their belief. Instead Eliphaz is seeking to force Job to ignore the implications of his experience and submerge his doubts beneath the cautious consensus of the sages. This Job remains steadfastly unwilling to do.

On the other hand, this reference to listening in on God's "council" has the further ironic effect of reminding the reader of the private knowledge that the opening chapters of the book provide of the heavenly conferences between God and *the* Satan. The reader *has* had the opportunity to do what Eliphaz suggests here. The reader *has* been able to "listen in on God's council," and that council has already exonerated Job as "blameless and upright, a man who fears God and shuns evil" (1:8). Thus the reader already knows that Job is right and the friends—in their reliance on the long tradition of the sages—are wrong.

15:9–10 / Eliphaz claims parity of knowledge with Job, in an apparent reply to Job's denial that his knowledge or wisdom is in any way inferior to that of the friends (12:1; 13:1). So Eliphaz asks, what could Job **know**, what **insights** might he have that the friends, and indeed all generations of sages, do not already know? The obvious answer—one that Eliphaz will not admit is possible—is that Job knows his own heart. He knows that he is innocent of any great evil deserving of the suffering he receives from God. This the reader knows as well. But for Eliphaz, the testimony of **the gray-haired and the aged** (again a reference to the long tradition of the sages) is enough. This testimony confirms the convictions of the friends that suffering is always justified and the consequence of human sinfulness. The reference to **men even older than your father** is simply another way of undermining the authority and validity of Job's words, since they are only the individual ruminations of a latecomer.

15:11 / Eliphaz claims that Job finds **God's consolations** of trifling significance and rejects them. Just what these "consolations" might be is a point of continuing discussion. Most refer to the divine revelation of the innate sinfulness of humans that Eliphaz described in his first speech (4:12–16) and to which he returns in 15:14–16 (see, e.g., Hartley, *Job,* p. 246). In this view the revelation consoles because it indicates that all humans—even the most righteous—sin occasionally and should expect to experience suffering without it undermining their confidence in the orderly nature of existence. Job is simply making too much of his suffering. The phrase **words spoken gently to you** contains a veiled threat. Job's *experience* has been anything but gentle! Eliphaz is most likely referring to the friends' attempts in general—and his own in particular—to encourage Job to submit to the consensus of the sages and to give up his angry struggle with God. The implied threat is that if Job ignores these gentle words, he can anticipate a harsher response in the future. Since Job has already experienced the worst that God can offer, and since death seems like a release from his suffering, this threat has little motivating force for him.

15:12–13 / Job has been **carried . . . away** by his **heart** to react to God in a rash and angry manner. We must remember that the "heart" is not simply the seat of emotions here, but the center of moral reflection and decision-making (see the discussion on 11:13–14 in §38). The implication is that Job's deep reflection on his experience and circumstances has led him to inappropriate conclusions and ultimately into **rage against God.** The phrase translated **your eyes flash** is difficult since the verb (Heb. *rzm*) appears only here. The NIV interprets it as an indication of the anger that verse 13 describes.

The phrase **vent your rage** is equally difficult. The Hebrew says, literally, "that you return to God your spirit [*ruakh*]." On the surface this might suggest that Job's anger against God places him in danger of giving up his life-sustaining *spirit* so that it returns to its source in God. While this is certainly part of the ironic and playful context in which Eliphaz speaks, most commentators understand *ruakh* here as a "state of mind" (Clines) or a "dominant mood" (Hartley). A "spirit" of anger leveled at God is influencing Job's thinking and preventing him from perceiving and accepting the "consolations" of God where they are to be found.

Additional Notes §51

15:11 / It is most likely that the Heb. *laʾat* is the combination of the preposition *le-* and the noun *ʾat*, meaning **gently**, rather than the verb *lʾt*, "cover; be secret."

15:12 / **Flash** (or perhaps "wink") is derived by transposing the consonants of the verb to *rmz*. Clines, *Job 1–20*, p. 342 (following Tur-Sinai), and Pope, *Job*, p. 116, understand the meaning to be "dwindle away; become weak" with the consequence that Job's "eyes" have failed to perceive the truth about God, and he has thus been led into faulty thinking and anger.

§52 *Human Corruption (Job 15:14–16)*

15:14–16 / Returning to the revelation of the essentially sinful nature of humans he originally described in 4:12–16, Eliphaz again seeks to persuade Job to put aside his angry quest and to accede to the consolations this view offers. The gist of Eliphaz's argument is that humans are incapable of being completely **pure** (Heb. *zkk*, see the related noun *zak* in 8:6) or **righteous** (Heb. *tsdq*). Even the **holy ones** (heavenly beings, angels) and **the heavens** themselves are not "pure" enough to earn God's **trust**, let alone humans who are **vile and corrupt.** These last two terms are the Hebrew verbs *tᶜb*, "vile" ("be loathed; be abhorrent") and *ʾlkh*, "corrupt." Both appear in the Niphal participle form, which links them together visually. Eliphaz also describes the human (*ʾish*) as so enmeshed in evil that it **drinks up evil** (*ᶜawlah*) **like water!** This description reflects an almost casual relationship to evil that has become commonplace in one's life. How could such a one possibly escape the disciplining punishment of God?

Eliphaz's implication, of course, is that Job falls under this general condemnation of human corruption and thus has no legitimate reason to balk at his suffering. Eliphaz completely ignores—or disregards—Job's continuing protestation of innocence. Job might even agree that humans are not perfectly sinless—he never claims they are—but his chief argument is that his punishment is out of proportion for any "crime" he might have committed (see 7:20–21). Neither has Job's scrupulous attention to the details of religious response even to *possible* offenses to God (1:5) met divine forgiveness or mercy. Thus Eliphaz continues to talk past Job without really addressing his arguments and complaints seriously.

§53 Deserved Torment (Job 15:17–35)

To buttress his argument, Eliphaz turns in the remainder of the chapter to what appears to be a series of traditional wisdom admonitions ("what wise men have declared") proclaiming the ultimate punishment of the wicked (esp. vv. 20–35). Eliphaz introduces these sayings—which were probably part of the common wisdom repertoire of *both* Job and his friends—as ancient and authoritative words received from the fathers (vv. 17–19), but which have been shaped so that their application to Job's situation is clear (vv. 21, 24–25, 27–29).

15:17–19 / Eliphaz calls Job to **listen** to his explanation of what he has **seen.** The call to "listen" is a typical wisdom introduction and usually implies the superior knowledge of the speaker (the sage) in contrast to that of the hearer (the student). Eliphaz omits here the common familial description of the hearer as "my son," perhaps as a harsh slap at Job's refusal to learn anything from his friends. Job is the "fool" who resists discipline and must, therefore, be answered "according to his folly, or he will be wise in his own eyes" (Prov. 26:5). In the Hebrew, the opening phrase begins with Eliphaz's intent to **explain** his point to Job, followed by the imperative demand that Job "listen." It is almost as if he must grab the attention of an unruly and inattentive child and coerce his participation: "I will explain to you, so *listen!*"

What Eliphaz proceeds to declare is something he has "seen." He may be referring again to the vision he reported in 4:12–16—a vision of the essentially sinful nature of humans who deserve the punishment they receive. Alternatively, he may be referring to a more general vision of the suffering of the wicked as laid out in the traditional sayings of the fathers (which he then offers in the verses that follow). In either event, Eliphaz is adding his personal confirmation to the testimony of the ancient fathers and sages.

What seems to be a parenthetical statement separates the call to "listen" from the proclamation of what Eliphaz has "seen." The statement in verse 19 proceeds from the reference to **their fathers** and describes an exclusive claim to **the land** at a time **when no alien passed among them.** The reference, if taken as the land promised to the fathers *of Israel,* represents a somewhat awkward statement in the face of the consistently *non-Israelite* identification of Job, his friends, and the context of the rest of the book (e.g., "people of the East" in 1:3). It is probable that Eliphaz speaks here of an early, unadulterated time in his own tribal history during which native wisdom was uninfluenced by any foreign contact and could thus be considered *pure.* Eliphaz, as a result, claims to be reporting authentic, unadulterated wisdom traditions in contrast to the newfangled ideas Job put forward.

15:20 / Rather than anticipating some future judgment meted out on the wicked as we have heard from the friends before (e.g., 4:7–9; 8:11–19, 22; 11:20), Eliphaz advances the argument significantly by declaring that, despite their seeming prosperity and impunity, nevertheless **the wicked man suffers torment.** Wealth and power offer no escape from these terrors as the wicked are beset from without and within.

All his days. This terror is not just an end-time judgment, but plagues the wicked throughout their lifetimes. The "torment" is extreme, as the verb *khyl* in the Hitpael stem, emphasizing the "continual and repeated writhing" associated with unbearable pain, indicates. (Having suffered through three sets of kidney stones, I have some idea of the kind of agony depicted here!) In the face of such constant suffering, **all the years** of the **ruthless** become an agonizing storage house of unremitting pain (the verb here is *tspn,* "store up").

15:21–22 / Paranoia sets in as every **sound** is **terrifying** and the wicked live in fear of **attack** by **marauders** (the participle of *shdd,* "destroy; devastate"). Even **darkness** feeds into this fear because the wicked **despairs of escaping** it (lit., "he can not be confident of returning from darkness"). Note how the theme of "darkness" returns several times in this passage (vv. 22, 23, 30). This individual carries a sense of dread like one who knows there is a "contract" out to kill him (lit., "he is spied out **for the sword**").

15:23–26 / The Hebrew text of verse 23 is a bit difficult, mostly because of the word ʾ*ayyeh,* translated in the NIV as

vultures. The literal meaning of the Hebrew is, "He wanders about for food; Where is it?" It is possible that this refers to the tenuousness of the life of the wicked, who rootlessly wanders and can find nothing to eat. The NIV has followed those who read *ʾayyeh* instead as *ʾayyah,* "vulture" (see Clines, *Job 1–20,* p. 341). Others read the verb (*ndd*) as "cast out," in which case the meaning would be that the wicked is fearful of being cast aside as food for a vulture. The image of **darkness** returns in this probable reference to the coming of death.

Two synonyms begin verse 24: **Distress and anguish.** These also terrify the wicked and **overwhelm him.** Anticipation is as bad as the reality, as these two causes of fear are **poised** for **attack.**

The cause for the terror that besets the wicked is his own relation to God (this is clearly intended as a warning to Job!). The accusation is two-fold and plays out over verses 25 and 26. The wicked person **shakes his fist at God,** taking a hostile attitude to him. In addition he **vaunts himself**—a use of the verb *gbr,* "be stronger," in the Hitpael stem to mean "make himself stronger (than God)." Having convinced themselves of their superiority, the wicked are emboldened to launch an attack directly at the deity while metaphorically trusting in the protection of a **thick, strong shield.**

15:27–28 / A second series of images describe the futility of the wicked person's existence. These revolve around the contrast between the apparent wealth and power of the wicked and the reality of their devastating insecurity. Verse 27 describes one who displays one's wealth by gaining excess weight through eating rich foods. In some societies, **fat** and physical heaviness reflect one's prosperity and security—a fat person is able to secure abundant food and need not fear starvation. Neither do those who are fat with a bulging **waist** usually engage in hard labor—another sign of wealth. The Hebrew here, literally, is "he covers his face with his fat," which suggests intriguingly that the wicked wealthy indeed *hide* behind their excesses.

Even though the wealthy show all the outward signs of security, the reality of their existence is far different. The wicked **inhabit** villages that have been **ruined**—possibly by military action—and **houses** that have been abandoned as unlivable. In an image particularly apt for the situation of the wicked, the **houses** are described as **crumbling to rubble** (lit., "preparing themselves for rubble"). The picture is of weakened structures on the brink of collapse, endangering all who remain within.

15:29 / The apparent **wealth** and power of the wicked do not last. The word NIV translates as "wealth" in this case is the Hebrew *khel,* which most often has the sense of "strength; power; defensive structures." The verb *qum,* "arise; stand up," intensifies this image of a defensive wall. Even those sources of security the wealthy depend on **will not endure.** Nor will their **possessions spread over the land.** All of these elements of the description of the wealthy wicked resonate clearly with the earlier picture of the blessed state of Job *before* the advent of his suffering (1:1–3). Eliphaz is informing Job, rather blatantly, that his great personal loss places him (in the friends' view) squarely in the category of the wicked described in these verses. Job's early wealth, says Eliphaz, was no more a sign of divine blessing, nor was it any more enduring, than the wealth and power of the wicked who will ultimately come to ruin.

15:30 / I end this section here at verse 30 because of the appearance in this verse of two images—**darkness** and fire—that also play concluding roles elsewhere (darkness in v. 22 and fire in v. 35). The central part of this description combines both darkness and fire and concludes with a return to this theme of "darkness." In verse 22, the wicked "despairs of escaping the darkness" (Heb. *lo' ya'amin shub minni khoshek*), while now the impossibility of **escape** is declared an inevitable reality (Heb. *lo' yasur minni khoshek*). The darkness appears to be metaphorical, since the destruction continues in terms of **flame** and wind.

Like a tender tree overwhelmed by a raging fire, the **shoots** of the wicked **wither.** This reference to "shoots" is a direct response to Job's earlier dismal evaluation of human vulnerability to death in 14:7–10. Eliphaz takes Job's image, of a tree cut down that returns to life with new "shoots" when water enlivens the apparently dead roots, and turns it into a condemnation of Job himself. Job contrasts the tree's hope for revival with a strong and general pessimism concerning a human's hope to return from death. Eliphaz here turns the tree into a metaphor for the hopelessness of *the wicked,* undermining Job's more general claim that *all humans* are weak by nature and therefore vulnerable to the powers of suffering and death through no fault of their own. Once again Eliphaz is claiming that Job's suffering is not the consequence of any tragic human flaw, but rather of his own choice for wickedness. He makes this point even more clearly when he links the source of suffering at the end of this verse to the **breath** of God's mouth (lit., "breath of *his* mouth"; emphasis added). This suffering is not just the inevitable result of innate human weakness, but divinely instituted discipline for human sin.

15:31–35 / The final section of chapter 15 both begins and ends with the theme of human deception (15:31, 35). Humans are characterized finally by deceit from their conception in the womb (15:35), but are warned not to trust in their own deceptions, since there is no profit in them (15:31). In between Eliphaz returns to the metaphor of plants and trees, in this case those that lose their fruit before it ripens.

In verses 31–34 Eliphaz measures the tendency of human beings to trust in their own strength and wealth and finds it wanting. Human power and riches are **worthless** (lit., "empty; vain") and do not reward human trust. The more literal rendering of this verse illustrates the wordplay and repetition: "Let him not trust in vanity [Heb. *shaw*] that leads astray, for vanity [Heb. *shawᵓ*] will be his exchange." A series of agricultural metaphors describe the wicked as offering evidence of fruitfulness that is ultimately shown to be deceptive. **Before his time** the wicked receives judgment for his sins so that **his branches will not flourish.** The verse is an almost exact negation of Psalm 1:3, where a tree metaphor describes the righteous: "He is like a tree planted by streams of water, which yields its fruit in season and whose leaf does not wither. Whatever he does prospers." The vocabulary is quite different, but the sentiments quite parallel (in a negative fashion). Like **a vine,** the wicked puts forth **grapes** that are **stripped** off before they ripen. Finally, the wicked is compared to an **olive tree** that puts forth **blossoms** that fall before they are pollinated. As a consequence, the **godless** as a group are considered **barren** (Heb. *galmud,* see 3:7), incapable of producing good and worthy only of destruction by **fire.** The fire imagery links this verse back to the "flame" that withers the shoots of the wicked at the end of the preceding section (v. 30).

In an imperfect extension of the metaphor of barrenness begun in verse 34, Eliphaz concludes his speech in verse 35 by describing the wicked as those who **conceive trouble and give birth to evil.** The metaphor is imperfect because those who are "barren" (v. 34) do not "conceive" or "give birth." The difficulty may be in the understanding of the Hebrew translated "barren" (*galmud*), which appears only in Job 3:7; 15:34; 30:3; and Isaiah 49:21. The idea of *human* barrenness is certainly present in the expression of Job's desire that the day of his own birth had instead been barren (3:7).

The section that began in verse 31 with a warning to the wicked not to be misled into believing their own deceptions now concludes with a last description of the wicked as one whose **womb fashions deceit.** Elsewhere the picture of the careful formation of a child in the mother's womb during the long months of gestation emphasizes divine care and protection (e.g., Pss. 22:9–10; 139:13). However, for Job (3:3–12)—and now for Eliphaz—the development of a child can be a tricky episode, with possibly negative results. Here the growth of the "child" in the womb is understood to be under the control of the wicked rather than God. Since Job is one of these deceitful humans, Eliphaz must conclude that he too deserves the judgment he experiences and can only hope for restoration through confession and repentance.

Additional Notes §53

15:17 / **Seen:** the verb is *khzh,* which can refer to seeing by means of a visionary experience. The noun for "vision" (Heb. *khazon*) shares the same root.

15:19 / The implication of foreign influence adulterating the purity of wisdom was certainly a thought that would resonate with the exilic Diaspora community, who came themselves to understand foreign influence as one of the most significant reasons the exile came upon Israel. Joel envisions a future when Jerusalem would experience a holiness it never had during Israel's residence in the land—a time described here in Job as a time when "never again will foreigners [Heb. *zarim*] invade her" (3:17). The verb translated "invade" (ʿ*br*) in 3:17 is the same one translated in 15:19 as **passed among them.**

15:23 / Many translations and commentators transpose the last two words of v. 23 (Heb. *yom khoshek,* "day of darkness") to the beginning of v. 24. This move is usually accompanied by emending the preceding word of v. 23 from *beyado* ("in his hand") to *pido* ("his ruin"). This leads to the translation of v. 24b as: "he knows that ruin is prepared for him." The beginning of v. 24, then, becomes: "The day of darkness terrifies him."

15:28 / The verb *shkn,* **"inhabit,** dwell," most often emphasizes the tenuousness of existence and the temporary nature of residence. The verb describes the type of dwelling associated with nomadic tent life, where one moves from place to place. The related noun is *mishkan,* "portable dwelling."

15:30 / Some commentators emend *shub,* "turn; return" in v. 22 to *sur,* "turn aside; flee away," on the basis of v. 30.

Because of the difficulty of the Heb. translated by NIV as **the breath of God's mouth,** numerous emendations have been suggested. Most seek to strengthen the verb *swr* into something more like "drive away (like a storm)," or to alter "his mouth" to "his fruit" or "his blossom." See Clines, *Job 1–20,* p. 344, for a discussion of the options. It may well be, however, that the "breath" (Heb. *ruakh*) mentioned here is intended to be that of the wicked (Job), rather than God. In vv. 2–3, Eliphaz begins his argument by discrediting the words of Job as "empty notions" (Heb. *daʿat ruakh*) and a "hot east wind" (*qadim*). In v. 13, he characterizes Job as so carried away that he vents his "rage" (*ruakh,* "spirit") against God by pouring out "words from [his] mouth." See also 6:26 and 8:2, where the friends' critique of Job is made in terms of "windy [*ruakh*] words." On one other occasion Job himself links his words with *ruakh.* In 7:11, he declares "I will not keep silent; I will speak out in the anguish of my spirit [*betsar rukhi*], I will complain in the bitterness of my soul." In this view it is the wicked who "turns aside in the wind/rage of his *own* mouth."

15:31 / Clines, *Job 1–20,* p. 344, rejects the "commercial metaphor" (**in return,** along with **paid in full** in v. 32) as out of place in the context of the plant metaphor. See Clines, *Job 1–20,* and also Hartley, *Job,* p. 250, for a discussion of other, non-commercial options.

15:32 / The first half of the sentence is a bit difficult because of uncertainty regarding the verb translated **paid in full** (Heb. *timmaleʾ*). The form is a Niphal imperfect, feminine singular, while the subjects usually suggested ("his time" or "the wicked himself") are masculine. This has led to a variety of emendations, most of which are not very persuasive. Perhaps a way forward is to take this verb as anticipating the feminine singular noun that follows (Heb. *wekippato,* "its branch"), so that the sentence would read: "Before its time its branch comes to fulfillment, but does not flourish." This would fit in with the following images of a vine that puts forth grapes that fall off before they are ripe and the olive tree that flowers but loses its blossoms before they are pollinated.

15:34 / The Heb. phrase *ʿadat khanep* suggests a close association between those of like character and mind. The shared characteristic in this case is "godlessness" (Heb. *khanep*).

Although the author is in the midst of shifting metaphors—from horticulture in vv. 32–33 to conception and childbirth in v. 35—the latter half of v. 34 does not seem to fit in *either* context. The references to **tents** and **bribes** are particularly awkward.

§54 Miserable Comforters (Job 16:1–6)

Job returns to the discussion even more hopeless than before. Whereas he had expressed a determination to carry his case before God when he last responded to Zophar (chs. 12–14), he now seems almost resigned to defeat and rejection by human beings and by God. By the end of this response to Eliphaz, Job declares his hopelessness and prepares to go down to *Sheol* unrequited (17:16).

16:1–3 / As often before, Job's response begins with a critique of his friends' lack of compassion and support. They are all **miserable comforters** (Heb. *menakhame ʿamal,* "comforters of trouble/labor"), perhaps meaning "comforters for whom their task is unwelcome *labor*" or "those whose comfort brings trouble." While the friends offer no true comfort, neither do they offer much in the way of helpful insight. Job has **heard** it all before and wishes their **long-winded speeches** (Heb. *dibre ruakh,* "windy words," see also 6:26; 8:2; 15:2, 13) would be done. Job wonders **what ails** (irritates? provokes?) the friends to keep them spouting such tired platitudes.

16:4–5 / Again Job compares himself with his comfortless comforters, and he even imagines a scenario in which they might switch places. He recognizes that he is capable of similar "speechifying" (and may even, as a reputable sage, *often* have spoken at length on many wise topics incorporating traditions from the past), and he has already shown himself able to make equally **fine speeches** in support of his own position. He could oppose the friends' view eloquently and **shake** his **head** at them (a sign of disapproval or contempt). For his part, however, Job claims he would offer true comfort, unlike the troublesome friends. His words would **encourage** (Heb. *ʾmts,* in the Piel stem, means "strengthen, make strong"), and his **comfort** would **bring relief.**

16:6 / Job returns from his imagining by remembering that, in his very real world, the presence or absence of words does not change suffering. While his imagined words of comfort would relieve his suffering friends, Job's real words pile up on one another and yet his **pain is not relieved.** The friends have railed against Job's many words (8:2; 11:2–3; 15:2–3, 13) and have encouraged silent submission, but Job replies here that even restraint has proven ineffective in causing suffering to **go away** (the description of Job's initial response to his suffering in chs. 1 and 2 provides evidence of an extended period of silence and restraint).

Additional Notes §54

16:4 / The Heb. is instructive as Job says: *lu yesh napshekem takhat napshi,* "if perhaps your soul (were to be) in the place of my soul" or "if (it were) your neck in place of my neck."

16:5 / Although the last phrase in v. 5 is a bit difficult in the Heb. owing to the lack of object for the verb (*khsk,* "restrain; hold back"), the overall meaning comes through. It is possible to read **my lips** as an object ("comfort will restrain my lips"), or to emend following the LXX ("the comfort of my lips I *will not* restrain"). Clines, *Job 1–20,* p. 369, supplies the object *keʾeb,* "pain," from the same verb (although in the Niphal stem rather than Qal!) in the next verse (v. 6): "the consolations of my lips would soothe your pain."

16:7 / Job turns from his disappointing friends to remonstrate with God, who is clearly the one behind all of Job's suffering. The friends are constant irritants, but God has **worn** Job **out**—an expression meaning to "try one's patience" or "frustrate (someone)." The friends are ineffectual humans, but Job expects better from God himself. Instead, God has **devastated** all of Job's associates. The phrase here would better be translated "appalled all my community of associates." The group implied by the Hebrew ʿeda is broader than NIV's more specific translation **household** would suggest. Also, the following verses describe how God's treatment of Job has left him at the mercy of those around him (including the friends!).

16:8–9 / Those around Job understand his suffering to be an attack by God. He is **bound** and his inability to escape becomes a **witness** to those who look on it as evidence of Job's sin. Similarly, the deterioration of his body through sickness (his **gauntness**) also **testifies against** him. God is the **opponent** who **assails** Job and **tears** him in **anger**. The Hebrew word order in verse 9 indicates that Job is emphasizing God's "anger" here: "His anger tears and he holds hostility towards me." The image is of the predatory beast tearing at the prey (Heb. trp usually refers to animals "tearing" their prey) that has been hunted down. Although "gnashing the teeth" at someone is often a sign of anger and frustration, the association with rending prey in this context intensifies the metaphor. The image calls to mind an animal baring its teeth and snarling to drive other contenders away from the prey. At the end of the verse, God has clearly become the "opponent" (Heb. tsar, "enemy, foe, opponent") who "pierces" Job with **his eyes.**

16:10–11 / God carries out his attack through the taunts and jeers of Job's human associates. Besides the friends' vocal opposition, there is little to suggest that Job has actually experienced attacks as extreme as those described here. This is most likely hyperbole, reflecting the isolation and rejection that Job associates with his lack of vindication. The phrase "with reproach they smite my cheek" most clearly indicates the metaphorical character of this attack. The suggestion is clear: the rebuke and ridicule of multiple detractors is ultimately the responsibility of God who fails to support Job, or to maintain his integrity openly. Instead of supporting him, God has **turned** Job **over to evil men and thrown** him **into the clutches of the wicked.**

Additional Notes §55

16:7 / The verb translated **devastated** (Heb. *shmm*) can mean either "make deserted/desolate" or "make disconcerted/awestruck." The latter would be more appropriate, as the group affected is understood to be Job's associates rather than his household.

16:8 / Many take this rare Heb. verb for **bound** (*qmt*) as related to the Syr. *qmt*, with the meaning "shrivel up." This would fit well with the parallel *kakhash*, "gauntness, leanness" in the second half of the verse. See the discussion in Hartley, *Job,* p. 258, and Clines, *Job 1–20,* p. 370.

The Heb. for **testifies** is, lit., "answers in my presence," although the context suggests a legal setting.

16:9 / The verb (Heb. *ltsh*) means "sharpen, forge, hammer, pierce (with eyes)" so that **piercing** is the action of the eyes, not a characteristic of them. The picture is one of sharpening the weapon in preparation for an attack. Following the verbs of "tearing" and "gnashing" in the first part of the verse, "piercing" takes on a whole new and more extreme nuance here.

16:11 / The Heb. here is difficult, esp. *ʿawil*, which normally means "young boy." Most emend to *ʿawwal*, "evil person" (NIV **evil men**). The verb **thrown** is rare and variously taken from *rth*, "wring out," or *yrt*, "thrust, push." The latter seems most likely in this context.

§56 Attacked by God (Job 16:12–14)

16:12 / Job turns again to describe God's attack in more direct terms. Except for the "archers" mentioned in verse 13, God is the sole active participant in this attack. The opening words emphasize the unexpected nature of the assault: **All was well with me.** Job was at ease and secure with no inkling of what was to come. The verb *prr,* **shattered,** which can mean "nullify, revoke, violate", as well as "break, shatter," suggests the sense of sudden violation. Job felt violated because the unanticipated dismantling of his confident reliance on God seemed to nullify and revoke his covenant relationship with God.

Job is mixing his metaphors here. From the legal arena of covenant revocation, he returns again to the picture of the predatory animal seizing its prey **by the neck** and crushing out its life. By the end of verse 12, we move on to the archery practice field where Job has become the **target.** The common thread that holds these diverse images together is Job's growing sense that God has personally attacked him.

16:13 / Having become the practice "target," Job now finds himself surrounded by God and his **archers,** who repeatedly pierce Job's **kidneys** with their arrows and spill his **gall on the ground.** Although the context seems to imply a group attack, the verbs are in the singular—indicating that, as in his description of his human detractors in verses 10–11, Job considers God the true enemy. Job depicts God as **without pity,** and his attack as deadly, piercing Job's inner organs and spilling "gall"—a symbol of bitterness and anger—on the ground.

16:14 / Using explosive language, Job describes God as a **warrior** rushing to hand-to-hand combat. Pressing the attack home, allowing no escape, he **bursts upon** Job and **rushes** at him **again and again.** The Hebrew employs repeated *assonance* to emphasize the repeated attacks: *yipretseni perets ʿal-pne-parets yaruts ʿalay kegibbor* (note the repetition of *prts* in the first, second and fifth words, as well as the additional *p*-in the fourth word and further-*ts* in the sixth). God is the enemy who overwhelms a weakened Job with his strength, allowing him no opportunity to defend himself.

Additional Notes §56

16:13 / The word *rab* means **archer** in other contexts, such as Prov. 26:10 and Jer. 50:29.

16:14 / The verb translated **burst** is Heb. *prts*, "break out, burst forth." The word can describe an unusually explosive birth (Gen. 38:29); a soldier breaking through defenses (Mic. 2:13); God's wrath breaking out (e.g., against Uzzah when he touched the ark of the covenant, 2 Sam. 6:8); holes being created in city walls to destroy them (2 Kgs. 14:13; Isa. 5:5; 30:13; Pss. 89:40; 144:14; Prov. 25:28).

§57 Sackcloth and Mourning (Job 16:15–17)

The attacks of God and humans have brought Job low in suffering and loss, so that he has assumed the posture of mourning—both for the loss of his children and for his own approaching and inevitable death.

16:15 / Job has donned the customary mourning garb of **sackcloth** over his cracked and scabby skin. The rough sacking would have been a constant irritation in his condition. It is probable that the image is more symbolic of Job's mourning than an attempt to describe reality at this point. Job has lost everything and mourning consumes him. The rest of the verse is clear in its literal sense, if not in its interpretation. Rather than NIV's **brow**, the Hebrew speaks of "thrusting my *horn* into the dust." The horn is a symbol of pride and strength and, metaphorically speaking, to exalt the horn is to honor someone (e.g., 1 Sam. 2:1; Ps. 112:9) as well as to give them strength and victory (e.g., 1 Sam. 2:10; Pss. 89:17, 24; 92:10; Lam. 2:17). Some commentators relate the thrusting of the horn into the dust with the action of a bull who dips his horns to the ground in submission. Most likely the metaphor—regardless of it precise origin—indicates Job's capitulation to the attacks against him. He has no hope of defending himself against God. This does not mean that Job has given up his quest for vindication. Instead, it emphasizes the unjust nature of the attack against one who cannot, and does not, seek to defend himself.

16:16–17 / Job's mourning is deep, sincere, and extended, as the physical effects indicate. His face is **red with weeping** and his eyes marked with **deep shadows**. Despite his apparent submission to God's attack (what else could he be expected to do?), Job continues to maintain his innocence. On two levels Job claims to be blameless: on the one hand he has committed no **violence** (Heb. *khamas*) which might deserve his punishment and, on the other hand, his **prayer is pure** and unadulterated, like the oil reserved for holy ritual. There is no fault to condemn Job and, even if there were, his scrupulous attention to the rituals of restoration should have led to mercy and deliverance.

Additional Notes §57

16:16 / Again, the term *tsalmawet* (lit., "shadow of death") appears to be a superlative expression meaning "darkest shadow." See the discussion on 3:4–5 in §7.

§58 Hope for Intercession (Job 16:18–22)

16:18–19 / Once again it is the lack of provocation for the attack that leads Job to call out for redress. His cry is to the **earth** that has experienced the pollution of Job's **blood** spilled in the violent attack. The Israelites thought blood spilled in violence actually corrupted the ground and prevented it from being used for anything productive. The Bible often depicts the earth as crying out to God to avenge a violent death and to cleanse the earth. See, for example, the response of the earth to the spilling of Abel's blood by his brother Cain in Genesis 4:10, as well as the reason behind the great flood in Genesis 6:10–13. Job calls on the "earth" to be his **witness** in **heaven,** a modified use of *merismus* drawing on the customary pairing of heaven and earth to describe the whole of creation. While many commentators ultimately consider *God* to be Job's intercessor, it may be that the cry of the earth in response to the spilling of Job's blood is in view here.

16:20 / **My intercessor.** Just who is this intercessor in whom Job places so much hope? The Hebrew word (*melits*) is not a common one and occurs only five times in the OT (twice in Job, here and in 33:23; also Gen. 42:23; 2 Chr. 32:31; Isa. 43:27). The sense in all of these passages seems to be "interpreter" or "go between." In the Hebrew text, the word is plural, leading some to suggest a masculine form of the noun *melitsah,* which is often taken to be derived from the Hiphil stem of the verb *lyts,* "mock, ridicule." In this case the phrase would mean something like "my scorners are my friends." This seems less likely than "intercessor," however, especially since the next verse focuses on pleading with God on behalf of another.

Most would affirm that the identity of the friendly intercessor is God himself. However, this seems more than awkward when Job also depicts God as the attacking enemy he needs to confront. If we read the word "my intercessor" as "interpreters of" (requiring no change of the consonantal text), and the following **friend** as "thoughts" (see Pope, *Job,* pp. 122, 125), the resulting phrase "interpreters of my thoughts to God" would make sense in light of verse 19, where there are two terms for mediator (NIV "witness" and "advocate"). While this does not completely settle the question of the intercessor's identity, it would shift the emphasis away from God to another antecedent—possibly Job's "cry" (v. 18) that ascends to heaven to interpret his thoughts directly in the presence of God himself.

The translation **my eyes pour out tears** is a rather expansive interpretation of a much briefer Hebrew phrase. Literally, the text says only "my eyes leak/drip." Just how this information fits the context about intermediation is unclear. It does show how emotionally strained Job is and how pleading his case before God is a matter of the greatest import, draining him of his normal defenses. Perhaps it is just such a tearful, emotional outburst that requires the kind of interpretation of Job's thoughts that he mentions in the first half of the verse.

16:21 / This verse presents the "intercessor" as a single individual (after the plural reference in the preceding verse). It is not uncommon—especially in poetry—for references to shift back and forth from singular to plural as the poet exploits a variety of metaphors to illumine his point. This shifting is not always apparent in translation, since the tendency is to iron out difficulties in a more consistent fashion. It is also clear that here Job is speaking more generally about the role of an intercessor rather than about the specific nature and identity of a particular person. The "intercessor" Job envisions would be able to do what Job fears he could not—the mediator will plead **with God** as easily as if he were a man pleading **for his friend.**

16:22 / The matter is urgent, because Job knows **only a few years** remain before his death—years Job would rather *not* spend in deep suffering. Using traditional language regarding *Sheol,* the abode of the dead, Job describes his conviction that death marks the end of his hope for vindication: **I go on the journey of no return.**

Additional Notes §58

16:19 / The affirming parallelism of this verse brings together two words for "witness; defender." The first (*ʿed*) is the common Heb., while the second (*sokhad*) is from the Aramaic. **Heaven** is thought to be "in the heights," as the use of *meromim,* "heights," to parallel "heaven" indicates.

16:21 / The reference to **his friend** in this verse is, of course, one of the strongest reasons for affirming the translation of *reʿay* in v. 20 as "my friend" rather than "thoughts." The argument is not definitive, however, as it may well be that the writer intended a play on these words, emphasizing this tension rather than creating a parallel between them.

16:22 / **I go on the journey of no return.** The Heb. is, lit., "and the path [from] which I will not return I will walk." See the discussion on 10:20–22 in §34.

§59 Surrounded by Mockers (Job 17:1–5)

Job's reflection on the nearness of death continues into, and indeed dominates, chapter 17. Death seems very real (vv. 1–5) and public vindication very far away (vv. 6–10). As a result, Job finds his sense of hope evaporating (vv. 11–16).

17:1–2 / **My spirit is broken.** Job laments the death of his hope. Cloaked in translation, "is broken" indicates that he *has been broken* by someone else. The breakage is not simply deterioration due to age, but the result of an active attack to destroy his spirit. We are not talking here of Job's "spirit" as his plucky will to live, but as the actual *animating life force* that comes from God and will ultimately return to God as well. The destruction or crushing of Job's life force sends him not into *depression,* but into *death!* Job's **days are cut short** (lit., "extinguished"), brought to an abrupt end before his time, so that only **the grave awaits.** The Hebrew here is literally "graves are mine," perhaps meaning something like "graves are all I have to look forward to."

Not only is the future nonexistent, but the present is troubled as well. Job responds with an oath to affirm the truth and extremity of his situation. Since **mockers** (lit., "mockery") **surround** him, his **eyes must** constantly **dwell on their hostility.**

17:3–4 / Since his human detractors surround him with mockery and scorn, Job can only turn to **God** for some understanding (however remote the possibility may be!). Although Job never actually mentions God in this verse, he is clearly addressing his plea to God. The NIV's translation of verse 3 seems a bit off-track here. The first half of the verse is fairly straightforward in the Hebrew: "Set, please, my pledge with you," asking God to keep close at hand the pledge Job has offered as surety for his claims (as an indication that God takes the matter seriously?). The second half of the verse is more difficult, primarily because of uncertainty regarding how to understand the Niphal form of the verb *tqʿ*, "strike/clap." The idiom "to clap hands" is well enough known as a symbolic conclusion to an agreement—much like our own practice of shaking hands to confirm our commitment to an arrangement. The Niphal here may express a sense of permission, so that the meaning of the second half of the verse would be: "Who (else) will allow (my hand) to be shaken?" (Both Hartley, *Job*, p. 266, and Clines, *Job 1–20*, p. 163, trace this suggestion back to Gordis.) Job is feeling completely isolated without any human support and he realizes that he can only find the vindication he desires with God—even though that may seem utterly impossible under the circumstances.

God has **closed to understanding** the **minds** of Job's human detractors. Although the vocabulary is different, the sentiment here is somewhat akin to the "hardening" of Pharaoh's heart (Exod. 7:3), or of Israel (Isa. 6:10). The Hebrew literally says here that God has hidden their hearts/minds from understanding—suggesting that understanding cannot find them in order to enlighten them regarding the truth! The reference to **triumph** is difficult, since the verb in question (Heb. *teromem*) literally means "you (God) will not exalt," and some sort of an object would normally follow. Scholars have suggested a variety of emendations, and NIV has opted for one expressing Job's hope that God will not exalt the enemies in their lack of insight.

17:5 / Job concludes this section with a rather obscure aphorism originally intended to encourage loyalty and friendship. Interpretation depends on the association of the opening words—*lekheleq*, "smooth talk/flattery; portion/reward" and *yaggid*, "he will declare." NIV's translation assumes that someone (the friends?) has *denounced* **friends** in order to gain some **reward**. This "reward" might be to prevent the undermining of the traditional wisdom worldview, with its assumption of retribution. The proverb is generally understood to say that those who are willing to deny the truth and to sacrifice a friend to protect themselves will nevertheless see their own **children fail** as a consequence. On the one hand, the reference to "children" offers a rather backhanded slap recalling Job's own early loss. The friends, thinking to shore up their world from the onslaught of Job's harsh critique, will experience themselves the painful loss they have tried to interpret as evidence of Job's sinfulness. On the other hand, the children may be "students" or "disciples" in the wisdom mode rather than physical children. In this case, the friends' attempts to protect the traditional wisdom worldview at the expense of their friend Job's integrity will ultimately lead to the demise of the whole wisdom enterprise as, literally, the "eyes of their students fail."

Additional Notes §59

17:2 / Verse 2 begins with the oath formula *ʾim loʾ*, "if not," in which the self-imprecation is implied but not stated. The sense is akin to: "If this is not true, may X happen to me," where the final phrase represents the omitted self-imprecation.

The verb **dwell** is the Heb. *lin*, "stay overnight," perhaps suggesting no escape even in the dark when the mockers cannot be seen. The Hebrew word translated **hostility** is *mar*, an adjective meaning "bitter; bitterness."

17:4 / **Triumph:** others understand that *God* will experience no exaltation through the humans' lack of illumination. See the discussions in Hartley, *Job*, p. 266, and Clines, *Job 1–20*, p. 373.

17:5 / Another understanding is that someone has spoken "flattery" to **friends.** How this would fit into Job's context is unclear. Clines, *Job 1–20*, p. 395, takes the proverb to describe, "the boastful man who calls his friends to a banquet when his larder is so empty that his children are starving." Clines has in mind those who mock Job, claiming "to have knowledge of the true situation, but their intellectual cupboard is bare, for their minds have been closed."

§60 A Byword to Everyone (Job 17:6–10)

17:6–7 / Returning to his lament concerning his dismal circumstances, Job places the blame squarely upon God, who **has made me a byword.** The Hebrew word *mashal*, "proverb," is common and describes making someone into a negative example through a proverb. Almost every proverbial statement expresses or implies such a negative admonition: "A wise son brings joy to his father, but a foolish son grief to his mother" (Prov. 10:1). Similarly, "Wise men store up knowledge, but the mouth of a fool invites ruin" (Prov. 10:14). Who would want to be identified with the second halves of these proverbs? And yet God has made Job into a negative admonition **to everyone.** Although the Hebrew text does not directly mention God, it is clear Job is referring to God. The translation "everyone" is an interpretive rendering of the literal Hebrew ʿammim, "peoples." Job means "all the peoples of the world" rather than just everyone in his local context!

Job has become not just an object of ridicule and warning, but a person to be despised and **a man in whose face people spit.** Spitting in someone's face is, of course, the ultimate act of rejection and degradation. By spitting in another's face one intends to express contempt and ultimately even to *dehumanize* the person. **My eyes have grown dim . . . my whole frame . . . a shadow.** Job's suffering and rejection have reduced him to a mere "shadow" of his former self. The eyes grow "dim" as the light of life departs at death. Job's "frame"—his physical structure indicated by posture—shrivels and fades as one affected by a wasting disease. The slow slide into oblivion is a response to the ongoing *anguish* (Heb. *kaʿas*) of his oppressing circumstances rather than just **grief** (NIV).

17:8–9 / Irony and sarcasm drip in the next few verses. Job's plight is a source of deep consternation (but *not* compassion!) for the **upright,** who are **appalled** at the realization that if this could happen to one who seemed to be the epitome of righteousness, it could happen to them as well. Because of their fear, the **innocent** (those who ground their hopes in the traditional understanding of retribution) **are aroused against** those they assume to be **ungodly.** Because their fixed view of the world prevents them from accepting the truth that the righteous indeed *do* suffer, they must label Job a sinner and array themselves against him in pitched battle.

Clines, rightly I think, takes verse 9 as a continuation of Job's ironic depiction of his righteous attackers. So committed are they to their worldview that nothing—no argument, however true or persuasive—will sway them. They **hold to their ways** and, under the attack of Job's contrary evidence, their determination only **grows stronger.** There is the possibility, of course, that Job is here talking in an exhortative plural of his own determination to remain undeterred by the ridicule of his opponents from pursuing his quest for vindication.

17:10 / Like a confident boxer taunting his opponent to take his best shot, Job calls his detractors to try again their best arguments against him. Assured that their arguments can only fail to impress or persuade, he returns their ridicule with biting words: **I will not find a wise man among you.**

Additional Notes §60

17:8 / Many commentators eliminate vv. 8–10 as out of place or an intrusion.

17:10 / The use of the Heb. verb *bwʾ*, "enter," may indicate the engagement in battle.

§61 Where Is My Hope? (Job 17:11–16)

Job's second reply to Eliphaz concludes with a pessimistic rumination on the nearness of death and his growing hopelessness regarding any resolution of his plea for vindication.

17:11–12 / The final movement begins with a general statement of Job's pessimistic outlook. His **days** are rushing to an end, his **plans** have been **shattered,** and the **desires** of his **heart** (the seat of moral reflection and decision-making, not emotion; see the discussion on 11:13–14 in §38) equally frustrated. By contrast, the attackers keep maintaining that Job can turn his circumstances around by a simple confession of sin. Job's sarcasm is evident as he characterizes the contradictions implied by their claims. They **turn night into day** and in the midst of Job's deepest **darkness** they almost cheerfully proclaim: "**Light is near.**"

These words remind me that often we, too, try to counter oppressive pain and sorrow with almost naïve affirmations of light. When we say to those who have been devastated by loss and who are teetering on the brink of losing faith as the result of their experience of the dark, "God meant this for the good! He is trying to teach you something through it! Just trust that everything is going to be all right!," we are most often showing little empathy or compassion for those who suffer. Our cheerful words of faith can be like rubbing salt in the wounds or slapping the face of one who is crying. Our words at such times may have more to do with shoring up *our* faith than with showing solidarity with our suffering friend. This may be our way of dealing with the attack on our carefully ordered world that their devastation represents. Job's caustic reply offers us wisdom. Those in deep pain and sorrow often need our love and compassion; our strong arms and anguished silence; our admission of the mystery of suffering and pain; our acknowledgement that others have traveled this road before.

17:13–16 / Job's response to his friends' unrealistic lightness is to delve more deeply into the darkness of his circumstance.

He imagines the worst as a way of testing his resolve. He intends his statement to shock. He begins, literally: "If I will hope," as if the cheerful prodding of his opponents has persuaded him. But as he continues, he shows how far from true this appearance is: "*Sheol* is my house." The result of such false hope is to dwell in *Sheol*, the abode of the dead! **I spread out my bed in darkness.** The promised "light" is not forthcoming as Job lies down in the eternal sleep of death, from which there is no return.

In words very close to the concluding verse of Psalm 88, where the narrator concludes: "You [God] have taken my companions and loved ones from me; the darkness is my closest friend" (Ps. 88:18), Job also describes the destructive terrors of the grave in terms of the closest familial relationships. So **corruption** becomes Job's **father** and the flesh-consuming **worm** is his **mother** or **sister.** This is full capitulation to the inevitable future that the friends, with their easy assumption of light in darkness, cannot bear to contemplate.

Job calls his hearers to join in a search for the **hope** the friends have offered so easily. Like one leading a group of small children in a game of "I Spy," Job asks, **where then is my hope? Who can see** it? Is it here? Is it there? Job's point is, of course, that it is ridiculous to search for something that one has no hope of finding.

There is some dispute regarding the translation of the first half of verse 16, although the meaning of the verse as a whole is fairly clear. The problem is in how one understands the obscure word *badde,* which is here translated "**gates** (of *Sheol*)." The Hebrew meaning is more usually "(carrying) poles" (as for the ark of the covenant) or "chambers" of a room. Neither of these seem a particularly apt description of *Sheol*. The most generally accepted emendation is to replace *badde* with the prepositional form ʿ*immadi,* "with me," following the lead of the LXX translation. Assuming an interrogative particle at the beginning produces a parallel with the second half of the verse: "Will it go down with me to *Sheol*, **Will we descend together into the dust?**"

Regardless of the resolution of this question, the meaning of the verse as a whole is unmistakable. Job anticipates that the only conclusion to the present state of affairs is his death. The friends offer false hope as a means of seducing Job into confessing sin he has not committed and submitting out of fear and self-preservation. Since Job steadfastly refuses to follow what he sees as a dishonest course, he is resigned to his inevitable demise.

Additional Notes §61

17:11   /   The Heb. *zimmah* can have the sense of a "cunning plan" or, more negatively, "infamy."

§62 Opening Criticism (Job 18:1–4)

Bildad's speech clearly falls into two major segments: the opening response caustically directed to Job (18:1–4); and a longer wisdom rumination or admonition concerning the ultimate destruction of the wicked (18:5–21). The commentators variously divide the latter section into subsections, but in my opinion no particular division is more persuasive than another. The discussions of Clines, *Job 1–20*, pp. 407–8, and Whybray, *Job*, pp. 89–91, however, are particularly helpful.

18:1 / The heat of Bildad's reply illustrates the friends' growing frustration (and perhaps desperation!) at Job's refusal to accede to their arguments. Unable to persuade him to acknowledge their superior wisdom or even to submit to the wisdom of the ages, Bildad lashes out and turns from persuasion to rather heavy-handed warning of the dreadful fate that awaits those who, like Job, refuse to confess their sin before God and humans.

18:2–3 / With an exasperated "How *long!*" (emphasis added; NIV **when**), Bildad explodes on the scene demanding that Job cease speaking. His outburst is tantamount to an admission that the friends are unable to answer Job's arguments or persuade him of their own views. The verb translated **end** here may be a jussive form expressing Bildad's desire that Job "shut up!" The result would sound something like: "How long (must I listen to this)? Put an end to words!" This is not a request for a time table, but a demand for Job's immediate silence and submission!

Bildad's assessment of Job is not just that he is unreasonable, but that he lacks the basic *perceptive ability* that is the hallmark of wisdom. Continuing in the jussive mood, he demands that Job **be sensible,** "perceive," or "understand" (the meaning of the Heb. verb *byn*) before they continue the discussion. This explains Job's refusal to capitulate to the friends' arguments as no failing in the friends, but a lack of intellect on the part of Job! "When you understand as much as I do," Bildad contends, **then we can talk.**

In fact, Bildad says, Job is treating the friends as if they have the diminished mental capacity of **cattle.** Large domesticated animals such as oxen were controlled and restrained in order to put them to the work of their human masters. Normally humans are considered superior in intellect to "cattle" (e.g., 35:11), but the animals can instruct and deepen the understanding of perceptive sages (see Job 12; Eccl. 3:18, 19). Elsewhere humans are negatively compared with "cattle" when the humans are considered senseless (Pss. 49:12, 20; 73:22) or resistant to instruction. While not a reference to "cattle," Psalm 32:9 offers a similar sentiment in its reference to horse and mule: "Do not be like the horse or the mule, which have no understanding but must be controlled by bit and bridle or they will not come to you." Bildad accuses Job of calling the friends **stupid,** when they are really established sages of reputable insight. He is not far from wrong, of course, because Job has disparaged their intellect on several occasions—usually in response to what he feels are their attempts to deny *his* wisdom (e.g., 12:2–4).

Heat and rage often come when we feel belittled and discounted. When we feel "less than" we often use anger as a protective wedge between ourselves and our attackers. They are wrong and their critique ridiculous! We reject their words and then do not take stock of their claims. Anger can also sometimes be a response of fear. When someone gets too close to our hidden truths, our response is sometimes to push them away with a burst of anger so that our inner turmoil is not brought out into the open. Perhaps Bildad's heat here is a way of cloaking the insecurity he is feeling as Job's critique of the wisdom worldview chips away at the foundational beliefs Bildad and the other friends had depended on for so long. Rather than allow Job's perceptions to reorder their world, they push him away with anger and cling to the comfort of the familiar.

18:4 / Bildad concludes his opening critique by describing the self-destructive consequences of Job's **anger.** Like an unruly child's tantrum, Job is to be ignored. Bildad does not validate Job's arguments as the logical conclusions of sagely wisdom—he has already called him *un*reasonable in verse 2. Job's words are instead, Bildad insists, the heated and chaotic outpourings of unrestrained "anger." His suffering has affected his reflective processes and his confusion has led him to lash out at anyone near. The end result, however, is more destructive to himself as he

tears himself **to pieces.** The "tearing" here is the Hebrew *trp*, most often associated with the rending of prey by the predatory beast. In his lashing out, Job is harming no one more than himself.

If Job thinks his arguments are effective in creating change, he is much mistaken according to Bildad, who asks rhetorically: **is the earth to be abandoned for your sake?** This is the equivalent of the common contemporary reproach: "The world does not revolve around you!" or "You are not the center of the universe!" In Bildad's opinion, Job thinks far too highly of himself, that God and the world should respond to his every word and thought. But Bildad places the world's concern with Job's plight at a much lower level. The order of the world will not be rearranged to accommodate him. Nor **must the rocks be moved from their place.**

Additional Notes §62

18:2 / **When:** the phrase (like the much more frequent *ᶜad matay*, "How long?") expresses anguished and desperate longing in the face of protracted suffering or rejection (Exod. 16:28; Num. 14:11; Josh. 18:3; Pss. 13:2, 3; 62:4; Jer. 47:6; Hab. 1:2), and is often directed to God in an attempt to encourage action on behalf of the human sufferer.

§63 The Fate of the Wicked (Job 18:5–21)

The rest of chapter 18 is an extended description of the fate of the wicked. Although Bildad never explicitly mentions Job here, it is clear that he is trotting out this warning in order to dissuade him from continuing on this path.

18:5–6 / **The lamp of the wicked is snuffed out.** Bildad's first images revolve around **light** and **dark.** The wicked person is like a lamp that is extinguished at night or a **fire** that has run out of fuel and **stops burning.** The image is of the approach and finality of death, which verse 6 makes more obvious still with the reference to **the light in his tent.** The "tent" is the abode, or home, of an individual. When battle ends in defeat, soldiers flee for their lives, each "to his tent" (1 Sam. 4:10; 2 Sam. 20:1). In the book of Job, the tent serves as a metaphor for the life one possesses and can lose. Three times in chapter 18 and again in chapter 20, the image of the tent describes the tenuous nature of human life (18:6, 14, 15; 20:26).

18:7–10 / Not only does the end seem near for the wicked, but daily life is full of danger. These four verses bring together no less than *six* terms describing a **trap** or **snare** usually employed to capture animals or enemies (*reshet,* **net** and *sebakah,* **mesh,** v. 8; *pakh,* **trap** and *tsammim,* "snare," v. 9; *khebel,* "tripline," **noose** and *malkudet,* "trap," "snare," v. 10). The wicked have become the hunted, who must constantly watch their steps and look over their shoulders. In this section Bildad is following the lead of Eliphaz, who in 15:20–35 first explored the continuing *present* torment of the wicked, preceding their ultimate destruction.

18:11–14 / In a scene which calls to mind the four horsemen in the book of Revelation (6:1–8), Bildad describes the progressive attack of the wicked by **calamity, disaster,** plague that **eats away . . . his skin,** and finally **death's firstborn.** The section begins with the more general proclamation that **terrors startle him on every side** ("terrors" is Heb. *ballakhah* [pl.], "overwhelm suddenly or unexpectedly"). Like a soldier fleeing from the enemy, he cannot escape the "terrors" that **dog his every step.**

"Calamity" and "disaster" wait anxiously for the slightest chink in their armor through which they can attack the wicked. The verbs heighten the tension as they describe these two opponents as **hungry** for the attack, and **ready** for the first sign of stumbling (NIV **falls,** Heb. *tselaᶜ,* "stumbling, slipping, falling"). Again the picture is that of a soldier attacked suddenly from ambush and pursued closely by his enemies, who are seeking every opportunity to carry out their attack and are ready to take full advantage of any sign of weariness or stumbling.

The image shifts in verse 13 from ambush to the particularly loathsome effects of a skin disease that "eats away parts of his skin." Some commentators, drawing on the reference to "death's first-born" (*bekor mawet*) in the latter half of this verse and **the king of terrors** in verse 14, see the personification of the god of death in these references. The Canaanites among whom Israel dwelled worshipped the god of death called Mot (a form of the Heb./Canaanite word *mawet,* "death"). While Mot is nowhere within the extant corpus of Canaanite texts called "the firstborn," he is known to be one of the children of the chief god El. There are also many references to Mot *consuming* by eating those who die. The dead then enter his abode through his throat and gullet. In this view, "firstborn" represents Death's title or rank, and it is this personified Death who "eats . . . his skin" and **devours** him. This is a strong image of the fearsome approach of death and the complete destruction it entails. Humans lose all dignity and become the "fodder" of death and *Sheol.*

In verse 14, we see the wicked **torn from . . . his tent.** Here is another use of the "tent" as metaphor for one's life (also vv. 6, 15). The wicked is then forced to march off to "the king of terrors," or Death personified. The word "terrors" links the end of this subsection back to its beginning in verse 11. It may be that the author is intimating that even Death does not *end* the "terrors" visited on the wicked, but offers the prospect of continuing torment even in the grave. While these verses do not express a clearly developed theology of punishment of the wicked through an eternity of afterlife, the ideas here are consistent with that later view and may represent early seeds of that future development.

18:15–17 / While the reference in verse 15 to the **tent** that is burned might seem to link this verse with the preceding subsection, it describes better the continuing destructive consequences of the torment of the wicked, which is the particular subject of the concluding sections of chapter 18. **Fire** and **sulfur** were used in warfare—first to destroy completely the towns, villages, and dwellings of the enemy, and then to render the very earth on which they stood infertile and inhospitable for further life. The wicked person's very life, as symbolized by "his tent," is destroyed so that only fire **resides** there. This offers a particularly interesting contrast to the statement in verse 6a that, "The light in his tent becomes dark."

Metaphors shift again in verse 16 to speak of the wicked in terms of a distressed and dying tree that shrivels up from **below** and from **above**—a modified use of *merismus* that emphasizes the totality of destruction. Finding insufficient water, the **roots dry up** and as a result the **branches wither.** The image is one of complete destruction and loss.

Even **memory** of the wicked **perishes from the earth.** Since there is no developed sense of life after death among the ancient Israelites, "memory" played an important role in carrying on the life of an individual and the influence of that person beyond the grave. For all memories of an individual to perish, as here, would mean that none of one's efforts had left a mark on the world and were thus of no consequence. This conclusion is much in line with Ecclesiastes' pessimistic evaluation of human endeavor as *hebel habelim*, "utterly worthless." The **name** of an individual is the public representation of his personhood. It is the means by which "memory" is carried on. Often the "name" indicated the character of, or at least the hopes attached to, the person, and many names expressed one's trust in the saving power of God. For the name to be forgotten then, means the end of one's hopes as the person has passed from memory into oblivion.

18:18–21 / Not only is the wicked forgotten and his life in this world relegated to insignificance, but Bildad also chronicles his death as imprisonment and exile. The wicked one is "shoved; pushed" (NIV **driven**) **from light into darkness**—an apt description" for one jailed in a dank cell. The deceased is **banished from the world** and bound in the confines of *Sheol* (from which there is no return). The contrasting interplay between light and darkness appeared earlier in Bildad's speech (v. 6), and now brackets the piece near the end.

The complete obliteration of the wicked continues with the lack of **offspring or descendants.** Where one cannot hope for personal immortality after death, children carry on the name and memory of the dead. So important was the place of the descendant in assuring the continuation of memory that, when one died childless, the rather extreme expectation of the levirate marriage was enacted to supply a descendant to carry on the name of the deceased (Deut. 25:5–10; Gen. 38). So terrible is it to be left childless, and thus with no continuing memory through descendants, that those who observe this obliteration are **appalled at his fate** and are **seized with horror.**

Bildad's speech concludes with the summary statement in verse 21: **Surely such is the dwelling of an evil man.** Although the noun for "evil man" (Heb. ʿawwal) is in the singular, the Hebrew speaks in the plural of "these . . . dwellings," possibly referring to the examples in the preceding verses of a life imagined as a tent or temporary dwelling in a variety of circumstances. The second half of the verse further defines the nature of the "evil man" as **one who knows not God.** Knowing God in this sense is not a matter of intellectual knowledge *about* God, but an experiential knowing of the *heart* that involves commitment and alignment with God's character and will. In this summary statement Bildad is claiming that Job speaks without any true understanding of who God is or any related commitment to God's purposes in the world—however mysterious they may be. For Bildad, knowing God means trusting him without questioning. Job, on the other hand, has a very different understanding about how to respond to his ongoing experience of God.

Additional Notes §63

18:11 / The verb *puls* (NIV "dog [step]") can also have the meaning "chase," leaving the impression of a breathless race for one's life!

18:13 / Some commentators suggest emending Heb. *badde,* "parts of," to *bidway,* "by disease." This also necessitates reading the verb "eats" as a passive form "is eaten." See the comments in Hartley, *Job,* p. 276. The discussion in Clines, *Job 1–20,* pp. 417–18, is particularly helpful. Hartley, *Job,* p. 277, is less accurate in reporting the evidence of the Ugaritic text *UT,* 67:1:19–20, where Mot is said to "consume clay [a probable reference to humanity] . . . by handfuls."

18:15 / **Fire** and **sulfur** can also be signs of *divine* destruction and judgment. See, e.g., Gen. 19:24; Deut. 29:23; Ps. 11:6; Isa. 34:9; Luke

17:29; Rev. 9:17–18. The Heb. is more difficult than the translation indicates. **Fire** is supplied from an emendation of the original *mibbeli lo*, "from nothing of his." This may mean nothing more than that nothing that belongs to the wicked is left in his completely destroyed **tent.**

18:20 / The balance reference to **men of the west** and **men of the east** is intended as a *merismus*, indicating "everyone." The Heb. terms are *ʾakharonim*, "those behind (him)" and *qadmonim*, "those in front (of him)." The directions "east" and "west" are derived from the positional orientation common in the ancient Near East. One fixed positions by facing the rising sun (east). In this manner, what was "before" (*qedem*) is east, what is "behind" (*ʾakharon*) is west, the "right hand" (*yamin*) is south, while the "left hand" (*semoʾl*) is north.

§64 God Has Wronged Me (Job 19:1–6)

Job's response to Bildad's second speech alternates between recrimination against his friends' lack of compassion and lament over the divine attack he is experiencing. The friends attack and torment Job because they are convinced he is at fault (19:4, 28). Job continues to claim his innocence and to call the friends to compassion and mutual support (19:21–22). He concludes with a warning that if the friends continue to align themselves with God's unwarranted attack on Job, they might find themselves the focus of a similar inexplicable outpouring of divine judgment (19:28–29).

19:1–2 / The friends, in their haste to justify God and thus to firm up their shaky worldview, **torment . . . and crush** Job in hopes of forcing an admission of sin from his lips. Their hopes are in vain, however, since Job remains committed to his innocence. Job begins his reply ironically by using the same frustrated cry (**How long?!**) with which Bildad began his second speech to Job (18:2). The mutual escalation of frustration is evident. Job seems to be saying, "I am just as irritated with your refusal to accept my protestations of innocence as you are with my rejection of your assumptions of retribution!" He characterizes the friends' speeches (he is speaking in the plural here) *not* as attempts at persuasion or even admonition, but as "torment" that seek by fear to force compliance and to "crush" any hopes Job might still harbor. They pulverize his already tenuous being (Heb. *nepesh*) like rocks ground to dust (*dkʾ* means to "crush" or "pulverize" rock).

19:3 / Job's use of hyperbole also betrays his frustration—his friends' attacks have been numerous, but hardly **Ten times** (unless we have lost something along the way). The friends have sought through their words to "disgrace" or "hurt" Job (Heb. *klm*, NIV **reproached**), by putting him to *public* disgrace. Job has desired a public acknowledgement of his integrity, but what he has received from the three friends is a public tirade and condemnation for sin. This is no private airing of differences. Job's words imply that the friends' **attack** is publicly known and detrimental to Job's public image as a sage and righteous man. The friends are not ashamed to attack Job openly and without justification.

19:4–5 / Again Job employs the adverb *ʾomnam*, "surely, without a doubt," to suggest a condition that is contrary to fact. When Job says **if it is true that I have gone astray** ("Even if it were true [which it is *not*]"), he is *not* opening the possibility that he has sinned. Rather, he is exploring the implications of the friends' accusations, which he continues to deny. Even if the friends' accusations of sin *were* true (which, Job says, they were *not*), then the sin would be a matter of **concern** between Job and God (Heb. *ʾitti talin meshugati*, lit. "against me my error will grumble/blame"). The friends are using Job's plight not as an opportunity to express their compassion, but as an occasion of weakness through which they can **exalt** themselves and gain the upper hand. The NIV's rather vague **use** cloaks the legal force behind the verb *tokikhi*, "argue against me (in court)." The friends are using Job's suffering (**humiliation;** Heb. *kherpah*, "reproach; disgrace; insult; scorn," implying a public context of rejection and disgrace) as evidence to convict him of sin in the eyes of the public.

19:6 / Job, however, remains undeterred and advances his claim that in fact **God has wronged me.** The verb *ʿwt* means to "make (something) crooked or perverted," skewing it from what is true or normal. This is almost diametrically opposed to the description of Job as *tam weyashar* ("blameless and upright") in the opening verses of the book. By extension, the verb means to "falsify" or "mislead." Job describes his plight as like that of the hunted animal entangled and drawn fast in the hunter's **net.** God is the hunter who has captured the hapless prey in his trap.

Additional Notes §64

19:6 / The NIV translation **wronged** is overly interpretive, in my opinion, since the verb means more accurately "pervert, mislead from what is normal." Job describes what has happened in his experience rather than evaluating it.

§65 Among God's Enemies (Job 19:7–12)

19:7 / Job shifts his focus now from the friends to the attack of God. His resignation mirrors the futility of his circumstance. Under attack by God, Job is nevertheless certain that his cries for redress will go unanswered. The NIV's translation, "**I've been wronged!**" misleads the reader to see a link with the preceding verse's "God has wronged me." Verse 7 uses entirely different vocabulary, however, which is much more like the cry of one attacked in a dark alley. Job says, more literally, "Behold, I cry, 'Violence!' but I am not answered." Job goes on to claim that **no justice** comes in response to his **call for help.** God comes off in this verse like an armed robber who attacks with impunity and, when hauled into court, gets off free!

19:8–9 / This image of armed robbery under cover of the dark continues in the following verses as the victim seeks to flee but is **blocked** from escaping. Cut off in a dead-end alley, he **cannot pass** (*gdr*, "to wall up; block by a wall") his attacker and is trapped **in darkness.** Defenseless and defeated the victim is **stripped** of his possessions, in this case his **honor** (Heb. *kabod,* "glory") and its symbolic **crown** (Heb. *ʿateret*). These same two words (along with the synonym *hadar,* "honor; majesty") appear in the description of God's amazing and undeserved gifting of humans in Psalm 8:5. Here Job depicts God as "stealing away" what he has so graciously given.

19:10–12 / Job is mixing his metaphors fluidly here. From the scene of armed robbery he shifts to the destruction of a **tree** (v. 10). And from there he moves at the end of this sub-section to describe God's approach as the advance of hostile **troops** (vv. 11–12). Picking up on the image of the dying tree employed as an admonition by Bildad in 18:16, Job subtly renews it as a sign of the hostility of God unleashed on his undeserving and unsuspecting subject. God **tears** Job **down on every side till** he is **gone.** This is clearly *more* than severe pruning by the gardener who hopes to enliven a failing tree. This is the final destruction of a rejected tree preceding its complete removal (**he uproots**). The symbolic nature of the uprooted tree is obvious since it is Job's **hope** that is in fact uprooted. Note that Job's hope does not fail on its own. Rather, it is forcibly removed and destroyed by the very one who should be the giver of hope!

This destructive assault against his hope leads Job to conclude that God has placed him on the list of **his enemies.** The only explanation Job can offer is that God's **anger burns against me** and so God wants only to see him suffer and disappear. The attack is engaged and God's troops **advance in force** to lay **siege . . . against** Job and **encamp around** his **tent.** Again the "tent" is the symbol of life (see Bildad's comments in 18:6, 14–15).

Additional Notes §65

19:7 / "Behold, I cry, 'Violence!' but I am not answered." The word is the Heb. *khamas*, "violence that sheds blood." This is the kind of violence that characterized the extreme evil of human beings that brought on the flood in Gen. 6:11–13.

19:12 / The noun *gadud*, **troops,** often has the more negative connotation "bandits, rebels, band of raiders."

§66 Loathsome to My Brothers (Job 19:13–20)

19:13–15 / Divine attack has left Job feeling isolated and abandoned. The list of those who avoid him because of what they consider evidence of divine rejection and hostility is long; the length emphasizes the *completeness* of his isolation. The list includes **brothers, acquaintances, kinsmen,** and **friends.** Even those who are considered outside his personal circle of intimacy—**guests** and the **maidservants**—consider Job a **stranger** and an **alien.** The last two terms are particularly poignant as they most often describe those who are outside the social fabric of the Israelite community (*zar,* "stranger") and who are excluded from the covenant faith that binds the Israelites together with their God (*nokri,* "alien"). Job blames God for the isolation he increasingly experiences, as the initial verb in these verses indicates. God **has alienated** (*hirkhiq,* "cause to withdraw to a distance") Job's associates so that *they* then *estrange* themselves and *forget* their former friend.

19:16–20 / The erosion of Job's status among family, associates, and friends affects even his **servant,** who dares to refuse to **answer** his master's summons—even when Job is reduced to begging.

Job turns from social isolation to his physical deterioration, which repels his former intimates. His **breath is offensive** (lit., "stinks") and repels his **wife;** he is **loathsome** (lit., "stinking") to his **own brothers.** Even **little boys,** who normally know to respect their elders, pick up on the general societal attitude toward Job and join in heaping **scorn** and **ridicule** on this object of communal rejection. Job's "mates" or "comrades," who could usually be counted on for support in any circumstance, **detest** him instead, and his loved ones have **turned against** him. Job's physical maladies have reduced him to **skin and bones** (lit., "to my skin and my flesh my skeleton clings") and he has escaped death for the moment, but only barely (by **the skin of my teeth**).

Additional Notes §66

19:15 / **Guests and maidservants:** rather than moving from extremely honored guests who are free to come and go to the more menial servants who are bound to the household, these nouns describe persons who are always distinguished from the intimate members of the family. (See the Sabbath commandment in Exod. 20:10, 12; Deut. 5:14, 16:11, 14.) Although Job is depicted as *non-Israelite*, the Israelite readers of this book would certainly understand the nuances of these terms in their own social and religious context.

19:16 / This kind of **servant** (Heb. ʿ*ebed*) would not be a slave or menial servant, but often "a dependent in a position of trust" (Holladay, *Concise Hebrew*, p. 262). This relationship heightens the pain of the servant's refusal.

19:17 / The idiom rendered **my own brothers** is the Heb. *bene bitni*, "sons of my belly/womb." The reference is to those born of the same "womb" or "mother" as Job.

19:19 / **Intimate friends:** the phrase includes the rather unusual alternative Heb. word for "man" (*mete*)—also known in the Ugaritic language (*mutu*)—combined with *sod*, "confidential talk; confidant."

§67 Yearning for Redemption (Job 19:21–27)

With a final plea to his friends to show compassion rather than sacrifice him to their compulsive need to justify God and retribution, Job almost inexplicably begins to resurrect the hope that has been systematically dismantled in the preceding verses. Having been brought through his present and continuing circumstances to confront the very worst possible explanation of his world—that God is the enemy who unjustly punishes the righteous—Job can no more surrender his trust in a God of love and mercy than can his friends. While Job's experience forces him to make room in his worldview for the innocent suffering of the righteous, he remains grounded in the belief that the God he worships is a God of truth and a lover of righteousness.

19:21–22 / Job seeks his friends' compassion (**have pity . . . have pity**). The Hebrew makes clear the tension between friendship and compassion when Job ironically says, literally: "Be gracious to me, be gracious to me. You *are* my friends [*after all*]" (emphasis added). Friendship entails compassionately taking the part of the suffering comrade and supporting him sympathetically in his trials. The friends of Job have steadfastly failed to do this. In their rush to judgment in order to shore up the shaky foundations of their retributive worldview, they have left friendship (and Job!) in the dust! Job goes on to state the obvious—**the hand of God has struck me.** The friends never debated this point. While in Job's mind God's attack is unwarranted and unjust, the friends assume that some failing in Job explains the attack.

It is enough for Job that he is under attack by God without having his friends join the pursuit. His question, **Will you never get enough of my flesh?,** offers an extreme image of scavenging animals surrounding the carcass of the fallen prey and vying with one another as they tear off pieces of flesh. If God is the predatory beast hunting down his prey, the friends are the scavenging jackals finishing off the scraps!

19:23–27 / Out of this circumstance of attack and isolation rises an expression of sublime hope, or at least intense desire—depending on which commentator you follow. The Hebrew is notoriously difficult at points and the sentiments expressed are less than crystal clear, lending themselves to a variety of interpretations. Verses 23–24 are the clearest part of the passage and express Job's sincere wish—not likely to be fulfilled—that his **words** be **recorded** and **written on a scroll**, or even **inscribed** permanently on a **rock forever.** This would give Job's case permanency, even after his death, which the preceding verses imply is imminent and unavoidable.

Beyond this initial wish, things get murky. The key to understanding verse 25 is to identify the **Redeemer** (Heb. *go*ʾ*el*) that Job so confidently describes. In Israel the *go*ʾ*el* was the individual responsible to aid extended family members whose inheritance was in danger of being lost, primarily because of death without an heir to carry on the family name, or in some instances because poverty had forced the sale of the family property. In the latter part of the book of Isaiah, in a circumstance that has some relevancy for Job's situation, God, who has appeared throughout the first 39 chapters as the Holy One of Israel standing in judgment over his sinful people, begins unexpectedly to be connected with hope as the *go*ʾ*el* of his people. In that case, the judge and punisher of Israel also becomes its redeemer. Of course the innocence of Job distinguishes his case from that of sinful Israel, but the point is clearly made that God can be *both* judge *and* redeemer.

This understanding paves the way for the most satisfying explanation of the identity of the "redeemer" Job so earnestly desires to see. Some interpreters would understand Job's "words," permanently "engraved in rock," to be his *go*ʾ*el* remaining even after his death, to plead his case in a sort of continuing public vindication. Others would think of some unknown heavenly advocate, a sort of counter to *the* Satan who accuses Job, who would arise to defend him. Clines (*Job 1–20*, pp. 457–66), who opts for and defends the first of these two options, offers extensive comments on all the possible interpretations of this passage. It seems most likely that Job here is grasping onto the hope—however impossible it may seem under the circumstances—that God at his core is essentially just, and that he will, if Job's case could only come before him, *necessarily* assume the role of advocate for the innocent and defenseless. The reader needs also to understand this expectation of a *go*ʾ*el*, linked with the preceding verses with *mi yitten* introducing impossible hopes, as Job's intense *desire* rather than an absolute knowledge or prediction of the future.

The second question in these verses concerns *when* Job anticipates seeing his advocate. In this life? Or in some resurrection life after his death? Commentators have defended both views, and the data are far from certain. The reference in verse 25 to the *goʾel* appearing **in the end** (Heb. *ʾakharon*, "behind; later; finally; last") is interpreted by some as an eschatological reference to the "last days." Job then "sees" the redeemer in a post-death resurrection experience at the end of time. The reference in verse 26 to **after my skin has been destroyed** is taken to indicate Job's death, so the subsequent expectation to see God **in my flesh** can only be in a resurrected body.

On the other hand, *ʾakharon* in verse 25 may mean nothing more than "later," or "afterwards," with no eschatological significance. In this view, the destruction of Job's "skin" is a reference to his extreme suffering and physical deterioration (boils, etc.) so that Job's hope to "see God" is an intense desire expressed against almost impossible odds. The end of verse 27—where he concludes his hopeful declaration with the poignant expression, **how my heart yearns within me!**—affirms that this "seeing" is bound up with Job's earnest *desire*. It seems more consistent that Job would be expressing in these verses his heartfelt desire that even though he has come so close to death and has almost no hope left, that even now—in this life—God might appear and provide vindication. This is part of Job's impossible dream and hope that he will carry to the end. The most cogent argument against the resurrection interpretation of these verses is that Job's certain knowledge that he will be resurrected to receive vindication after his death would severely undermine the remainder of the book, and especially Job's continued reference to the terror of death (23:17; 26:6; 30:23).

Job's hope, he states, includes a direct encounter with God, **"with my own eyes."** The emphatic structure of the verse places the pronoun "I" (Heb. *ʾani*) before the verb to mean **I myself.** According to Job's heartfelt desire, this seeing would be *direct* and *intimately personal* contact with God. In a counter to the circumstances of verse 15, where even the least intimate participants in Job's household consider him a "stranger" (Heb. *zar*) and an "alien" (Heb. *nokri*)—persons outside the social and religious community of Israel—Job declares that he will see God *not* as a *stranger* (Heb. *zar*). Job desires full restoration in his relationship with

God—not just to see him from the outside or to receive some cold, technical vindication.

Job's passionate conclusion, "How my heart yearns within me!" leaves no doubt concerning the intensity of his desire. The rather enigmatic Hebrew (lit., "My kidneys are consumed in my bosom") is either a sign of deep, passionate longing, or of complete emotional exhaustion. The kidneys are the center of deep-seated emotion, while the bosom is the place where one clings to that which is most deeply beloved. This deep desire to see God engages Job such that it *consumes* his greatest emotions and passions.

Additional Notes §67

19:23 / **Oh, that** . . . The Heb. construction *mi yitten*, "who will give," throughout Job (6:8; 11:5; 13:5; 14:4, 13) consistently expresses an intense desire that is nevertheless impossible, or at best unlikely. See the discussion on 14:4 in §47 with regard to *mi yitten.*

19:25 / The NIV attempts to decide the issue for the reader by capitalizing **Redeemer** to identify this figure with God himself. However, there is no capitalization in Heb., and the move is a matter of interpretive preemption. On the concept of Heb. *goʾel,* the story of Naomi and Ruth comes to mind, where Boaz is persuaded to assume the role of *goʾel.* See also Lev. 25:25.

§68 Judgment for the Hunters (Job 19:28–29)

19:28–29 / At the end of his speech Job issues a warning to the friends. The friends, in their haste to defend God from Job's attack, and in their hurry to protect their carefully ordered world from the implications of Job's suffering, have unwittingly placed themselves in a vulnerable position should his claims prove to be true (as the reader knows they must!). Job characterizes the friends' assault with two phrases: a) they **hound him,** and b) they claim **the root of the trouble lies in him** (Job). These two encapsulate Job's offense, which has grown throughout the dialogue. The friends show little compassion as companions and fellow sufferers, rather they exhort each other to "hound" (Heb. *rdp,* lit., "pursue") Job as an enemy. In addition they refuse to accept any evidence of Job's innocence, preferring to understand his suffering as well-deserved punishment for the sinful "trouble" that "lies in him." This absolves them from having to struggle with the enigma of innocent suffering and a God who would allow such suffering to happen.

The friends' failure to allow the truth of Job's situation and claims to penetrate their consciousness is like the willful rejection of the charmer's influence by the cobra that stops up its ears (Ps. 58:5), or the rebellious people of Israel who are prevented from seeing and hearing the truth of Isaiah's message lest they avoid the intended divine destruction (Isa. 6:9–10). So, too, Job's friends **should fear the sword** themselves. Trusting in their secure world of retribution, the friends are ripe for the same destruction Job experiences. If they would learn from him, they might be prepared for the future.

The last half of verse 29 is difficult and variously translated (and emended). The biggest question is how to relate the word **wrath** (Heb. *khemah,* "heat, rage, anger") to the following phrase, **punishment by the sword.** One solution is to understand *khemah* as referring to the friends' anger, expressed in their cold pursuit of Job. This kind of anger deserves punishment by the sword.

Hartley (*Job,* p. 298) follows this track and additionally reads *khemah,* "anger," as the plural pronoun *hemah,* "these"—a reference to the friends' multiple acts of hostility and pursuit. In other words, the friends are making themselves vulnerable to the kind of divine punishment Job has already received. Others would take *khemah* as a reference to *divine* **wrath** (as presumably NIV), and see that divine wrath *brings* punishment. The variety of possibilities makes little difference to the general sense of the verse: that the friends are in danger of experiencing punishment for their failure to deal rightly with Job. We see the results of this failure at the end of the book (42:7–10) when God himself rebukes the friends and they must make a sin offering to avert the consequences of their "folly." Job's final caution is to remind the friends that their insistence that suffering is a judgment for sin will come back to haunt them when they themselves come to experience **judgment** through the "punishment by the sword."

§69 Rejection of Discipline (Job 20:1–3)

20:1–3 / Zophar, in his second (and final!) speech, makes little attempt to respond to the words Job has just spoken. After an initial angry reaction to what he perceives as Job's attempts to "discipline" (NIV **rebuke,** at the beginning of v. 3) an already established group of sages, he launches into a traditional wisdom discourse on the fate of the wicked. His obvious assumption is that Job is firmly entrenched in this category and has little, if any, chance of avoiding a similar fate. Thus his speech is less a cautionary warning encouraging Job to repent than it is a dismissive consignment of Job to his deserved punishment.

The **troubled thoughts** by which he claims to be **greatly disturbed** initially compel Zophar to answer Job. The cause of his disturbance is not so much that Job's condition is inexplicable, or that his claims (if proven true) would turn Zophar's secure world upside-down, as it is a sense of pique that Job does not recognize his status as a sage (or that of the other friends for that matter). Job's attempts to "discipline" the sages, as if they are naïve, untutored school boys, **dishonors** and offends Zophar's sense of identity. He sets out to counter Job's criticism with an answer drawn from **understanding** (the accumulated perception of sages).

Additional Notes §69

20:3 / The meaning of the Heb. *ruakh mibbinati* (lit., "a spirit from my understanding") is not clear here. The NIV takes it as a sign of *inspiration.*

§70 The Premature Death of the Wicked (Job 20:4–11)

20:4–5 / As often in the dialogue section, Zophar couches his answer as disparaging sarcasm in the form of a question. Zophar appeals to the common store of wisdom knowledge collected **from of old** and even suggests that this body of observational and experiential knowledge extends back to the beginnings of human life on the earth. As a recognized sage, Job would be a student (and even master) of this traditional knowledge of the sages and would be expected to accept inferences drawn from its interpretation. Bildad (8:8–9) and Eliphaz (15:18–19) have made similar appeals to the collection of traditional wisdom. According to Zophar, what Job should accept, on the basis of this long tradition, is that any apparent prosperity of **the wicked** can only be **brief.** Their **mirth** and **joy** last **but a moment.** He also characterizes the "the wicked" as **the godless** (Heb. *khanep,* "those estranged from God"). It quickly becomes clear in Zophar's speech that he has already consigned Job to this category of those who are estranged from God, and that he has given up any hope of persuading him to change. Zophar intends this rehearsal of traditional sentiments regarding the fate of the wicked more as a pronouncement of judgment than as an encouragement to repent.

20:6–9 / The wicked will perish completely. Regardless of his stature (Heb. *si',* "height, exalted position," NIV **pride**) within the community, even though he is so elevated that he scrapes **the clouds, he will perish forever, like his own dung.** The contrast could not be greater—from the heights of human glory to the ignobility of human waste! The mighty wicked will disappear altogether. Those who have remarked his prominence before will now look around in bewilderment asking, "**Where is he?**" The wicked have all the substantiality of **a dream** or **a vision of the night** and will fly **away** like a bird, **banished** when the morning comes. The destruction is so complete that it is almost as if the

wicked has been *vaporized!* In a repetition of the thought of verse
7, verse 9 concludes by describing the utter invisibility of the
wicked to **the eye that saw him;** even **his place** (the space he occupied on the earth?) will no longer **look on him.**

20:10–11 / Even the wealth the wicked has accumulated
will not remain. Either he will be forced to repay **the poor** he has
exploited or, upon his death, **his children** will be unable to enjoy
their inheritance but will have to spend it to **make amends.** Although the wicked's **bones**—the structural support of the body
that often symbolize the strength of life—are filled with **youthful
vigor,** that vigor will not preserve him but will join him **in the dust**
of death.

Additional Notes §70

20:4 / The Heb. interrogative particle introduces this verse,
but the NIV translation **surely you know** obscures the meaning. This
form of sarcastic debate must have characterized some forms of wisdom
interaction.

§71 The Gluttony of Wickedness (Job 20:12–23)

20:12–15 / In this section Zophar compares the wealth and success of the wicked to overindulgence at a feast, or a life of gourmandizing. Like a food addict who consumes what destroys him, the wicked savors **evil** as something **sweet in his mouth.** Rolling it about in his mouth to prolong the pleasure, **he cannot bear to let it go.** Yet, like the one who consistently and perniciously overindulges in rich foods, there is ultimately a heavy price to pay. The pleasure of excessive riches accumulated and "consumed" by the wicked will not stay with them, but **will turn sour** like the **venom of serpents,** upsetting the **stomach** so that the **riches** are **spit out.** This is no accidental loss, for **God** is actively at work to **make his stomach vomit them up.** Perhaps the writer had witnessed the sickness and death of one who had been struck by a poisonous serpent and draws his description from the torment of the dying. The description is certainly graphic enough and harsh enough to suspect that it is based upon actual observance.

20:16 / The deceptive food of "riches," while seeming sweet, has in fact the same effect as sucking **the poison of serpents.** There may be some implied criticism in the use of the verb *ynq* ("suck")—normally used for a child nursing its mother—to describe the wicked person's consumption of evil. Perhaps the wicked is being called the child of a serpent, an image of evil. In this case, however, the feeding child is not nourished, since it consumes "poison" and **the fangs of the adder will kill him.** Like both Eliphaz (15:20–35) and Bildad (18:7–10) before him, Zophar now contends that the punishment of the wicked is not to be delayed to some unspecified future, but comes upon them presently as a consequence of their immersion in evil.

20:17–19 / Zophar does not discuss the fate of the wicked in terms of loss. Death from the serpent's venom destroys all hope of enjoying the wealth accumulated through the exploitation of the poor. The Hebrew couches the pronouncement against

enjoyment in the jussive verbal form, expressing the will of the
narrator rather than simple description of future consequence.
The speaker's desire is that the wicked, "May . . . not see the
streams . . . of honey and cream." Both **honey and cream** occur together in a variety of contexts, often as simple, rustic foods used to
sustain life in a crisis. Here and in 29:6, however, "honey and
cream" indicate abundance and excess, the results of the wicked's
toil and **trading**.

Because of his churning belly, the wicked will **give back un-
eaten** what he **toiled** long and hard to possess. He will be unable
to **enjoy the profit** of his treacherous dealings. What tastes sweet
and appears so desirable is, in reality, poison and lethal in its consequences (Prov. 9:17; 20:17). The reason for this judgment is
clear: the wicked amasses wealth by oppressing **the poor**. The
terms here are extreme—"crush" and "abandon"—as if the poor
have been mercilessly attacked and left for dead by the road. Similarly, the wicked have **seized houses** they **did not build**.

20:20–23 / These verses turn from the poisonous consequences of filling oneself with what is evil to the insatiable **craving**
for evil that consumes all and yet leaves no satisfaction. A more
literal translation of the first half of verse 20 is: "He knows no
contentment in his belly." Although NIV takes the second half of
verse 20 to mean that the *wealth* of the wicked cannot deliver from
this addictive craving for evil, it is more likely that it is *what he desires* (and endlessly consumes!) that offers no satisfaction or escape. The Hebrew *khamud* is a passive participle describing "that
which is coveted, desired," and only by extension becomes one's
"treasure."

Exhaustive consumption in search of satisfaction is ultimately frustrated when there is at last nothing more to consume,
and yet the craving still abides deep within. Perhaps linking more
explicitly the wicked's exploitive greed for possessions with the
metaphorical lust for food, the last half of verse 21 admonishes
that the **prosperity** for which he has striven without satisfaction
will itself **not endure**.

In what may be an intentional allusion to Job's own circumstance, Zophar describes how, **in the midst of his plenty**, the
wicked is overtaken by **distress**. The second half of the verse further defines this "distress" as **the full force of misery**. This kind of
misery is not just an unpleasant emotional state, but comes as the
result of exhausting human labor or toil. The noun *ʿamel* is related

to the verb *ʿml*, by which Ecclesiastes characterizes the profitless toil of humans which cannot provide ultimate security or satisfaction. Far from providing security and freedom from such physical toil, the wealth of the wicked is fleeting and leads ultimately to far more misery and distress than the common laborer will ever know!

Concluding the food metaphor of the preceding verses, Zophar once again clearly links the misery of the wicked with divine judgment. Just when the wicked has **filled his belly**—thinking to satisfy his craving—God brings judgment in the form of **burning anger** and raining **blows**. The former (Heb. *kharon ʾappo*) seems to link back to Job's complaint in 19:11 that God's "anger burns against me" (Heb. *wayyakhar ʿalay ʾappo*). Zophar clearly places Job in the category of the insatiable wicked he has just described.

Additional Notes §71

20:16 / **Serpents:** both John the Baptist (Matt. 3:7; Luke 3:7) and Jesus (Matt. 12:34; 23:33) use the similar image of the "brood of vipers" to critique the sincerity of the Pharisees and Sadducees. Note particularly Jesus' statement in Matt. 12:34–35: "You brood of vipers, how can you who are evil say anything good? For out of the overflow of the heart the mouth speaks. The good man brings good things out of the good stored up in him, and the evil man brings evil things out of the evil stored up in him." Another interesting parallel to Job 20:14–16 is found in Jeremiah's description of Nebuchadnezzar, king of Babylon: "[He] has devoured us, he has thrown us into confusion, he has made us an empty jar. Like a serpent he has swallowed us and filled his stomach with our delicacies, and then has spewed us out" (Jer. 51:34).

20:17 / The words for flowing water sources pile up in this verse, emphasizing the abundance of **honey and cream** that are being cut off from the wicked. Three terms appear: *pelaggah,* "(man-made) water course/channel," *nahar,* "river," and *nakhal,* "seasonal stream." In 2 Sam. 17:29, David's party, on the run from Absalom's army, are supplied with "honey and cream." In Isa. 7:15, 22, "honey and cream" is infant food and the simple fare of those left behind in the devastated land following the exile.

20:19 / **Seized houses:** the verb is *gzl,* "rob, take by force." Elsewhere, to occupy houses you did not build is the epitome of ease and pleasure. Deut. 6:10–11 and Josh. 24:13 describe God's gift to Israel of the land of Canaan in similar terms.

20:21 / Clines, *Job 1–20*, p. 493, suggests that the Heb. *tub* (NIV **prosperity**) ought here be taken as "the edible 'produce' of the land . . . since the food metaphor is still dominant." This food source does not continue, he says, "because the greedy evildoer has consumed everything that came into his hands."

20:23 / The translation of Heb. *lekhum* as **blows** is problematic, since the word occurs only here and in Zeph. 1:17, where it is often rendered "flesh" or "entrails." The consonants of the root are associated with food (*lekhem*, "bread") and eating (*lkhm*, "dine; eat") as well as with fighting and battle (*milkhamah*, "war; battle" and *lkhm*, "do battle; fight"). Different translations of the Job passage offer a variety of possibilities, including: "[God] will rain down [his anger] upon his flesh" (NASB), or "as his food" (RSV), as well as NIV's "his blows upon him." For further discussion of the possibilities see Hartley, *Job*, p. 303, and Clines, *Job 1–20*, pp. 477–78.

The noun **burning** and the verb "burns" (19:11) share the same root, *khrh*, while the noun for **anger** (*ʾap*) is the same in both cases.

§72 A Certain End (Job 20:24–29)

20:24–26 / The shift in verse 23 from images of food and gluttony to divine judgment prepares the way for the battle imagery of verses 24–25. Like a soldier fleeing before a warrior with **an iron weapon,** the wicked, seeking to avoid the consequences of his evil, may run directly into the path of the **bronze-tipped arrow** of divine judgment. Like Amos' man who "fled from a lion only to meet a bear" and then escaped to the safety of his own house "only to have a snake bite him" (Amos 5:19), the judgment of the wicked is inevitable and unavoidable. This graphic portrayal describes the mortal blow struck by the archer, whose arrow **pierces** the fleeing wicked through his back and into the **liver.** The arrow may be removed, but the damage is already done so that **terrors . . . come over him**—presumably because of the approach of death. The return in verse 26 to images of **darkness** and **fire** that consume **his tent** emphasizes the finality of his certain end. Bildad introduced these images in his last speech (18:6, 14, 15), and Job employed them himself to describe God's hostile attack against him (19:8, 12). Zophar's use of these same images here in his description of the complete and utter destruction of the wicked leaves little doubt about his intent to consign Job firmly to this category and its consequences. Although much of what Job had possessed or held dear—**his treasures,** as Zophar calls them—has already been taken from him, Zophar holds out hope only for more loss as even **what is left** in his tent will be consumed in the wrath of God unleashed upon him.

20:27–29 / Job consistently refuses to admit any guilt, but now, Zophar says, the very **heavens will expose his guilt** while the **earth will rise up** to testify **against him.** In a similar image in Isaiah 1:2, the heavens and the earth are called to witness God's accusation against Israel. Here, Zophar says that judgment for Job will be swift, final, and complete as **his house** (an image that can refer both to his physical abode and to his family of descendants) will be carried off in a **flood** on the **day of God's wrath.**

Zophar concludes what turns out to be his final speech with a summary verse that attributes the fate of the wicked to the active judgment of God, who both **allots** and **appointed** this dismal but certain end for those who choose the way of wickedness.

Additional Notes §72

20:28 / **A flood:** the Heb. *yebul* is most often translated "produce; food," and an emendation to *nabal*, "river; flood" is often suggested here. A simple transposition of characters in the consonantal text would produce *yubal*, which is translated "stream" in Jer. 17:8. Some sort of threatening water would seem required by the parallel *niggarot*, "gushing waters," in the second half of the verse.

§73 The Inexplicable Prosperity of the Wicked (Job 21:1–16)

In chapter 21, Job responds to Zophar's accusations by thoroughly deconstructing the foundation on which they rest. Zophar has claimed that the wicked perish both in an ultimate sense and in their relentless quest for that which does not satisfy—the gnawing greed that consumes the wicked from the inside out. Job assesses Zophar's claims as so much "nonsense" and "falsehood" (v. 34) when held up to the mirror of real life as Job both knows and describes it. Far from suffering agonizing lives and deaths, the wicked in Job's world prosper beyond imagination. And they do so even as they shove any relationship with God away and deny him any effective power over their lives (vv. 14–16). The key problem that stalks Job throughout this chapter is that God *is not powerless to act or to judge.* And yet, the fact is that such wicked arrogance and injustice continues unchecked and untested in the face of God, who is the Almighty!

21:1–3 / As we have seen before, Job is no stranger to sarcasm. In the tradition of the sages he can trade barbs and biting satire with the best. **Listen carefully to my words.** In an opening sortie that recalls the original intent of the three friends to "sympathize with" Job "and comfort him" (2:11), Job calls his talkative friends to return to the empathic silence with which their visit began (2:12–13). The Hebrew construction here (imperfect followed by the infinitive absolute of the same root) usually describes *continual activity* for an extended period. If the friends continually listen to Job, they cannot be speaking and preparing their rebuttals to his arguments!

What Job desires from his friends is the **consolation** promised by their initial silent support. In 15:11, Eliphaz described the speeches of the friends as, "God's consolations . . . words spoken gently to you [Job]." But what Job has received instead are endless words seeking to convince, persuade, rebuke, and now condemn.

How like Job's friends we can be when confronted by a complaining, weeping, suffering friend whose experience threatens to undermine our carefully constructed theology of a God who always blesses his faithful servants and punishes the wicked of our world. We practically fall all over ourselves spouting words of orthodox "truth" in our rush to convince our suffering companion (or is it ourselves?) of their distorted perspective. As Job sarcastically reveals, the best "gift" (consolation) we can offer in such circumstances is often to *shut up!* Our silent presence and support—our acceptance of our hurting friend despite their anger and doubt— these are the encircling arms of love that the broken soul craves and needs.

The Hebrew translated "**bear with me**," can have a double meaning that Job shrewdly exploits. On the one hand, the verb can mean "to lift up, bear" something, even something heavy or unpleasant—like an ox "bearing" a yoke, or a constantly whining friend! The word can also, however, mean "carry" or "support" someone in need. While Job is sarcastically asking his friends to be quiet and "put up" with him while he is speaking, he is at the same time reminding them of their forgotten responsibility as friends to bear him up in supportive arms of love.

After I have spoken, mock on. Job has little confidence that his friends will renew their original supportive care. The matter has gone too far and they are too invested in refuting his threatening words to go back now. Realistically, Job realizes the best he can hope for is their grudging silence while he speaks. Despairing of any change on their part, he fully expects them to "mock on" when he falls silent. It is certainly interesting that from this point on the friends' verbal attack begins to lose steam and their dialogue rapidly draws to an end. Eliphaz speaks but thirty verses in his third speech (22:1–30), while Bildad can muster only six verses (25:1–6) and Zophar none at all. In a sense, they finally give Job what he asks: silence—although it is not as *supportive* as he would have wished.

21:4–6 / These three verses set the tone for the rest of the chapter. Two rhetorical questions introduce the essential issue. Job is **impatient** because his **complaint** is **directed** not **to man**, but to God. Were human agency the cause of Job's suffering he would have no complaint. Humans are weak and unable to control their own circumstances, let alone those of another. Their actions are controlled by their desires, and their good intentions are constantly undermined by their lack of power and control. But the fact is, Job claims rhetorically, God is in control in this world, just as the friends have claimed. God is powerful and in control, *and yet* the wicked pursue their evil with impunity and all this great evil has come on one who is acknowledged by all to be *tam weyashar,* "blameless and upright" (1:1).

Look at me. If the friends have any lingering questions as to the legitimacy of Job's annoyance, they need only to "look at" him. The Hebrew verb is *pnh,* "turn (your face) *and look,"* which may suggest that the friends are having difficulty maintaining eye contact. Certainly they have lost sight of the severity of Job's suffering in their haste to prove him wrong. He tells them to **be astonished.** To look at Job, to really see his suffering and to empathize with his plight, is to be astounded by the lack of congruence between the theory of retribution and Job's actual experience. As their first sight of Job (2:12–13) reduced the friends to silent weeping, so now they need to renew their awareness, and as a result become both astounded and silenced. Further, he tells them, **clap your hand over your mouth.** As is often the case in our society today, to cover one's gaping mouth with a hand is a gesture of extreme astonishment. In Job's case it has the added benefit of silencing his detractors.

Job uses his own response as an appropriate model and tells the friends, **I am terrified.** Job is "terrified" not just by the intensity of his suffering, but also because of what this undeserved suffering says about the character of Almighty God and the nature of the world in which he rules. This is no mere mental contemplation of philosophical possibilities. Job does not simply **think about** the problem of innocent human suffering—the word is actually *remembers* (Heb. *zkr*), and Job is remembering from personal experience. If God is indeed both powerful and in control (as the friends and Job all attest); if nevertheless the righteous suffer innocently and extremely as Job has; if at the same time the wicked arrogantly defy God while living at ease; if this describes the real world, then what is left for anyone but **trembling** and terror?

21:7 / Job now embarks on the first of two excurses regarding the failure of retribution. In this first one (vv. 7–16), his focus is the charmed lives of the wicked. The second excursus (vv. 17–21) will lay the responsibility for this failure squarely at the feet of God. But here Job describes with utter astonishment (and disdain!) the sleek and pampered lives of the arrogant wicked. He begins with a plaintive question that sets the theme: **Why do the wicked live on, growing old and increasing in power?** Not only do the wicked live to a ripe old age—a sign of blessing—but they also increase in strength and influence. The Hebrew phrase for "increasing in power" (*gaberu khayil*) is related to the social designation *gibbor khayil,* "men of influence." These are the powerful social elite who gain influence in society by their "strength" (the meaning of the root *gbr*) and "wealth" (one of the derived meanings of *khayil*). So the wicked achieve all the benefits of righteousness in this life (venerable, influential old age) without any pretense of living lives connected to or in obedience to God!

21:8 / For the Israelites, **children** were the continuation of their lives. While resurrection and immortality were not established hopes within Israel's theological understanding, they considered descendants and a continued line to be the blessing of God. To be cut off without a descendant was to be cursed or punished by God himself (Ps. 37:28; Isa. 48:18–19). Job turns the world of retribution on its ear by highlighting that the evil ones live long enough to see their children and grandchildren not just born, but also **established around them** as mature adults.

21:9–13 / Not only do the wicked live long, they also live well. There is no pin to burst their bubble. All goes well for them. **Their homes** are never robbed or subjected to drive-by shootings. They live in secure gated communities with surveillance and security systems to protect them. Private security firms watch over them and public police respond quickly to their 911 calls. Those who look on from the outside can only conclude that God is on their side, or at least is unconcerned to judge them, since **the rod of God** never seems to come down upon them.

Their financial dealings multiply their wealth without any setbacks. I have a brother-in-law who is an expert breeder of purebred cattle. Every year during the breeding season he must exercise constant vigilance to keep the number of "open" (those not impregnated) cows to a minimum. Even in these days of increased skill in artificial insemination, success can never approach 100%. Not so with Job's arrogant wicked. **Their bulls never fail ...** **their cows** (always!) **calve and do not miscarry.** This is clearly hyperbole to emphasize the utter reversal of expectations according to the theory of retribution. Every one of the Israelite patriarchs and matriarchs had difficulty producing children in response to the sure promises of God, but these wicked humans who refuse to acknowledge the claim of God on their lives have a perfect record of fertility—even among their cattle!

The prolificacy of the wicked produces **children** without number—**flocks** of them! The author is playing on the preceding description of unchecked propagation among the herds to transition to the unrestrained joy of the abundant descendants of the wicked. This puts the lie to the traditional assumption that the descendants of the wicked will experience cursing and punishment (Prov. 20:7; Ps. 37:28). These **little ones** skip and **dance about** in evidence of their peaceful environment and indulgent lifestyle. Musical entertainment is most often a by-product of leisure time and affluence. When one is pressed to eke out the bare necessities of life, there is little time or energy left to perform, **sing,** and **make merry** on the **tambourine, harp,** or **flute.**

Easy come, easy go. Contrary to all retributive expectation, the wicked live long lives of ease and prosperity and, when it comes time to die, they go quickly without lingering in suffering and pain. Job's own state is obviously the intended contrasting counterpoint: the righteous who receives what the wicked should, while the wicked luxuriate in the blessings that have passed Job by. Job's experience practically "quotes" Ecclesiastes here: "There is something else meaningless that occurs on earth: righteous men who get what the wicked deserve, and wicked men who get what the righteous deserve. This too, I say, is meaningless" (8:14). This is not the momentary "joy of the godless" that "lasts but a moment" as Zophar claimed (20:5). This is a lifetime of comfortable ease and a swift, easy departure. Job's own life could not present a greater contrast.

21:14–15 / In these verses Job describes the inward disposition of the wicked in their own words. The report as direct quote, **they say,** removes any doubt as to the character of these individuals. This is no hypothesis based on external observation, but personal testimony from the heart of the wicked themselves. Even more, the speech of the wicked is no pompous bluff expressed to human companions. Rather, it is a caustic rejection thrown directly **to God. "Leave us alone!"** The Hebrew verb here is *swr,* "turn away; turn aside." It describes a decisive and complete avoidance. Exactly the same idiom (*swr + min*) affirms Job's committed and blameless character when he is said to "turn from evil" (*wesar mera͗,* 1:1, 8; 2:3).

The attitude of the wicked is diametrically opposed to the traditional Israelite grounding of faith in the fear of God—a recognition of one's utter dependence and reliance on God—that is both the beginning and end of the wisdom enterprise. These speakers have *no* fear of the Almighty, but pack him unceremoniously off to the furthest hinterlands of their awareness, demanding that he turn decisively away from any contact or attempts to influence them.

Continuing with their scathing rejection addressed directly to God, the wicked announce their total lack of interest in anything to do with God or his purposes. God's **ways** are the expected patterns of human behavior that acknowledge divine lordship and seek to align human living with the will and purpose of God. To **know** the ways of God is to follow the path of blessing that is known and watched over by God himself (Ps. 1:6). The wicked **have no desire** to know any path of blessing from God, since they experience blessing enough traveling their own independent way. To acknowledge (or **desire**) God's ways would require submission to his will and purpose: something the wicked have no intention of doing. Pharaoh says to Moses, "Who is the LORD, that I should obey him and let Israel go? I do not know the LORD and I will not let Israel go" (Exod. 5:2). The Hebrew in Job is different, but the attitude that the wicked express, resisting any call to submit to God, is the same: **Who is the Almighty, that we should serve him?**

Similarly they deny that they can achieve any **gain** by acknowledging their dependence on God through **praying**. They evaluate any relation to God on the basis of human profit or utilitarian value. Since the wicked already experience abundant riches and carefree lives without acknowledging God, why should they change? This is, of course, the exact contradiction of *the* Satan's insinuation in the prologue that humans (and especially Job) fear God only because they receive benefit from the transaction. Here Job demonstrates that the blessings of an abundant and influential life are no sure guarantee of submission to God's will and purpose. The Hebrew verb for "praying" here (*pgᶜ*) has a more desperate edge to it. This is not the usual verb for "pray" (Heb. *pll*, "intercede; pray"), but a much less common form with hostile overtones. In some contexts the verb means to "meet/encounter with hostility," in others it takes on the sense to "entreat" or "plead." The wicked, by their refusal to "plead," resist demeaning their own power and control by admitting their need for anything other than themselves (similar to the sentiments of the wicked expressed in Ps. 10:1–13).

21:16 / Job ends this section with a subtle rebuttal of the arrogant speech of the wicked. Like the sages, they have observed their easy life and the utter lack of consequences for their evil. Moreover, they have decided that God is not a factor they need to consider in life—he offers no restraint for evil and no incentive for righteous action. As a result, they have written God out of the equation and rely only on their own ability to wrest the good out of life by their own power. Job, on the other hand, sees the same facts of life but offers a different conclusion. The **counsel of the wicked** (forget God, self-power rules) is not trustworthy and Job stays **aloof,** keeping his distance from it. Regardless of the apparent evidence, Job is convinced that human power or endeavor is *not* the source of **prosperity.** Their prosperity **is not in their own hands,** but in the hands of God alone.

This conclusion is consistent with Job's argument thus far. The problem Job encounters is not that God is powerless or out of control. God's power is robust and Job sees his control everywhere displayed. Job's problem is that life is not turning out the way he expected according to the accepted wisdom tradition. If God is indeed powerful and sovereign, why do the wicked continue to prosper while the righteous perish? Nevertheless, Job refuses to simply join the ranks of the arrogant wicked and curse God (as *the* Satan predicted and Job's wife encouraged). Confused, frustrated, angry, and near despair, he remains faithful.

Additional Notes §73

21:4 / **Impatient:** the Heb. idiom (*tiqtsar rukhi*) has more the sense of "be annoyed/despondent" than simply "impatient."

21:8 / On the importance of **children,** see Ps. 127:3–5; Prov. 17:6. On the importance of descendants as tradition bearers, see Exod. 12:26; Deut. 4:9–10; 11:19. On children as recipients of punishment for the fathers' sins, see Exod. 20:5; 34:7; Num. 14:18; Deut. 5:9; 24:16.

21:12 / The three instruments mentioned here, **tambourine, harp,** and **flute** (*ketop, kinnor, ʿugab*), are variously understood. Musical instruments are notoriously difficult to identify. The *ketop* (mentioned some thirty times in the OT) is often considered a tambourine or timbrel that was struck or shaken. The *kinnor* (mentioned six times, four in the Psalms) is understood to be a stringed lyre or harp that was plucked or strummed. The last, *ʿugab* (Ps. 150:4), is more elusive. Some suggest it was another form of stringed instrument and others suggest a type of wind-blown flute.

21:13 / *Shalom*, the Heb. for "peace, wholeness," is not behind the NIV translation **in peace** here. As the textual note suggests, the Heb. is *regaʿ*, "quickly." The emphasis seems to be on the fact that in contrast to Job's lingering malaise, the wicked depart this life with no delay or extended suffering.

21:14 / The images in this section, and particularly the language of vv. 14 and 18, suggest to me that the retributive theology of Ps. 1 may lurk behind Job's comments here. If so, Job is contesting a naïve reading of that psalm in the light of his own experience.

21:16 / Once again, as in v. 14, Job's words here appear to draw on the text of Ps. 1. Job takes the stance encouraged in Ps. 1 as he refuses to be drawn into the arrogant rejection of God modeled by the wicked. He himself models the role of the "blessed" one who does not associate with the "counsel of the wicked." The Heb. of this phrase (*ʿatsat reshaʿim*) is identical to that employed in Ps. 1:1.

§74 God Annuls Retribution (Job 21:17–21)

Job's acknowledgment of God's power and control (albeit in a rather pessimistic context) does not mean that he has capitulated and given up his fight. He leaps immediately back into the fray. In the preceding verses, Job focused on the blessed life of abundance the wicked, who live merry and die easy, enjoy. In what follows, Job shifts his emphasis to the expected judgment (according to the theory of retribution) that the wicked seem consistently to avoid. On the one hand, God's blessing appears to be misdirected; on the other, his judgment fails to materialize. Job seems to be interacting here with a retributive proverbial tradition that has passed on its expectation for the judgment of the wicked in colorful aphorisms. He begins with a rather scathing question—"how often?"—and then proceeds to quote a series of traditional proverbs of retribution that do not, in Job's experience, describe reality. (For other examples of the traditional viewpoint, see Pss. 14; 53; 37; 49).

21:17–18 / In Proverbs 24:19–20, we find the extended proverb: "Do not fret because of evil men or be envious of the wicked, for the evil man has no future hope, and *the lamp of the wicked will be snuffed out*" (emphasis added). Job's reference to **the lamp of the wicked** may indicate a familiarity with this particular proverb, or with the sentiments it expresses. Bildad had trotted out a near quote of this proverb in 18:5 "The lamp [Heb. ʾor, 'light'] of the wicked is snuffed out." In response to this traditional expectation of sure judgment for the wicked, Job asks, **how often?** (Heb. *kammah*, "like when?"). Job's "show me!" attitude grows out of his own personal experience to the contrary.

Job refers to yet another proverbial tradition: that **calamity** (Heb. ʾedam) will **come upon** the wicked. It may be that he is simply reading on in his text of the book of Proverbs to encounter the next aphorism: "Fear the LORD and the king, my son, and do not join with the rebellious, for those two will send sudden destruction [Heb. ʾedam] upon them, and who knows what calamities they can bring?" (Prov. 24:21–22). Once again Job responds to these inflated hopes with a rather sour, "So when did this ever *really* happen to the wicked?" The **fate God allots in his anger** seems to remain far from the wicked.

In images that once again invite comparison with Psalm 1, Job scorns the traditional equation of the wicked to wind-blown **chaff** scattered to the four winds. Like the **straw** that remains after the harvesters have taken the good grain, the wicked are considered unstable, rootless, and ready to be blown away. Or, "like chaff," the husk winnowed from the kernel at the threshing floor, the ungrounded wicked will be swept away to destruction. Psalm 1 contrasts the rootless instability of the wicked with the firm grounding of the righteous tree, which remains deeply rooted and fruitful. "Not so!," counters Job, for the wicked instead live long, prosperous lives while the righteous experience desperation, loss, and torment.

21:19–21 / In these verses, Job seeks to head off what must have been a common contemporary explanation for the delayed (or nonexistent!) punishment of the wicked. Drawing on the classic picture of YHWH as the "jealous, but compassionate God," the friends offer Job one answer that he wishes to confront here and now. Their answer is most likely based on Exodus 34:6–7 and Numbers 14:18, which describe YHWH as: "The LORD, the LORD, the compassionate and gracious God, slow to anger, abounding in love and faithfulness, maintaining love to thousands, and forgiving wickedness, rebellion and sin. Yet he does not leave the guilty unpunished; he punishes the children and their children for the sin of the fathers to the third and fourth generation" (Exod. 34:7). Might it be that God's compassion and graciousness explain the delay of punishment for the wicked? And since guilt will not go unpunished, the children ultimately receive the punishment for their fathers' sins, even to the third and fourth generation. This perspective could even provide a cogent reason for Job's own suffering—not his own sin, but that of his father, or grandfather, or even great-grandfather may be the reason for punishment here (it is interesting, however, that Job's friends never make this connection). But such an idea of God meting out punishment on innocent descendants, while the wicked progenitors get away completely unscathed, leaves Job (and many of the prophets, and *me!*) cold and more than a little bit angry.

Job says God should **repay the man himself.** Passing the judgment upon fathers to their children is *not* just retribution in Job's view. It has nothing to do with reaping what one sows. Neither does such misdirected punishment serve any instructive or disciplinary purpose. What lesson can the innocent, suffering children learn to shape their lives in alignment with the will and purposes of God? For either reason—judgment or instruction—it is necessary, Job thinks, for the perpetrator to receive the punishment so that **he will know it.** When **his own eyes see his destruction** then the wicked will know that God is powerful, in control, and cares what the wicked (and the righteous) do. This sort of appropriate response, Job indicates, would give the lie to the arrogant assumptions of the wicked expressed in verses 14–15. To **drink of the wrath of the Almighty** (Heb. *shadday*) is to experience the anger of God poured out on sin. The idiom refers perhaps to a cup of poison (one of the alternate meanings of the Heb. *khemah*, "heat, rage, poison," translated "wrath" here) employed as a form of execution.

For what does he care? Job concludes his plea for direct punishment of the wicked (which is another way of criticizing the current *lack* of punishment being meted out) by pointing out how their callous self-concern renders any deflection of punishment onto their descendants an ineffective form of judgment. In Job's estimation, the hard-hearted wicked have no concern for what happens even to their own children, as long as their own lives remain trouble (and judgment) free! They will be unmoved by anything less than direct, personal pain and punishment.

Additional Notes §74

21:17 / In two passages in Jeremiah, the word **calamity** appears in the context of destructive winds and scattering, as in the following verses of Job. First, in a pronouncement of judgment on Israel, God declares: "Like a wind from the east, I will scatter them before their enemies; I will show them my back and not my face in the day of their disaster" (Jer. 18:17). And later in a message against Kedar and Hazor, enemies of Israel: "Their camels will become plunder, and their large herds will be booty. I will scatter to the winds those who are in distant places and will bring disaster on them from every side" (Jer. 49:32). These verses offer interesting parallels to the situation of the man Job. In the first, the word translated "enemies" is the Heb. *ʾoyeb* that is closely related consonantally to the name *ʾiyyob*, "Job." It would have been easy to read this text as, "I will scatter them before *Job*" (emphasis added). Regardless, the text describes destruction and scattering as "calamity" brought on as divine judgment. The first half of the second verse resonates with the experiences of Job in chs. 1 and 2. Plundering enemies and destructive winds make clear connections.

21:19 / NIV suggests that Job is *quoting* his opponents' views here by placing their editorial gloss, **it is said,** in brackets. Neither of these words, nor the brackets, appear in the Heb. text.

21:20 / One thinks immediately of Socrates drinking hemlock, but the OT contains many references to drinking the cup or the wine of divine wrath. Both God's blessing and his wrath can be viewed as stored in a cup, and those that experience either are said to drink from it. Perhaps the image is retributive in nature. God has but one cup, but what one receives from it depends upon one's relation to God. See Pss. 16:5; 23:5; 116:13; Isa. 51:22; Jer. 25:15; Rev. 14:10. Might this idea stand behind Paul's exhortations to caution regarding the cup of the Eucharist (1 Cor. 10:16–21; 11:25–29)?

§75 Death, an Inadequate Punishment
(Job 21:22–34)

In this final section of his response to Zophar, Job seeks to drive home the inadequacy of death as punishment for a life of wickedness. At the beginning (vv. 22–26) and end (vv. 32–33) he emphasizes the democratic nature of death—it comes to all, rich or poor, wicked or righteous, throughout the ages. As a common experience of humanity death cannot bear the weight of divine punishment, since all die.

21:22–26 / The section begins with an acknowledgement of God's sovereign knowledge and control. **Can anyone teach knowledge to God?** Job delivers his opening rhetorical question with tongue firmly planted in cheek. On one level, the humor is obvious because it is patently ridiculous to think that mortals can instruct the Almighty! But for the reader a more subtle smile is in order, for it seems that instruct is precisely what Job intends to do here! By describing the incongruity of a life in which the wicked prosper and the righteous suffer, and by confronting the thickheadedness of the friends who keep on spouting the truisms of retribution in the face of repeated evidence to the contrary, Job is certainly seeking to inform God of the baffling nature of life and to force a response.

Job continues to affirm the sovereign power of God. For, he says, **even the highest** must submit to divine judgment. Again, Job is not denying God's power and control. He simply does not understand why God displays his sovereign power in the way he does. While none can escape the exercise of divine judgment, there seems little to distinguish God's treatment of the righteous or wicked. Job drives home this failure of retributive theology subtly, without ever mentioning the righteous or wicked overtly. But Job establishes his intent clearly within the broader context of his life experience.

Job sets the deaths of two persons side by side. One **dies in full vigor** while the other **dies in bitterness of soul.** One had experienced the fullness of life—**completely secure and at ease . . . well nourished**—while the other experienced only "bitterness of soul," **never having enjoyed anything good.** Now . . . let's guess . . . which of these represents Job and which the wicked?

With all of the anticipated consequences of retribution turned neatly on their ear in this life (life as Job and most of us experience it), where can one possibly hope to encounter divine justice? Certainly *not* in any future life, Job hastens to note, for, when it comes to the end, there these two persons lie, **side by side . . . in the dust,** with nothing yet to set them apart, as **worms cover them both.** So, to paraphrase the common dictum, "Life's a pain, and then you die."

21:27–30 / One (or more) of Job's friends must have opened his mouth to protest, but Job quickly shuts them off with a hasty **I know full well what you are thinking.** Job will have his say and wants no interruptions. He uses their imagined protest as fodder for his ruminations. The Hebrew words for **schemes** (*makhashebot,* "well considered plan") and **wrong** (*mezimmah,* "deliberation; plot [usually evil]") suggest that Job thinks the friends are plotting and scheming in order to do him harm.

You say: Job encapsulates the friends' protest in a single rhetorical sentence that ties his own experience together with that of the wicked. Whether it is accurate or not, Job's perception of the friends' developing rhetoric is that they increasingly understand Job to be guilty and deserving of the punishment he is receiving. **Where now is the great man's house?** It seems unlikely that this is a reference to the destruction of the houses of the wicked as a consequence of divine judgment, although this does seem to be the intent of the explicit parallel phrase, **the tents where wicked men lived.** If this question intends merely to claim that the wicked do get their just desserts in this life, as their homes and possessions are taken from them, it would seem the friends have not been listening very closely to Job's speech! The thrust of what he is really saying seems to be that even if the wicked do live easy, comfortable lives, where is all their wealth and comfort now that they are dead? This is somewhat equivalent to our own admonition, "You can't take it with you!," and suggests that death is the ultimate divine judgment for the sins of the wicked. More subtly, however,

the question is a rather ham-fisted reference to the earlier losses of
Job, and serves to indict Job along with the wicked.
 Have you never questioned . . . ? The search for knowledge
and understanding should drive a sage to ferret out sources of information from the distant reaches of the earth. Those **who travel,**
who have extensive experience of the diverse cultures and peoples
of the world, can expand radically the personal knowledge and experience of a single sage who is willing to ask and to learn. Job is
saying that if the friends think retribution has brought about the
destruction of all the houses of the wicked, then they simply have
not looked far enough or listened carefully enough to the **accounts**
of those who have intimate knowledge of the realities of the world.
 Often, Job says, **the evil man is spared.** Broad experience of
reality shows, Job claims, that the homes of the wealthy wicked
stand firm in the face of disaster, natural or otherwise. Those with
wealth build strong homes capable of withstanding earthquake
and windstorm. They place them within protected compounds
and hire security guards to watch over them. They receive preferential treatment in the face of the threat of fire. The phrase **the day
of calamity** (Heb. *leyom ʾed*) links back to Job's earlier words in
verse 17. As then, Job remains convinced that the wicked escape
the effects of "calamity" and even remain secure from **the day of
wrath.** This is the flip-side of Job's earlier claims (vv. 7–13). There
the wicked experience everything good. Here they manage to
avoid anything evil.

 21:31–33 / The wicked person lives a carefree life in part
because no one **repays him** or is willing to confront his evil acts **to
his face.** The way of the wicked is a life path, a direction toward
which the individual faces and makes progress. For humans the
choice is between the way of God, that is known by him and leads
to him, or the way of the wicked, that leads away from God. This
imagery of the "ways" a human can choose to travel in life is behind the biblical understanding of repentance as "turning" or "re-
orientation." The Hebrew *shub*, "turn; return; repent" exhorts
sinners to turn away from the path of wickedness and reorient
themselves to the right path that leads to God. Repentance, then,
is an active turning *from* evil (Pss. 34:14; 37:27; Job 1:1). The acts of
the wicked show them to be on the way of evil. The pointed message of verse 31, however, is that it seems to Job that even God is
unwilling to confront the evil of the wicked—a far larger problem
than the fact that no human will confront evil.

This speech has twice already referred to the deaths of the wicked. In verse 13, Job described the long and prosperous lives and quick and easy deaths of the wicked. In verse 23, Job noted that death comes to the wicked in "full vigor" and that they have a sense of complete security and ease. Now he says that even death cannot end the preferential care of the prosperous wicked. After death the wicked is **carried to the grave** and **his tomb** is guarded and protected. An interesting parallel hit the papers in southern California lately. A city government was sued because the city had exercised great care in maintaining the "white" cemetery in town while allowing the "black" cemetery to fall into disrepair. In Job's experience the rich wicked are well cared for in death as in life. Even the **soil in the valley** seems to respond preferentially to the wicked's interment by being **sweet to him.**

During life no confrontation mars the joyous prosperity of the wicked; no judgment, divine or human, calls them to account for their evil deeds. And death, contrary to the imagined objections of the friends in verse 28, offers only careful protection and continued sweetness. Where is the judgment in that? Without any clear reference to a developed hope for resurrection and life after death, Job has removed either possibility as a source of judgment for the arrogant wicked. They live; they die; and nowhere do they suffer or receive appropriate recompense for their evil.

As the final deflation of the friends' claim that death is the ultimate judgment, Job points to the endless commonality of death for all humans. Regardless of their state of righteousness or wickedness, **all men follow after** the wicked into death, and a **countless throng** precedes them. If death is the common experience of *all* humans—rich or poor, righteous or wicked—how can it serve as any form of judgment?

21:34 / **So how can you console me with your nonsense?** And so Job concludes his response to Zophar's second speech as he began—with caustic sarcasm. There is no consolation to be found in words that do not align with reality. When put to the test of the real world, the friends' **answers** are reduced to so much **falsehood.** The drift of Job's argument in this chapter has been fairly clear. The friends' claims that God will ultimately judge and punish the wicked—in this life or through death—are not grounded in real experience of the world. In the real world, the wicked live prosperous lives, die easy deaths, and occupy opulent tombs carefully protected in the most pleasant valleys. No one confronts human evil in this life—certainly not God!—and death holds no terror. As a result, holding firmly to the idea of retribution seems the equivalent of "nonsense," or even outright "falsehood."

Additional Notes §75

21:23 / The Heb. for **full vigor** is *ᶜetsem tummo,* "whole of body." The adjective *tummo* is related to the word *tam,* which describes the integrated character of Job in 1:1.

21:25 / The Heb. for **bitterness of soul** is *nepesh marah,* where *nepesh* describes the essential human self animated by the divine breath, or spirit. The *nepesh* is also the place of deepest personal reflection, so that a "bitter *nepesh*" is the result of deep personal dissatisfaction and desperation.

Job describes both men with food and consumption images. Of the first individual (v. 23), the Heb. says, lit., "his buckets are filled with milk" and the "marrow of his bones are watered" (meaning his bones remain resilient rather than dry and brittle). In contrast, the second individual dies "having never eaten any good thing" (v. 25).

21:27 / The verb translated **wrong me,** *khamas,* means to "do violence; bloodletting." It was for this kind of violence that God brought the flood on the earth (Gen. 6:11–13).

21:30 / Although by the choice of the translation **day of wrath** here NIV seems to intend a link to the day of *divine* wrath, the Heb. (*ᶜabarot,* "anger, rage, fury") seems to reflect fits of anger and rage that are not necessarily divine. Although the word does occur (Isa. 13:9) in a reference to the "day of YHWH," it is included as *one* of a list of words describing the fearsome character of divine wrath. In Isa. 16:9, the term describes the anger not of YHWH, but of Moab. Perhaps the reference here in Job is to human pillaging and looting (which are fearsome enough), rather than to divine wrath.

§76 No Gain for God (Job 22:1–5)

The "third dialogue cycle" begins again with Eliphaz and his response to Job. He begins with a series of rhetorical questions that recall the tactics of his earlier two speeches (4:1–5:27; 15:1–35). In those utterances Eliphaz sought to undermine Job's claims of innocence by arguing that *no human* can be declared innocent before God (4:7–9, 17–19; 15:14–16). Since even the angels—who stand above humans in Eliphaz's understanding of creation order—are charged "with error" by God (4:18–19; 15:15–16; see also Ps. 8:5), how then can sinful humans hope to escape the divine punishment they *all* deserve? Now Eliphaz takes a further step to argue that God remains essentially unaffected by human conduct—whether exceedingly wicked or exceedingly righteous—and thus we can trust his judgments in all cases to be unbiased. As a result, since Job is suffering harshly, his sin must be richly deserved. Whybray expresses this well: "God cannot be affected by or derive any advantage from human behaviour: he is self-sufficient and entirely impartial, utterly unmoved by earthbound motives. Therefore, if he has rebuked Job and become his adversary, Job cannot, as he has maintained, be innocent. Job's treatment by God proves his guilt" (*Job,* p. 104).

Ironically, Eliphaz lays the groundwork here for the very character of God Job has been supposing. Eliphaz does not, apparently, see that in his attempt to eliminate any undue influence on the judgment of God, he has set the central principle of retribution on its ear. If God gives to each human according to what his or her actions deserve, as retribution demands, then his judgments *are* linked to human conduct. In 7:20, however, Job posits that human sin does *not* affect God. If God is free to act without respect to human behavior, then he is free to allow the wicked to prosper and the righteous to suffer as Job has suggested. This transcendent aloofness of God from human conduct that Eliphaz supposes would seem to sound the death knell for any tit-for-tat understanding of retribution. Perhaps this is why the friends fall so rapidly silent after this speech!

Eliphaz begins his speech with eight consecutive rhetorical questions grouped in pairs. In the Hebrew text this produces a noticeable string of four verses (vv. 2–5) beginning with the letter *he* down the right-hand margin. Each of these initial letters is the sign of a coming question (called *he interrogative*) and governs both interrogatives in the same verse. The result is a remarkable visual as well as thematic grouping of these four verses.

22:1–2 / The first two rhetorical questions are more general in nature. Eliphaz twice questions how humans can provide **benefit to God,** employing a different subject for the verb (Heb. *skn,* "be of use; service; benefit") each time. At first it is the Hebrew *geber,* "man; warrior," who is at issue. The term *geber* emphasizes the strength of the human being, as opposed to *ʾenosh,* that most often stresses human weakness (Ps. 8:4). This is no common human being, but a prime example. Yet even such a strong warrior is unable to offer any "benefit" to God. The second question raises the stakes by introducing *maskil* as its subject. This term describes one who is particularly skilled in wisdom understanding. If the strongest warrior is unable to influence God, and even the wisest sage (particularly revered by Job and his friends) has no affect on God's judgments, then God's decrees must surely remain unimpeachable.

22:3 / Eliphaz continues with two additional queries that extend the emphasis of the first verse and link more directly with Job's claims of innocence. Here Eliphaz subtly begins the indictment of Job that will occupy the central part of his speech and that will take on much harsher rhetoric before it is done. Two terms, **pleasure** and **gain,** are perhaps intended to circumscribe the whole of divine motivation. "Pleasure" (Heb. *khepets*) is that which gives one delight, while "gain" (Heb. *betsaʿ*) is material profit, often gained by violent action. According to Eliphaz, Shaddai receives no "pleasure," nor does he "gain" anything, from Job's supposed righteousness or from his claims to keep to **blameless ways.** Eliphaz couches his questions in verse 2 in indefinite third-person references to any *geber* or *maskil.* Here, however, he pointedly draws his circle of accusation around Job with second-person singular masculine verbs, **you were righteous** and, literally, "you made your ways blameless." Far from accepting Job's claims of innocence and righteousness, Eliphaz casts aspersions on Job by using the conditional particle *ki*, "if." It becomes increasingly clear that Eliphaz has no doubt that Job's claims are patently false.

22:4 / Eliphaz begins to reveal his own estimation of Job's character in the next pair of sarcastic questions. Having established that God is beyond the influence of Job's presumed righteousness, Eliphaz can only conclude that Job's suffering is in fact the just rebuke of God who **brings charges against** Job for his sin. The sarcasm is a slap at Job, as if to say, "If you are really as innocent as you claim, would God be rebuking you and taking you to court? Ridiculous!" Interestingly, Eliphaz uses words here that are reminiscent of his earlier encouragement of Job: "Should not your piety be your confidence and your blameless ways your hope?" (4:6).

22:5 / Eliphaz's final two rhetorical questions reveal his true estimation of Job's wickedness. **Is not your wickedness great? Are not your sins endless?** These words provide a fitting conclusion to Eliphaz's developing argument. God cannot be swayed from exercising justice. Suffering is the consequence of divine judgment. Job *must be* deeply enmeshed in sin. The verse also provides a transition to the second part of Eliphaz's speech, which will outline his harsh condemnation of Job's sin and give specific examples.

Eliphaz's certainty concerning Job's great sinfulness must necessarily stand in tension with the reader's equal certainty of his innocence. The opening prologue has established beyond any doubt that Job is "blameless" (*tam*) and "upright" (*yashar*)—a conclusion drawn from the observation of the narrator (1:1) as well as the confirmation of God himself (1:8; 2:3). Consequently the careful reader is aware from the outset that Eliphaz is *wrong* and that his catalogue of sins is either imaginary or erroneously presumed.

22:6 / **You demanded security.** Eliphaz draws his accusations from covenantal expectations—particularly those laws having to do with loans, interest, and pledges taken to secure them. Eliphaz accuses Job of demanding "security" for a loan—some sort of pledge the borrower would give to ensure future payment. Such a pledge was usually of value and could be used to personally identify the borrower, so that the lender would be assured of repayment. In Genesis 38, Judah gives the supposed prostitute whose services he had employed his personal seal, cord, and staff as a "pledge" of his intent to pay in full. Deuteronomy 24:6 cautions against taking the source of a person's livelihood (in this case a pair of millstones) as security, since the loss of livelihood would inhibit the borrower's ability to repay his debt. Eliphaz's accusation is based on the assumption that no one should ever take "security" **for no reason**—perhaps this implies that he questions the sincere intent of the borrower to repay. Eliphaz accuses Job of taking a pledge even when there was "no reason."

The second half of verse 6 is probably related to the first. The act of stripping is an extreme form of taking a pledge to secure a loan. Job is described as being so concerned to secure his investment that he takes the very clothes off the debtor's back to provide security. Exodus 22:25–27 exhorts Israel to compassionate lending to those in need. Usury (the charging of interest) is prohibited among fellow Israelites. A person's cloak *may* be taken as a pledge to secure a loan, but it must be returned to the debtor every evening by sunset so that he may wrap himself in it to sleep warmly. Job, by contrast, is accused of taking not only the outer cloak, but also the inner garments, leaving the debtor unprotected, undignified, and completely **naked**. This extreme action adds, of course, to the condemnation of Job.

22:7–9 / **You gave no water.** In addition to extreme self-interest in the practice of money lending, Eliphaz accuses Job of exercising no compassion in his relations with the unfortunate members of society. Here **the weary, the hungry, widows, and fatherless** are all categories of unprotected persons within society to whom the wealthy and secure are often exhorted to show compassion and care. The first two ("weary" and "hungry") are common characteristics of the poor (Heb. *'ani*), and the latter two ("widows" and "fatherless") describe categories of persons whose vulnerability in society is linked to their lack of any male representative. The law frequently enjoins Israelites—and kings in particular—to care for the needy and to protect the rights of those left defenseless in society: "Do not deprive the alien or the fatherless of justice, or take the cloak of the widow as a pledge" (Deut. 24:17; also 14:28–29; 26:12–13; 27:19). Eliphaz accuses Job of having no compassion or even a sense of responsibility toward these groups of persons in need.

The central verse of this subsection (v. 8) recalls Job's importance and influence in society *before* his calamity. His wealth and possessions had made him a force to be reckoned with in his community, **a powerful man**. Some commentators suggest that this verse implies that Job entered into abusive power relationships to wrest family land from the poor and to expand his own holdings at their expense. Power—as we all know—can corrupt the powerful and, as the "greatest man among all the people of the East" (1:3), Job was capable of doing either great good or great harm. Eliphaz suggests that all of Job's greatness is *self*-focused so that he has no compassion for the unfortunate, and that he refuses to use his power to benefit the powerless "widows" and "fatherless." Once again the reader must be aware that Eliphaz's accusations do not line up with what we have come to know of Job in the prologue—he is *tam weyashar*—and thus innocent of these charges. Eliphaz, on the other hand, is unaware of the divine affirmation of Job and must consequently make his decisions regarding Job on the basis of his own firmly established worldview—one that can only associate extreme and extended pain and suffering with divine judgment for sin. Job suffers; Job refuses to admit any sin; Job thereby refuses any reconciliation to God; Job must therefore be sinful and deserving of any suffering he receives.

The picture of the abusive powerful that Eliphaz builds up and then links to Job is one Job himself would acknowledge and decry in others. In Job's experience, however, such abuse of power and exploitation of the poor and powerless receive no divine punishment. As Job has just indicated in chapter 21, the wicked live long, pain-free, and prosperous lives and are even honored in death. Job would heartily agree that wicked persons such as the ones Eliphaz describes *ought* to suffer and die as punishment for their sins. Job simply disagrees, on the one hand, that in real experience such divine justice is consistently meted out. On the other hand, Job continues to deny that he should be counted among the wicked.

22:10–11 / **That is why** . . . Eliphaz concludes his direct accusations of Job with a summary linking Job's sufferings with his supposed abusive conduct. The introductory phrase (Heb. ʿal ken) means something like "for these previously stated reasons" or "on the basis of the evidence just presented." Having exposed your utter wickedness, Eliphaz is saying, we now know why you are surrounded by **snares** and subjected to **sudden peril.** Verse 10 compares these "snares" and "peril" to impenetrable **dark** and an overwhelming **flood of water.**

Additional Notes §77

22:6 / There is certainly a play on words here, since *the* Satan uses the same term **for no reason** (Heb. *khinnam*) to question Job's willingness to "fear God for nothing" (1:9). Both *the* Satan and Eliphaz insinuate that Job is a person motivated by *self-interest* and *profit* rather than true faithfulness to God and the covenant.

22:11 / The Heb. of the first phrase (ʾo khoshek loʾ tirʾeh) means "or darkness *so that* you cannot see," while the second (shipʿat-mayim tekasseka) means "a quantity/abundance of water *so that* it will cover you."

§78 Job among the Wicked (Job 22:12–20)

22:12 / In this section, Eliphaz interacts directly with statements from Job's most recent discourse in chapter 21 (particularly vv. 14–18). The segment begins with a description of the elevated loftiness of God who is **in the heights of heaven.** He sits among the **highest stars,** whose visible presence in the night sky impresses upon earth-bound humans the moral and spatial distance that separates them from their God (Ps. 8). From this vantage point, Eliphaz suggests, God is able to survey the whole earth and is thus privy to all the acts of humankind. Nothing they do escapes him!

22:13–14 / **Yet you say, "What does God know?"** The description of God's elevated position is intended to put the lie to this claim that his accuser places in Job's mouth. The statement, however, is a less than accurate summary of Job's complaint in chapter 21. There he did not claim that God was *unaware* of human evil, only that he has failed thus far to exact punishment for it! Job had in fact assumed that God's knowledge exceeded that of humans (21:22) so that it was impossible to "teach knowledge to God." Eliphaz's words—"Yet you say"—echo Job's own words describing the rejection by the wicked of any divine authority over their lives ("Yet they say to God, 'Leave us alone!'" 21:14).

Eliphaz attributes to Job the notion that God is so withdrawn into **darkness** and **thick clouds** that **he does not see** the evil that humans do so that he is unable to **judge through such darkness.** For Job, however, darkness represents not divine ignorance, but judgment. Early on Job curses the day of his birth and wishes it had been shrouded in darkness and clouds—unable to come to the light of day (3:4–6). In 19:8, "darkness" is the means by which God "shrouded" Job's "paths" and rendered Job's understanding (and not God's!) opaque. Darkness is no hindrance to God's knowledge, since, "He reveals the deep things of darkness and brings deep shadows into the light" (12:22). God's lack of response to evil in general, and Job's experience of it in particular, cannot, therefore, be the result of divine ignorance. Consequently, the words Eliphaz places in Job's mouth are a bit twisted and may in fact represent a *third* viewpoint—over against Eliphaz and Job—concerning how to resolve the question of the delay of divine judgment.

Eliphaz's distorted quote of Job presents a picture of a decidedly transcendent deity, far removed from the human realm, moving about **the vaulted heavens** blissfully ignorant of human pain and suffering. Such a view runs contrary to that actually espoused by Job on at least one major point. Job's complaint is grounded in his firm belief that God is well aware of what is happening in the human sphere and quite capable of acting to affect the world. Thus Job's real question is: What kind of God can know that evil lurks in the world bringing low the righteous *without acting in response?*

22:15–16 / Eliphaz cautions Job that an attitude that dismisses God's awareness of or concern for human activity is doomed to failure and is tantamount to taking the well-worn **path that evil men have trod.** Job is in danger of entering this path of denial, Eliphaz infers, and must now decide to turn back in order to have any hope of escaping the inevitable consequences. If he refuses to turn aside, Job will experience the same fate as these wicked who **were carried off before their time** (untimely death is often considered the result of divine punishment for sin), and whose **foundations** have been **washed away by a flood.**

22:17–18 / **Leave us alone! What can the Almighty do to us?** These wicked, says Eliphaz, deny the power of God to intervene in human affairs, failing to see that God is the source of all the **good things**—the wealth and provisions—with which they **filled their houses.** Job himself similarly describes the wicked's rejection of God in 21:14: "Yet they say to God, 'Leave us alone! We have no desire to know your ways.' " By associating Job with the rebellious wicked, Eliphaz intends to subject Job to self-condemnation. Assuming the inevitability of judgment on such self-focused and unrepentant wicked persons, Eliphaz takes care to **stand aloof from the counsel of the wicked,** claiming to disassociate himself from them completely.

22:19–20 / **The righteous see their ruin and rejoice.** From their positions of aloofness the righteous are able to observe the anticipated destruction of the wicked. Eliphaz is, of course, describing the logical outworking of retributive theology, according to which the righteous prosper while the wicked perish. In such a world it seems easy to distinguish between these two opposing groups, since what they receive in life indicates their character and God's response to it. The picture of the righteous rejoicing at the destruction of the wicked may give us pause (as well it might), since it does not seem to accord well with Jesus' command that we love our enemies. In this context and worldview, however, these wicked are the enemies of God who have rejected his working in their lives. The rejoicing is an expression of thanksgiving for the sure structures of retribution that offer security and hope to Eliphaz and his compatriots. It is clear by this point in the dialogue that Eliphaz considers Job to be moving toward the wicked. His graphic description of the destruction of the **foes** of the righteous and the burning of **their wealth** by **fire** is a commentary on Job's own experience (chs. 1 and 2) and a warning for him to acknowledge his sin and to seek restoration on the right path.

Additional Notes §78

22:12 / God's elevated position in the heavens is often related to the path of the sun overhead. In Mesopotamian mythology, the sun god (Sumerian *Utu* or Semitic *Shamash*) is considered the divine judge, since he arcs overhead during the day and sees all that humans do in the world. This is why evildoers often reserve their activities for the nighttime darkness when the sun god is unable to see them (Pss. 19, 104, 139; John 3:19–20). Similarly in Egypt the sun god (Ra, or Atum) surveys the world from the heights of heaven and notes what humans are about. The rather unique *Hymn to the Aton* written by the reformist (or heretic—depending on which side you were on!) Pharaoh, Akh-en-aten, has some clear parallels with Ps. 104 and illustrates the same theme of the sun as heavenly observer of human activity (*ANET*, pp. 369–71).

22:18 / The phrase **counsel of the wicked** is the same as that employed in Ps. 1:1 to describe the righteous one "who does not walk in the counsel of the wicked" (Heb. *beʿatsat reshaʿim*, in both cases). Both verses assume that the duty of the righteous is to avoid association with those self-focused persons who deny the power of God in their lives.

22:20 / Destruction by **fire,** in Job and elsewhere in Scripture, often indicates *divine* presence (e.g., Exod. 3:2; 13:21; 19:18; 24:17) and particularly *divine* punishment (e.g., Exod. 32:20; Num. 11:1–3; 16:35; Deut. 4:11–15, 24; 7:5, 25). Eliphaz used the image of divine destruction by fire in 15:34, as did Bildad (18:15) and Zophar (20:26). Job, however, never employs fire imagery in this way.

§79 Submit and Be at Peace (Job 22:21–30)

22:21–22 / Submit. The opening imperative of verse 21 (Heb. *hasken*) is variously translated "Submit" (NIV), "Yield" (NASB), "Make peace" (NJB), or "Agree" (RSV). According to Clines, "this is the language one uses for friends who have fallen out with one another" rather than repentance or submission. [D. J. A. Clines graciously provided the author with an electronic pre-publication copy of his *Job 21–37* (Word Biblical Commentary; Nashville, Tenn.: Nelson, 2006).—Ed.] See Clines, *Job 21–37*, p. 562. It seems to me that "agree" is the best option here. Eliphaz still hopes that Job will be reconciled with God, although he stands on the brink of disaster. If Job lays aside his differences, then he will **be at peace** with God, with the result that he will experience **prosperity** once again.

Eliphaz cautions Job to be receptive to divine instruction (Heb. *torah*). His opening imperative, **accept,** is softened by the addition of the particle *na'* (marking an entreaty or exhortation), so that the demand has a more pleading tone. While the Hebrew for **instruction** (*torah*) is often used to describe the commandments of Yahweh embedded in the Torah (Law) of Moses, here the word most likely refers to the instruction of the sages, of whom Yahweh is chief. As sages commonly memorize and meditate upon the traditional teachings of those sages who have gone before, Job is encouraged to treasure (another imperative, NIV "lay up") the divine **words** of wisdom in his **heart**. The heart, as we have seen (see the discussion on on 11:13–14 in §38), is the place of deep reflection where moral decisions are made. The problem for Job is that, although he would *like* a word from God, he receives instead only unexplained trouble and pain. Eliphaz's admonition implies that Job's suffering is indeed an expression of the divine will and a word from God that Job ought to hear and accept.

22:23–24 / If you return to the Almighty. Eliphaz's admonition continues with two conditional phrases indicating a bright future in return for Job's willingness to change his stance.

To "return" is to reorient oneself on a new path directed toward God. Eliphaz assumes that Job needs such a change of direction to leave the "old path" (v. 15) that the wicked follow. Then, he says, **you will be restored** (Heb. Niphal imperfect *tibbaneh,* "you will be *re*built" [emphasis added]). Eliphaz qualifies the nature of this return he envisions with further conditions.

Clines suggests that the conditional statements end with verse 23a and that the statements in verses 23b–25 are instead *promises* that will result from turning to God (*Job 21–37,* pp. 564–66). However, most commentators and translations, as Clines himself admits, understand these verses as continued conditional statements. Although **if you remove wickedness far from your tent** may seem to imply that Job is presently committing evil that he needs to stop, the verb (*tarkhiq,* "put far away; make distant") means to keep "wickedness" (*ʿawlah*) at a distance. Zophar made a similar appeal in his first speech (11:13–14) using very similar terms: "if you put away (*tarkhiq*) the sin that is in your hand and allow no evil (*ʿawlah*) to dwell in your tent." Of course, since the reader already knows that Job is a righteous person who consistently "shuns evil" (1:1, 8; 2:3), Eliphaz's admonition is misguided.

Besides avoiding association with wickedness, Eliphaz warns Job to give up any expectation of wealth and prosperity: **assign your nuggets to the dust.** It does seem a bit odd, as Clines notes (*Job 21–37,* pp. 564–66), that Job, who has lost everything of profit or value, should be exhorted to lay his gold in "dust." If these are indeed promises, the sense would be that Job's gold will be as abundant as dust, and as plentiful as **rocks in the ravines.**

22:25–26 / Eliphaz employs an extended wordplay to draw his exhortation along. He encourages Job to give up his hopes in, or reliance on, wealth or gold (NIV "nuggets," Heb. *betser*) by casting it among the "rocks" (Heb. *betsur*) of the ravines. If he is willing to do this, **then the Almighty will be your gold** (Heb. *betser*) and **choicest silver.** This whole conversation plays around *the* Satan's initial question (1:9) concerning whether completely selfless allegiance to God is possible for humans. Eliphaz restates the question in its crassest, most materialistic terms: is Job willing to give up material wealth in order to gain the treasure of God's very self? But this return to the original question—that Job effectively answered by faithfully enduring the tests in chapters 1 and 2—seems to miss the point of the continuing dialogue. Job has long since moved beyond the question of material wealth and is now seeking something at once more modest and yet infinitely more important: a public acknowledgement of his essential righteousness, even in his impoverished state.

Eliphaz continues by unpacking the value of God to a faithful Job in relational terms. Job will **find delight in the Almighty**, rather than the continuing hostility he currently experiences. The Hebrew here (*ʿal shadday titʿaggag*) means "to take exquisite delight in the Almighty." The phrase appears only one other time, in Isaiah 58:14, in a very similar context. There Yahweh speaks through the prophet to encourage his people to return to their faithful relationship with him. In a similarly conditional statement, God says, "If you keep your feet from breaking the Sabbath and from doing as you please on my holy day, . . . and if you honor it by not going your own way and not doing as you please or speaking idle words, then you will find your joy in the LORD (*titʿaggag ʿal yhwh*)." Both the Job and the Isaiah passages introduce the result of turning to God with the temporal adjective *ʾaz*, **then,** making the connection between these contexts even clearer. The parallel with Israel suggests that Eliphaz assumes Job *is* sinning and needs to stop in order to experience restoration. The NIV obscures a causal link between God becoming Job's "gold" and Job "finding delight" in the Almighty. In the Hebrew text, verse 25 begins with the particle *ki* ("for; because") that most often introduces a causal clause. In this case the Almighty becomes Job's "gold" *because* Job returns to a state of finding "delight" in God. Once again the emphasis is upon renewed *relationship* rather than human profit or gain. This construction is also used in the first speech of Zophar (11:15), a passage to which Eliphaz seems to make frequent reference here.

The conclusion of verse 26 provides a transition to the next two verses. Having returned to a relationship of "delight" with God, Job will **lift up** his **face** to bask in God's glorious presence like the warm and healing rays of the sun. Lifting up one's "face to God" is an indication that one is free from guilt and prepared for an open relationship of blessing. Note, in contrast, Ezra's response to recognizing the postexilic Jerusalem community's guilt before God: "O my God, I am too ashamed and disgraced to lift up my face to you, my God, because our sins are higher than our heads and our guilt has reached to the heavens" (Ezra 9:6). Once again, Eliphaz seems to be drawing on Zophar's first speech, which instructed Job that putting away evil and returning to God would allow him to "lift up [his] face without shame" and to "stand firm . . . without fear" (11:15).

22:27–28 / In the last four verses of his speech, Eliphaz turns from *relational restoration* to the effective consequences of being at peace with God. A restored Job will be able to communicate with God, and will intercede successfully for the deliverance of others. **You will pray . . . and he will hear.** The restored relationship Eliphaz envisions will result in renewed communication between Job and God. The tense silence Job now experiences will be replaced by divine response to his pleading. The structure of interaction here is reminiscent of the lament form: the supplicant pleads to God for deliverance from trouble; God hears and graciously responds; in gratitude, the supplicant is to **fulfill vows** made to God during the time of trouble (Ps. 66, esp. vv. 13–15). In the lament psalms, fulfilling one's "vows" most often means offering a *Todah* sacrifice of thanksgiving in the temple, accompanied by a song testifying to the deliverance granted by God. Eliphaz encourages Job by assuring him that returning to God will lead to just such a celebratory event.

What you decide on will be done. Not only will channels of communication be opened between Job and God, but God will respond positively to Job's prayers. The NIV's "What you decide on" is a little pallid for the meaning of the Hebrew verb *gzr*. In Esther, this same root describes what King Xerxes "had decreed" concerning his rebellious wife, Vashti (Esth. 2:1). Eliphaz pictures God as hastening to carry out the decisions and decrees of Job.

Eliphaz returns to the sun imagery of verse 26 when he says that **light will shine on** Job's **ways.** There Job lifted up his face to God as to the warmth of the sun. Here restored relationship means that God's light and warmth will shine on all that Job does. This would be a remarkable change in contrast to Job's current experience that is consistently painted in somber terms of darkness. It also contrasts with Eliphaz's use of darkness as an indication of divine judgment for sin in verse 11.

22:29 / There are textual difficulties in the last two verses of chapter 22. The Hebrew of the opening half of verse 29 reads something like: "They bring low and you say 'Arrogance!'" Translators offer a variety of improvements, most depending rather circularly on what the sentence is thought to mean. Some assume the intercessory activity of Job is intended, and thus render the initial verb in the passive ("[When] they [others] are brought low . . .") and read the noun "pride/arrogance" as an imperative: "Lift up!" (This is the approach NIV takes.) According to this interpretation, therefore, Job calls for the elevation of those who are abased and God responds by saving **the downcast.**

Others understand *Job* as the one who is **brought low,** but he responds confidently because it is a source of pride to be abased since God **will save** "the downcast" (NKJV). Still others omit any reference to Job speaking and understand the verse proverbially: "For God abases the proud, but he saves the lowly" (RSV). It is important to note that the construction translated "the downcast" by NIV is more literally rendered "the cast down of eyes." In light of the description of lifting the face to God as an indication of one's innocence, it would seem that God is delivering those who acknowledge their guilt rather than those who have been oppressed by others.

22:30 / He will deliver even one who is not innocent. This translation comes out of another difficult text. The particle *ʾi,* which is taken as "not" here, occurs nowhere else in the OT with this meaning. Some translators omit this particle altogether and read "He [God] delivers the innocent" (NASB; RSV). In this case, God's treatment of the innocent becomes an encouragement to Job to take stock of his own circumstances, since "you will be delivered through the cleanness of your hands" (RSV).

On the other hand, those who understand *ʾi* to be negative assume that Eliphaz believes a restored Job will become such an effective intermediary that even those who are "not innocent" **will be delivered** due to the **cleanness of** Job's **hands.** Perhaps, however, the solution is to be found in the comparison between verses 29 and 30. In verse 29, God delivers those who are "cast down of eyes"—who acknowledge their guilt. It may be in verse 30 that those who are "not innocent" are those who *acknowledge their guilt* like their counterparts in the preceding verse. In both of these instances, however, the effective factor in motivating God to gracious action is Job's ability to contact and influence God through restored relationship.

While Eliphaz seems to return at the end of his speech to his belief that Job can be restored to right relationship with God, and thus experience a renewed effectiveness in intermediation for others, the harsh and contrasting images he introduced earlier in the chapter (vv. 5–11) of Job as hardened oppressor suggest an ongoing suspicion that Job is less innocent than he claims. This assessment aligns with the growing accusations of the other friends, but it stands in contradiction to the reader's privileged insight into Job's character afforded by the prologue (1:1, 8; 2:3).

Additional Notes §79

22:21 / The last phrase of the verse is a bit difficult. The verb form consistently translated **will come to you** (Heb. *teboʾatka*) contains an unexplained -*at* expansion before the second-person masculine singular pronominal suffix -*ka*. This has led some to identify the form as a miswritten form of the noun *tebuʾa* (construct *tebuʾat*) meaning "increase; income," in which case the phrase would mean: "your increase (will be) good."

22:27 / The word translated **pray** (Heb. *taʿtir*) has more the emphatic sense of "plead; petition."

22:28 / The Heb. that NIV translates **will be done** is not a passive, and a better rendering would be in the active, as "he will establish it." Job does not simply create events by speaking like God in Gen. 1, but God establishes what Job decrees.

§80 Taking God to Court (Job 23:1–7)

23:1 / One can hardly call Job's words in chapters 23 and 24 a *response* to Eliphaz's third speech. Job takes no notice of his friend or his argument, but he begins instead to consider the feasibility and benefit of bringing God to court so he might hope to find just resolution to his complaint. In chapter 23 Job reflects, at first confidently but ultimately with increasing terror, on the difficulty of locating God and securing his presence for the legal proceedings.

23:2 / Job says, **my complaint is bitter.** Once again the Hebrew text is less than transparent. The word translated "bitter" (Heb. *meri*) normally means "rebellious; obstinate" (NASB; NJB). The NIV assumes instead a form of the adjective/noun *mar*, "bitter; bitterness." For **his hand is heavy,** most translations (like NIV) emend the original Hebrew *yadi*, "my hand" to *yado*, "his [God's] hand" (emphasis added), although there is no textual evidence in support of this change. NKJV follows the Hebrew and interprets the "heavy hand" as a reference to Job's listlessness in the face of suffering.

23:3 / **If only I knew where to find him.** The continuation of his ceaseless suffering leads Job to consider how to bring God into court so that a just verdict might resolve this suffering. The immediate difficulty that arises, however, is how to serve the subpoena on a transcendent deity who remains so truly hidden. The first "if only" is the translation of the Hebrew idiom *mi yitten,* "who will give"—an interrogative expressing the desperate desire of the speaker, who has no real hope of fulfillment. In **if only I could go to his dwelling,** the Hebrew for "dwelling" (*tekunah*) refers to a fixed place where one can always be found (like a permanent address). In this sense, God's "dwelling" is certainly outside Job's world and thus beyond approach. Eliphaz envisioned God as *up* in the heavens, from which vantage point he could observe all that humans did (22:12). Like a frustrated process server unable to serve papers on an elusive witness, Job senses his hopes for confrontation are futile unless God is willing to make his presence known. The implications are clear: God does not always appear present to humans and his presence can be neither coerced nor commanded. God remains free to appear or not to appear, to act or not to act, as *he* wishes.

23:4–5 / I would state my case. If God could be found and forced to appear, Job would prepare an articulate case to present. Behind NIV's low-key "state" is the Hebrew verb ʿ*rk*, "lay out in order; arrange carefully." What Job would carefully lay out before God is *mishpat*—a legal term describing the statement of what should have occurred in a particular case (see the discussion on 13:17–18 in §44). Usually the judge pronounces *mishpat* after having considered all of the evidence in a case. Here Job uses the term to describe his own presentation of the facts of his circumstance, which he assumes cannot be denied. Job is ready to fill his **mouth with arguments,** to answer any criticisms of his case that might arise. Certainly his dialogue with the friends thus far proves his ability to press his views in light of unremitting opposition.

I would find out what he would answer me. A legal confrontation would afford Job the opportunity to express his own views, but it would also allow him to hear and **consider** the divine case. Both of these aspects of communication are missing at this point in Job's experience, and both are important elements of the intimate relationship Job seeks. As in a marriage or any relationship, it is important for Job to be heard by God and to hear God in return. In fact, this is what ultimately happens in the theophany. Despite God's bombastic approach, it is clear that his coming is a response to Job's complaint and desire for meeting. Job has been heard! Job also sees and hears God in return, even if Job's specific questions are not directly addressed. Job says he would **consider what he would say.** It seems more important in this context for Job to *hear* God than to *understand* God. To engage God in meaningful conversation is of more significance than achieving complete understanding. Thus the fact that Job will "consider" the divine response does not assume that he will either understand or agree with it. This is important in light of the nature of his eventual theophanic encounter with God in chapters 38–42.

23:6–7 / Would he oppose me . . . ? Job is confident that such an encounter as he envisions would not result in divine opposition. The NIV renders the Hebrew *yarib*, which means

something like "legally accuse someone of breach of covenant," as
"oppose." The prophets often employ the verb and its related
noun, *rib,* to describe Yahweh's contention against his rebellious
people for their failure to keep their covenant obligations. The obligations at issue in the Prophets are the commandments laid
down in the Mosaic Torah. The book of Job uses these terms infrequently (13:19; 23:6; 31:15; 33:13), and with the more general
meaning "raise questions about one's fulfillment of their obligations of relationship." Job's confidence in this instance is more the
result of his satisfaction that his case is unimpeachable than his
trust in the nature of God. Job's earlier comment, "I know I will be
vindicated. Can anyone bring charges against me? If so, I will be silent and die" (13:18–19), implies the same kind of confidence. The
Hebrew phrase *yarib ʿimmadi* in 13:19 is also found here in verse 6,
press charges against me.

Would he oppose me with great power? Clines understands this phrase to mean great *legal* power (*Job 21–37,* p. 595). As
both defendant and deciding judge, God is thoroughly in charge
and capable of determining the outcome of the proceedings regardless of Job's presentation. Job has covered this ground in a
more pessimistic way in his response to Bildad's first speech,
where he expects to be condemned by God regardless of his innocence (9:2–3, 14–16, 19–21):

> But how can a mortal be righteous before God? Though one
> wished to dispute with him, he could not answer him one time
> out of a thousand. . . . How then can I find words to argue with
> him? Though I were innocent, I could not answer him; I could
> only plead with my Judge for mercy. Even if I summoned him and
> he responded, I do not believe he would give me a hearing. . . .
> Even if I were innocent, my mouth would condemn me; if I were
> blameless, it would pronounce me guilty.

His anxieties there are largely due to his sense of the overwhelming power of God, against which no human can stand. While
nothing seems to have changed with regard to God's dominance,
perhaps Job has been emboldened by his success in silencing his
friends to invest more confidence in the persuasive character of
his case. In any event, he appears now to hope that God will not
use abusive power to subvert justice.

No, he would not "press charges." Here we have another
phrase that is difficult for two reasons. In the first instance, the positioning of the negative (*loʾ*) before the particle *ʾak,* "surely,"
raises the question of whether "no" is an independent and em-

phatic rejection of the preceding question ("Would he oppose me with great power? No!"), or whether it serves to negate the following phrase ("[Surely] he would not press charges against me"). A brief survey of ten different translations reveals that only the NIV takes the negative as governing the second half of verse 6. All of the others render the latter part of this verse in some positive way, often with the sense of "Surely he will give heed to me" (including KJV; NKJV; NAB; NASB; RSV; NRSV; NJB; YLT).

The second difficulty in this part of the verse is the phrase *yasim bi* (NIV "press charges against me"). Translated literally, "He [God] will set with me," there appears to be some omission here. Many supply *libbo*, "his [God's] heart," so that the result ("set his heart with me") describes God giving close attention to Job. The NIV translation reads the preposition *b-* in *bi* as an adversative meaning "against me," which explains the application of the preceding negative to this phrase. Even so, NIV must supply a missing word equivalent to the translation "charges" in order to fill this phrase out. Regardless of which alternative one adopts, it remains clear that Job anticipates an encounter in which he would be free to make his case without intimidation, and that he therefore hopes for a fair hearing.

There an upright man could present his case before him. By "there" Job means *wherever* this transcendent God can be run to ground and subpoenaed to appear. A legal setting or courtroom comes to mind. "Upright" (Heb. *yashar*) is what Job has claimed to be all along, and what the reader has known of his character since both the narrator and God confirmed it in chapters 1 and 2. Job's growing confidence and determination rest on his personal knowledge of his righteousness as well as on the persuasive effect of his argument as honed in debate with the friends.

And, he says, **I would be delivered forever.** The verb here (*waʾapalletah*) is cohortative in form and expresses the will or desire of the speaker. While the Hebrew *netsakh*, "forever," does not have the technical sense of "eternity," it does indicate a stable endurance, perhaps equivalent to "in perpetuity." Others understand the term to mean "successful," with the sense that Job is expecting to win his court contest. The **judge** is, of course, God himself. The consonantal text of this phrase (*mishopti*) could also be read as "my case" (*mishpati*).

Additional Notes §80

23:3 / All of the Heb. imperfect forms in vv. 2–7 represent subjunctive expressions of possible future events that are less than likely to occur. All depend on God being found and cornered into a meeting.

There is only one *mi yitten* at the beginning of this verse, but it seems to govern both halves of the verse. See the discussion on 14:4 in §47 with regard to *mi yitten*.

This difficulty in locating God may indicate an exilic origin for the book of Job. Most often God's **dwelling** is associated with the temple, or the heavenly abode that is linked for humans to the temple. With the temple destroyed, or at least far removed from the Diaspora community, the exiles might well lament, **if only I knew where to find him . . . if only I could go to his dwelling!**

23:7 / NRSV takes *mishopti*, "from my judge," to mean "by the agency of my judge" so that the verse describes the ruling of the judge [God] in Job's favor.

§81 Faith in Spite of an Invisible God (Job 23:8–12)

23:8–9 / All of Job's hopes for a favorable settlement of his case hinge on the feasibility of bringing God into a face-to-face meeting in court. Despite his confidence in his innocence and the persuasive nature of his case, Job is becoming less hopeful that God will show up to hear his arguments. These two verses imagine the fruitlessness of any search to discover God's whereabouts in the world of human experience.

While the directional terms **east, west, north,** and **south** translate the sense of the Hebrew into terms that are meaningful for our modern directional thinking, the Hebrew words describe the personal positioning of the individual (see, e.g., RSV and NASB). "East" is *qedem,* or what is "before" a person, while "west" translates *ʾakhor,* or what is "behind." Similarly, "north" is *semoʾl,* "left hand," and "south" is *yamin,* "right hand" (G. H. Wilson, "Orientation," *ISBE* 3, p. 615). No matter which direction Job explores, his hidden God is nowhere to be found. This search emphasizes poignantly the deep sense of isolation and abandonment Job is experiencing—especially in contrast to the affirmation of the inescapability of divine presence the psalmist offers Psalm 139:7–12.

But if I go . . . he is not there. Job begins by describing the futility of searching for God. His failure to find God is not for lack of trying. Humans cannot find God through their own endeavor, but only through God's gracious self-revelation. The flip side of this gracious divine condescension—as Job knows only too well—is that when God chooses to remain hidden, humans cannot force an appearance.

When he is at work . . . when he turns. God's apparent absence does not mean that he is not still at work in human affairs. Job knows God is active, but this only sharpens his personal sense of abandonment. **I do not see . . . I catch no glimpse.** One gets the sense of Job frantically scanning the horizon to no avail. Wherever Job looks, God's work and person remain obscure.

23:10–12 / **But he knows the way that I take.** God may not be visible to Job, but God sees Job. From his distant isolation in the heavens (or from around the corner, or just over the next hill!), God observes and "knows" what Job is doing. The "way" (Heb. *derek*) is a life path directed toward a particular goal and conclusion. Job has properly oriented his life toward God and therefore he is blameless. Job assumes that since God observes everything, he surely knows this and must confirm Job's righteous behavior.

When he refers to the fact that God **has tested me,** Job does not know that a conversation between *the* Satan and God set this test of his present suffering in motion. What he means here is that God, in his constant observation of humans, is able to weigh and analyze human actions in order to determine their true motivation. Job described this divine scrutiny of humans more negatively in an earlier speech (7:18). Later, Elihu will call for an extreme testing of Job "to the utmost" as punishment for what Elihu considers wicked answers (34:36). The verb for "testing" in all these instances (Heb. *bkhn,* "prove; test; try") usually occurs in the context of metallurgy and the assay of precious metals, in particular gold. This process of "testing" subjects the metal-bearing ore to extreme heat to burn off impurities so that only the refined metal remains. Job is confident that such testing will prove him faithful.

My feet have closely followed his steps. Job employs two images to describe his careful pursuit of the "way" established by God. Like the child trying to follow precisely in the footsteps of a parent, Job claims to have "closely followed" God's "steps" (lit., "my feet have grasped his steps"). Similarly, he claims to have followed the path blazed by God **without turning aside.** Making God the model for his own steps assures Job that his life path is without offense to God.

I have not departed. Job now speaks more directly of the manner in which he has kept to the path set by God. Here he describes following the divinely marked path as keeping God's **commands.** While God's "commands" (Heb. *mitswah*) might refer to the divine expectations laid out in *the* Torah, they are most likely the wise instruction of the divine sage to whom Eliphaz referred Job in 22:22.

I have treasured. In a parallel but *positive* image, Job claims to have "stored up" **the words of his mouth** as one would amass treasure (as in 22:25) or accumulate necessary provisions for the future. The word translated by NIV as **more than my daily bread** (Heb. *mekhuqqi*) represents a textual problem as the varied translations indicate. The Hebrew word normally means "statute, ordinance" and by extension "limit, boundary." Neither option seems appropriate here, so some translations read instead *bekheqi,* "in my bosom" (Ps. 74:11)—the place where Job treasures or stores the divine word (NJB; RSV). Others (including NIV) ground their reading in a very rare use of *khoq,* "statute; ordinance," to refer to the portion of a sacrifice allotted to the priest and translate "more than my necessary food" (NASB) or **more than my daily bread** (NIV).

There is an artful chiastic arrangement of the segments of verses 11–12 as the phrases move from positive to negative and then from negative to positive. "I have kept to his way / without turning aside / I have not departed from the commands / I have treasured the words of his mouth."

At the end of chapter 23, Job's renewed consideration of the absolute freedom of God, that renders any human attempts to sway him not only futile but also fearsome, tempers his confidence.

23:13 / The construction **he stands alone** is difficult, largely because of the obscurity of the phrase *beʾekhad* (lit., "in/with/by one"). Translators have generally followed one of two paths. The NIV (along with the NASB; NRSV; RSV; NKJV and others) understands the expression as one of divine uniqueness or immutability. Others (Pope, *Job*; Clines, *Job 21–37*; NAB; NJB; REB) emend the Hebrew to *bakhar*, "he has decided," and take it to mean that a divine decision, once taken, is unchangeable.

The Hebrew is not as confrontational as the NIV translation, **who can oppose him?**, suggests. The verb (*yashib*, "cause to return/turn aside") has more the sense of persuading someone to change rather than opposition. The idea is that God is a free agent who acts out of his own will and is not subject to human pressure or persuasion. Despite his confidence in the validity of his cause and the unimpeachable nature of his arguments, Job must acknowledge that ultimately God **does whatever he pleases.**

23:14 / **He carries out his decree against me.** If God is free to do what he wants, then what Job is currently experiencing must represent the will and purpose of God. How can Job hope to change the unchangeable God? He fears that **many such plans he still has in store.** The freedom of God is a cause of great anxiety. It is comforting to accept, as do the friends, a rather mechanistic cause-and-effect view of God which enables humans to more accurately predict God's responses. To accept God's freedom from manipulation and control is to acknowledge one's vulnerability in the extreme. Job's acceptance that his current state may reflect the inscrutable will and purpose of a sovereign God leaves him with the unsettling conclusion that more of the same may yet be "in store" (lit., "and such as these, many [are] with him").

23:15 / **That is why I am terrified.** Job realizes and articulates the fact that the freedom of God to act in uncontrollable
ways is a source of great terror for humans. The Hebrew for **when
I think of all this** is, more literally, "I perceive; comprehend." Job
is therefore coming to an understanding of what God's freedom
means for humans who are dependent on him. When Job truly
understands his vulnerability, fear is the result: **I fear him.** Unfortunately, NIV's choice to use "fear" to translate the Hebrew *pkhd*
obscures the important distinction between this kind of "dread"
or "anxiety" and the "fear of God" (always the verb *yr³*) that is
the appropriate attitude of reliance on the grace and mercy of
God. Job is *not* claiming that dwelling almost compulsively on
God's freedom encourages Job to adopt an appropriate attitude
of reliance. Instead, this kind of "fear" can create a barrier of terrible dread that separates rather than binds together God and
human being.

23:16 / **God has made my heart faint . . . has terrified
me.** The anxious dread that Job experiences is not an attitude he
chooses, but a response to the activity of God. God's freedom that
allows Job to suffer so desperately, even though he is righteous,
produces an unstable world which reduces even the faithful heart
to quivering.

23:17 / **Yet I am not silenced by the darkness.** Unfortunately chapter 23 closes with another difficult passage. The most
significant problems are: (1) the meaning of the verb *nitsmatti* (NIV
"be silenced"; NJB "destroy"; RSV "be hemmed in"); (2) the function of the negative particle *lo³*, "not," in the first half of the verse;
and (3) a difficult prepositional phrase (*mippenay,* "from my face")
that begins the second half of the verse. There are three primary
interpretive options here. First, it may mean that Job remains determined in the face of the terrors of darkness that threaten (so
NIV; NASB). This option requires retaining the negative particle as
active in both halves of the verse; assuming the translation "be
silenced"; and emending the prepositional phrase *mippenay* to
the object of the verb "cover" in the second half of the verse. The
second option is that Job desires to hide himself in darkness from
divine terror (so NAB; NRSV). This option is accomplished by understanding the negative particle as an *asseverative* form expressing the desire of the speaker ("Oh that . . ." or "If only . . ."). The
third option is to eliminate the negative particle altogether, in
which case Job is simply acknowledging the continuing threat of

overwhelming darkness (so RSV). In light of Job's continuing desire to argue his case in the presence of God, the NIV translation
seems to capture the undiminished determination of this beaten
but unbowed combatant.

Additional Notes §82

23:17 / See the rather lengthy but astute and comprehensive
discussion of the issues and possibilities in the notes of Clines' commentary on this verse (Clines, *Job 21–37*, pp. 580–81).

§83 No Time Set for Judgment (Job 24:1–17)

While there is a general consensus that the first 17 verses of the chapter represent the speech of Job, some translations and commentaries make a variety of attempts to reassign parts of the material in chapter 24 to speakers other than Job. Scholars claim that rearrangement is necessary because the sentiments in certain verses (particularly vv. 18–24) are contrary to those Job expresses earlier in the chapter. Some (including Clines, *Job 21–37*, pp. 667–69) reassign these verses to create a later speech for Zophar, who is otherwise entirely omitted from the third cycle of speeches. Others (e.g., NJB) shift verses 18–24 to follow chapter 27, but apparently retain Job as speaker (although the point of such an adjustment without change of speaker is not clear and would seem to undermine the reason for the emendation). Those who leave these verses in their present context as the speech of Job do so either by allowing contradictions to stand without explanation or by reinterpreting the passage in line with Job's primary views.

There is no evidence from any known manuscripts to support these various rearrangements. Rather, they rely wholly on the commentators' assumptions regarding what is or is not an appropriate view for Job to hold. These hypothetical reconstructions are exactly that—hypothetical—and may tell us as much about the assumptions of the constructor(s) as they do about the purposes and meanings of the book of Job. For this reason, I prefer to read these verses as they currently stand in the Hebrew text and seek to understand any tensions these verses raise in terms of their implications for the meaning of the book in its canonical form. This is not an easy task, and we must exercise humility in our attempts to bring clarity to this difficult text.

24:1 / On the question of **times for judgment,** the word "judgment" (*mishpat*) does not occur in the Hebrew, but is drawn by inference from the broader context. The more literal rendering would be: "Why are not times stored up by Shadday?" The "times"

might refer to what is appropriate for the various events of life—
assuming a quasi-determination by God. Or, more likely here,
they might describe moments of divine appearance, so that humans might know his coming in advance and anticipate his appearing. Alternatively, the "times" might represent moments set
aside for the judgment of human wrongs, such as those described
in the following verses. "Knowing the times" means understanding how to act appropriately in different life situations. Such times
are opportunities for human action or response and always involve decisions to choose the right way. Only the sages, with their
careful attention to and reflection on life's events and intricate relationships, are able to become "those who know the times" (Esth.
1:13). The "times" (or circumstances) of a human's life are "in the
hand" of God, or under his authority (Ps. 31:15; also Dan. 2:21;
7:25). But, since humans must choose how to respond to life's circumstances, life is not fixed or predetermined. The times humans
experience may be either good or bad (Prov. 24:10; Job 38:23; Eccl.
7:14), and one must choose the appropriate response to each
(Job 27:10; Prov. 17:17).

    Why does the Almighty not set . . . ? It may be that Job is as-
suming that God "stores up" or records human choices of wrong
actions. Thus these "times" (moments of decision) might serve as
the basis of divine judgment. Job seems to be saying that it appears God takes no notice of human choices for good or evil, since
the righteous suffer while the evil live on without punishment.

    To **know** God is to enter into an intimate experiential rela-
tionship with him that involves both reliance and loyalty. This is no
intellectual knowledge *about* God, but the kind of mutual knowing
that grows from long-term commitment. Hosea describes Israel's
sinful state that deserves judgment as "*lack* of knowledge," or a failure to acknowledge, and expresses his greatest condemnation of
the people of God when he says "there is . . . no acknowledgement
of God in the land" (Hos. 4:1 NIV). The consequence of such lack of
knowledge is destruction (Job 18:5–21; Hos. 4:6). Knowing God is
the essence of relationship, and is more vital even than ritual observance (Hos. 6:6; Amos 3:2). But God judges Israel's *claims* to know
him as false unless they also demonstrate faithfulness, loyalty, compassion, and justice (Hos. 4:1–3; 5:4; 6:1–6; 8:1–8).

    The assumption of "judgment" in the preceding phrase
means that NIV must render the second half of the verse compati-
bly, with **look in vain for such days.** The Hebrew says only that
"those who know him do not see his days." While this *could* refer

to times of judgment established by God—days that are nowhere to be seen—it is equally feasible that these "days" are simply times of divine appearance to humans. While it is true that Job goes on in the rest of this section to lament the unchallenged evil of humans, the emphasis in this verse seems to be on the absence of God from the scene and the resultant lack of "attention to business." If God did not choose to absent himself, then he would have to act in judgment on the wickedness that otherwise runs rampant.

24:2–4 / **Men move boundary stones.** The NIV needlessly masculinizes the indefinite plural of the Hebrew "they remove," while NJB identifies the actors as "the wicked." To obscure the inheritance boundaries established during the conquest is considered a covenant breach deserving of a curse (Deut. 19:14; 27:17; Prov. 22:28; 23:10). The verb behind "stolen" in **flocks they have stolen** suggests a particularly violent act of "stripping away." These thieves who keep their stolen property in plain sight (**they pasture**) exhibit a sort of open disdain.

Verses 3 and 4 describe acts of oppression directed toward the defenseless of society. The **orphan** has no father and **widow** no husband to provide identity and security in a male-dominated society. The **needy** and **poor** are powerless groups disenfranchised because of their lack of resources and social stature. These groups of disadvantaged persons are frequently understood to fall under the special concern of God, who oversees their well-being and acts to punish those who abuse or oppress them. Their inclusion here, as objects of exploitation by the wicked, emphasizes Job's point that God has so removed himself from active participation in human affairs that he fails to defend those who are forced to rely solely on him.

A **pledge** is an item of property offered as security for a loan. God commands the Israelites to exercise compassion in regards to pledges taken from the poor and defenseless (see the discussion on 22:6 in §77). These wicked persons Job is describing, however, feared no reprisal from God and arrogantly violated their covenant obligations and societal expectations.

They thrust . . . from the path. They further display their arrogance through lack of common courtesy—shoving the poor and powerless aside as they shoulder their way along. **And . . . into hiding.** The verb translated **force** (Heb. *khbʾ*) occurs in this particular stem (a *passive* Pual) only here, so the meaning is somewhat obscure. The subject of the verb is most likely **the poor of the land** rather than the wicked, as NIV assumes. Holladay captures the sense with his suggested translation, "[they] have to go into hiding" (lit., "they are made to be hiding ones," Holladay, *Concise Hebrew*, p. 93; see also NJB, "have to keep out of sight"). On the one hand, the implication may be that the wicked so hound the poor in order to exploit them that they must flee common society to escape constant victimization. On the other hand, this may be an attempt to express the very "invisibility" of the poor and powerless that we experience in our present context. Those who have enough often do not wish to be reminded of the suffering of the "less fortunate." Even this term we use deflects responsibility by assuming that poverty is the result of "fortune" or "chance" rather than exploitive persons and societal systems that allow such exploitation. Similarly, the term "marginalized" reflects how the poor are pushed to the periphery where they are less visible and can be more easily ignored.

24:5–8 / **Like wild donkeys in the desert.** The wild donkey, or onager, was known for its untamable character and occupation of remote, uninhabited wilderness areas (Job 11:12; 39:5–8; Hos. 8:19; Jer. 2:24). In Job 39:5–8, God will describe the onager as one of his precious creatures that continues to elude the exploitation of human utility. Even there, however, the emphasis is on the remoteness of the donkey's native habitat and the animal's ceaseless search for food. The poor, having taken themselves into hiding from the exploitation of the wicked in the previous verse, are **foraging food** in the desert steppe lands for a meager subsistence to keep their children alive. While Clines questions whether this picture is a real one in light of the later description of these same poor in obviously paid agricultural pursuits (vv. 6, 10–11; Clines, *Job 21–37*, pp. 605–6), it seems likely that those living on the desperate edges of society might resort to such scavenging in order to survive—especially during those months when agricultural labor was not available.

They gather fodder . . . and glean. This activity is not necessarily paid labor, but possibly gleaning allowed after the paid laborers finished the primary harvest. Verses 7–9 describe rough living conditions that would make sense for those who had taken themselves off to isolated areas to avoid oppression by the wicked. The remote areas of the southern Negev, the shores of the Dead Sea, and the Arabah of the Jordan were known as hideouts for such disaffected persons who fled society for reasons of debt, oppression, or political conflict. David, for example, while being pursued by Saul, withdraws to these same areas and is able to gather to himself a large body of similarly displaced persons (1 Sam. 18–31). It is certainly possible that we have an account of two groups of impoverished persons: those who escape oppression by withdrawing to remote regions and eking out a meager existence there; and those who support themselves by hiring out as agricultural laborers—perhaps even working on the lands they had lost to the oppressive wicked.

Lacking clothes . . . naked. It seems unlikely that significant groups of impoverished persons were reduced to absolute nakedness. This hyperbolic language, however, illustrates the plight of the poor and emphasizes the callous disregard of the wicked. The law commands creditors to return garments taken as pledges of repayment of debt to their owners at night so they can keep warm (e.g., Exod. 22:25–27). Those who have only the clothes on their backs to offer as security for a loan are certainly the most destitute. To strip such persons naked so that they have **nothing to cover themselves in the cold** is an act of great disgrace and humiliation. Clines (*Job 21–37*, p. 606) suggests rightly that it is unlikely the poor were left "stark naked" but merely without their protective outer cloak. Clearly these wicked exploiters have regard for neither human dignity nor the law.

Hounded into the hinterlands and without resources or protection, the poor find themselves at the mercy of the elements, **drenched by mountain rains.** "Mountain rains" are the heaviest and would most likely fall during the winter months when lower temperatures would be a complicating factor as well. Without **shelter,** the marginalized must live among the rocks or in caves.

24:9 / As Clines suggests (*Job 21–37*, p. 607 begins to repeat the pattern established in verses 2–8. That section began by describing the oppressive activity of the wicked and then shifted to an extended account of the plight of the oppressed poor. So here verse 9 describes the wicked taking advantage of the powerless, while verses 10–12 return to the distress of the oppressed. When the poor lack property, they have only their clothing to offer as pledges for loans. When even their garments have been given up, only their children, whose labor could apply toward the debt, remain. The language of infants **snatched from the breast** is surely hyperbolic, but it underlines the extreme suffering of the poor and the calumny of the wicked who prey upon them. The whole point of this section is, however, *not* primarily the guilt of the wicked that deserves judgment, but the disconcerting realization that God—who ought to act to punish their wicked deeds—remains offstage, allowing evil to continue unabated.

24:10–12 / Lacking clothes, they go about naked. Job stresses the degradation and humility of nakedness by repeating this theme. Whereas in verse 7 the nakedness of the poor is more a matter of personal discomfort in the cold night, here it is a visible sign of public humiliation in broad daylight. The poor **carry the sheaves,** engaging in agricultural labor probably as a result of their debt to rich land owners. They must harvest the grain from their creditors' fields, some of which may have originally been their own, **but still** they **go hungry.** The laborers cannot enjoy the produce of the harvest because it does not belong to them, but to the creditors. While it is unlikely that the landowner would actually allow the laborers to starve, the hyperbolic language once again drives home the disparity between the oppressed and the oppressors who control all the means of production and exploit the laborers for their own enrichment and comfort.

They crush olives. Olives were crushed to produce olive oil, one of the most important sources of food and commercial export in the region. The impoverished debtors, therefore, must produce the commodities that support the life of ease for the rich, but they receive no real benefit for their labor. Also, **they tread the winepresses.** We have now covered the basic food groups of the region: grain, olive oil, and wine. The poor are the labor force and produce the commodities that sustain life and provide comfort. Verse 10 tells us that the poor labor and go **hungry;** verse 11 tells us that their work does nothing to relieve their **thirst.** The law demands that even the ox that grinds at the mill should not be muzzled to prevent it from satisfying its hunger by eating as it labors (Deut. 25:4). The poor, however, are not accorded the same dignity and compassion as the animal.

The groans of the dying rise from the city. Job brings this section to a close with a clear statement about the consequences of divine abandonment. In the "city," where those driven from the land congregate to find a means of subsistence, the oppressed are "dying" and are left to merely groan. While the noun translated "dying" here can mean more generally "men" (Deut. 2:34) or "people" (Gen. 34:30), it can also be associated with the participle of the verbal root for death (Heb. *mwt*), as here.

NIV often translates the Hebrew *nepesh* as "soul," as here in **the souls of the wounded.** (NIV is not alone in this tendency: see also KJV; NAB; NASB; NKJV; RSV; and YLT; but contrast NJB, "gasp"; and NRSV, "throat.") This has the unfortunate effect of leading the reader to assume the same sort of dichotomy between mortal, physical body and immaterial, eternal soul that is characteristic of ancient Greek philosophical understanding. For the Hebrews, however, the *nepesh* is the physical person animated by the "spirit" or "breath" of God (Heb. *ruakh*). The divine spirit gives life to the individual, who becomes a *nepesh khayyah* "living being" (Gen. 2:7). At death, the divine spirit returns to God while the *nepesh* returns to its unanimated state, and ultimately decays to dust (Gen. 3:19; Eccl. 12:7). When the *nepesh* speaks, it voices the deepest longings of the human being so vulnerably dependent on the grace of God. Here "the wounded" **cry out** with groans longing **for help** from God, who remains absent.

But God charges no one with wrongdoing. The Hebrew phrase is less than clear due to two difficulties. First, the verb *yasim* (as in 23:6) usually means "to set; appoint" rather than "to charge." As in 23:6, the translators have interpreted the meaning based on their understanding of the context. Second, the consonantal form of the word rendered "wrongdoing" could also be read as "prayer." Those translators (like NIV) who take the phrase to indicate God's failure to render judgment on the wicked read *tiplah,* "what is insipid or unseemly," while others interpret the phrase to indicate that God is ignoring the *tepillah,* or "prayer," of the oppressed. Both options make for awkward Hebrew, but both make basically the same point: God does not seem to judge evil or deliver the powerless either immediately or consistently. The wicked oppress the poor mercilessly, and the poor as a result are destitute and humiliated, but God is nowhere seen to respond to the cries of the despairing, nor does he call the wicked to account. Thus the whole theology of retribution upon which the friends (and Job) have relied in the past appears not to correspond to honest observation of life experience.

24:13–17 / In an extended reflection reminiscent of Proverbs 1–9 or Ecclesiastes, Job now develops the theme of darkness that steadily enshrouds these verses as he considers **those who rebel against the light.** The NT describes the condition of all humanity in similar terms: "Light has come into the world, but men loved darkness instead of light because their deeds were evil. Everyone who does evil hates the light, and will not come into the light for fear that his deeds will be exposed" (John 3:19–21). For Job, the wicked are "those who rebel against the light." They have chosen to depart from the **ways** illuminated by God's light and refuse to **stay** (Heb. "dwell; take up residence") **in its paths.** There may be an intentional allusion to Psalm 1:1 here. The wicked are the opposite of the "blessed one" in Psalm 1, who avoids association with evildoers and refuses to take up residence with them. The wicked **do not know** the "ways" of light—not out of ignorance but because they actively choose not to associate with them. Therefore, they have no *experience* of the light because they spend all their time in darkness.

When daylight is gone. Without emendation the Hebrew would better express the time *before* dawn (so Hartley, *Job*, pp. 348–50; Clines, *Job 21–37*, p. 612), suggesting that the murderous wicked are eager to begin their oppressive activities. They kill **the poor and needy** (categories of oppressed persons seen above in v. 4, along with the orphan and widow in v. 3). In their eager exploitation of the poor and defenseless, the wicked—like murderers—bring their victims' lives to an end with callous disregard. The first phrase of **in the night . . . like a thief** forms a sort of *merismus,* in which the whole of a matter is suggested by the listing of its parts, with the initial reference to "daylight" at the beginning of verse 14. The wicked get up early to pursue their evil plans and they continue their ways into the darkness of night. There is *no* time—day or night—that is free from their oppression.

The eye of the adulterer. It is unlikely that Job is primarily concerned with adultery here, but—building on the atmosphere of devious stealth associated with the "thief" in the preceding line—he adds the image of a wayward husband slipping through the darkened alleyways to avoid detection as an apt analogy for the sneaky actions of the wicked. Opening a window to the self-deceptive thought of the wicked, Job quotes the false hopes of the philanderer, **he thinks,** who has already been spied in his pursuit of lust but **keeps his face concealed.** Even though he knows he cannot avoid detection, the wicked cannot hold back but rushes headlong to commit evil. Wrapping his face in his cloak—like a perpetrator filmed on his way from police van to booking—is as much self-delusion ("If I can't see you, you can't see me!") as a hope for true anonymity.

Returning to the theft imagery with **men break into houses,** Job contrasts the nefarious activity of robbers **in the dark** with their hiding away **by day.** Their withdrawal is the result of their conscious rebellion against the way of light (v. 13), for they **want nothing to do with** it (Heb. "they do not know").

Because of their predilection to evil deeds, **deep darkness is their morning,** the wicked person's natural element. Like a worker on nightshift, the beginning of their "day" ("their morning") is the time when honest persons are asleep. This is a mark of evil's direct opposition to good.

Since the Hebrew for **they make friends** literally means "to know from acquaintance," some take this line to mean that the wicked are themselves terrified of the dark. Others turn the first line of verse 17 around to mean that "morning" is as nighttime for the wicked, who are fearful to live in the light where their evil deeds can be seen and judged. In this case the **terrors of the darkness** beset the wicked during the daylight hours. The NIV is probably on the right track here, however, and the sense is something like our rather cynical observation that "familiarity breeds contempt." The wicked have become immune to the "terrors of the darkness" by long familiarity with them. Job is using light and dark with symbolic connotations in these verses. Although much wickedness does take place under the cover of night, Job is decrying the exploitation of the poor by the wicked *whenever* it occurs—day or night.

Additional Notes §83

24:1 / NJB capitalizes **Day,** apparently suggesting that this is a reference to the eschatological Day of Yahweh—traditionally a time of judgment.

24:3 / Neither was such compassion regarding pledges unique to the Israelites. The Code of Hammurabi contains a regulation fining an individual a third of a mina of silver for taking an **ox in pledge** (§241).

24:6 / The verb translated **glean** here (Heb. *lqsh*) occurs only here, and some translate it as "despoil" (Holladay, *Concise Hebrew,* p. 179), suggesting that the poor were taking grapes by stealth.

24:12 / This urban desperation is a phenomenon common to many industrializing societies. As farming is mechanized, requiring fewer laborers to support the many, excess agricultural laborers often flood the growing urban centers in search of jobs to support their families. This in turn creates a cheap labor force for urban industries, who often exploit the workers to increase productivity and profit. Thus the **groans of the dying** is an apt description of the plight of workers in many periods of the industrialization of our contemporary world.

24:13 / This focus on **light** recalls Eliphaz's use of sun imagery for God in 22:12, 26. For Eliphaz, darkness is an evidence of divine judgment for human sin. Here Job understands the dark as the choice of the wicked, the better to pursue their evil deeds without discovery.

24:14 / Clines tries a bit too hard in questioning how a murderer would profit from killing such impoverished persons. His conclusion is that *anyone* who is murdered, regardless of wealth or station in life, is an oppressed person (Clines, *Job 21–37*, p. 612). While this is true, it undermines Job's essential focus on those impoverished by circumstance.

24:16 / The Heb. for **break into houses** says, lit., "dig into houses," possibly because the walls of many houses were composed of dried mud or mud brick. The same idea is also found in the Code of Hammurabi (§21): "If a seignior made a breach in a house, they shall put him to death in front of that breach and wall him in." Pritchard, p. 141. See also Exod. 22:2.

24:17 / See the discussion of 3:4–5 in §7 with regard to deep darkness.

§84 The Fate of the Wicked (Job 24:18–25)

As we have noted, some question the placement of verses 18–24 as part of Job's speech. This material can be read as exhibiting confidence in the working of retributive theology in the judgment of the wicked. Such confidence does not seem to fit well with Job's critique up to this point in chapter 24 and throughout the book as a whole. Job's chief point in the first 17 verses of this chapter has been that the wicked mercilessly oppress the poor and defenseless without any opposition or judgment from God. In Job's recent personal experience, God appears absent from and unconcerned about the human world. For this reason, some commentators and translations move verses 18–24 in order to place them in the mouth of someone other than Job.

Clines, for example, sets these verses after 27:7–17, where they expand Zophar's third speech (*Job 21–37*, pp. 667–69). NJB leaves these words in the mouth of Job but places them after 27:23, as more appropriate in a context where Job is cursing the wicked and expressing his *desire for* (rather than certainty of) judgment on them. The NIV leaves the verses in place, noting in the *Study Bible* that "it is also legitimate to translate the verses as Job's call for redress against evildoers" by reading certain verbs as jussives that express the will of the speaker (Job): "May their portion be cursed . . . may the grave snatch away," and the like. Hartley concurs in taking these verses as Job's curses on the wicked (*Job*, pp. 350–54), and this approach seems to me the most appropriate way forward if we are to retain the canonical arrangement. Otherwise one must assume that Job's state of turmoil has so weakened his ability to maintain a consistent argument that he falls back here on the traditional retributive thinking which so influenced his early life as a sage.

24:18–20 / Job begins this section by describing the tenuous nature of the wicked: **they are foam** (Heb. *qal*, "light; insignificant") or flotsam floating **on the surface of the water.** Often

rushing streams bear along tiny bits of leaves, wood, and other
rubbish that swirl downstream in the current and eddies with no
control over their ultimate destination. Such are the wicked, says
Job: insignificant trash swept along, they know not where, in the
currents of life.

Further, he says, **their portion of the land is cursed.** The
"portion" is the ancestral allotment of land going back to the conquest and passed down by inheritance to subsequent generations.
The cursing of the "portion" may be the result of the wicked
breaking covenant obligations to the poor and defenseless. As a
result of their oppressive acts, the curses of Deuteronomy 28 are
unleashed on them. If Job is not envisioning a certain future retribution, he is at least calling here for divine enactment of the covenant provisions. This curse would effectively end the productivity
of the property of the wicked. In the wake of the curse, **no one
goes to the vineyards.** The grapes are withered and the vines
shriveled. There is no reason to approach the vineyards since
there is no life there. This may also refer symbolically to the shriv-
eling up of the wicked even in life, such that those who had formerly sought their company shun them. This would also describe
Job's experience despite his righteousness, and he appears to be
wishing his own unjust suffering on the wicked who truly deserve it, according to retributive theology.

As heat and drought snatch away the melted snow. The
verse describes metaphorically the abrupt demise of the wicked
for which Job hopes. In the preceding verse the curse has destroyed the productivity of the wicked's portion; they, like Job, are
reduced to poverty. Now **the grave** (Heb. *sheʾol*, "abode of the
dead") **snatches away** the sinful wicked like "melted snow" that
can neither stop the heat nor prevent its own destruction.

The womb forgets them. The loss of a mother's love for the
child she bore is a harsh metaphor for absolute abandonment. Yet
this is what Job wishes for the wicked. The "womb" (Heb. *rekhem*)
is related to the Hebrew term for "compassion" (*rakhamim*), which
describes feelings like those of a mother for the child of her womb.
Here Job desires to revoke even that loving bond. "The womb forgets" having ever borne the child who has grown into a wicked
adult. A disturbing image of death drawn from the decay of
corpses in "the grave" (v. 19) or bodies left exposed on the ground—
the worm feasts—pictures the ultimate abandonment of the evildoers in death. The image is even grosser than the translation admits. The Hebrew verb (*mtq*) means "to consider sweet" or even

"to suck." The "worm" relishes the flesh of the wicked like a delicate dessert course (see also 21:26).

It is one thing to be forgotten, quite another to be **no longer remembered.** These wicked people are significant only because of the pain they produce during their lives. When they are gone, Job suggests, there will be no reason ever to call them to mind again. As we have seen, in a culture with no developed understanding of a life after death memory is the closest thing to eternal life one can hope to achieve. In Job's estimation, the wicked have no such hope. Perhaps the image **broken like a tree** is of a once mighty tree shattered by lightning (Ps. 105:32–33) or broken down by a strong wind (Ps. 29; Job 19:10). The destruction of trees is often a metaphor for divine judgment (Isa. 10:28; Ezek. 17:24; Dan. 4). Like trees unable to protect themselves from the destructive power of the storm, so Job desires these wicked to be broken down in divine judgment.

24:21 / **They prey on the barren and childless woman.** The passage turns rather abruptly from the expected end of the wicked to their evil deeds. The word translated "prey" (Heb. $r^{\flat}h$, "graze; feed") is more pastoral than the translation indicates. Some take the phrase to mean that the wicked "consort" (Heb. $r^{\flat}h$, "have dealings with") with young women, but produce no children. Perhaps they seek out "barren" women to seduce precisely so that children will not complicate their affairs. The lack of children might be just another indication of the curse that renders all of their entanglements unproductive. The fact that they **to the widow show no kindness** is but another sign of the wickedness of those who exploit the powerless.

24:22 / **God drags away the mighty by his power.** The Hebrew text does not mention God here, although he seems the logical subject. Elsewhere the term "mighty" (Heb. $^{\flat}abbirim$) describes obstinate and violent persons who resist God, so it seems natural to assume a reference to the wicked here (Job 34:20; Isa. 46:12). They may be "mighty" by human standards, but they are no match for God in "his power." RSV translates this phrase as "God prolongs the life of the mighty"—taking the long lives of the wicked as another contradiction of retribution. This translation would seem to require an object explaining what is "drawn out" (Ps. 36:10; Jer. 31:3; Neh. 10:3). Here the object is "the mighty," so the meaning is most likely "to carry off; drag away"—as the prey of a hunter in a net (Ps. 28:3). The Hebrew for **they become**

established means, literally, "he will stand/rise up," seemingly implying "to take one's position in life." Understanding **they have no assurance of life** as Job's desire for the wicked means that he *hopes* they will be unable to find security in life.

24:23 / He may let them rest in a feeling of security. This verse continues the contrast begun in the last verse between the confidence of the wicked and the tenuous reality of their existence under divine scrutiny and judgment. God may allow them a period of respite in which a false sense of security grows, but Job longs for a day when divine justice will reign and the wicked receive what they deserve. Far from a description of divine protection, **his eyes are on their ways** is instead a warning of divine watchfulness as prelude to judgment (2 Sam. 22:28; Jer. 16:17; Job 34:21; see also Clines, *Job 21–37*, p. 672). Although he delays now, God knows their ways and will ultimately bring them to justice— at least, Job hopes so!

24:24 / Since God is the one who lifts up (**they are exalted**) and brings low (**they are brought low;** see also Ps. 75:7), the rise of the wicked to power is no independent achievement but remains subject to the permissive will of God. When God decides to act, those who are at the peak of their human power will be **gone.** God is the true actor behind the seeming vagaries of human existence. The phrase **and gathered up** may also be taken as a jussive form expressing Job's desire: "Let them be gathered up!" This gathering up of the wicked **like all others** may refer to the common destiny of all humans in the grave (v. 19). Job has already mentioned this destiny in 21:22–26. Despite their arrogant dismissal of God and their confidence, the wicked can no more escape the inevitability of death than those impoverished persons they drove to the grave (v. 14). Lest there be any doubt of his meaning, Job concludes with an obvious agricultural simile: **they are cut off like heads of grain.** As grain grows up until the stalks ripen into mature heads and then are "cut off" in the harvest, so the seeming unencumbered growth of the wicked and their power will end when the moment for judgment arrives.

In the mouth of Job, these words suggest that he has not yet given up on a God who rules justly. If Job had abandoned any hope of divine sovereignty and justice, his tireless labor to bring God to account would hardly make *any* sense. While God is free to act in ways that humans do not understand; while tit-for-tat retribution clearly fails as an adequate explanation of the experience of

Job and other righteous sufferers, Job still agrees with the psalmist that God is "not a God who takes pleasure in evil; with [him] the wicked cannot dwell" (Ps. 5:4). Thus, brought to court and confronted with the unavoidable facts of Job's circumstance, God would have to rule justly . . . he could in fact do no other! This is the foundation of Job's hope. This conviction in the face of confusion induced by his contradictory experience is one plausible explanation for Job's apparent waffling—his failure to adopt a consistently pessimistic and negative evaluation towards God. As was the case in the initial and second tests, Job remains unwilling to "curse God and die," preferring instead to hang on to faith while pursuing God for understanding and resolution.

24:25 / **If this is not so.** Job ends his speech with a challenge—since his friends fail to take up this challenge, the dialogue rapidly dwindles to an end. Bildad's five-verse response (25:2–6) covers no new ground and serves little purpose other than to introduce Job's final monologue (26:1–31:40) and to demonstrate convincingly the friends' ultimate failure to answer Job, who asks **who can prove me false?** The verb (Heb. *yakzibeni*) means, more literally, "who can make me a liar?" Job claims that his views are the result of observations and experiences that should convince anyone. He issues the challenge not only to the friends but also to readers through the ages to the present. Who can deny the truth of what Job claims? Who can deny that the wicked oppress the powerless with impunity, and that the righteous are not uniformly spared from suffering, poverty, or death? God's justice does not prevent enduring injustice. Who can **reduce my words to nothing?** Job's critique of human life remains valid to the present day. No one has convincingly refuted his allegations. Understanding continues to elude us, despite many and vigorous attempts. As a result we tend, like the friends, either to fall back without question on an assumption of retribution, or to dwindle into uncomfortable silence.

Additional Notes §84

24:21 / See the discussion on this verse in Clines (*Job 21–37*, p. 671). He takes these women as the wives of the wicked, whose barrenness is a sign of divine judgment.

§85 God Is in Control, Humans Are Unrighteous Maggots (Job 25:1–6)

Here, in his final speaking appearance, Bildad makes but a weak and truncated response to Job's long, impassioned plea. Some commentators restore a longer speech here by transposing verses from the extended speech of Job that follows (chs. 26–31). In what follows, however, we take Bildad's brief speech as an intentional indication of the faltering of the friends' arguments in their failure to persuade Job. Later Elihu will declare his disdain for the friends because of their inability to respond effectively to Job's claims (32:1–3, 11–12, 15–16). Following Job's long reply to Bildad, Zophar does not offer a third speech at all, which accentuates the dwindling argumentation from the friends. (Although many commentators also reconstruct a third speech for Zophar out of the extended material attributed to Job in chs. 27–31.) This trailing away of speech is an effective way to suggest that the friends are at last silenced—unable to mount new arguments to oppose Job.

25:1–3 / Bildad's final argument is simple enough, although not new: God is exalted and firmly in control. If he rules even over the powerful heavenly beings and can call on them to enforce his will, how can mere humans resist? Since humans are by nature sinful and weak, they cannot expect to be pure before God and—as lowly maggots—they must accept God's judgment.

Dominion and awe belong to God. God is in control of his heavenly abode. While the Hebrew does not actually mention **heaven** here, "his heights" refers to the exalted dwelling place of God. The term for "awe" (Heb. *pakhad*) has an even more fearful edge, meaning "dread." The word **order** translates the Hebrew word *shalom*, "peace; wholeness." God's domain above has been knit into holy unity. There is no conflict there between oppressed and oppressor.

Can his forces be numbered? The Hebrew for "forces" (*gedudayw*) indicates God's irresistible power as well as his immense control in bringing "order" to this myriad of beings. **Upon whom does**

his light not rise, is another use of sun imagery to emphasize the all-encompassing nature of God's sovereignty and blessing. As the sun arcs overhead, so God sees all that occurs in the human world. As the sun shines down the warmth of its life-giving rays on all who see it, so the blessings of God are available to all.

25:4–6 / How . . . can a man be righteous before God . . . one born of woman be pure? Bildad returns to an old argument that Eliphaz formulated in his first speech (4:15–19), and restated in his second speech (15:14–16) in very similar words: "What is man, that he could be pure, or one born of woman, that he could be righteous?" The translation "man" is once again more masculine than necessary, since the Hebrew ʾenosh most often means "human being," with emphasis on weakness and finitude (Pss. 8:4; 144:3; Job 7:17; 9:2; 15:14). Job is also aware that human weakness makes it difficult to "be righteous before God" (9:2), but for him the problem is not the inevitability of sin but the impossibility of maintaining one's innocence in the face of the overwhelming power of God that prevents the recognition of human righteousness (as in his own case!).

The divinely created elements of the night sky, **the moon and the stars** (Ps. 8:3–4), are far removed from the pain, suffering, and sin of human life. Yet, uncolored as they are by evil and trouble, even the "moon" and "stars" fail to measure up to the standard of purity in God's **eyes.** The reference to the divine eyes reminds the reader once again of God's scrutiny of human activity with a view to judging evil (vv. 2–3). If these exalted heavenly bodies cannot satisfy God's demand for purity, what chance has weak and limited **man** (ʾenosh)? By contrast, says Bildad, a man is a **maggot** and a **worm.** These terms describe insect larvae that invade plants and meal (toleʿa, Exod. 16:20; Jonah 4:7; Deut. 28:29; Exod. 25:4), rotting meat, or corpses (rimmah, Exod. 16:24). The contact with dead flesh is especially repugnant and symbolic of death and uncleanness. Calling humans by these terms is declaring their essential sinfulness, deserving of judgment.

Additional Notes §85

25:4 / It is a bit odd that, in 9:2, NIV translates ʾenosh as "mortal," while retaining "man" in 7:17; 15:14; and 25:4.

§86 Sarcastic Introduction (Job 26:1–4)

Job's response to Bildad's third speech is extended (six chapters long)—even for the usually loquacious Job! Many commentators divide up the chapters attributed to Job to supply an extension to Bildad's brief speech, as well as to wholly reconstruct a missing third speech for Zophar. Such reconstruction, however, can only proceed on a presumptive assumption of what each speaker would have said—and is thus controlled ultimately by the reconstructor's theory rather than challenged and shaped by the text's own structure. There is no clear consensus regarding how the materials in chapters 26–31 ought to be sorted among the various possible speakers. In what follows, therefore, we honor the existing form of the text and seek to explore the effects of its final shape on the reader.

26:1–3 / As has increasingly been the case in Job's responses, he begins here with words dripping with sarcasm. In what amounts to pseudo-praise for his friend's **insight**, Job spends two verses underlining Bildad's failure (and that of the other friends as well) to address the needs of those with whom Job has been driven by circumstance to cast his lot: **the powerless** and **feeble**. The poetic structure of these verses employs artful parallel and a final chiastic twist. Each verse begins with the interrogative *meh* or *mah*, "What? How?" followed by a second-person singular perfect verb indicating Bildad's ineffectiveness, and then proceeds to a negative prepositional phrase describing the object. A literal translation would read something like this:

> How you have helped (the one who has) no power (*koakh*),
> you have delivered (the) arm (that has) no strength (ʿ*oz*).
> How you have advised (the one who has) no wisdom (*khokmah*),
> And good counsel (*tushiyyah*) to many you have made known.

Job has his tongue firmly placed in his cheek again here, and this becomes clearer still when we compare this passage to his hymnic celebration of God in 12:13–16. There, in very similar words and concepts, Job declares that wisdom (*khokmah*), power (*geburah*), counsel (*ʿetsah*), and understanding (*tebunah*) belong to God alone (12:13) and that strength (*ʿoz*) and effective counsel (*tushiyyah*) are his as well. The parallels between these two passages indicate that here Job is ridiculing his friends because they believe they can achieve understanding reserved only for God. In reality, Job is saying, their "wisdom" is folly in the extreme since it fabricates a world in which retribution works absolutely, but it contradicts the clear teaching of the real world in which righteous lives are crushed with loss and suffering.

26:4 / **Who has helped you?** Still in the midst of his ridicule, Job feigns amazement at the profundity of his friend's **words.** They must be the result of some sort of inspiration from outside Bildad's own understanding! The Hebrew translated "**whose spirit,**" is, more correctly, "breath"—indicating a belief in a direct form of inspiration. Job, in his sarcasm, is actually denying Bildad's understanding and ridiculing the thought that his insights might be inspired. Later, however, Elihu will return to this theme in his rebuke of Job. In 32:8 and 33:4 he will equate the "spirit of God" (*ruakh ʾel*) with the "breath of Shaddai" (*nishmat shadday*) and proclaim that this breath, or spirit, is the foundation of human perception and the source of human life. In both of these later passages, Elihu will insist that it is the indwelling "breath" of God that gives his words authority that Job must heed (32:6–10; 33:1–5).

§87 A Maggot's View of God's Power
(Job 26:5–14)

In 25:6, at the end of his last speech and just before Job's present response, Bildad characterizes weak and sinful humans as unclean maggots before God. As such, they deserve any suffering they endure in this life. Far from silencing Job, this rather unfeeling evaluation of the predicament of suffering humans precipitated Job's caustic response in the first verses of chapter 26. Bildad's words could only be spoken by one who has little compassion and no personal experience of the kind of suffering and loss known by Job and the other "maggots" of the real world. Now, however, Job counters this by describing the effects of divine power on the world of powerless humans. What will become clear in these verses is that Job believes not only that God is fully aware and fully in control of all the deepest recesses of the world, but also that the consequences of this divine knowledge and power—from a "maggot's eye view"—are painful in the extreme!

26:5–6 / **The dead are in deep anguish.** Job refers to the "dead" here with the Hebrew *repaʾim*, which is related to the verbal root *rpʾ*, "heal." As Hartley and others indicate, this suggests an understanding that the departed dead have power to accomplish healing. There is, perhaps, some sense of differentiated status among the inhabitants of *Sheol:* the more elevated *repaʾim* and the more general *shokenim*, or "inhabitants." The phrase "deep anguish" translates the Hebrew verb *khwl*, "to writhe" ostensibly in fear or pain. Thus it seems that even the dead cannot escape the fear and pain of God's inexorable scrutiny (compare the more positive understanding of divine inescapability in Ps. 139:1–12, esp. v. 8). In the ancient cosmology, the flat plate of the earth and the arching dome of the sky held off the chaotic waters above and below the earth so that humans, animals, and plants could exist in this protected space. Job pictures *Sheol*, the abode of the dead (**those beneath the waters**), lying beneath the earth—and even beneath the waters below the earth. God, therefore, is capable of penetrating these most far removed and hidden places where living humans could never hope to come. And **all that live in them** are, of course, the sea creatures that inhabit the oceans and seas connected with these chaotic waters under the earth. **Death is naked . . . Destruction lies uncovered.** Using nakedness as a symbol of ultimate vulnerability, Job reaffirms the preceding verse by describing the abode of the dead as laid bare to the penetrating gaze of God. We use similar idioms to describe unwilling exposure of our innermost thoughts or our most hidden deeds. "Death" translates the Hebrew *she'ol*, the abode of the dead, while "destruction" renders the frequent synonym for *Sheol, abaddon.*

26:7–11 / A series of participles that describe the absolute power of God over his creation link the first three verses of this section (vv. 7–9). God acts and the impossible happens. **He spreads out the northern skies over empty space.** The poet has creation in mind. In the beginning, the earth was *tohu wabohu*, "formless and empty" (Gen. 1:2). Job says God created "the northern skies" (or "the north," which is often associated with the abode of God) by spreading it out like a tent over *tohu*, NIV "empty space" or "formless nothingness." Amazingly, God's tent requires no tent pole to support it. Like a lamp or adornment hung from the center of a tent, and again with no visible support, God **suspends the earth over nothing** (or, as NASB and RSV suggest, "*from* nothing," emphasis added).

He wraps up the waters in his clouds. The clouds obviously contain water, which is dispensed in the form of rain. But, unlike a bulging water skin stretched beyond its limits, the clouds **do** not **burst** (except metaphorically). **He covers the face of the full moon.** The Hebrew word translated "full moon" (*kisseh*) is problematic. Some, as NIV, emend vowel pointing to the Hebrew noun *keseh*, "full moon." Others, like Hartley, assume a minor consonantal change to *kisse'* ("chair; throne") and translate "his throne," as a reference to God's throne that serves as a sign of his creation authority. Since the rest of the allusions in these verses are to God's activity in creation, the reference to the "full moon" seems more likely to me. Comparable enthronement images in the Ugaritic myths of Baal and Anat, however, mean that "his throne" is not entirely outside the realm of possibility. Whether the "full moon" or "his throne," Yahweh is actively in control of the natural phenomena employed to obscure it, **spreading his clouds over it.** Clouds covering the "full moon" provide a particularly dark and murky context for Job's pessimistic ruminations. **He marks out the horizon.** God's creative power extends to establishing the limits and order of the expanse of creation. The "horizon" (Heb. *khoq*) can also mean "statute; ordinance" prescribing a particular course of action. Here it describes the prescribed limit that marks the **boundary between light and darkness.** In the beginning, when "darkness was over the surface of the [watery] deep" (Gen. 1:2), God created "light" and "separated the light from the darkness" (Gen. 1:4). In Job 38:8–11, God uses the same term *khoq*, to describe how he set limits for the sea at creation: "I fixed limits for it and . . . I said, 'This far you may come and no farther; here is where your proud waves halt.'" Job has in mind here this great power of God that holds even the watery seas of chaos at bay. **The pillars of the heavens quake.** Describing the "heavens" as if they are the ceiling of a room or the roof of a building supported on "pillars," Job illustrates the fearful effects of God's creative control on the very elements of creation itself. So **his rebuke** most likely refers to God's restriction of the chaotic waters to prescribed boundaries, as in the preceding verse. As in Job 38, God sets these limitations by conveying a restrictive verbal command to the seas. Other passages depict God rebuking or subduing the rebellious waters by force (Pss. 18:15; 104:6–9; Isa. 50:2). Even the physical creation quakes in response to the display of divine power.

26:12–14 / In these last verses of the chapter, Job continues to describe God's fearsome creative power. The imagery shifts, however, to incorporate even more mythological elements of the conflict between God and the great chaotic sea monster Rahab. As in verses 7–9, repeated prepositional phrases link verses 12 and 13: **By his power . . . by his wisdom . . . By his breath** (*bekokho . . . bitbunato . . . berukho . . .*). The movement is from turmoil to stable order, from churning seas to fair skies. The poet also artfully parallels more naturalistic imagery (**he churned up the sea**) with mythological conflict (**he cut Rahab to pieces**), allowing the reader to see the two as reflexes of one another. Similarly, while Job describes God's method in physical terms ("he cut Rahab to pieces," **his hand pierced the gliding serpent**), suggesting actual combat, he introduces a moderating emphasis on God's effective wisdom as the force behind creation stability ("by his wisdom"). The aura of conflict and the subjugation of chaotic powers emphasize the fearsome nature of God's sovereign control over the universe— power that should give any human considerable pause.

And these are but the outer fringe of his works. Job concludes this chapter with an awe-filled reflection on how little even these powerful creation narratives tell us about the true nature of God. With all of their powerful display of divine control, these narratives communicate only the "outer fringe" of God's activities. The "outer fringe" (Heb. *qetsot derakayw*) is literally the "ends of his ways," so the idea is rather like spying on God from afar with a telescope or trying to know him from third-hand reports.

Our knowledge of God is like a **whisper** that is **faint,** difficult to hear and even more difficult to understand. Note the interplay in the last half of this verse between the "whisper" of what we truly know about God and the **thunder** (Heb. *raʿam*) that the display of his power produces. Surely Job has in mind here trying to discern the "whisper" of God's just care and compassion toward the faithful righteous ones in the midst of the clapping "thunder," of the crushing pain and suffering the friends attribute to divine retribution.

Additional Notes §87

26:5–14 / NJB conjecturally places 26:1–4 *after* vv. 5–14 and understands the latter verses to supply a continuation of Bildad's rather brief final speech.

26:5 / De Moor considers the word *repaʾim* related to a similar Ugaritic word to be a reference first to powerful living persons and later to prominent persons among the dead. See Johannes C. de Moor, "Rapiʾuma—Rephaim." *ZAW* 88 (1976), 323–45.

26:7 / Hartley, *Job,* p. 365, reads *tohu* as referring to the "watery chaos" that God placed under orderly restriction in creation.

26:9 / On "his throne" for **full moon,** see Hartley, *Job,* p. 366. Compare also Marduk's erection of his throne after defeating the sea god Yamm, in the Baal-Anat texts from Ugarit; Pritchard, pp. 92–100.

§88 Job's Vow of Continued Integrity (Job 27:1–6)

27:1 / And Job continued his discourse. In light of the ongoing scholarly discussions regarding the appropriate arrangement of the latter chapters of the dialogue section, it is worth noting that the Hebrew text *does* contain notices intended to mark out the identity of the speakers along the way. Immediately following the truncated final speech of Bildad (25:1–6), chapter 26 begins (v. 1) with the heading typically employed throughout the dialogue section to introduce the next speaker: "Then Job replied" (*wayaʿan ʾiyyob wayyoʾmar*). Chapter 27, however, employs for the first time in the dialogue a new type of heading that indicates a *continuation* of the *same* speaker, in this case Job: **And Job continued his discourse** (*wayyosep ʾiyyob seʾet meshalo wayyoʾmar*). This phrase occurs twice more in the book: once to mark the continuation of Job's long final monologue (29:1), and once to indicate that Elihu is continuing his extended discourse (36:1). These notices indicate that, early in the history of the text, these long speeches were understood to be assigned to particular speakers. These markers may have been part of the original text, to prevent the reader from becoming lost and confused in these unusually long speeches. If, on the other hand, a helpful scribe added these notices later, we should understand them as honest attempts to assist the reader—not an ignorant (or worse, *devious!*) attempt to mislead and confuse. There is no evidence, to my knowledge, of any manuscript tradition that omits or otherwise rearranges these markers.

27:2–3 / As surely as God lives. Job begins with an oath formula, swearing by the very life of God himself! The reference to God's life (Heb. *khay*) draws on the certainty of divine endurance to indicate Job's confidence in the validity of his oath. God "lives" forever and thus remains forever able to affirm or deny Job's oath. In the phrase **as long as I have life within me**, "life" is

actually the word *nishmah*, "breath." Since God is the source of
human breath and life, Job's oath acknowledges his complete vulnerability to the one who can uphold or reject him—an indication
of his absolute confidence and sincerity. Job's *nepesh* (NIV **soul,**
better "being; self") is animated by **the breath of God** which can
be withdrawn whenever God wills. Job is putting it all on the line
here. He holds nothing back.

Not only does Job acknowledge his complete vulnerability
to God (the meaning of "fear of God" in the OT), but he also admits
that he must ultimately depend on one who seems his enemy,
who has denied me justice. The Hebrew phrase translated "denied me justice" has more the sense of "turned my judgment
aside." The judgment is the statement of *mishpat* that the judge
gives to indicate the proper course of action in a case under consideration. Job fully believes that he has fulfilled the demands of
mishpat and, if God is unwilling to acknowledge Job's righteousness, then God himself must have twisted *mishpat* in order to put
Job in the wrong. As a result, God has made Job **taste bitterness of
soul.** "Taste bitterness" is a highly interpretive rendering of the
Hebrew verb, which is more accurately translated "make bitter."
"Soul" is, again, *not* the eternal and immaterial soul that inhabits
the physical body in life and departs at death, as in Greek thought
(see the discussion on 24:10–12 in §83). Rather, the Hebrew word
nepesh refers to the physical being that God animates by his spirit.
The *nepesh* is the place where humans do their deepest reflection
and where their greatest sense of self resides. For the *nepesh* to
be made bitter would bring the value of one's very life or self
into question.

27:4–6 / I will not . . . The translation of vows such as
these is somewhat difficult. In the Hebrew, verses 4 and 5 both
begin with the particle *ʾim*, "if," which introduces in each case a
negative conditional clause describing what Job vows never to do.
In a spoken oath, a self-imprecation would have followed as a
"then . . ." clause in order to spell out the consequences expected
to befall one who failed to fulfill the vow (something like: "May
my nose fall off!" or "May my brain shrivel up like a pea!"). In
most cases those self-imprecations have been omitted from our
biblical texts—perhaps because the editors believed in the effective power of such curses and found such written threats disturbing. As a result, translators usually render such vows without the
"if . . ." introduction.

Job expresses each of the three parts of his vow in a single verse. First, he says, **my lips will not speak wickedness . . . my tongue . . . deceit.** He swears that he will die as he has lived thus far: in honest, unvarnished expressions of the truth. His reference to "my lips" takes us back to the end of the second test in 2:10. There the narrator's evaluation affirms Job's faithful endurance in the face of suffering: "In all this, Job did not sin in what he said." The final phrase is literally "with his lips," using the Hebrew *sapa*, "lip," as in this passage. Thus Job is vowing never to "curse God to his face" as *the* Satan had claimed he inevitably would. "Deceit" is more "rebellious treachery" than deceptive misleading.

I will never admit . . . In the second part of his vow (v. 5), Job resolves never to surrender his **integrity** in the face of false accusation. The verse opens in the Hebrew with the interjection *khalilah li,* "accursed to me." Here Job's self-imprecation stands in the text. Our translators evidence some of the hesitancy of the ancient editors when they translate, rather cryptically, "Far be it from me . . ." (NASB; RSV; NJB), or turn it into a negative (NIV's "never"). The translation **you are in the right** obscures the legal nature of the Hebrew (*ʾatsdiq ʾetkem*), which means "declare you righteous." This is how a judge would exonerate the party who had met the demands of *mishpat* in a court case. In the Hebrew, "you" is clearly *plural,* signifying that Job is responding to all of the friends, and not just Bildad (or God!). As in the preceding verse, Job vows to maintain this stance to death, **till I die.** The verb "die" (*gawaʿ*) is used only in Job (10:18; 29:18) and means "gasp for breath (in death)" and may refer to the "death rattle" among the dying. The Hebrew verb translated, "**I will not deny,**" is the same as that used to express God's denial of justice to Job in 27:2. Job refuses to be forced by suffering, or by the insistent pressure of his friends, or even by the continued abandonment of God, to admit wrong falsely in order to achieve relief. The term "integrity" here is the Hebrew *tummah,* related to the affirmation of Job's "blameless" character (Heb. *tam*) in chapters 1 and 2. This idea of maintaining his "integrity" becomes increasingly important for Job as he moves toward the end of his speeches. He has remained faithful in the face of complete loss, and he asks only that God publicly declare his righteousness.

I will maintain my righteousness. The third part of Job's vow is a more positive action. In verses 4 and 5, he has taken an essentially passive but resistant stance: "my lips will not speak . . . I will never admit . . . I will not deny." Now, however, he promises to continue actively to **maintain** his righteous character. "Maintain" has the sense of "make firm/strong" and "to hold firmly on to" at the same time. Like a tenacious bulldog, Job vows not to let integrity slip from his grasp, to **never let go of it.** Nor will he abandon what he knows to be true in the face of opposition and suffering. So convinced is he of his rightness, Job anticipates no inner doubts to undermine his resolve: **my conscience will not reproach me.** "My conscience" is actually "my heart"—the place of deep reflection and moral decision-making. As he reflects deeply, Job is confident his moral decisions give no cause for self-doubt. Here is an integrated person: one who is able to stand up to external "reproach" because of a deep inner sense of personal integrity that is not just a matter of convenience, but the very fabric of life.

Additional Notes §88

27:1 / The heading found in 26:1 ("Then Job replied") introduces alternating speeches in the dialogue section, differing only in the name of the speaker: 4:1 (Eliphaz); 6:1; 9:1; 12:1; 16:1; 19:1; 21:1; 23:1; 26:1 (Job); 8:1 (Bildad); 11:1 (Zophar); 15:1 (Eliphaz); 18:1 (Bildad); 20:1 (Zophar); 22:1 (Eliphaz); 25:1 (Bildad). The Heb. translated, "**And Job continued his discourse,**" lit. means, "And Job continued to lift up his *mashal* and he said." The term *mashal* describes a more general form of wisdom speech, normally translated "proverb." (See the discussion in the additional note on 3:2 in §7.) The phrase here is identical to that in 29:1. Other than the omission of the phrase *se'et meshalo*, "to lift up his *mashal*," the marker in Elihu's long speech (36:1) is also identical: *wayyosep 'elihu' wayyo'mar:* "And Elihu continued and he said."

§89 Friends Consigned to Fate of the Wicked (Job 27:7–12)

27:7 / Job's words turn outward now in an imprecation on his **enemies** and **adversaries.** Although in the Hebrew these words are both singular, it seems clear that their immediate reference is to Job's three "friends" who have steadily "raised themselves up" in opposition to Job. The verse begins with a jussive, **may,** which indicates that Job is expressing his wish for these opponents and which confirms the imprecatory nature of this verse. He wants these opponents—surely the friends—to experience the fate of **the wicked** and **the unjust.** There is, of course, more than a little irony in this wish, since in Job's experience "the wicked" and "unjust" often live long, prosperous lives and die unpunished! Job, on the other hand, has experienced great suffering and his friends consider him to be among "the wicked." Job is saying something like: "Since you are convinced of my guilt, and believe my suffering to be just, may you, who are no more righteous than I, receive similar justice for your own deeds." Rather ironically, I think, Job continues to refer to himself as "the wicked" in these verses, implicitly placing quotation marks around the word to indicate that this is the friends' estimation of Job and not his own. In this way he is able to speak of the traditional view of the retributive judgment on "the wicked" and "unjust" in ways that actually reflect his own experience of undeserved suffering.

27:8–10 / **For what hope has the godless?** Job's ironic tone continues into verse 8 as he speaks of the hopeless circumstance of "the godless" (Heb. *khanep,* "profane; irreligious person"). Again, Job's friends consider him to be the "godless" one because of his experience of divine abandonment. If Job, who is righteous, receives no response from God, how is his "hope" any different than that of the "the godless"? Job's righteousness has presented no barrier to his also being **cut off.** The verb (*bts*^c) is active (contra NIV's passive translation) and God is the subject here,

as in the second half of this verse. This kind of cutting off is especially violent and often describes "armed robbery" to achieve
profit or gain by violating another person. Using the noun from
this same root, Eliphaz denies that God receives "gain" (*betsaᶜ*)
from the righteous behavior of humans (22:3). God is clearly the
protagonist here as he **takes away** (or "draws out") the life-giving
breath from a person's being. These words help us to understand
a little of how Job feels about God leaving him to experience the
punishment deserved by "the godless."

Does God listen to his cry? Job has certainly cried out to
God to no avail, for God does not "listen" to the cries of "wicked"
Job in his **distress.** The Hebrew word translated "listen" does not
mean simply hear, but has the sense of heed or pay attention, with
an expectation of response. God does not respond to Job. How,
then, is his "hope" for a divine hearing any greater than that of the
truly "wicked" person who refuses even to acknowledge the effective presence and authority of God (21:14–15; 22:17)? **Will he find
delight . . . Will he call upon God?** This is certainly a swipe at
Eliphaz's contention (22:26–27) that, if Job would only submit to
God, he would "find delight in the Almighty" with the result that
God would hear his prayers and restore him. Job is reminding his
friends that, according to their own words, the wicked (among
whom they now include Job) have little interest in God, nor
do they expect God to intervene in their affairs. Therefore, the
wicked will not turn to God or "call upon" him. Job, however,
continues to "call upon God at all times," seeking him even during his great suffering, and yet he receives no more response than
the wicked.

27:11 / **I will teach you.** Using the verb (*yrh*) from which
the noun Torah ("instruction; guidelines") derives, Job offers to reveal to the friends how **the power of God** *really* works. Job is seeking to explain the implications of his own personal experience of
God that these friends are unable to access on their own. Job's experience is, of course, contrary to the retributive worldview that
the friends, in their ignorance, espouse. Job is not "wicked" as his
friends suppose, and yet he experiences the punishment intended
for those who arrogantly reject the authority of God. The "power
of God" is, literally, "in the hand of God"—a way to describe being
under the authority and control of another. When he speaks of
the ways of the Almighty (lit., "what is with God") he is referring
to that knowledge of God that remains distant from humans

because it is far from their common experience. **I will not conceal.**
What Job is implying here is that the friends, by assuming a retributive worldview that does not accord with real experience, are actually concealing the true nature of God and thus leading others
into a false relationship with him. Job wants no part of such a distorted understanding of God and "will not conceal" the painful possibilities of a life lived vulnerably exposed to "the power
of God."

27:12 / **You have all seen this yourselves.** What Job is declaring to the friends (and to the reader!) is no hidden, esoteric
knowledge known only to Job, but the results of plain observation
and experience of life in the real world. As trained practitioners
of the traditions of the sages, the friends ought to see all the incon-
sistencies that Job describes. Their failure to acknowledge the
truth that stares them in the face renders their retributive pro-
nouncements so much **meaningless talk.** This last phrase is from
the Hebrew *hebel tehbalu* ("vanity you are vainly speaking"), a
combination of noun and verb from the same root (*hbl*) that is
behind Ecclesiastes' thematic saying, "Meaningless! Meaningless!
. . . Utterly meaningless! Everything is meaningless" (*habel habalim
. . . habel habalim hakkol habel,* Eccl. 1:2; 12:8). If their philosophy cannot stand up to the evidence of the real world, it is ultimately
worthless.

§90 Utter Destruction of the Wicked/Friends (Job 27:13–23)

Job goes on in this final section of chapter 27 to describe the fate of the wicked. It seems clear from the preceding verses that Job is doing two unexpected things here. On the one hand, he continues to parallel his own innocent suffering with that understood as divine judgment on the wicked. While the friends have assigned Job to the category of those deserving judgment, the reader knows that they are wrong. By the obvious parallels, Job is driving home (to the reader at least) his contention that retributive theology is an inadequate explanation of the human experience of pain and suffering. On the other hand, since Job has in the earlier section identified his opponents as "the wicked" and "the unjust" (v. 7), the punishments he describes here serve as an additional warning to the friends of the consequences of their continued opposition to Job.

27:13 / **Here is the fate.** The word "fate" is not a particularly apt translation of the Hebrew *kheleq*. Here, as well as elsewhere in Job and Scripture as a whole, the word refers to the "portion" allotted to one as their *due*. In this sense it describes the portion of the sacrifice allotted to the priests or, in other contexts, the portion of the land allotted to the tribes in the conquest. The parallel use of *nakhalah*, "inheritance" (NIV **heritage**), in the second half of this verse captures this relationship between one's *kheleq* and the division of the land. Job ironically uses these terms, with their long association with divine blessing for God's people, to describe divine punishment for wickedness. God remains the active force in the verse as he **allots** the punishment the wicked man **receives.** Those who receive this "heritage" from God, **the wicked** man (*ʾadam rashaʿ*) and the **ruthless** (*ʿaritsim*), deserve all they get.

27:14–15 / To remind the reader (and the friends) of his own experience of loss, Job describes the vulnerability of the

children of the wicked. **However many** they may be (Job himself had seven sons and three daughters), they could be gone in an instant—as Job knows full well from experience. The children of the wicked meet their end in any number of ways, including **the sword,** starvation, or **plague.** The sectarian scrolls from Qumran use the word *sharid*, **those who survive,** to refer most often to "refugees" or "escapees" who flee in battle (this is perhaps connected to the "sword" that decimates the "children" above). The connotation, therefore, is stronger than the idea of surviving a deceased person that is common in obituaries. The phrase **their widows will not weep** is plural, so it refers to the spouses of the deceased children. Their lack of weeping may indicate that they, too, are dead, rather than callously indifferent.

27:16–17 / **Though he heaps up** . . . Wealth and possessions are no guarantee of security. Heaping up **silver like dust** obviously refers to amassing great wealth—similar to Job at the beginning of chapter 1. Closets of fine garments **like piles of clay** represent expendable capital and luxurious living, especially when contrasted with the plight of the poor who, deprived of their outer garments by their oppressive creditors, must lie down naked to sleep at night (22:6; 24:7, 10). The "piles of clay" (Heb. *khomer*) may be mounds of mortar or the large woven baskets—with a capacity of a little more than 100 gallons or three bushels—in which these building materials were carried.

The phrase **what he lays up** refers to the possessions amassed in the previous verse. Notice how the poet artistically reverses the order of possessions considered in order to form a *chiasm:* **the righteous will wear** . . . **the innocent will divide.** In verse 16 the wicked lay up "silver" and then piles of "clothes." Here in verse 17 the righteous first "wear" the garments and then the innocent "divide" the gathered **silver.** These two groups—the "righteous" and the "innocent"—are of course the very groups oppressed by the "wicked," and who ought to be blessed by God. Job's ironic eye does not miss the lack of congruity between the picture in this verse and his own experience of loss. Even as a person acknowledged as "blameless and upright" (1:1, 8; 2: 3), all the blessings of family and possessions that made him "the greatest man among all the people of the East" (1:3) did not survive the onslaught of a single afternoon!

27:18–19 / From wealth and possessions Job now considers protective shelter. He imaginatively views the mansion of the rich wicked as a fragile **moth's cocoon** that is easily destroyed.

Those assigned to protect the ripening harvest from plundering thieves built temporary lean-tos to provide shade in the heat of the day. Never intended to remain permanently, such a **hut made by a watchman** collapsed quickly into decay when no longer needed. Similarly the home of Job's eldest son offered little protection to Job's children, as it collapsed on their heads when struck by a strong wind from the desert (1:18–19).

He lies down . . . he opens his eyes. This image emphasizes the unexpected rapidity with which the wicked's prosperity disappears. Like an investor caught napping when the stock market tanks, overnight he goes from being **wealthy** to being impoverished; **all is gone.**

27:20–23 / These last four verses describe the **terrors** that attack the wicked who has lost all sources of security in life. Wealth, clothing, family, protective shelter, secure sleep—all of these necessities of life are gone and replaced by the constant battering of destructive forces described as **a tempest.**

I spent my youth in southeast Texas, not far from the Gulf of Mexico and near the Louisiana border. Every year as summer came to an end and the school year began, life was carried along by the rhythm of tropical storms and hurricanes that frequently battered the coast and inland plains. The "tempest" Job describes sounds like a particularly nasty hurricane from my childhood. The wicked is overtaken by a **flood,** and I remember having up to three feet of water surrounding our home on at least one occasion. The storm **snatches him away in the night,** and I remember falling to sleep to the sound of howling winds and waking up the next morning to find trees blown down and roofs ripped off buildings. Job's storm **hurls itself against** the wicked **without mercy,** and I am reminded of the oil tankers blown ashore and left grounded by the winds and the swath of death and destruction in the wake of the passing hurricane. The wicked **flees headlong,** and I remember the year we packed a few things in the car and headed inland to escape the worst of the storm.

The **power** of the storm is so great that it dwarfs the wicked oppressors. They may wield life and death power over the poor and defenseless, but the storm remains unimpressed. **It claps its hands in derision and hisses him out of his place.** There is no stopping or standing in the way of such power. The "place" of the wicked is the space his body occupies—the evidence of his continued existence. In Job, to be removed from one's "place," so that the place cannot remember you, is to exist no longer (7:10; 8:18; 20:9). This storm and its consequences very closely parallel Job's own experience of suffering. In 7:10 he fears just such a destruction awaits him, and so he becomes determined to seek vindication before he goes (7:11; 27:2–6).

As chapter 27 comes to an end, we see that Job has been using these imaginative descriptions of the judgment awaiting the wicked to remind his friends that their refusal to acknowledge the evidence of his observations and experiences of life—evidence that calls into question the validity of their own blind commitment to retribution—will not save them from suffering similar consequences themselves. Ignorance is no excuse in wisdom circles—especially willful ignorance maintained by keeping one's eyes tightly shut against the truth. If Job is blameless, as he claims (and as the reader *knows* him to be), then his suffering like the wicked in this chapter is more than sufficient evidence that *any* righteous person—including the three friends—can suffer as if they were wicked (v. 7).

Additional Notes §90

27:13 / More broadly, the term ʿaritsim, **ruthless,** has the sense of violent, fearsome power and oppression, or refers to those who perpetrate such abuse on others. In 6:23 the word stands in parallel with tsar, "opponent; oppressor."

27:14 / Again, NIV's use of **fate** is distracting since the phrase says merely "theirs (is) the sword." The word translated **plague** is actually "death," mawet, rather than deber.

27:17 / The **innocent** (naqi) are not sinless, but have been declared innocent in specific circumstances, esp. of accusation of violent bloodletting.

27:19 / The phrase **he opens his eyes** may mean something like our similar idiom: "in the blink of an eye."

§91 Excursus: A Poem of the Elusive Nature of Wisdom (Job 28:1–28)

We encounter in these 28 verses a wisdom poem of exquisite beauty. Some commentators declare it to be an independent composition which, in its original form, had nothing at all to do with the book of Job. According to this view, the poem was later imported into the book to serve as the words of Job or some other speaker. Clines, for example, proposes to read this chapter as the conclusion of the Elihu speeches (chs. 32–37), which Clines further relocates after the concluding addresses of the friends and prior to Job's final monologue (this reconstruction is quite complicated, see Clines, *Job 21–37*, pp. 908–9).

There is, however, good reason to think that this poem expresses the sentiments of Job—at least in the canonical form of the book. There is no textual evidence to support any of the proposed rearrangements, and notices within the Hebrew text itself are best understood as encouraging the reader to consider these words as from the mouth of Job. As we have seen, chapter 27 begins, "And Job continued his discourse" (*wayyosep ʾiyyob śʾet meshalo wayyoʾmar*). This type of notice in Job regularly indicates the *continuation of speech by the same speaker* (27:1; 29:1; 36:1). Following chapter 28, the identical phrase appears in 29:1 to indicate once again that this is a continuation of Job's speech. Such a notice would hardly seem necessary without the intervening material of chapter 28. It seems clear that sandwiching this wisdom poem between two chapters bearing identical continuation formulas binds this poem into the context of Job's ongoing speech.

In addition, a careful comparison of the contents of chapter 28 with the speeches of the friends, Elihu, and Job, demonstrates that these verses have a much closer affinity to the words of Job than to any of the other speakers (see esp. the fine study by S. A. Magallanes). As a result of these considerations it seems not only plausible, but indeed preferable, to read chapter 28 as the continued expression of Job himself. As it currently stands, the poem brings Job's dialogue with the friends to its definitive end, and it opens the way to Job's long monologue that prepares for his ultimate meeting with God. The poem is divided into three segments, each of which we will treat separately in what follows.

§92 Humans Uncover the Earth's Most Hidden Riches (Job 28:1–11)

The composition begins with a description of the effectiveness of human ingenuity and effort to ferret out precious metals and gems from their most hidden places in the remote depths of the earth. Humans are incredibly resourceful, the poet says, in discovering valuable ores beneath the earth's crust. Humans are equally diligent in their pursuit of these commodities into the depths, regardless of the danger and effort required.

28:1–2 / **There is a mine for silver.** Having just returned from a visit to a Welsh slate mine, I am newly impressed by the effort and courage required by those who spend significant segments of their lives underground, lighted only by candles, working in poor air, breathing in dust, and laboring intensely in restricted spaces far below the surface of the earth in order to bring up the desired materials. Such underground mining was common in the ancient world, with extensive operations going back into prehistoric times, at least as far as the Paleolithic period. I have also visited Egyptian copper mines at Timnah in the Arabah desert, a region exploited as well during the reign of Solomon (966–922 B.C.). Here the poet reminds readers that humans know where to find "silver" and how to create "a mine" to extract and exploit it.

The phrase **a place where gold is refined** parallels the first half of the verse and expands on the theme of human effectiveness in exploiting precious commodities hidden in the earth. The process of refining here seems to require washing and filtering pulverized ore in order to separate gold from the waste. Since gold is heavier, the lighter waste could be poured off after rinsing, and the precious metal would be left behind, perhaps in a process similar to panning for gold in the American West. The point is that humans are adept at finding gold, mining it, and separating it from the worthless host rock in which it hides.

Iron is taken . . . copper is smelted. This verse continues to parallel the first, describing the discovery of one metal ("iron") and the refinement of another ("copper"). "Iron" became the primary source of military weaponry (Josh. 17:16–18; Judg. 1:19; 4:3, 13; 1 Sam. 17:7). It was prized because of its enduring hardness and gradually replaced bronze, which was a hardened mixture of "copper" and tin. Smelting—which involves removing metals from ore and eliminating impurities from the metal by means of heat—occurs at lower temperatures for copper. Iron, however, requires higher temperatures, so this process developed later with the design of some sort of air bellows to force hotter fires. At least at an early point in Israel's history, it seems that the Philistines may have enjoyed a monopoly on the technique necessary to work iron efficiently (1 Sam. 13:19–22).

28:3–4 / Man puts an end. These two verses, stressing remoteness and hiddenness, emphasize human diligence in discovering and accessing precious minerals and gems. The underground **darkness** in which **ore** has hidden for millennia is brought to "an end" by the intrusive lamps illuminating the burrowing paths of the miners (the early Welsh slate miners lighted their way using only candles). Through the spreading web of tunnels within a mine, humans follow the veins of ore to their **farthest recesses,** leaving no valuable rock unturned. The verb translated **searches** here (Heb. *khaqar*) has the sense "dig deeply; investigate thoroughly; search out," a meaning entirely appropriate for the probing excavations of miners. This **blackest darkness** under the surface of the earth does not deter humans. If you have ever been in an unlighted subterranean cavern or deep mine tunnel, you know just how dark *absolute* darkness can be! Yet, even in prehistoric times, before the advent of technology to support tunnel walls or to bring fresh air to deep excavations, humans braved the dangers and discomforts to find and remove commodities they found precious. It is slightly unclear here whether the first of two successive words for "darkness" (*ʾopel*, "darkness, gloom") reinforces the second (*wetsalmawet*, "deepest darkness") emphatically (as in NIV), or whether it instead modifies the preceding word for **ore** (*ʾeben*, "stone; rock") as in NJB, "black rock."

Far from . . . While the literal rendering of this verse is somewhat difficult, the description of the remoteness of the miner's pursuits is clear. The activities take place *meʿim gar*, "(away) from those who dwell temporarily." The effect of *gar*, rather than *yashab*,

"settle down; dwell permanently," is to emphasize again how remote mining is from inhabited cities and villages. In the first half
of the verse, the miner **cuts a shaft** (Heb. "channel; river bed").
The verb, *parats,* "break (violently) through," can describe the
breach of the wall of a city under attack. These places are uninhabited, however, since they are **forgotten by the foot of man** (i.e., are
off the beaten path). In the search for new ore deposits the miner
dangles and sways, descending steep rock faces suspended on
ropes to find and excavate ore. This may also describe the exploration of subterranean caverns. The verse stresses again that these
sites are **far from men.**

28:5–6 / The poet communicates a sense of the unexpected and awe-inspiring nature of the subterranean world to
those who are primarily acquainted with working the surface soil
for agricultural production. On its surface, **the earth** produces
fields of grain and other crops from which humans produce their
food (Heb. *lekhem,* "bread"). But, beneath the surface where miners go, the world **is transformed** (lit., "turns over against itself").
Beneath the earth there is evidence of violent turmoil in which
the rock has been melted and changed **as by fire.** And rather
than **food,** the **rocks** and **dust** of this hidden world yield **sapphires** and **gold,** treasures unknown to those limited to experience above ground.

28:7–8 / Even the wild animals who wander the hinterlands beyond human settlement have no experience of this world
under the earth. **No bird of prey** or falcon, circling high in the
heavens and from whom no part of the earth's surface is hidden,
is able to observe this hidden realm. **Proud beasts:** the Hebrew
speaks literally of "sons of the arrogant" here, and the same
phrase appears in 41:26 to describe arrogant humans. But in this
context, and parallel with *shakhal,* **lion,** in the second half of the
verse, the NIV translation seems most likely in this case. The point
seems to be that even the most "noble" of the "beasts"—the prowl-
ing "lion"—has no contact with the remote and hidden world
of mining.

28:9–11 / Removed far from human habitation, hidden
from access even by wild animals that roam the wilderness areas,
and shielded from the far-seeing eyes of the high-flying birds
of prey soaring above the earth, this underground wonderland
of precious stones and metals would seem perfectly hidden and

inaccessible. But in these three verses the poet returns to praise the human skills of discovery and exploitation of the earth's buried resources with which the poem began (vv. 1–4). Undeterred by the remote setting and difficult labor, the miner's **hand assaults the flinty rock,** and digging down through the earth **lays bare the roots of the mountains.** After cutting river-like **tunnels** through solid **rock** with primitive tools, none of the earth's most precious **treasures** can escape. The miner explores the **sources of the rivers** where they begin deep under the mountains, and **brings . . . to light** the **hidden** treasures discovered there. So humans, in the poet's view, are masters at discovering and digging up the treasures hidden beneath the earth's surface. Against all odds and expectations, they brave isolation, fearsome darkness, and life-threatening danger to find and exploit the resources of the earth; *nothing* seems able to escape them!

Additional Notes §92

28:1 / The NIV translation of this verse obscures the fact that the Heb. begins with the particle *ki,* that often expresses a causal relationship with what precedes. Most translations, however, render the particle in this case with some form of emphasis: "surely" or "indeed." The Heb. term translated **mine** (*motsaʾ*) means, lit., "place of going forth; source."

28:3 / See the discussion in the additional note on 3:5 in §7 with reference to blackest darkness.

28:5 / The same verb translated **is transformed** appears in 20:14 to describe the nauseating turmoil in the stomach of one who has ingested poison or venom.

28:11 / **He searches the sources of the rivers and brings hidden things to light** is more difficult in the Heb. and may alternatively be read: "He binds (dams up?) the sources of the rivers, and brings out to the light what is hidden (under the water?)."

Humans may be immensely skilled at mining, but their seemingly unstoppable skills do not transfer to the search for wisdom. Like the various treasures of the earth mentioned in the preceding verses—silver, gold, copper, iron, precious stones—wisdom was long ago woven into the very fabric of God's world at the moment of creation. The sages in general, and Job's friends in particular, assume that one can find and exploit this orderly wisdom much like the physical resources of the earth. The process is not easy, of course—it takes patience, diligence, care, and intelligence over generations—but with time, they believe, God's wisdom yields to the scrutiny of the sages, and mastery over wisdom offers mastery over life. This is precisely the stance the three friends take in their dialogue with Job (and it is a view that Job probably espoused himself before his experience of devastating loss!). The world works according to discoverable principles, and Job needs to submit to those principles in order to achieve and maintain a life of wisdom and blessing. The wise prosper while the wicked perish—it is as simple as that—and since Job is suffering, he must have departed somehow from the way of life to which he needs to return.

In Job's mouth, the words of chapter 28 stand firmly against the common assumptions of the sages that the three friends represent. As we will soon see, all the skill, diligence, and bravery of determined humans are ultimately of no avail in wresting an understanding of wisdom from the creation.

28:12–14 / But where can wisdom be found? This segment of the poem begins with a matched pair of questions that set the tone for what follows. While there is a place to discover "silver" and "gold" (vv. 1–2), no one seems to have any idea where to start looking for "wisdom." The Wisdom literature often parallels "wisdom" (*khokmah*) and **understanding** (*binah*). These terms reflect the range and effect of the wisdom enterprise: to gain knowledge of the world (*binah*) and to achieve mastery (*khokmah*) that leads to benefit in life. This poem begins to state clearly what Job's arguments to the friends thus far have only illustrated less explicitly: that even sages are unable to understand fully God's world and what he is doing in it (see, e.g., Eccl. 8:16–17). Treating "wisdom" like a commodity to be "found" and possessed (like gold or silver) is thoroughly to misunderstand what wisdom is. Such an approach has nothing to offer an upright person like Job, who experiences horrendous loss and suffering in spite of his committed righteousness. Elsewhere the sages assume that they *can* find wisdom if they search it out with the same diligence as miners searching for precious commodities from the earth (see, e.g., Prov. 2:1–5; 3:13–15; 8:10–11).

Man does not comprehend its worth. The translation "worth" is one way to understand the Hebrew *ʿerkah*. The root of the word describes an orderly arrangement or preparation. In this sense the poet may be saying that humans do not know how to arrange the many facets of wisdom in an orderly fashion so as to understand it. The NIV draws on a secondary meaning, "arrange in order; assess/evaluate." Other commentators choose a different nuance of the root that emphasizes "stretching out; length" and interpret the word as an indication of the impenetrable distance that separates humans from the discovery of true wisdom (RSV; NJB). The latter seems more in line with the context that stresses the inability of humans to uncover wisdom despite diligent pursuit. They know the *value* of wisdom; they are just unable to *locate* it since wisdom **cannot be found in the land of the living.**

The deep . . . the sea. Where might wisdom lurk? Genesis 1 depicts these watery masses as antedating the orderly creation of the world. While the earth was still without form and void (Gen. 1:2), darkness covered the face of "the deep" and the waters were swept by the spirit, or wind, of God. God established boundaries for these primeval waters in creation, but these regions remain inaccessible to the investigative inquiries of humans. Here these primeval witnesses to creation testify to what humans cannot know by personal examination: It (wisdom) **is not in/with me.** Even with all the modern technological marvels of twenty-first-century oceanography that allow humans to explore the darkened depths of the deepest ocean trenches and beam back live video, wisdom is nowhere to be found.

28:15–16 / **It cannot be bought.** Not only does wisdom elude discovery, but even if it were to be found it is far too precious for humans to purchase and possess. Wisdom is not a commodity that can be bartered for **gold.** It does not appear on the NASDAQ index. There is no way to determine its value in terms of **silver.** Even precious stones (**onyx** and **sapphires**) and the much desired **gold of Ophir** cannot equal the value of wisdom. Here the poet lists all of the most esteemed indicators of great wealth in the ancient Near East. None of these precious materials—which were themselves rooted out from remote and inaccessible places under the earth (see the discussion on 28:1–11 in §92)—can provide *in any quantity* a suitable exchange for wisdom.

28:17–19 / The list of valuables that cannot match wisdom goes on and on. **Neither gold nor crystal** can be laid alongside of it. Nor do **jewels of gold** constitute a worthy exchange. **Coral and jasper** fade from memory beside wisdom and even **rubies** are an inadequate replacement. Equally inadequate are **topaz of Cush** and **pure gold.** Obviously the poet is moving beyond strict monetary value to consider the aesthetic appeal of these items. They are not just investments piled up in treasure houses to secure a financial future, but they are artistic ornaments worn for personal adornment and displayed for their beauty. Similarly, wisdom has a beauty that exceeds any practical value that might be assigned to it. (Prov. 3:22; 25:12, for example, equate wisdom and speech influenced by wisdom with personal ornamentation.) It is this combination of value and beauty that draws the wise to seek it above all things.

Additional Notes §93

28:12 / NIV's **dwell** is not actually in the Heb. text, but is an interpretive translation of the more literal "where is the place of understanding?"

28:16 / The location of Ophir is still debated, with possibilities including Arabia, South Arabia, India, and South or East Africa. In 1 Kgs. 9:26–28 Solomon's trade fleets sail for Ophir from Ezion Geber on the Gulf of Aqaba.

This passage uses several different Heb. words for **gold:** *ketem,* vv. 16, 19; *zahab,* v. 17; *paz,* v. 17.

28:17 / The phrase **jewels of gold** is a rather awkward translation of the Heb. *keli paz,* "vessel of gold" (NASB, "articles of gold"; NJB, "vase of gold").

§94 The Way to Wisdom (Job 28:20–28)

Having described in detail the priceless, yet utterly elusive, nature of wisdom—constantly enticing humans to great efforts to secure it while remaining always just outside their grasp—the poet now offers to provide the treasure map to the hidden stash. There *is* a way to wisdom, the poet claims, but it requires special guidance and direction to reach it. Almost like unrolling an ancient parchment pirate's map marked with X's to indicate where the gold is buried, the narrating voice beckons the reader to digest the coded words and follow the measured paces to uncover the prize!

28:20 / **Where then does wisdom come from?** Except for one verb, this verse is identical to verse 12, which began the immediately preceding section. There the question was "where can wisdom *be found?*" (emphasis added), emphasizing the elusive nature of wisdom and the continual failure of humans to find it. Here, however, the poet replaces the passive verb *timmatseʾ*, "be found," with the active *taboʾ*, "come." Wisdom is no longer a hidden commodity waiting to be found, but a dynamic, living force that comes in its own time to those who know how to receive it. **Where does understanding dwell?** The second half of the verse remains unchanged from verse 12, since the source of wisdom is the same. Here, however, the question is not so much about exploring and discovering where wisdom dwells as it is about the futility of unaided human endeavor to reach it.

28:21–22 / These verses follow up on the latter question to emphasize again the inaccessibility of wisdom to humans. The first verse is a summary reminder of the more extended arguments put forth in verses 1–19. **It is hidden . . . concealed.** The verb *neʿelmah*, "concealed," communicates a sense of *intentional* obscurity. Wisdom is not difficult to obtain because of where it is located—it has, rather, been intentionally withheld. As we will see, however, wisdom is *not* some sort of *esoteric* knowledge available only to the few who have been initiated into the mysteries of the fellowship. Instead, the poet is claiming that wisdom comes to those who inculcate the appropriate attitude of receptivity expounded at the end of this section. The phrase **from the eyes of every living thing** recalls and summarizes the argument put forth in verses 12–19. Compare in particular the opening statement of this section in verse 13b: "It cannot be found in the land of the living." Further, **concealed . . . from the birds of the air** clearly refers back to verses 1–18, which described how humans are able to dig out precious ore located in inaccessible places: "No bird of prey knows that hidden path; no falcon's eye has seen it" (v. 7). Wisdom is no less hidden, but remains even more elusive since **Destruction and Death say, "Only a rumor of it has reached our ears."** If indeed wisdom cannot be found "in the land of the living," and is only a "rumor" in the abode of the dead, then what hope can humans have of finding and possessing it on their own? Wisdom cannot be found; it cannot be taken by force or guile. It can only come to those who prepare themselves for its coming. Having once again established the ultimate futility of any human endeavor to wrest wisdom and understanding from the world in order to gain mastery over life, the poet now removes the ties from the parchment scroll and begins to unroll the treasure map.

28:23–24 / **God understands the way.** The first step to finding true wisdom is to recognize that God does not suffer from the same restrictive impediments as humans. God knows "the way" to wisdom and has drawn up the map, **and he alone knows where it dwells.** The Hebrew here emphasizes the sole knowledge of God by placing the pronoun *hu$^{)}$*, "he," in an unusual position *before* the verb. Since the verb itself contains the pronoun, the word order has the effect of emphasizing the subject: "He, himself" or, as in NIV, "he alone." Where humans fail, God is unhindered.

God **views . . . and sees**: his vision is keener even that of the high-flying birds of prey who soar high above the earth and drop like stones to capture the smallest field mouse. His vision also extends to **the ends of the earth** and includes **everything under the heavens.** This *merismus* ("heavens . . . earth") indicates complete vision and knowledge of everything that is.

28:25–27 / God's knowledge of the world is not only a matter of perspective, but also of authority. He knows not only because he surveys the world with all-seeing eyes, but also because he created the world and all that is in it. The fact that **he established the force of the wind** and **measured out the waters** indicates his infinite concern with the details of creation. One can almost see God holding up an anemometer into the wind or pouring out the oceans in five gallon buckets! This sort of involvement confirms his intimate knowledge of the whole of creation. Even the seemingly unruly elements of the natural world, **rain** and **thunderstorm,** turn out to be under the orderly authority of God, who oversees their progress. What animals cannot see and humans cannot find, God knows from the inside out—because he made it all.

Then **he looked at wisdom.** The sages proclaimed wisdom as the "first" of God's creations (Prov. 8:22–31), a master artisan who, along with God, participated in the creation of the world and rejoiced in it (see also Ecclesiasticus 1:9–10). God created wisdom at the beginning of creation and **appraised it.** The Hebrew verb *spr* means basically "count up; measure," but it can also have the sense of "proclaim; declare." It is as if a traveler returning from a foreign journey must count up and declare to U.S. Customs the value of items purchased while abroad. Again, the idea is that God, having created wisdom himself, truly knows its value and worth. That he **confirmed it and tested it** sounds a bit like an investor investigating the worth of a stock or mutual fund! The first verb (Heb. *kun*) has to do with "making something firm" or establishing it. Having created wisdom, God makes sure it will not fade away but is well grounded. The verb translated "tested" (*khqr*) is already familiar to us from its use to describe humanity's endeavor to "search out" riches from the earth (v. 3). God is able to accomplish what humans cannot—searching out wisdom (NRSV; NASB).

28:28 / **And he said to man.** God created wisdom; he knows its whereabouts; he knows its worth. And so he reveals to humans what they have been unable to discover on their own. And in these few words, the wisdom of the ages since the moment of creation *comes to humans on its own terms*. It is not a precious commodity to be possessed, but a companion and guide for the journey. **The fear of the Lord . . . to shun evil.** With these words the book of Job comes full-circle to its beginning. The reader is expected to remember that these phrases are precisely those that characterized Job in the beginning. He is not only "blameless and upright," but also one who "fears God and shuns evil" (1:1, 8; 2:3).

What a radical redefinition of the nature of true **wisdom and . . . understanding!** To be truly wise is not to be able to perceive the divinely instituted order that permeates creation, nor is "understanding" to gain mastery over life as Job's friends have suggested all along. Instead, true "wisdom" is "fear of the Lord." Of course, this does not mean that we are to *be afraid* of God (Exod. 20:20), but rather that we realize and live according to the recognition that we are entirely dependent on God and his mercy in all things. "Fear of God" is an admission of human powerlessness and submission to the power of God (see the discussion on 1:1 in §1 with regard to the "fear of God"). True wisdom, then, is not to gain *mastery* over life but to acknowledge *dependence* on God! And it is this acceptance of personal powerlessness and reliance on the power of God that enables humans to "turn from evil" (a better translation than NIV's **shun**). In the mouth of Job, then, this poem in chapter 28 emphasizes the failure of the friends' arguments by undermining the very structure of their worldview. It is no wonder that the friends never return to the debate!

Additional Notes §94

28:28 / It is interesting that the text at this point reads **Lord** in upper-and lower-case letters. This tells us that the Heb. is not *'elohim* (which would have been translated "God"), as in the original description of Job (1:1, 8). Nor is it the divine name *Yahweh,* which would have been printed LORD, in small capitals. Instead, the Heb. is *'adonay,* the more common term of respect that traditionally replaced the divine name in the public reading of the text. This is not so unusual since, in the dialogue section, the divine name *Yahweh* appears only once (in the speech of Job in 12:9). It seems clear, however, that by using *'adonay* the poet intends to direct the reader to Yahweh as the appropriate subject of human relationship.

Shun seems to imply complete avoidance of evil, while "turn" acknowledges that humans sin and will need to reorient themselves to God in order to leave evil behind.

§95 Longing for God's Intimate Presence (Job 29:1–6)

After the dialogue with the friends ends, Job's continuing monologue takes on a new character. It is as if Job is turning his back on the friends and lifting his face towards the heavens. In chapters 29–31 Job puts his case before God in its final form. He moves from a longing reflection on a lost past (ch. 29), through a final lament for his present circumstances (ch. 30), to posting an affidavit of innocence with the highest court, calling for a response from God (ch. 31).

29:1–3 / **How I long for the months gone by.** Job begins his wistful reminiscence with a desire to recapture the untroubled days of the past. The reference to "months gone by" suggests that the book has covered a brief, rather than drawn-out, period of loss and dialogue. Job has enjoyed comfortable abundance throughout most of his life, in contrast to this brief but intense season of loss and suffering. In Job's earlier life, he had enjoyed the protective care of God, **when God watched over me.** As *the* Satan suggested early on (1:10), Job experienced a divinely erected hedge of protection around him and all that was his. The Hebrew for **when his lamp shone upon my head** suggests a more active role for God than the translation indicates. The Hebrew verb means something like "let shine" or "made shine"—God is demonstrating some sort of benevolence to Job by beaming life-giving light down on him. It was **by his light** that Job **walked.** The "lamp" here is primarily a source of guidance rather than blessing. It lights Job's way in **darkness,** much as David recalls in 2 Samuel 22:29: "You are my lamp, O LORD; the LORD turns my darkness into light." In Psalm 119:105, God's word is a "lamp" to the psalmist's feet "and a light for [his] path." Elsewhere, however, God's "lamp" is a means of scrutinizing the inner recesses of humans: "The lamp of the LORD searches the spirit of a man; it searches out his inmost being" (Prov. 20:27). In his righteousness, Job has nothing to fear from such scrutiny. Indeed, he longs for the time when God's light drove away the darkness that now threatens to engulf him.

29:4–6 / The Hebrew for **when I was in my prime** is obscure primarily because of the uncertain meaning of the word translated "prime" (Heb. *khorep*), which may have something to do with harvest time, winter lambs, or perhaps young manhood. In the phrase **God's intimate friendship,** the Hebrew for "friendship" (*sod*) has more the sense of "secret counsel/conversation." NIV assumes, perhaps, that there was more of a friendship in Job's earlier relationship with God than this noun suggests. While Job may have felt that his relationship with God consisted of secret communication between superior and subordinate, at least it was direct and clear—and this is something Job misses in his present distance from God. There is no mention of blessing in the original Hebrew in the phrase translated **blessed my house.** The sense is that the intimate counsel from God to Job results in direction and thus benefit for his whole house. Job's emphasis is more on his need for communication and direction from God than longing for restored blessing.

The statement, **when the Almighty was still with me,** offers a glimpse into what Job considers his present state. His focus remains on the loss of relationship with God rather than on loss of possessions and wealth. Job is keenly aware of his feelings of abandonment by God. When Job says, **my children were around me,** it sounds as if he is recalling his sons and daughters prior to their destruction. The Hebrew is a bit more ambiguous than that, as the word for "my children" here is not the expected *benay,* "my sons/children," but *na'aray,* "my youths/servants" (the translations fairly consistently read "children" here). While this could refer to Job's own children, it might also refer to the youths of his household, or perhaps the pupils who followed his wisdom instruction. In the following verses, Job is clearly speaking of public respect and deference in response to his reputation. This would lead me to understand *na'aray* as "youths/pupils" rather than his own children.

The metaphor **my path was drenched with cream** speaks of comfort and smoothness. People's respect for Job eases his way in society, as others clear his path. While "cream" (Heb. "curds") was also a sign of wealth and luxury, here it seems to indicate Job's smooth progression in life. In another image of almost impossible smoothness and ease, **the rock poured out ... streams of olive oil,**

Job recalls a time when even the craggy rocks seemed to ooze with lubricating oil. These verses remind me of watching an aged Hasidic zaddik, "spiritual leader" (lit. "righteous one"), surrounded by his young disciples, who ushered him securely through the bustling streets of the old city of Jerusalem. Two respectfully gripped his elbows to steady and guide him, others went before to clear the way, while a rear guard followed protectively behind. This was not so much a sign of the zaddik's wealth as a public display of respect and honor for his venerable wisdom.

Additional Notes §95

29:6 / The translation **cream** assumes an emendation of the Heb. from *behemah*, "with heat/rage," to *bekhemah*, "with curds." The two words sound nearly identical.

§96 Longing for Community Respect
(Job 29:7–17)

The easing of Job's way that verse 6 describes can be either a sign of divine blessing or an outpouring of public honor and respect. In verses 7–17, however, it becomes increasingly clear that Job is focused on public acknowledgement of his wise and righteous behavior. Wherever Job appeared in public, people met him with deference and solicitude befitting his honored position in society.

29:7–8 / **When I went to the gate of the city.** The city gate is the place where the elders, sages, or rulers decided matters of business, justice, and social order. Job goes to the city gate, not to seek a decision, but to take his **seat in the public square** in order to render judgment. In the Hebrew, Job "established" rather than **took** his seat. The picture may be of setting up a mobile chair or throne, but it also has connotations of establishing his authority firmly—perhaps through consistently wise decisions.

When Job appeared, everyone demonstrated respect. The **young men . . . stepped aside.** The "young men" translates the same Hebrew word (naʿar / naʿarim) rendered "children" in verse 5. Here, however, it clearly refers to the younger members of society rather than Job's own offspring. The Hebrew verb translated "stepped aside" (khbʾ) means "hide oneself." Perhaps this is the equivalent of our idiomatic statement that "children should be seen but not heard." Out of respect for the august wisdom of Job, the younger citizens know their place and withdraw silently to the fringes of the discussion. Also in deference to Job, **the old men rose to their feet.** By using this less common word (yashish) for aged persons, the author creates a *merismus* which mentions the extremes (youths/elderly) to indicate everyone in between as well. *Everyone* respects Job and responds deferentially to his presence.

29:9–11 / The word for **chief men** here can also refer to "princes" or those of noble birth. These are certainly members of the highest levels of society. These men **refrained from speaking** and even **covered their mouths with their hands,** another sign of respect. When confronted by the awesome presence of God, Job will respond in a similar manner (40:4). In **the voices of the nobles were hushed,** the word for "nobles" (*negidim*) might better be rendered "leaders." Job's appearance silences even these leading figures, so that it appears that **their tongues stuck to the roof of their mouths,** a sign of their nervousness at being in the presence of such a respected person. The respectful silence Job remembers certainly contrasts with the vocal opposition of his friends during the dialogue. Convinced of his sinfulness, they are no longer respectful but oppose him vociferously.

Whoever heard me spoke well of me. Silence was only a first response to the presence of Job. All those who heard Job speak later pronounced him blessed. The Hebrew here is the verb *ʾshr,* of the same root as the wisdom term *ʾashre* that describes the state of wholeness and rightness reserved for those who fear God and follow his path (Ps. 1:1). Unlike Job's three friends, those who heard Job in the past declared him worthy of such an exalted state of divine approval.

In addition, he says, **those who saw me commended me.** Hearing and seeing are two different forms of evidence of Job's character. The one (hearing) responds to the words with which Job articulates his wisdom and worldview. When he speaks, people find Job to be faultless—even blessed. At the end of chapter 2, the narrator evaluates Job's response to his enormous loss in similar terms: "In all this, Job did not sin in what he said" (2:10). The other evidence involves watching—even scrutinizing—Job's actions in response to the events of his life. Words and deeds may sometimes be at odds with one another, and consistency between one's spoken words and one's actions is an essential measure of integrity. Those who know Job find no fault with him in either sphere. In all he says and does, Job is commendable. This commendation of Job early on perhaps anticipates his ultimate approval by God (42:7). Those who hear and see Job in the dialogue section of the book, noting his reaction to divinely imposed suffering and false accusation by his peers, must find him equally faultless in both word and deed.

29:12–14 / Two segments of three verses each (12–14; 15–17) lay the foundation of this public respect for Job. Verse 12 begins with the Hebrew particle *ki*, "**because.**" Each segment describes Job's praiseworthy actions toward the poor and needy. Given the preceding verses recalling Job taking up his seat in the city gate, these verses almost seem like an honorific summary of a prestigious career as attorney or judge dedicated to upholding the cause of the poor and defenseless of society. Such a past career may also explain Job's desire for a judicial-style confrontation with God. As one familiar with court proceedings, Job would logically look to this sort of context for resolution.

The defenseless persons for whom Job has served as advocate and defender include **the poor** (Heb. ʿ*ani*), or those who are suffering oppression by the more powerful, as well as **the fatherless** (*yatom*), or orphans with no male guardian to assist them by securing rights in a patriarchal society (see the discussion in the additional note on 6:27 in §17). Job **rescued** these defenseless persons.

The man who was dying. While the Hebrew participle (ʾ*obed*, "perishing one") may mean "dying," in the extended context it seems better to understand that the reference is to defenseless persons who are perishing because of the oppression of the powerful. Thus those delivered from oppression would naturally pronounce blessing on their deliverers. **I made the widow's heart sing.** Widows, like orphans, are left without a male protector in society. Protection by a wise and powerful person can lead such persons to "sing" for joy.

As we have seen before, **righteousness** and **justice** are legal terms employed in deciding cases in court. The metaphorical description of these characteristics as **clothing** that Job **put on** like a **robe** or **turban** may provide additional support for the idea that Job is being depicted as a judge marked out by special official dress.

29:15–17 / **I was eyes to the blind and feet to the lame.** The catalogue of unprotected persons whom Job defends continues with those whose physical disabilities leave them at a disadvantage. Job is their advocate and helper. The **needy** (Heb. ʾ*ebyonim*) are those who are truly destitute in society. Like a **father,** Job must have seen to their needs. The reference to **the case of the stranger** also calls up the context of a law court. The "case" is more specifically a suit over breach of covenant (Heb. *rib*). **I took up.** Job investigates the case of "one I do not know" as thoroughly as those of well-known celebrities or his friends. For Job, justice is not a matter of wealth or reputation but of searching out the facts of each case. **I broke the fangs of the wicked.** The metaphor of an attacking beast summarizes Job's deliverance of the oppressed and powerless. Like a shepherd protecting his sheep from a predatory lion, Job frees the innocent **victims** from the **teeth** of their oppressors by breaking their powerful hold over the weak.

Additional Notes §96

29:10 / The phrase **their tongues stuck to the roof of their mouths** elsewhere indicates the extreme dryness of mouth that comes as the result of heightened stress and anxiety. In Lam. 4:4, sucklings are thus affected by thirst, while in Ps. 137:6 it is the agony of loss and ridicule that creates this condition.

29:16 / The Heb. verb behind NIV's **I took up** (*khqr*) is better translated as, "I dig out," or "I search out diligently."

29:18–20 / I thought. Job's longing gaze shifts now from the public approbation he experienced in the past to remembering his earlier expectation of a long and fruitful life. **I will die in my own house.** Job alludes to a comfortable death surrounded by family with the noun *qen*, "nest" (NIV **house**). The word elsewhere describes nests of birds, but it can also metaphorically describe close-knit family. Prolonged life, **my days as numerous as the grains of sand,** is a sign of divine blessing. Job had assumed he would live far beyond the norm.

My roots will reach to the water. Like the fruitful tree described in Psalm 1, Job will send his "roots" down deep to the source of life-giving "water." As an additional sign of divine care Job anticipated **dew** would **lie all night on** the **branches** of his metaphorical life-tree.

My glory will remain fresh in me. Human "glory" is the visible essence of a person that commands respect. To see God's "glory" is to see his very core substance—his essential holiness that confronts human sinfulness and threatens its very existence. Job's "glory" is his blameless and upright character described in the opening chapters and contested in the dialogue with the friends. Now Job longs to return to the earlier days when all those who knew him unquestionably acknowledged his integrity. In the phrase, **the bow ever new in my hand,** some commentators take the "bow" as a metaphor for Job's manliness or strength which is constantly renewed. Clines, however, reminds us that the bow is always a weapon used with destructive intent toward other humans or animals. He views the bow as a symbol of "power over others" that is necessary to maintain Job's position in society (*Job, 21–37,* p. 992). This is perhaps a bit too one-sided a view, as the bow can be a powerful tool in *defense* of others, as well. Perhaps the "bow" ought to be understood as the power resident in Job's unquestioned wisdom. Those wielding such power can use it to destroy the wicked and fools while defending and preserving those oppressed ones who rely on their protection. So, as a whole, these verses represent Job's longing for a return to a past in which everyone recognized his wisdom and he could anticipate a long and fruitful life enlivened by the life-giving water of God.

Additional Notes §97

29:19 / Although the **dew** in Israel is short-lived and quickly burns off in the heat of the early morning, its presence during the night and pre-dawn hours provides significant moisture to sustain and enliven plants.

§98 Longing for Community Influence (Job 29:21–25)

Job concludes this chapter, and his longing backward glance, with a lament for the loss of influence in his community. In the earlier segment (vv. 7–17), Job focused on the respect that those who knew him and heard his wisdom teaching held for him. Here the emphasis is on the effects his words and deeds had in shaping and guiding his community.

29:21–22 / **Men listened ... expectantly, waiting in silence for my counsel.** Again silence demonstrates the respect of those who surround Job. But the purpose of their expectant "silence" is to receive the guidance of his "counsel." **After I had spoken, they spoke no more.** What a studied contrast with the dialogue with the friends! In the past, Job suggests, further comment was unnecessary because people took his "counsel" as respected wisdom. There was no reason to argue, since those who heard it respected and accepted Job's wisdom. The friends, on the other hand, show no respect and take every opportunity to undermine Job and question his words. The Hebrew for **my words fell gently on their ears** draws on the image of dripping honey (or dew?), which is a symbol of luxury and abundance. The listeners heard Job's words as a gift of sweetness rather than harsh or unwelcome prodding and coercion.

29:23 / **They waited ... as for showers ... the spring rain.** The imagery of joyful blessings of abundance continues with these references to "showers" and "spring rain." Since Israel and its surroundings are arid lands—a desert, really—rain was an absolute necessity to sustain agriculture and human life. Without rain, the seasonal stream beds quickly dried up and the cisterns carved by inhabitants of the hill country would be empty as well. Those who chose to live in these inhospitable regions located themselves near water sources such as streams and springs or created aqueducts to channel precious water from its source to villages or fields. A literal translation of the Hebrew of the last half of verse 23 captures the expectancy of the people waiting for the enlivening words of Job: "Their mouths they opened wide for the spring rain."

29:24–25 / **When I smiled at them.** The Hebrew more literally reads: "I laughed to them." Job's joy was infectious! Job's good favor was such a precious commodity that the people **scarcely believed** their good fortune when they experienced it. The words **the light of my face** are most familiar to us as an indication of *divine* blessing. The traditional priestly blessing in Numbers 6:24–26 indicates, "The LORD bless you and keep you; the LORD make his face shine upon you and be gracious to you; the LORD turn his face toward you and give you peace." Job's presence and guidance provided a similar blessing. So **precious** was the "light of [his] face" to his fellows that they took care not to allow a single bit to be lost (Heb. "they did not allow it to fall").

I chose the way for them. Job's influence is clear. He chose the direction the community would take. None opposed him, but all accepted his counsel confidently. Job was their **chief,** decisive in all things. **I dwelt as a king among his troops.** As the king commands and the troops obey, so Job's word effectively mobilized his people. Job concludes with a bite of sarcasm: **like one who comforts mourners.** Job remembers his own role as one concerned to bring comfort to friends who were mourning. His own friends, however, could only sit silently and then they turned to dispute Job's lamenting words and reject his claims of innocence.

§99 Mocked by the Banished (Job 30:1–8)

Following his memories of the life he once lived, Job moves on in chapter 30 to his final lament as he describes the radical transformation brought on by his intense and public suffering. The three-fold repetition of the temporal particle "and now" (Heb. *we'attah*) punctuates the chapter at the beginning of verses 1, 9, and 16. The particle effectively shifts the discussion from the backward reflection of chapter 29 to the present experience of Job and provides us with three roughly equal segments: verses 1–8; 9–15; and 16–23. The exclamation of certainty (Heb. *'ak,* "surely") then introduces Job's concluding lament.

30:1–2 / **But now they mock me.** Job begins his final lament by illustrating how removed his present experience is from the respect and influence of his past. Those who had respectfully withdrawn and kept their silence now return with loud ridicule and rejection. The Hebrew for **men younger than I** (*tse'irim*) emphasizes both the youth and insignificance of those who attack Job. These are not the respectful young men (*na'arim*) who honored Job, but rebellious rabble who respect no one. Further, he says, they are those **whose fathers I would have disdained.** Although what we understand as a biased statement of class distinction offends our modern egalitarian sensibilities, we may also have experienced the venom of those who, trapped by various family dynamics, societal pressures, and unwise personal choices, have come to the point where they cannot affirm wisdom or accede to any authority. Instead, they spill out ridicule and rejection on all. Clines reminds us that Job also clearly had detractors from higher levels of society—his friends, for example—and his caustic words may represent the self-serving attempts of the deeply wounded to discredit his detractors (*Job 21–37,* pp. 996–97). But the primary point Job is making in these verses is that his fall has been great—almost complete. From the heights of public honor and respect, he has now tumbled to such an extent that even those relegated to the fringes of acceptable society find themselves superior to him and laugh.

Job refuses to entrust the safety of his herd to the "fathers" of those who mock him. This may suggest a lack of responsibility on their part, an attitude that may have communicated itself to their children. Job does not actually describe the "fathers" as **dogs**—a harshly offensive insult. Instead, he questions the wisdom of giving to men such as these the responsibility to protect his animals. The implication is that the "dogs" provide a more effective deterrent to loss and attack. The insult may be veiled in this way, but it is stinging nonetheless. Clines also suggests that Job may be quoting his pre-suffering evaluation of these fringe dwellers (*Job 21–37*, p. 999)—an opinion derived from his enjoyment of the lofty heights of social approbation. Or it may be that he is mouthing the broad assessment of society concerning this group. Now Job must acknowledge that those who are considered insignificant by societal standards nevertheless stand above him in judgment.

Of what use . . . ? Job draws out his reasons for rejecting the "fathers," whom he here declares useless for protecting the herds. Their uselessness is connected with their lack of **vigor** that renders the **strength of their hands** ineffective. Thus it is not so much who these men *are* that Job rejects, but their history of lethargic ineptitude.

30:3–7 / Some commentators suggest that these verses are more sympathetic to the impoverished persons they describe than Job's opening comments. As a result, some seek to relocate this passage to chapter 24, which also considers the poor. This seems an unnecessary dislocation. The opening verses—particularly verse 2—establish the context for understanding this description of the poor. The lack of vigor that characterizes their lives and diminishes the **strength of their hands** brings on their desperate circumstances. Again, while we may be discomfited by a blanket description of certain groups as "lazy and shiftless," we have to admit that some in any class of persons may willfully adopt such attitudes. If Job is speaking more illustratively than specifically, then his observations are more inwardly turned than outwardly directed. He is more concerned to indicate the depths of his own decline than to impute sloth and indolence to any particular person or an entire class of people.

Haggard from want. The circumstances of these marginalized people are desperate. They inhabit the desolate regions outside common society and eke out a tenuous existence from natural plants and roots. Because they are **banished,** their isolation is not a matter of choice or rugged individualism. They are outcasts who are removed from society and prevented from returning. While the Hebrew stops short of calling them criminals, these wanderers, who are **shouted at as if they were thieves,** are certainly subject to suspicion regarding their motivations. Landless (homeless) persons at all times have experienced similar treatment. Those who have property to protect clearly assume that those reduced to desperation will resort to theft in order to save their lives or better their lot. Again Job focuses not so much on the character of real people, but develops a context to demonstrate the depths of his own loss of status and esteem.

Reduced to almost animal-like conditions, these "banished" ones are forced to live in the open or seek protection in remote caves in the many wadis and stream beds that cut through the uninhabited regions. The animal imagery continues as the outcasts **brayed** like wild donkeys **among the bushes** and **huddled in the undergrowth.** These are indeed the most peripheral of humans, cast out to live like animals away from civilized society.

30:8 / The description of the outcasts concludes with a summary verse that reaffirms the negative character of the group and their rejection by society. **A base and nameless brood.** Behind NIV's "base" is the Hebrew phrase *bene nabal,* "sons of a fool/foolishness." The fool is not someone with diminished mental capacity, but one who *willfully* chooses to reject the instruction and discipline of wisdom. As the insignificant mockers of Job refuse to acknowledge and respect his wisdom, so their ancestors are presumed to be equally rebellious and foolish.

Not only are they foolish, but they are also "nameless." This does not mean that they are anonymous unknowns. To have a name is to possess a worthy reputation in society. To be considered "nameless" is never to have proved oneself worthy in the sight of one's community. The result of rebellious folly is loss of respect and ultimate banishment from common society, and so **they were driven out of the land.** Thus the desperate straits in which these persons find themselves result from their own refusal to operate wisely and with discipline. Again, we must remember that Job intends his critique of this group to set the context from his own fall from grace. Those society has "driven out" as worthless rebels are now in a position superior to Job and able to subject him to their own mocking evaluation.

Additional Notes §99

30:3–8 / Note the similarity between this passage in Job and the description of the banishment of the Babylonian king, Nebuchadnezzar, who was driven out to live as an animal until he acknowledged the sovereignty of Yahweh (Dan. 4).

§100 Abandoned by God and Beset by Terrors (Job 30:9–15)

30:9–10 / **And now their sons mock me in song.** The second appearance of the temporal particle "and now," at the beginning of verse 9, returns us to the context of the mocking younger generation: insignificant sons of banished fathers. In the Hebrew, Job has "become their song" (*neginatam*), the source of their rollicking amusement and derision. **They detest me.** Job describes a common phenomenon. When those who have long enjoyed respect, influence, and power fall from their exalted positions, many times those who have long been subject to them respond with great anger and cruelty. Often the anger is deserved—as in the case of callous despots who ruled their people with fear and torture—but it need not always be so. In our own time particularly, the general public seems to feed on the downfall of prominent public figures and respond to their moments of weakness with caustic glee.

Even these ragamuffins, fringe children of disrespected families, **keep their distance** and do not want to associate with Job! It is as if homeless street people cross to the other side of the street to avoid contact. To **spit** in someone's **face** is the ultimate insult of rejection and degradation. In 17:6, Job describes himself in similar terms and attributes his fall to such depths to the action of God. Jesus experiences the same kind of final rejection as he approaches the end of his earthly life (Matt. 26:67; also Num. 12:14; Deut. 25:9).

30:11 / The Hebrew in this verse is somewhat obscure. The individual words are clear enough for the most part, but the meaning is vague. **Now that God has unstrung my bow.** The Hebrew does not mention God, but it is a likely interpretation from the context. Rather than "bow," some manuscripts read "*his* [God's] bow*string*" while others supply an alternate reading "*my* [Job's] bowstring." NIV's translation "unstrung my bow" seems to capture the basic meaning of the phrase.

But what is Job's bow[string], and what does it mean that God has unstrung it? In 29:20, the image of the bow describes Job's power either to defend the poor and oppressed or, as Clines suggests, to maintain his own influential position in society (*Job 21–37*, p. 992; see the discussion on 29:18–20 in §97). The Hebrew for **afflicted me** can also have the sense of "humbled me," but in any event God is the force behind Job's decline and suffering. The Hebrew for **they throw off restraint in my presence** is again less direct, reading literally, "(the) halter from my face they send away." The halter (Heb. *resen*) is a form of restraint for horses and mules. In Psalm 32:9, these animals are considered resistant and rebellious unless restrained by a halter. In Isaiah 30:28, a halter leads the rebellious people away from their God. While it is possible in Job to read this phrase as describing the removal of restraint from *Job* ["from my face"], it is probably best to read, as in NIV, that it is Job's detractors who cast off restraint when they sense because of his downfall that they no longer need to fear the protective power of God in his behalf. God has "unstrung" Job's power and so his enemies have no fear of him.

30:12–13 / **On my right.** Job now follows on with the militant image of the unstrung bow to describe the attack of his enemies as a one-sided military engagement. In **the tribe attacks,** the Hebrew word for "tribe" (*pirkhakh*) occurs only here in the entire OT, but it is derived from a root associated with poultry and their young. Some commentators prefer to translate it as "brood"— a possible reference to the children of insignificant fathers mentioned in the preceding verses. Others take the imagery to describe "rabble" or an undisciplined "mob" (See *HALOT*, p. 7728). These rise up against Job, taking advantage of his defenseless state. Another difficult phrase in the Hebrew is, **they lay snares for my feet** (lit., "my foot they send away"). The variety of different translations indicate this difficulty. Whether Job's enemies snare his feet (NIV), thrust his feet aside (NASB), or drive Job forth (RSV), it is evident he feels under attack. The Hebrew phrase translated "**build . . . siege ramps**" (*wayyasollu ʿalay ʾorkhot ʾedam*, "they cast up against me paths of destruction"), occurs only here, although a similar construction appears in 19:12: "they cast up against me their way" (*wayyasollu ʿalay darkam*, NIV "they build a siege ramp against me").

They break up my road. This is no road crew repairing a worn highway, filling in potholes. The "road" is a metaphor for

Job's path in life, and his mockers are more like bomber pilots destroying supply bridges and roads to prevent the passage of needed supplies and relief troops. Their purpose is to bring Job down and to hinder him from reaching his goal: God. Others take **they succeed in destroying me** to mean that the detractors "profit" or "benefit" from Job's destruction. Just how this might be is not clear. The Hebrew for **without anyone's helping them** is not clear, and others translate "and no one restrains them." In this case it would be God who fails to act on Job's behalf.

30:14–15 / **They advance.** Job returns to the military imagery of attack by siege. Job is the city whose walls are breached, and enemy troops pour in **through a gaping breach.** The Hebrew verb (*hitgalgalu*) describes the soldiers **rolling in** through the rubble of the protective wall like a flash flood or successive waves pounding on the shore. **Terrors overwhelm me.** The "terrors" are in reality the *demons* of the underworld who "pursue" Job like the attacking soldiers of the preceding verses. What is at stake, what is threatened, is Job's **dignity.** This is not the public reputation associated with the Hebrew *kabod*, "glory," but the more inward personal sense of nobility and self-confidence (*nedibah*). Job's attackers have been so overwhelming that his very sense of self is severely undermined. In **driven away as by the wind** the parallel with Psalm 1:4 is clear. There it is the insignificant wicked who are driven away like chaff. Here the tables are unexpectedly turned so that righteous Job experiences the judgment the wicked deserve. It is perhaps a bit more than just **safety** that **vanishes** here. The Hebrew word is *yeshuʿah*, "salvation; deliverance." Hope for deliverance from attack is fading like an insubstantial **cloud.** Job intimates that his hopes for divine deliverance from his present suffering are teetering on the brink.

Additional Notes §100

30:9 / The headings of the Psalms employ the term *neginah* to prompt accompaniment "with stringed instruments." See also Lam. 3:14, where the word is paralleled by *sekhoq*, "laughter, derision, sport."

§101 God the Enemy (Job 30:16–23)

30:16–17 / **And now . . .** appears again, this time introducing the third major section of the chapter. This temporal particle serves to remind the reader of the contrast between Job's earlier experience and his present suffering. In these verses Job clearly articulates his sense that God is behind his collapse and ongoing rejection by society. When he says **my life ebbs away,** his "life" here is his *nepesh,* the animated self that is totally dependent on God for its continued existence. Job's *nepesh* "pours itself out" like water onto dry sand, communicating that he feels close to giving up in death. He is in the **grip** of great **suffering** as **night pierces** his **bones** and he is subject to unceasing **gnawing pains.**

30:18–19 / In sharp irony Job speaks of the **great power** and inescapable closeness of **God,** who is near to Job **like clothing.** But these are not the comfortable or protective clothes one might choose and wear gladly. Instead, Job describes God as an ill-fitting garment of rough material that **binds** Job and chafes him around the **neck.** Job has been seeking God—demanding he appear in court—and yet Job has been unable to find even a whisper of God's caring presence. But, as this verse shows, divine *judgment* seems entirely too close, inescapable, and unrelenting. **He throws me into the mud.** God is the one behind Job's decline and fall from respect and influence to ignominious ridicule and weakness. The only comparison Job can find for his extremity is **dust and ashes—** twin symbols of mourning and death.

30:20–23 / **I cry out to you.** Job's lot is not the consequence of his failure to entreat God. The verb "cry out" is from a root (*shwᶜ*) related to the noun *yeshuᶜah,* "deliverance; salvation." The verb is in the *imperfect,* indicating that Job's pleas for deliverance are ongoing. And yet God continually fails to reply in the face of Job's pleas: **but you do not answer. I stand up, but you merely look at me.** Job knows that God is aware of his plight and his pleas. When Job takes a "stand," God fastens his eyes upon him. The verb *hitbonen* implies close attention and scrutiny rather than a casual glance. God is carefully aware and attentive, but he makes no move to deliver Job from his difficulty.

You turn on me ruthlessly. The verb describes an unexpected flip-flop so contrary to normal experience as to be nearly impossible. In Jeremiah 13:23, the prophet uses this same verb to question the possibility of an Ethiopian "changing" his skin or a leopard its spots. Job expects divine deliverance but, contrary to all expectation, when God *does* act it is to **attack** Job "ruthlessly" **with the might of** his **hand.**

You snatch me up. Job returns to the imagery of the wind blowing about insignificant litter (vv. 14–15). Like threshed grain is tossed into a stiff breeze to allow the worthless chaff to be blown away, so Job feels as if God has thrown him headlong into a **storm** to be driven **before the wind** so he can **toss** him **about** like chaff. Job concludes this section with the pessimistic observation that the only logical conclusion of such a state of affairs is **death.** God is indeed active in relation to Job—not to accomplish the deliverance of his faithful one, but to **bring** him **down** to *Sheol,* **the place appointed for all the living.**

Additional Notes §101

30:21 / The adverb *ʾakzar,* NIV **ruthlessly,** is perhaps better translated "cruelly." See Deut. 32:33; Lam. 4:3 and the related noun *ʾakzeriyyut,* "cruelty" (Prov. 27:4).

30:24–25 / A shift away from direct address of God distinguishes the final segment of chapter 30. Job laments here in intense personal reflection. "I" language predominates in these verses, as Job lays out his unexpected suffering in the starkest terms. **Surely . . .** Job opens with an appeal to common social propriety. It is socially unthinkable, he says, to kick a person when he is down: **no one lays a hand on a broken man.** Job describes the sufferer in extreme terms as a "ruin" (Heb. ʿi). When such a one **cries for help in his distress,** others have the decency to come to his aid, or at least to leave him alone. Job himself has responded to **those in trouble** with similar compassion. He has **grieved** alongside the **poor.**

30:26–27 / Job's own experience at the hand of God defies all social convention and common expectation. Job waits expectantly (NIV **hoped**) for **good, but evil came.** He anticipated (NIV **looked for**) **light,** but only **darkness** arrived. Job does not directly indict God in these verses as he speaks only of his contrary experiences—not their origin. But it is clear, after his direct speech to God in verses 18–23, that God is behind Job's suffering.

Like a victim of virulent food poisoning (or the effects of venom as in 20:14–16), Job's internal organs seethe and boil (NIV **churning inside me**) without ceasing. Since **days of suffering confront me** (Heb. "come to meet me"), Job has only more affliction to look forward to.

30:28–30 / **I go about blackened.** The NIV takes the participle *qoder* ("be black") as a description of the externally visible effects of Job's illness. Others take the term to refer to the black garb of mourning (NASB) or the somber gloom of depression (NRSV; NJB). Still others emend *beloʾ khammah* ("not in the heat/ sun") to *beloʾ nekhmah,* "without comfort" (see the thorough discussion of v. 28 in Clines, *Job 21–37,* p. 1010, for this and other suggestions). Job's pleas **in the assembly**—probably a reference to the worship setting—are apparently met with deaf ears. The effects of Job's suffering are a darkening of his skin ("blackened," v. 28; "black," v. 30), burning **fever,** and social avoidance (v. 29). Rather than human companionship, he finds himself consorting with **jackals** and **owls,** animals often associated with remote, desolate locations removed from human occupation.

30:31 / This last verse takes an artistic turn as Job comments, rather obliquely, on his personal response to these unexpected and crushing circumstances. The *kinnor* is a stringed instrument used to accompany singing. The Psalms refer to it as part of Israelite worship (81:3). In Isaiah, the *kinnor* forms part of pagan worship (5:12), but playing the instrument is also one of the skills associated with prostitutes (23:16) and those who participate in joyous revels (24:8). In keeping with the tenor of the rest of chapter 30, Job seems here to be stressing his experience that is contrary to expectation. Rather than joy, his **harp is tuned to mourning** and his **flute to the sound of wailing.**

Additional Notes §102

30:27 / The Heb. for **churning inside me** is a graphic description of an internal gastric upset. The "boiling" of the inner organs will not be "silent," calling to mind the noisy gurgling of a stomach and bowels in extreme distress.

§103 Introduction: God Is Judge of Wicked (Job 31:1–4)

Chapter 31 is Job's last speech. His only contributions hereafter are his rather terse responses (40:3–5; 42:1–6) to the questioning of God from the theophanic whirlwind. In this chapter Job concludes his plea for confrontation with God by offering an affidavit affirming his own innocence. This is more than just a protestation, and it has all the earmarks of a legal challenge in court that demands a response from the other party in the case.

The affidavit takes the form of a series of oaths introduced by the particle *ʾim,* "if." Job expresses the related "then . . ." clause in only a few cases, leaving most of these oaths without a clearly anticipated consequence. In this legal setting, the obvious result of being proven false would be to lose one's case or to be convicted. There is considerable disagreement over how many oaths of disavowal Job uses in the affidavit. The particle *ʾim* occurs seventeen times by my count, which parallels the maximum number of oaths assumed by some commentators. Others group these occurrences of *ʾim* into lesser series of oaths (see the discussion of this speech in Clines, *Job 21–37,* p. 1013, for the variety of options). The most likely division of the materials is into an introductory opening followed by a series of *seven* disavowals, as indicated below.

Job begins his legal case by affirming God's power and responsibility to judge the wicked. God is the one who sees all that humans do and has the power to render justice accordingly. Job is leading up to his series of claims of innocence that occupy the rest of the chapter. He wants to make it clear from the beginning that God is in a position to *know* the truth of what Job claims. That fact, coupled with the assumption that God is *able* to render justice, makes Job's experience of suffering even more acute.

31:1 / **I made a covenant with my eyes.** Since the purpose of this introductory section is to lead up to Job's disclaimers, this first verse seems a bit awkward. Some commentators have called it misplaced and suggest moving it to another location (see Clines, *Job 21–37*, pp. 960, 1014, for an extended discussion of the possibilities). While the verse may in fact be dislocated, there is no textual evidence and it is impossible to know with certainty whether it ought to be completely removed, or where it should be relocated. The same sort of awkwardness occurs at the very end of the chapter. Job's final disavowal (vv. 38–40) rather unexpectedly follows his explosive summary of his affidavit's purpose (vv. 35–37) that sets the stage for God's response. This beginning and ending bear the marks of an intentional editorial strategy. We will, therefore, simply accept this initial awkwardness and proceed.

The opening verse does not appear to be one of Job's disavowals, since there is no *ʾim*, "if" introduction as there is in all the other cases, nor is there any statement of consequences as there is in several of the disavowals. It is, instead, an affirmation of a *positive* commitment that characterizes Job's approach to all such circumstances in life. Prior to any temptation to err, he has adopted a path of action that keeps his way secure. The "covenant" is a commitment between Job's heart (the source of moral decision-making) and his eyes (the source of input to the senses). In this covenant the heart has determined beforehand the appropriate course of action so that in the event of tempting input from the "eyes," the right decision will prevail. This is, of course, an instructive example for us. The commitments we make out of knowledge of what is right and true can stand in the face of temptation and lead us in "paths of righteousness." Despite its awkwardness, this verse serves as a fitting example of Job's commitment to the right way and of the preparation he has made to fulfill this commitment.

NIV makes this avowal **not to look** more straightforward than it is in the Hebrew. The phrase is actually a question introduced by the interrogative *mah* ("how?"). The question emphasizes his commitment, as he asks, almost in a state of amazement, how one who has made such a "covenant" could then violate it. The term **lustfully** does not appear in the Hebrew text, which says simply, "How will I gaze intently at a young woman?" The lustful nature of the gaze is an interpretation by the translators that may be correct, but it prevents readers from making that conclusion on their own. Many translations render the word for **at a girl** as "virgin," perhaps to accentuate the sense of violation Job disclaims. The Hebrew is the noun *betulah*, which most likely refers to a woman of marriageable age rather than a virgin. Genesis 24:16 describes Rebekah as "very beautiful, a *betulah*; no man had ever lain with her." It would hardly be necessary to explain her lack of sexual experience if the noun *betulah* meant in and of itself "a virgin" (see also Judg. 21:12).

31:2–4 / **For what is man's lot . . . his heritage.** The term "lot" is an unfortunate choice here since it suggests "fate" or "destiny" that comes by chance, while the Hebrew *kheleq*, "portion," means that which is *allotted* to one by another—in this case, **God.** The second term, "heritage" (*nakhalah*), affirms this understanding of *kheleq*, since *nakhalah* also describes the "inheritance" one receives from another. The "lot" one receives is not by chance but comes "from God above," **the Almighty on high.** The description affirms that "God," from his exalted position, is able to see and know all that humans do, and is responsible for delivering to each the "portion" or "heritage" that is due. It is very important at this point for Job to establish clearly that what he receives in his suffering is the consequence of divine power, however unfitting a response it may seem to the blameless life Job has lived.

Job answers his own question with a seeming affirmation of retributive theology. When God metes out the "lot" or "heritage" of each human, the **wicked** and **those who do wrong** ought to receive **ruin** and **disaster.** However, Job is *not* acceding to the friends' contention that one can reverse this equation and determine by their "lot" whether humans are righteous or "wicked." He is instead stressing the *inappropriateness* of his own "heritage" of suffering. In a world where retribution ought to reign, Job's life and his experience of suffering are like the explosion of a fragmenting grenade that shreds one's carefully constructed understanding and hopes into indecipherable chaos.

Does he not see . . . ? Job agonizes: if God is above all and sees all, how can he not see that Job's life is blameless? Of course, the reader already knows that God is fully aware and has affirmed Job's righteousness from the beginning. The lack of congruity between a blameless life and a portion of suffering drives Job to seek resolution in the only way possible: confrontation with God himself. If Job is indeed blameless and yet receives a heritage of suffering, then it seems the only answer must rest with God. Either God does not see Job's blameless way, or God is not in the business of retributive distribution.

§104 The First Disavowal: Deceit and Greed (Job 31:5–8)

Verse 5 presents Job's first disavowal. He casts this series of protestations of innocence in the form of an oath. Any failure to fulfill these oaths invites disastrous consequences. All of these disclaimers involve the themes of deceit and greed and are concerned primarily with integrity in dealings with others.

31:5–6 / **If I have walked in falsehood . . . hurried after deceit.** The Hebrew of this first phrase is, more accurately, "walked with what is empty/worthless" (*shaw*ᵓ), although the parallel in the next phrase with "deceit" (*mirmah*) confirms the sense of prevarication. Job denies having abused his associates with misleading language in order to gain the upper hand. The image of **honest scales** in verse 6 suggests that he refers to a business context, although this is not certain. The picture is of the merchant whose scales are under investigation by the regulating authorities. Job has no fear, if weighed in "honest scales" by God. He knows that his "integrity" (a better rendering than NIV's **I am blameless**) will be demonstrated. This is probably not intended to raise questions about God's honesty, as if he might manipulate the "scales" in order to prove Job wrong (e.g., Amos 8:5). It is, rather, a case of judgment in kind, where God measures Job's integrity on the scale of his own deeds and relationships.

31:7–8 / Job now turns from deception to greed: **if my steps have turned from the path.** Verse 7 illustrates a progression: wandering from the "path," following temptations introduced by the **eyes** (also v. 1), all resulting in defilement of the **hands,** possibly through theft. I can almost visualize the scene in a crowded Middle Eastern *souk,* or open air market, where merchants have their items on open display. If one's **heart** (again, the source of moral decision-making) is **led** astray by the "eyes" to desire something spied among the wares, it is an easy matter to *bend* (a good rendering of the verb behind NIV's **turned**) one's normally straight "path" to approach, in the crush of people, and steal the item away. Metaphorically, such a theft would certainly cling to the "hands" as much as any wound or bruise.

Verse 8 outlines the consequence should Job's denials be proven false. If he has taken from others by means of deception or even theft, he will suffer similar loss. Although the image is clearly agricultural, it is subject to a variety of understandings. Will **others eat** Job's produce because they *steal* it? Will they receive his goods as a judgment against Job in court? Or is it because he will die and leave his crops to those who come after him (Eccl. 2:18–21)? A *double entendre* lurks behind the words **my crops . . . uprooted.** While the word rendered "crops" here (Heb. *tse'etsa'im*) can refer to plants, it also alludes on a number of occasions to *human* offspring. Surely this calls to mind Job's own offspring, who were "uprooted" in the opening chapter of the book (1:18–19).

Additional Notes §104

31:7 / The Heb. phrase here is not about *ritual defilement* but injury that marks the **hands.** The verb *dabaq* means "cling to" rather than **defiled,** while *m'um* (*mum*) describes a bruise or wound rather than a leprous spot.

§105 The Second Disavowal: Adulterous Lust (Job 31:9–12)

Job now turns from general deceit and dishonesty to more specific offenses of adulterous lust. Several *double entendres* characterize these verses: the terms for "be opened; opening" (NIV "enticed"; "door"), "grind," and "kneel over" (NIV "sleep with") also intentionally allude to the acts of sexual misconduct they disapprove.

31:9–10 / **If my heart has been enticed.** Again Job begins with the temptation to the "heart," for this place of decision must be involved first for the offensive act to take place. The verb "enticed" means more literally "be opened," and refers also to the sexual act of "opening" a woman by intercourse. Here, however, it is the "heart" that is first opened by lust. The Hebrew translated **by a woman** does not intend to lay blame on the woman for exercising seductive wiles. Rather, it criticizes the man's "heart" for being opened "concerning the woman." This seems to imply a predisposition or readiness on the part of the "heart" to pursue adulterous thoughts and acts. When the "heart" is open, the decision is already made and the act will inevitably follow. The verb translated **lurked** (*ʾrb*) suggests "lying in wait" with premeditation—often to attack or do harm to another. Here the man is the predator waiting to approach his **neighbor's** wife with adulterous intent.

In the Hebrew for **may my wife grind another man's grain,** there is no mention of "grain." It reads simply, "may my wife grind for another." While the image is certainly that of grinding grain to produce flour, the *innuendo* suggests an act of sexual congress. Job denies any such wrongdoing himself, and he takes an oath calling down parallel consequences to establish his own innocence: "If I have seduced another man's wife, may the same happen to me!" The use of the plural to describe **other men** who would "kneel over" (NIV **sleep with**) Job's wife indicates that his oath intensifies the nature of the consequence. A single adulterous act on his part would be repaid with multiple encounters between his wife and others. The language is harsh, but one must remember that Job is absolutely certain of his own innocence and never anticipates that the consequence would be realized.

31:11–12 / **For that would have been shameful.** Job recognizes that to enter into premeditated lurking with adulterous intent would be a highly offensive act. The term "shameful" (*zimmah*) can be a technical, legal term describing condemned acts with sexual overtones (Judg. 20:6; Jer. 13:27; Lev. 18:17; 19:29; 20:14). Such willfully sinful acts should and will be judged, Job says. The result of such "shameful" acts is both a complete destruction of the participant and the positive benefits that sprang from his life. Like a **fire** that consumes all in its path, lust can destroy all of life even to the gates of **Destruction** (Heb. *ʾabbadon*), a reference to *Sheol*, the abode of the dead.

§106 The Third Disavowal: Inequity and Injustice (Job 31:13–15)

Job claims to have performed with justice and equity even in relation to his underlings and servants. The setting is one of legal dispute between master and servant. Job intends, therefore, this parallel between this situation he imagines and the relationship between himself and God. What Job wishes is for God to give the same account of himself in court as Job offers here.

31:13 / **If I have denied justice.** The circumstance implies that Job is in the position to determine "justice" (*mishpat*) for the complaining servants. Perhaps he envisions himself in the role of judge with the power to determine the outcome of the case and the consequences for the parties. If so, he refuses to exploit the power inherent in the circumstance. Clearly the **grievance against me** (*rib*) is a legal complaint brought in court, not the informal grumbling of employees. Similarly, by his signed affidavit Job has elevated his complaint against God from grumbling to a formal legal suit demanding response. The question now is this: will God, who is both judge and defendant in the suit, deny Job's claim out of hand, or answer as Job is doing here?

31:14–15 / Employing a chiastic structure, Job considers his response should God appear to confront him: **what will I do . . . What will I answer?** This confrontation is, of course, exactly what Job wants! But here he is using his desire to meet God in court to buttress his claim of innocence. What person, guilty of refusing justice to others, would actually call down upon himself a confrontation with God? Only the innocent would willingly enter into a suit with the Almighty. Job has passed beyond his earlier fear that God's powerful speech can turn even the words of the innocent into convicting evidence against him (9:14–20). The verb translated **when called to account**, *pqd*, means "to visit in order to scrutinize/examine carefully." This is the activity of a judge who carefully considers all aspects of a case and testimony in order to render a just decision.

Job's words **he who made me** reveal a certain egalitarian sense of human worth before God. God is the creator of both master and servant and the divine creation **in the womb** precedes any "elevation" of position by virtue of birth or skill or human effort. These words do not erase any trace of class distinction in ancient Israel (or Uz!), but Job does envision here the equal right of all parties to just treatment in court. Job is accepting God as just arbiter between rich and poor, powerful and powerless. He is also hoping for similar treatment in his own confrontation with God.

§107 The Fourth Disavowal: Lack of Compassion (Job 31:16–23)

The fourth oath is almost twice the length of the first three. It might be possible to divide this section at verse 19, where a new *ʾim*, "if," clause punctuates Job's speech. Thematically, however, the whole section seems to hang around Job's denial that he failed to demonstrate proper compassion for the traditional list of disenfranchised members of society: *dal*, "poor"; *ʾalmanah*, "widow"; *yatom*, "orphan" (twice); *ʾebyon*, "needy." In addition, the final verses of this section provide both a self-imprecation to balance out the list of oaths (v. 22) and a summary response (v. 23) that draws the whole section to a close. For these reasons I will allow this segment to stand as a cohesive unit with subdivisions.

31:16–18 / If I have denied the desires of the poor. The "poor" here are the *dallim,* a term which emphasizes "weakness" and "thinness," perhaps as the result of poor nutrition as a consequence of their poverty. Job is claiming never to have withheld from such persons their "desires." In such desperate circumstances he is speaking of the basic necessities of life that are lacking, rather than frivolous wants. Job goes on to speak of food and clothing, indicating the kind of "desires" that occupy those who are poor. Widows are another group of powerless persons, particularly in a patriarchal society, because of their lack of a male representative. Compare the desperation of Naomi and Ruth, when they find themselves on the fringes of Israelite society as widowed, childless women dependent on charity for daily survival (e.g., Ruth 2:2, 7, 15–16; see the discussion in the additional note on 6:27 in §17 with regard to widows and orphans). When the **eyes ... grow weary,** death is not far away, since the eyes lose their light and focus as life slips away. Lackluster eyes can also be the result of suffering and hunger, with consequent loss of vitality.

The NIV chooses a fairly loose translation in verse 17, **if I have kept my bread to myself,** that captures the general sense of the Hebrew but does not convey the more specific intention. The "bread" is more literally a "scrap" or "fragment" of food, suggesting a refusal to share even one's cast-off scraps with the hungry poor. The Hebrew says, literally: "(If) I ate my scrap alone," conveying the picture of a friendless miser avoiding company and resisting any call to hospitality or generosity. The second half of the verse reads, literally: "(If) the fatherless has not eaten from me," driving home the condemned refusal to share with the needy that Job disavows.

A sort of parenthesis interrupts the string of "if" clauses in verse 18, as Job protests in order to offset the accusations of his failure of compassion: **but from my youth I reared him.** Eliphaz raised similar issues in his condemnation of Job in 24:6–9 (see Job's own comments in 29:12–16). The Hebrew is a bit difficult here and the translations diverge. The verb (*gedelani*) means something like "he made me grow up" and is unlikely in this context. Some emend the form to say "I reared him" (NIV; NRSV), others read "he grew up (with) me" (NASB). The NJB goes even farther afield with "I, whom God has fostered." (See Clines, *Job 21–37*, p. 1022, for a clear description of all the possibilities.) If we understand this line to be parallel with the next, then the sense is probably: "I raised him (the orphan) . . . I guided her (the widow)." This seems the proper understanding. In both lines the statement generates a hyperbolic image of the infant Job assuming a protective paternal role over the fatherless or guiding the **widow** while Job is yet in his mother's womb. Both "widow" and "orphan" are representatives of multiple needy persons who have received Job's assistance, rather than specific individuals.

Because our modern sensibilities with regard to the poor may be disturbed by Job's views, a brief word about how we approach any text from an alien culture is helpful. It is clear that in these verses the narrator/author is doing little or nothing to confront the systemic evils of a society in which the acquisition of wealth by a few (such as Job!) places many in desperate circumstances and ultimately forces their dependence on the *largesse* of the powerful elite. It is questionable, I think, to derive a negative picture of Job as a hypocrite or as naïvely self-deceptive because our own sensibilities (heightened by other OT and NT teachings concerning care for the poor and needy, the examples of Jesus, and contemporary social sensitivities) are offended by a cultural setting that is distant from our own. The original readers of this text most likely shared the worldview of the author and did not experience the contradictions that we do—at least not in the same way. While it is an important aspect of biblical exegesis in any age to allow our own experiences to enter into the interpretive process and thus to highlight incongruities of life and text that we must explore, it is nevertheless wrongheaded, in my opinion, to allow our own sensibilities to rewrite the text in ways that obscure or undermine its original intention. If, by our modern standards, Job is an unthinking exploiter of the poor who excuses his exploitation by virtue of his attention to the needs of the poor in largely isolated and limited acts of *largesse,* we could see Job as ultimately vain, misguided, deceptive, and deserving of the judgment of suffering and loss he receives. Such a view would cast doubt on the motivation behind his interactions with friends and with God, and would undermine the credibility of the ultimate resolution of the book in God's appearance, his questioning of Job, and his affirmation of Job in 42:7. This is certainly *not* the view of Job that the author/narrator of the book espouses, and if we read Job (book and man) in this way we follow our own issues rather than allowing ourselves to be confronted by those of the book. The unfortunate effect is that we excuse ourselves because of our cultural "superiority" and ignore the message because we do not agree with the messenger.

I do not mean that our cultural discomfort with Job's easy acceptance of his privileged social position is wrong or even inconsequential. This lack of comfort should force us to look further to understand the whole of scriptural teaching on the issue. I simply say the obvious: the revelation of Scripture in a particular time and place means that revelation comes to us in an alien cultural garb that we must see and understood for what it is. The book of Job is not about whether systemic social evil exists—it certainly did exist, and it still does. Nor is the book concerned with whether the powerful elite like Job (and most of us) are complicit with that evil in ways they are naïvely unaware—Job was, and so are we. Other books in the OT (e.g., Proverbs, Ecclesiastes) *do* focus on these issues and offer sweeping condemnation of such entrenched evil. However, Job is, at the core, concerned with whether or not God is worth holding onto in faithful committed relationship, even when we do not see or experience the benefit of our faith in this life—or have any hope of it in another life. Our own concerns are legitimate and we need to explore them, but they ought not to cause us to dismiss the response the book of Job offers to this key issue that still remains a vital one for our contemporary human experience.

31:19–20 / Job returns to his oath by shifting the focus to those who lack adequate clothing: **if I have seen anyone perishing.** It is unlikely the Hebrew means that these persons are actually "perishing" because they have no clothes. The "perishing" (Heb. *ʾobed*) are a category of destitute persons like the **needy** in the second half of the verse. These impoverished persons are identified by their **lack of** adequate **clothing** for social respectability and personal protection from the elements. The joyful response of the poor to Job's ministrations, **and his heart did not bless me,** affirms his generous action and contradicts the accusation of compassionless disregard. It is in fact the "loins" of the poor that "bless" Job. As the loins are often understood as the seat of procreative power, Job's compassionate covering of the poor may save lives and secure the existence of future descendants. Clines (*Job 21–37*, pp. 1022–23) sees the loins as the portion of the body particularly warmed by a **fleece** wrapped around the waist.

31:21–22 / The words **if I have raised my hand** may refer to a threatening gesture, as if preparing to strike with the fist or slap with the hand (Isa. 13:2). An awareness that the powerful wealthy had more **influence** than the **fatherless** (because the latter had less stature and power in society) might encourage such intimidation of others **in court.** Job is claiming never to have abused his position to undermine the cause of the poor.

The self-imprecation set as a consequence for failure to fulfill the preceding oath is: **then let my arm fall . . . be broken.** By his willingness to suffer such extreme punishment Job intends to proclaim his innocence. The consequence here—an "arm" that falls "from the shoulder" or is violently "broken" **off at the joint**—is particularly apt to the threat foresworn. Job imagines God intervening to break the arm of the intimidator in order to protect the rights and person of the defenseless poor.

31:23 / **For I dreaded destruction from God.** Job's concluding remarks offer insight into his hesitancy to abuse his social capital in order to intimidate and abuse the poor. It is his dread of divine punishment and his sense of God's exalted **splendor** that hold Job back from selfish exploitation of personal power. These two motivations balance one another out somewhat. Job is not hesitant to act simply because he fears punishment. He is, above all, restrained because of his awareness of God's majesty of character. Self-preservation alone does not govern Job's actions. He also desires to be aligned with the essential character of God, who is opposed to evil and is compassionate to the defenseless. As Psalm 5:4 affirms, God is "not a God who takes pleasure in evil, with [him] the wicked cannot dwell." Job desires above all to dwell with God, and so he shuns behaviors that would exclude him from the divine presence. He remains "blameless and upright," fearing God and turning from evil (1:1).

Additional Notes §107

31:16–23 / Clines' description of the structure of this section is apt: "The structure of this strophe seems to be a long series of five 'if'-clauses, from v. 16 to v. 21 . . . , interrupted by a parenthesis in v. 18 and concluded by a self-imprecation in v. 22 and a motive clause in v. 23" (*Job 21–37*, p. 1021).

31:21 / The **court** is actually the "gate" of the city, where economic and legal proceedings take place as a regular matter of course. This is not necessarily a legal venue, but in any social transaction those of greater social standing might disenfranchise the powerless.

§108 The Fifth Disavowal: Trusting Wealth and Other Gods (Job 31:24–28)

The fifth set of oaths revolves around the twin concerns of trust in the accumulation of wealth and worshipping other gods. The beginning of the book describes Job as a man of great wealth who nevertheless loses everything. In all of that extreme loss, however, he remains blameless and undeterred from following after God.

31:24–25 / The oath describes an accumulation of **gold** that becomes a false basis of self-confidence. The second half of the verse even imagines that the oath taker is talking to his treasure: "(If) I have said to gold, 'My trust!' " This reminds us of stereotypical images of misers crooning to their piles of coins, or perhaps Gollum in Tolkien's *Lord of the Rings* murmuring to his "precious" ring. The picture is extreme and communicates Job's sarcastic rejection of the charges leveled against him. Not only does Job refuse to **trust** in gold, but he also denies having **rejoiced over** his former riches. His disavowal here is consistent with his response to the loss of his family and possessions at the end of chapter 1: "Naked I came from my mother's womb, and naked I will depart. The LORD gave and the LORD has taken away; may the name of the LORD be praised" (1:21). These are not the words of a miser, or of one who trusts and delights in the security of wealth. Job, instead, claims to delight and trust in God alone. Job denies having relied on his own effort and accumulation of riches, on **the fortune my hands had gained.** In contrast to the depiction in chapter 28 of the expenditure of immense human effort and ingenuity to extract gold and precious stones from the bowels of the earth, Job's life reflects his dedication instead to the pursuit of wisdom, which can only be found in the fear of God (28:28).

31:26–27 / Job now turns to consider the secret worship of **sun** and **moon.** There are numerous references to the worship of celestial bodies in Israel, so it must represent a real temptation faced by many (Lev. 26:30; 2 Kgs. 23:5, 11; 2 Chr. 14:5; 34:4, 7; Isa. 17:8; 27:9; Ezek. 6:4, 6; 8:16). Job denies even **secretly** adoring these created celestial lights. The enticement of the **heart** in verse 27 represents another use of the Hebrew word for "open" in a metaphorical sense for sexual congress (see the discussion on 31:9–10 in §105). Habel (*Job*, p. 437) has noted the parallels between this worship of the "sun" and "moon" and adultery. In each there is seduction of the heart, secrecy, kissing, and betrayal—and each betrayal is condemned and punishable (see also Clines, *Job 21–37*, pp. 1025–27, for an insightful and eloquent discussion of the seductive character of such worship).

31:28 / The fifth disavowal concludes by declaring Job's motivation for resisting the seductive draw of wealth and false worship: **these also would be sins to be judged.** As he made clear in verse 23, Job's action is in one sense a response to his awareness of the consequence of punishment, as God condemns those who worship "sun" and "moon" to death (Deut. 17:2–7). But Job's sensitivities are based as much on his fear of God as on his fear of punishment: **I would have been unfaithful to God on high.** Like "sun" and "moon," God is "on high" in the heavens. But, as creator of all, he is worthy of worship—unlike the created lights on display there.

§109 The Sixth Disavowal: Inhospitality and Secret Sin (Job 31:29–34)

In his sixth set of denials, Job returns to explaining his relationships with others. This section considers three different areas: Job's attitude toward his "enemies"; his response to men of his household and strangers who depend on his hospitality; and finally his avoidance of secret sins known only to himself.

31:29–30 / **If I have rejoiced . . . gloated.** One might, perhaps, be excused for experiencing a sense of satisfaction at the downfall of a particularly vicious enemy. Indeed, the psalmists often seek divine punishment for those who pursue the faithful relentlessly. Here Job's enemies are those "who hate me"—those who reflect this inner motivation and completely reject Job—rather than those who simply trouble his life. The **misfortune** does not refer to minor mishaps or irritants but to absolute "destruction" or even "extinction" of his enemies. It is the kind of word (Heb. *pid*) used elsewhere in Job to describe the desperate circumstance of those who suffer like Job (see 12:5; 30:24; also Prov. 24:22). The term for **trouble** here (*ra*ᶜ) can mean "evil" or "wickedness." In a backhanded way, Job is lashing back at those who have rejoiced at his downfall. The phrase **that came to him** suggests that the suffering of Job's enemies is the result of divinely appointed punishment rather than vengeance meted out by Job or others. Job claims not even to take joy in seeming happenstance that lays his opponents low.

Invoking **a curse against** one's enemies was a time-honored way of enlisting divine aid when one felt particularly impotent to act against others. The phrase more literally says, "to ask with an oath his life." The consonantal text could also read, "to *Sheol . . .* his being!"—the equivalent of, "To hell with him!" The imprecator actively participates in the anticipated demise by envisioning and articulating the desired fate of the enemy, while allowing God to bring the punishment to fruition. So here we have moved from enjoying the unexpected misfortune of the enemy to actively seeking his destruction. Job is, of course, claiming not to have **allowed** his **mouth to sin** in either of these ways.

31:31–32 / Job now asserts his open generosity. His hospitality is so great that **the men of** his **household** are unable to recall any guest who has departed Job's house stomach empty. Job welcomes even the passing **stranger** without reservation since his **door was always open to the traveler.**

31:33–34 / Job concludes this sixth disavowal by denying any hidden sin kept **concealed** from others but left to work out its fearful consequences deep in his **heart.** The description of the fear of discovery engendered by hidden sin, and the toll it takes on the one who strives to live a double life—innocent to outward observation, but enslaved to evil within—is finely etched. Such a person often lives in fear of **the crowd,** feeling that all around can plainly see the hidden sin. Shrinking from the anticipated **contempt of the clans** (perhaps better "families"), the sinner withdraws silently from social contact and refuses even to **go outside.** Such is not his case, Job declares, precisely because he has no transgression to hide.

Additional Notes §109

31:30 / **I have not allowed my mouth to sin.** While the words are slightly different, the sentiment is almost the same as the earlier statement in 2:10: "In all this, Job did not sin in what he said" (lit., "with his lips"). We are probably expected to remember this earlier disclaimer here at the end of Job's speeches.

31:31 / The **men of my household have never said . . .** The use of the Heb. idiom *mi yitten,* "who will give . . . ?" (meaning there is no one who could provide evidence of having left Job's table unsatisfied), signals the exhaustive nature of this claim. See the discussion on 14:4 in §47 with regard to *mi yitten.*

31:32 / The phrase **my door was always open to the traveler** may be better translated, "my door was always open to the *road,*" suggesting that Job's open door stands as an invitation for weary travelers to turn in for hospitality.

§110 Desire for a Day in Court (Job 31:35–37)

Toward the end of Job's legal affidavit, we encounter the second awkwardness of arrangement similar to that in verse 1. There the opening statement of Job's covenant not to lust after a woman seems awkwardly placed *before* his description of God's role as judge of humanity. Here Job's desire to meet God in court seems to explode from his lips even before he expresses his final disavowal. Some commentators have relocated these three verses to the end of Job's speech, just before the concluding postscript: "The words of Job are ended" (v. 40c). Because these awkward assertions occur at the beginning and end, however, it seems they form a sort of *inclusio* around the chapter. This unexpected outburst at the end emphasizes the emotion behind Job's desire to see God—emotion that escapes his ability to carefully control it and present it in an orderly fashion.

31:35 / **Oh, that I had some one to hear me!** Job's desire for a hearing is palpable. He employs the idiomatic expression *mi yitten* that expresses a deeply held desire that is unlikely to be fulfilled. His friends have failed to pay unbiased attention to his struggle. They have sought to maintain their life-long commitment to retribution in the face of Job's experience of innocent suffering. Now Job desires a public opportunity to defend his innocence in court. **I sign now my defense.** Like a witness who signs the written record of her deposition, Job is willing to put his "mark" on the final affidavit of his personal testimony.

The words **let the Almighty answer me** comprise the subpoena for God to appear in court. Job has stated his case, but he has thus far received only silence in reply. The friends have been vociferous in their attempts to undermine Job's claims. But God, the only party besides Job who can know the truth of the matter, has yet to present evidence. The translation, "**let my accuser,**" turns the original Hebrew a bit. The more literal meaning is, "the man of my law suit." It is not so much that Job thinks of God accusing him, as that he is naming God as the other party in his legal action.

The Hebrew behind **put his indictment in writing** again opposes the NIV translation at this point. The "indictment" (actually "document," a possible reference to the other party's written testimony, like Job's affidavit) is viewed as already written. Either this phrase connects to the opening phrase at the beginning of the verse—"Oh, that I had . . . !" (as in the NRSV)—or it links forward to the opening statement of verse 36—"Surely I would wear it [the document] on my shoulder" (as in the NASB and NJB). Job wants to see God's evidence in his case because he is confident it will exonerate him. The idiomatic expression here, however, indicates that Job has little hope that such evidence is forthcoming. The NIV's use of the terms "accuser" and "indictment" implies that God is opposed to Job and laying out a case against him. The Hebrew seems to suggest that Job expects God's evidence to confirm what Job has already claimed. Job's purpose, then, is not to set God in the wrong, but to gain public vindication of his integrity by means of God's sworn deposition.

31:36–37 / Surely I would wear it on my shoulder . . . put it on like a crown. Since Job expects God's testimony to exonerate him, he would want to publish the deposition abroad in the most public fashion possible. It would be somewhat like wearing a sandwich board advertisement in the street. This statement seems to affirm that Job does not view God's document as an indictment, but as testimony to the truth of Job's claims. **I would give him an account.** Job has nothing to fear from God's testimony, and once cleared he would be free to "account" for his actions without being misunderstood. With his slate cleared and public vindication realized, Job's reputation would be restored beyond question and he would be able to **approach** God **like a prince,** as the blameless and upright person we have known him to be from the opening pages of the book.

Additional Notes §110

31:35 / See the discussions on 11:5 in §36 and on 14:4 in §47 with regard to *mi yitten*.

§111 The Seventh Disavowal: Abuse of Land and Tenants (Job 31:38–40)

The final disavowal takes aim primarily at Job's relationship to the physical earth under his authority and the "tenants" who farm the land on his behalf. He depicts the land itself as able to cry out in objection to abuses perpetrated by the overlord against the "land" and the farmers. In the end (v. 40) the consequence envisioned for proof of abuse is a sort of retributive tit-for-tat—the destruction of the productive capacity of the land. He who abuses the land will lose all profit from it.

31:38–39 / In **if my land cries out against me** the imperfect verb for "cries out" (*tizᶜaq*) might better be rendered with a subjunctive force: "would/should cry out." Here the land is given a voice to register its complaint. This may be another legal image of the plaintiff testifying in a court setting. The personification of Job's arable soil continues with a picture of the multiple furrows of his plowed fields as individuals who together weep in response to his treatment: **and all its furrows are wet with tears.** Again we must remember that these are not *actual* complaints but *hypothetical* accusations Job introduces as part of his statement of innocence. The nature of the hypothetical complaint—just *how* Job is supposed to have abused the "land" and its **tenants**—does not become clear until the next verse.

At first glance the complaint **if I have devoured its yield without payment** seems directed toward the "tenants" rather than the "land." However, failure to fertilize the land or to allow its time in fallow years (Exod. 23:10–11; 26:34–35; Lev. 25:2–7) might be seen as lack of "payment." Alternatively the "land" may stand in solidarity with the "tenants," who work directly with the soil to make it fruitful and to harvest its crops. The phrase **or broken the spirits** of its "tenants" says, literally: "If I have caused the owners (of the land) to breathe out the *nepesh*." This might refer to causing their death, but it more likely suggests desperation and grief. The loss of timely wages would make it difficult for these farmers to keep food on their tables and would increase the stress and sorrow of their lives.

31:40 / The oath, **let briers come up instead of wheat and weeds instead of barley,** enjoins an appropriate retribution for land and farmers. Should Job be proved to have abused the land and those who work it, then he will reap no benefit from the land but only useless "briers" and "weeds." He is, of course, referring to *divine* punishment since no human court could control the production of the land in this way. This calls to mind the consequences of human sin in Genesis 3, where fruitless toil produces thorns and thistles, because the ground has been cursed as a punishment for human disobedience (Gen. 3:17–19).

The words of Job are ended. This brief postscript signals the conclusion of Job's final monologue (and indeed his whole presentation in the dialogue section). The choice of terms is striking, since the editor/author does not employ the more common verb for completion (*klh*) that appears in the similar postscript at the conclusion of David's prayers in Psalm 72:20 ("Finished are the prayers of David, son of Jesse"). Here the verb is *tmm*, "complete; finished," the same root used at the beginning of the book to affirm Job's blameless innocence. While it is obvious that the intention of this phrase is to mark the conclusion of Job's presentation of his case, the use of this particular verb offers a not-so-subtle affirmation of the blameless and complete quality of Job's words. Those commentators who depict Job as in the wrong and who see God's theophany as a *rebuke* of Job's attempt to place God in the wrong do not note the clear connection this final statement makes with the view of Job in the opening chapters.

The author of Job leaves very little to chance, and so it is probable that this postscript, with its word choice, is intentional. This reaffirms for the reader that Job, who survived the initial tests and did not sin, either by putting God in the wrong (1:22) or by what he said (2:10), remains *tam*, "blameless," in all that he has said to the end of chapter 31. This also anticipates God's final affirmation of Job before the three friends in the epilogue: "you have not spoken of me what is right, as my servant Job has" (42:7).

Additional Notes §111

31:38 / The earth, or **land,** is personified in other places (Jer. 12:4; Joel 2:21) and cries out against injustice perpetrated on it in Gen. 4:10.

31:39 / **If I have devoured its yield without payment:** Clines mentions the possibility that Job might have planted in some manner prohibited in Israelite law—such as two types of seeds (Lev. 19:19; Deut. 29:9)—but he thinks it unlikely since such care has been taken throughout the book to maintain Job's status as a non-Israelite (*Job 21–37,* p. 1032).

The term **tenants** here is *ba͑aleha,* normally "owners." Since the land is Job's, Clines suggests an emendation of the initial consonant to create *po͑aleha,* "workers" (*Job 21–37,* p. 1032). This seems consistent with the intent of the passage.

31:40 / The structures of the two postscripts, here and in Ps. 72:20, are almost identical. The order of the Heb. here, "Completed [*tammu*] are the words of Job," parallels that in Ps. 72:20, "Finished [*kallu*] are the prayers of David." See also the related but less similar concluding formulas in Jer. 48:47 and 51:64. See the discussion on 1:1 in §1 with regard to *tam.*

§112 Excursus: The Friends Conclude and Elihu Begins (Job 32:1–37:24)

Had the third cycle of dialogue between Job and his three friends been complete, we would expect to find Zophar's concluding speech in response to Job at this point. However, at least in the canonical form of the book, Bildad's truncated final speech (25:1–6), Job's expanded concluding speech (chs. 26–31), the complete absence of any final speech by Zophar, and the opening comments in the following Elihu section, press the reader to understand this collapse of the last dialogue cycle in another way. Contrary to those commentators who reallocate portions of Job's long speech in order to create a balanced and complete third cycle of dialogues, it is my opinion that the text makes sense—even *more* sense—in its present state.

The fact that Bildad's speech in 25:1–6 is truncated suggests that the friends are running out of steam and are unable to come up with new and persuasive arguments in response to Job. Job, therefore, is free to expand his own comments beyond the norm for the dialogue section—and he is met only by stony *silence.* Zophar neither interrupts nor responds to Job's words, and the concluding postscript in 31:40 does not lead us even to expect him to do so.

The prose link to the Elihu monologues understands the friends' silence as an indication that they have failed to counter the declarations of Job and that they have given up any attempt to do so. Their silence paves the way for Elihu's entrance.

As a result of these factors, there is a sort of logic to the present state of the text—a logic that seems artistically appropriate. I read the text as it is, then, as purposeful and resist the temptation to arrange the text to suit my personal understanding of what the text *should* mean.

Now that the friends' speeches have ceased and Job has made his final, extended plea for a day in court, an unexpected character appears on the scene. Elihu, son of Barakel the Buzite, of the family of Ram, seems to arrive out of nowhere. The six chapters of Elihu's monologues distinguish themselves from the preceding dialogue in several ways. First is the fact of Elihu's absence from the rest of the book. The first thirty-one chapters do not mention Elihu at all. Nor does Elihu appear in the theophanic chapters (chs. 38–42:6) or the epilogue, where God rebukes only the *three* friends of Job (42:7). Second, Elihu is the only individual other than God and the narrator to mention Job *by name*, and he does so no less than ten times in these six chapters. Besides the Elihu speeches, the book refers to Job by name only in the prose prologue (eleven times) and epilogue (seven times), in the narrator's prose link (32:1–4) introducing the Elihu speeches (four times), and in the headings introducing his own speeches and the postscript concluding the poetic dialogue section (twelve times). Third, in the Elihu section, the standard formula for introducing new speakers (*wayyaʿan . . . wayyoʾmar,* "and [X] answered and said") is twice (34:1; 35:1) employed inappropriately to mark the *continuation* of Elihu's uninterrupted speech instead of the usual formula used for this purpose (*wayyosep . . . wayyoʾmar,* "and [X] continued and he said").

Factors such as these have led many commentators to suggest that the Elihu speeches are a later addition to the poetic section of the book. Some would excise them altogether. Others wish to relocate these chapters to somewhere else in the book. Clines, for instance, would place the Elihu speeches following Job's response to Bildad in chapters 26–27, and would take the wisdom poem in 28 as Elihu's concluding word (*Job 21–37*). Such extensive relocations of material seem unwarranted since they are not based on any textual evidence, and no one has offered a persuasive explanation for how the book might have become so confused. Such wholesale readjustments rely entirely on the emender's intuitive (but completely *hypothetical*) sense of what the book *must* have said.

For this reason especially, I will consider the Elihu speeches in their present location between the final speech of Job and the theophanic appearance of God. While I do not deny that these chapters *may well* have come to this position at a later date than the rest of the poetical segments, there is no reason to assume from a canonical point of view that any earlier form of the book—without the Elihu speeches—would or should bear any greater weight of authority than the present, final form. The alternative form of the introductory formula that announces the theophany in 38:1 (*wayyaʿan yhwh ʾet ʾiyyob . . . wayyoʾmar,* "Then the LORD answered

Job . . . He said") makes it clear, by referring to Job as the recipient of the divine address, that the Elihu chapters must have already intervened between Job's speech and the theophany. Otherwise it would have been unnecessary to clarify to whom God was speaking.

In their present position, the Elihu speeches produce three significant effects on the reader. First, the speeches *delay* the coming of the theophany in response to Job's legal affidavit in chapter 31. This prevents God from seeming to respond too quickly to the beck and call of Job, and it emphasizes God's freedom to appear or not. This message of freedom is one of the implications of Job's submission in 42:1–6 and must have been directed to the community of readers who were struggling with the continued absence of God in their own experience. The delay has the added *dramatic* effect of increasing the tension of expectation in the narrative. Job has thrown down the gauntlet, so to speak, and yet God does not come!

The second effect of the Elihu speeches is to *anticipate* the rather bombastic character of the divine appearance. In chapter 37, in particular, Elihu describes God in ways that foreshadow the theophanic chapters. God's voice is a thunderous roar (37:1–5). His coming is a downpour of rain or snow that stops human labor and drives animals into hiding (37:6–13). Like God, Elihu employs rhetorical questions (37:14–20) to emphasize human inability to fully grasp and understand the divine activity. Elihu concludes this chapter (37:21–23) with the image of God coming "in golden splendor . . . awesome majesty"—a clear anticipation of the theophanic appearance of God only a few verses later.

The third effect of the Elihu speeches is to prepare the reader for the restoration of Job and the *unspoken* vindication that the theophanic appearance offers. While God never once publicly declares Job righteous as Job so fervently desires, the Elihu speeches prepare us to understand God's coming as a vindication of Job's blameless character. Elihu tells Job (and the reader) that he need not complain of God's silence, since God has already spoken in the misery that has attached itself to Job (33:14–22). God has already decided Job's case, and his suffering is God's word of judgment for Job's sin (34:7–12). God does not continue to speak to those he has already condemned and so will not come in response to Job's pleas. So, regardless of whether the Elihu speeches form an original part of the literary complex of Job or represent a later independent insertion into the book, this block of material in its present position affects the final form of the book and has all the earmarks of purposeful placement.

§113 Connecting Links (Job 32:1–5)

The first chapter of Elihu's speech introduces the rest of what he has to say. Here Elihu seeks to legitimate his youthful audacity in the face of the august wisdom of age (32:6–10), goes on to speak of his frustration with the inept attempts of the three friends to answer Job (32:11–16), and intimates a sort of prophetic compulsion to legitimate his words (32:17–22). Only then, at the beginning of chapter 33, does he start to formulate his own response to what Job has said.

A brief section of prose (32:1–5) introduces the Elihu monologues, with the ostensible purpose of linking these speeches with the preceding dialogue section. These verses explain why there has been no mention of Elihu to this point and provide a legitimate reason for his late entry into the discussion. While this section might represent an attempt to bind a later independent text into the original book, there is no more reason to excise these chapters from the canonical form of the book than there is to excise chapter 28, or even the prose prologue and epilogue.

32:1 / **So these three men stopped.** The intent to connect back to the dialogue section is clear. If the Elihu speeches are a later addition, the final editors have artfully incorporated them into the fabric of the book. "Stopped" is the same verb (*shbt*) that describes God's own cessation of creative activity at the end of the first account of creation (Gen. 2:2). While in Genesis the term is often translated "rest," in order to link it with the human rest instituted in the Sabbath, here the more appropriate meaning is "cease, desist, end." Just as a rolling stone that comes "to rest" has "stopped" or "ended" its motion, so the three friends of Job have "stopped" any attempt to dissuade him.

The expression **because he was righteous in his own eyes** is not found elsewhere in the OT. A similar idiom, "be wise in his own eyes," has negative connotations—human pride leads one to reject the wisdom of God and thus to take the wrong path in life (Prov. 3:7; 26:5, 12; 28:11; Eccl. 2:14; Isa. 5:21). As wisdom and righteousness are often synonymous in the Wisdom literature, it appears that this statement levels a charge of pride and self-deception at Job. These words certainly express the opinion of Job's friends at this point, as well as that of the new speaker, Elihu. It is unlikely, however, that this evaluation of Job also represents the *narrator's* point of view. In Proverbs 3:7, the call not to be wise in one's own eyes parallels the contrasting plea to "fear the LORD and shun evil." This latter exhortation mirrors both the narrator's and God's consistent assessment of Job as a man who "feared God and shunned evil." It seems improbable that this assessment would now change, especially following so closely on the conclusion of Job's speeches with the superscript that also implies his words were "blameless." The statement does, however, set up an expectation for the general tenor of Elihu's comments.

32:2–3 / **Elihu son of Barakel the Buzite, of the family of Ram.** The fullest patronymic of any character in the book introduces this new character. The name "Barakel" means "God has blessed," and it occurs only here and in 32:6. "Buzite" designates an inhabitant of Buz, a place and people associated loosely with areas around Edom in Jeremiah 25:23. Thus "Elihu" seems also to be a non-Israelite from the same general region as Job. The Buzite "family of Ram" is otherwise unknown. Elihu **became very angry with Job.** The verb *khrh*, "be angry," occurs three times in 32:2–3, emphasizing the anger Elihu expresses. The object of Elihu's anger is clearly Job, and the reason is quickly stated—**for justifying himself.** In the Hebrew, the verb means "make righteous" and shares the root (*tsdq*) with the noun *tsedeq*, "righteousness." This verbal link also brings Elihu's critique back to the friends' evaluation of Job in 32:1. Both the friends and Elihu share a common estimation of Job's failing. The construction used here for **rather than God** is more *comparative* than *contrastive* and is perhaps better rendered *"more than* God." Thus Elihu is angry because he perceives that Job is more concerned to declare *himself* righteous than to excuse God from involvement in his suffering.

He was also angry with the three friends. While Job is clearly the primary target of Elihu's ire, the friends do not escape unscathed. Their failure to **refute Job** effectively exposed them to Elihu's scorn and dismissal. To Elihu, the friends' failure to clarify the inadequacy of Job's claims is like a panel of judges declaring a legal conviction in a case based on unclear and faulty

evidence—**and yet they had condemned him.** Elihu here anticipates God's ultimate rejection of the friends' arguments in the
epilogue (42:7). His anger with the friends' response implies that
Elihu thinks himself able to succeed where they have failed. He has
confidence that his words will offer an effective rebuttal of Job.

32:4–5 / **Elihu had waited.** Verse 4 explains why Elihu
has not appeared before this point in the book. This may be the
"special pleading" of a later redactor who inserted the Elihu material at this point. He waited **because they were older than he.**
Since wisdom is often associated with age and experience, Elihu's
reasons for delay are linked to his relative youth and respect for
his elders. His compulsion to speak at this point is thus a further
testimony of the inadequacy of the friends' arguments. It is difficult to imagine brash Elihu sitting quietly aside during the whole
dialogue, and his biting sarcasm evidences little respect for the
friends. In any event, these verses provide a plausible—if not
completely convincing—explanation for Elihu's delayed entrance
into the debate.

The narrator's actual words are stronger than the NIV's, **the
three men had nothing more to say.** It is not so much that the
friends had run out of words, as there "was no answer in their
mouth." This remark suggests that Elihu understands the friends
as *incapable* of answering Job. The Hebrew phrase for **his anger
was aroused** almost exactly mirrors the expression that begins
verse 2. Together the two statements form an *inclusio* around the
prose introduction of Elihu in 32:2–5, which is now concluded in
preparation for Elihu's speech proper.

32:6–7 / **So Elihu son of Barakel the Buzite said.** Elihu's first monologue begins with the same introductory formula used to introduce the speeches of Job and the friends in the dialogue section. This formula (*wayyaʿan* [X] *wayyoʾmar*, "and [X] answered and said") indicates a new speaker who responds to a preceding speech by another. (The one exception to this rule is the appearance of this formula to introduce the very first speech of Job [3:2] that opens the dialogue section and is thus *not* responding to a preceding speech by another.) This connecting formula links what Elihu is about to say to the discussion carried on in the earlier discourses. Although 31:40 recorded the end of that dialogue, the same connective formula softens the apparent intrusion of the Elihu discourse. We will see, however, several more instances of this formula in the Elihu speeches where he is not responding to anyone.

I am young . . . you are old. Elihu himself affirms the editorial explanation in the prose link for his delayed appearance. Elihu's speeches reveal a sort of brash, arrogant edge that may reflect a youthful sense of confidence. The word for "young" here has additional connotations of insignificance of standing, besides age. Elihu is acknowledging that he does not have an established reputation as a sage. Elihu's words here suggest a respect for aged wisdom that his biting words in what follows do not affirm. The verb translated "**fearful**" probably means something more like "timid, reluctant, or reticent." The "fear" comes in with **not daring to tell you what I know.** The verb *yrʾ* means "be afraid; fear" rather than "daring." The point remains clear, however. Elihu claims that his respect for aged wisdom and his own humility concerning his lack of stature delayed his entry into the discussion.

Age should speak; advanced years should teach wisdom. Elihu continues his justification with a further description of his deference to established sages. He employs jussives here to emphasize his conclusion that the recognized sages should have preference in such a discussion. This observation is about to change, however.

32:8–10 / **But it is the spirit in a man ... the breath of the Almighty.** In contrast to age and experience, Elihu suggests it is in reality the presence of divine inspiration in weak humans (Heb. *ʾenosh*) that provides the basis for **understanding.** This is a different understanding of the "spirit" (*ruakh*) and "breath" (*nishmah*) than that which the OT most commonly expresses. The usual understanding is that the divine spirit or breath animates humans and thus makes them into "living beings." This animation is for *all* humans and is an indication of their complete dependence on God for life and breath (e.g., Gen. 2:7). Wisdom is usually associated with the accumulation of observation and experience over a lifetime—thus the expectation that the aged are more perceptive than the inexperienced young. **It is not only the old who are wise.** Elihu indicates that this divine spirit can enlighten anyone, regardless of age and experience. **Therefore ... Listen to me.** His conclusion provides the basis for his own entry into the discussion where elder friends have been ineffective.

§115 Refusal to Wait (Job 32:11–16)

Elihu describes how he has waited during the long dialogue exchange. While his words seem to offer an outward semblance of respect for age and wisdom, he grows increasingly scornful of the friends' feeble attempts to counter Job's arguments.

32:11–12 / I waited ... I listened ... I gave you my full attention. While these expressions continue to explain Elihu's late entry into the discussion, they also affirm his complete familiarity with the arguments of the dialogue partners. Although silent, he claims, he was attentive and fully engaged in the conversation. Elihu's description of the friends **searching for words** could be understood either as an example of their care and diligent selection of arguments, or it could indicate their desperate attempts to find a satisfactory refutation. Regardless of their diligence or desperation, Elihu says, **none of you has answered his arguments.** Elihu's estimation affirms the interpretation of the truncation and disappearance of the final speeches of Bildad and Zophar as signs of their inability to mount additional arguments rather than textual disarray. This would imply that the textual disorder (if it is not part of the literary creation intended by the original author) was already present when the Elihu speeches were added to the book.

32:13–14 / Do not say "We have found wisdom." Elihu is no passive pluralist who is satisfied to retreat into a confidence in personal wisdom—"I know what I believe!"—while allowing that the contrasting viewpoints of others are equally valid. This hallmark of contemporary, pluralistic society ("whatever is good for you is good for you") is abhorrent to Elihu, who follows the dictum of Proverb 26:5: "Answer a fool according to his folly, or he will be wise in his own eyes." "Do not say," Elihu contends, **let God refute him, not man.** To leave Job's refutation up to God is to admit defeat. The consummate apologist, Elihu must defend the faith and set Job straight or see his own worldview crumble.

Elihu claims to bring new insight to the discourse. Job has not had to respond to Elihu before now, **not . . . against me,** so Job's previous victory over the friends cannot undermine the **arguments** that Elihu is about to set forth. Again, Elihu separates himself from the earlier speeches in a bid to legitimate his late entry into the discussion. Regardless of his claims, however, it is difficult to see much that is new in his arguments.

32:15–16 / **They . . . have no more to say.** Elihu interprets the friends' silence as evidence of the failure of their arguments. **They are dismayed . . . words have failed them.** It is not that the friends have completed their arguments and are satisfied with their statement of the case. They realize their failure and sink into despairing silence because they can find nothing more to say. (This is also further evidence that the dwindling speeches of the friends were part of the text read by the one who added the Elihu speeches.)

Must I wait, now that they are silent? If we had any doubts, we are now disabused of any hope that Elihu would restrain his speech. And yet the introduction still goes on for another six verses! This long, repetitious introduction is intended, I think, to let us see Elihu as the rather pompous windbag that he is. His remarks drag on, constantly circling back upon themselves and reemphasizing the same two issues: the friends' failure and his confident expectation that he will supply the ultimate refutation of Job's claims. We are prepared for a rather brash and overblown attack, but we remain wary that his words will offer any true resolution.

§116 Compulsion to Speak (Job 32:17–22)

Elihu styles his contribution as prophetic speech delivered with a sense of compulsion. His claim concerning the divine origin of his words is an attempt to legitimate his insights before he even expresses them. There is a certain similarity between Elihu's depiction of words bottled up and threatening to explode and Jeremiah's inability to refrain from speaking once the prophetic urgency is upon him: "his word is in my heart like a fire, a fire shut up in my bones; I am weary of holding it in, indeed, I cannot" (Jer. 20:9).

32:17 / **I too will have my say.** The time of reticence and patience is over. As Elihu prepares to speak he says he **will tell what I know,** which is perhaps a claim of special understanding given from God.

32:18–19 / **I am full of words.** Elihu makes what amounts to a subtle claim of divine inspiration and compulsion behind his words. The friends and Job have drawn on a lifetime of personal observation and experience, along with the traditions of the sages passed down through generations of wisdom teaching. The extended and passionate preparation for Elihu's speech leads the reader to expect just such an uninterrupted gush of words as appears in chapters 33:8–37. The **spirit** is actually "in my belly," according to the Hebrew. The belly is usually the origin of passions rather than reflective consideration. The verb for **compels me** can mean "harass; press into a corner; urge to speak." Elihu is unable to escape the building internal pressure to speak out, which is **like bottled-up wine.** Of course there were no wine *bottles* in this context, but **wineskins.** The picture is similar to that Jesus uses in his parable: "Neither do men pour new wine into old wineskins. If they do, the skins will burst, the wine will run out and the wineskins will be ruined" (Matt. 9:17; also Mark 2:22; Luke 5:37–38). The Greek translation of Job 32:19 employs the same noun (*askos*, "leather bottle") as appears in the NT passages. It may well be that

Jesus is familiar with this image from Job and employs it for his own purposes. Evidently the early fermentation process creates sufficient gas that "wineskins" weakened by age are unable to withstand the expansion and crack under the strain. The phrase **ready to burst** is an apt description of Elihu's explosion of words after having been restrained for so long.

32:20 / **I must speak.** Although the Hebrew does not carry quite the same sense of necessity, the jussive form expresses the urgent desire of the speaker to let his words out of confinement. As in the case of Jeremiah (20:9), the only way to **find relief** from the building sense of compulsion is to speak out. Thus, Elihu claims, his words are not his own. Rather, they are divine speech that he can no longer hold back. It is never entirely clear how the narrator evaluates Elihu's claims or his words, since the evaluative comments in the epilogue address only the *three* friends of Job. However, the rather abrupt interruption of Elihu's long monologue by the theophanic appearance of God, who is responding to Job, completely ignores Elihu and seems to brush his words aside. Elihu simply evaporates as soon as God appears.

32:21–22 / **I will show partiality to no one.** A chiastic structure (in which elements are stated in one line and then reversed in the second) binds these two verses together. In the first verse, Elihu will not "show partiality" (Heb. *nasaʾ pani*, "lift up the face"), nor will he **flatter** (Heb. *knh*, "give a name of honor") to anyone. In the next verse, he is not **skilled in flattery** (Heb. *knh*) because God would **take** him **away** (Heb. *nsʾ*, "lift up"). Again, Elihu intends these claims to legitimate what he is about to say as the "unvarnished truth."

33:1–3 / I almost laugh every time I read the opening words of this chapter: **But now, Job, listen to my words; pay attention to everything I say.** It sounds as if Elihu is finally ready to provide substantive comment and critique . . . but his self-inflating introductory words go on for another *seven verses!* (If Hollywood were casting the role of Elihu, I think the only possible choice would be the marvelous comedic actor John Cleese in his Basil Fawlty incarnation, spouting his righteous indignation with an exaggerated posh accent and rolling eyes.) **I am about to open my mouth.** Surely the author of this material is toying humorously with the reader. Clearly Elihu's "mouth" has been "open" for some time now. The Hebrew for **my words are on the tip of my tongue** says, literally, "my tongue speaks in my palate." This refers perhaps to shaping words in the mouth before expressing them out loud (so NJB).

Elihu goes on to stress again the validity of his words. They proceed from **an upright heart** with honorable purpose. The Hebrew word translated **sincerely** has connotations of purity brought about by polishing away adulterating grime to leave his **lips** clear and shining. He claims therefore to have carefully constructed his argument rather than giving a quick, unconsidered response.

33:4–5 / **The Spirit of God has made me.** While this may be no more than Elihu's attempt to establish his common humanity with Job, it sounds more like intimidation—as if Elihu is claiming to be an agent of God rather than an ordinary human debater. The divine spirit, or **breath,** is the life force that animates a human during her life and returns to God at her death. It is the ultimate reminder of human dependency on the creator—the essence of "fear of God." In verse 6, Elihu will more humbly describe his status as equal with that of Job, but it seems that with these words at this particular juncture he intends to establish his own special relationship with God that gives his words authority.

Answer me then, if you can. The almost "throwaway" phrase "if you can" suggests that Elihu thinks just the opposite. Job will be unable to answer Elihu's arguments—this time it will be Job who will be silenced. Elihu invites response and expects confrontation: **prepare yourself and confront me.** Interestingly enough, Job never *does* respond to Elihu. But the reader is not left with the impression that Elihu's analysis of things has won the day. First, the end of chapter 31 notified us that "the words of Job are ended." So we are not surprised that he has nothing more to say. Apparently Elihu's words do not elicit further comment from Job, who has no need to revise his statement. Second, because God's theophanic appearance abruptly preempts Elihu's speech in mid-course, there is little or no opportunity for Job to respond to Elihu.

33:6–7 / **I am just like you.** The Hebrew says, literally, "I am like your mouth to God." Perhaps Elihu is claiming that his words are as valid as Job's rather than humbly seeking to establish common ground with his opponent. The reference **taken from clay** is, of course, to the creation of humanity in Genesis 2:7 where the term is *ʿapar,* "dust," rather than *khomer,* "clay." "Clay" is a building material in Exodus 1:14 and Job 4:19. There are other references to clay being used for creating pots and other vessels (Jer. 18:4, 6; Isa. 29:16), and clay can also be a metaphor for humans, as the creation of God (Isa. 45:9; 64:7; Job 10:9). The use of clay for creating humans is a common motif in Mesopotamian myths of creation as well (see, for example, the "Creation of Man by the Mother Goddess" in *ANET,* 99–100). Here Elihu seems to be staking out a common humanity which should relieve Job of **fear** or **alarm.** Although Elihu denies any heavy-handed attempt to force a reaction from Job, **nor should my hand be heavy upon you,** his words increasingly reflect just such a coercive attitude.

§118 Summary of Job's Claims (Job 33:8–13)

33:8–9 / **But you have said . . . I heard.** At long last Elihu begins his substantive critique of Job's claims with a quote. The question arises immediately whether Elihu's quote fairly represents Job's statements. This precise quote is found nowhere in the book of Job and so can only be a loose summary of the implications of Job's speech from Elihu's point of view. We shall take each part of the quote individually. **I am pure and without sin.** The first word, "pure" (Heb. adj. *zak*), occurs six times in the book of Job, five of which are in the mouths of Job's accusers (Bildad in 8:6; 25:5; Zophar in 11:4; Eliphaz in 15:15; and Elihu here in v. 8). Job uses the word only once, in 16:17, when he describes the oppressive suffering he has received from God even though his "hands have been free of violence and [his] prayer is pure [*zakka*]." The term generally describes olive oil that has been purified by straining, and by extension refers to a life free from lingering, willful sin.

The second term, **without sin** (Heb. *beli pasha*ᶜ), refers to an avoidance of sins of rebellion against God. Elihu uses the term four times (here in v. 9; 34:6, 37; 35:6), and Bildad once (8:4) when he is accusing Job. Job himself employs the term four times. In the first of these occurrences (7:20–21) Job offers a *hypothetical* situation (which he obviously does not believe to be the case): "If I have sinned . . . Why do you not pardon my offenses (*pish*ᶜ*i*) and forgive my sins (ᶜ*awoni*)?" Once, in 14:17, Job uses the term in an expression of hope that confrontation with God will lead ultimately to restoration and divine removal of any offense or sin that might separate them. Twice (in 13:23 and 31:33) Job calls for God to show him his offenses so that they might be atoned for and restoration might be accomplished. What Job claims in all of these passages is lack of any *awareness* of sin that could account for the ferocity of suffering he experiences. He will not repent for sin of which he is unaware, but he is willing to be instructed. The friends have failed to enlighten him as to his misdeeds. Elihu's accusation fails to acknowledge this willingness on Job's part.

Elihu paints Job as an arrogant rebel refusing to admit to any sin, rather than as one who is confident that no sin can be found to establish his guilt.

I am clean and free from guilt. This phrase parallels the preceding one, with much the same thrust. The term "clean" (Heb. *khap*) has the sense of being washed clean of dirt and grime. This is consistent with the view of Job as one who does not claim sinless perfection, but who faithfully employs the available mechanisms to restore right relationship with God. The last phrase, "free from guilt" (*ʿawon*), refers not to freedom from some internal emotional feeling of guilt, but means, rather, that a judge pronouncing *mishpat* in his case would have to declare Job, "Not guilty!"

33:10 / Yet God has found fault with me. The Hebrew does not name God, but God seems to be the logical subject of the phrase. Elihu does appear to capture Job's essential complaint at this point. Although legally innocent, Job still experiences God pursuing him like a criminal. The Hebrew actually says, "he has found *opposition* to me"—the point being not that God has declared Job guilty or declared his sin, but that he **considers** Job **his enemy** by heaping up undeserved punishment on him. This is an accurate summary of what Job has previously claimed and the latter phrase is an allusion to Job's question directed to God in 13:24: "Why do you hide your face and consider me your enemy?"

33:11 / He fastens my feet in shackles; he keeps close watch on all my paths. Elihu quotes almost directly from Job's statement in 13:27. In that context, Job feels certain that his case warrants vindication (13:18) and invites proof to the contrary (13:19). He seeks a meeting with God where each may examine the other (13:22), and then he requests an accounting of the wrongs for which he is being punished (13:23). The section concludes with Job lamenting the failure of God to appear and his treatment of Job as an enemy (13:24), then he describes the suffering he experiences at the hand of a hostile God (13:25–28). Elihu seems to catch the heart of Job's complaint: Job is **in shackles,** unable to escape from his torment while God scrutinizes every step he takes.

33:12 / Having stated his version of Job's complaint, Elihu opens his critique. What remains unclear in this verse is exactly what is offensive to Elihu. Is it Job's reported claim of complete innocence? Is it his assessment of the reality of divinely induced suffering? Or has Job's temerity in approaching God to demand an explanation and personal vindication offended Elihu? When Elihu says that Job is **not right,** he negates the verb *tsadaq,* "be righteous," that regularly describes fulfillment of expectations in a legal case. In 13:18 Job anticipated vindication, while Elihu here pronounces a verdict of "guilty!" **God is greater than man.** This response to Job's complaint seems to emphasize divine power rather than justice or righteousness. God's power so overwhelms weak and fragile humans (the term translated "man" is *ʾenosh,* stressing human weakness) that they ought to simply accept their lot without complaint.

33:13 / **Why do you complain to him.** The Hebrew word translated "complain" is stronger than this translation suggests. The verb *ryb* most often means to pursue a legal dispute in court. The prophets use the verb and its cognate noun, *rib,* to describe God's legal complaint against an unfaithful people who have broken their covenant agreement with him (Hos. 4:1; Mic. 6:1–2). While Elihu says that God **answers none of man's words,** Job's complaint has primarily been that God does not answer Job's complaint (rather than those of humanity in general). The NIV inserts the word "man's" into a text that actually reads "his words," which leaves the pronoun more ambiguous—as varying translations indicate (NASB "His [God's] doings"; NRSV "my [Job's] words"; NJB "to you [Job]").

Additional Notes §118

33:9 / The declaration of *mishpat* is the formal conclusion to a law case in which the judge, having considered all of the evidence, renders judgment on each party by declaring them guilty or not guilty— much like a modern jury rendering a verdict after deliberation. See the discussion on 13:17–18 in §44 with regard to *mishpat.*

§119 Rebuttal: God Speaks in Visions (Job 33:14–18)

33:14 / **For God does speak.** Job is wrong, Elihu claims, because God does communicate to humans on multiple occasions—**now one way, now another**—but humans are not attentive enough to **perceive it.** The verb for "perceive" (Heb. *shur*) has the sense of stooping down to give close attention to something.

33:15–16 / **In a dream, in a vision of the night.** The first medium of divine communication is by revelation in dreams and visions. The OT describes many such nocturnal moments of divine manifestation. Moderns are often quick to discount dreams as the result of stress or indigestion ("too much bad pizza"), although Freud understood dreams to be an expression of the unconscious. For the ancients, dream interpretation was an important way to gain insight into the will and purposes of the divine (see, e.g., Joseph in Gen. 37; 40–41; Gideon in Judg. 7:9–15; and Daniel in Dan. 4:4–27). Often the phrase **deep sleep falls** indicates a divinely-induced sleep in preparation for God's action or communication (Gen. 2:21; 1 Sam. 26:12; Isa. 29:10).

The purpose of this divine encounter through dream is to provide a preemptive warning to dissuade humans from continuing in a path of sin: **he may speak . . . and terrify them with warnings.** The term "warnings" (Heb. *musaram*) could be read as "their warning/instruction" and has the sense of "discipline" or "instructive chastisement." Here terror is not God's punishment for human sin but a means of discipline to bring them back to the right path.

33:17–18 / These two verses clarify the purpose of God's terrifying discipline: **to turn man from wrongdoing.** The NIV has (rightly, I think) interpreted the neutral term *maʿaseh* ("deed; doing") as "wrongdoing" requiring discipline. Divine discipline and terror have a way of undoing human **pride** so that one is willing to submit humbly to God's instruction. The **soul** here is the Hebrew *nepesh*, which is *not* the eternal, immaterial soul in Greek-influenced Christian thought, but rather the animated physical being which constitutes all that a human being is in life. It is one's most personal self and identity. The ultimate end of humans who pursue their own way in the world is **the pit**—a frequent synonym for *Sheol*, the abode of the dead. God's discipline is intended to **preserve** (or "withhold") submissive humans from death. The Hebrew for **from perishing by the sword** is difficult and literally means something like "[and preserve] his life from crossing over the water canal." Some translators (e.g., NRSV; NJB) take this as a reference to the river separating life from death. Others (e.g., NASB) think the word for "water canal" (Heb. *shelakh*) is a mistake for the similar word *Sheol* (Heb. *she'ol*). The NIV bases its translation on a related noun (*shelakh*) that includes an "uncertain metal weapon" among its possible meanings—thus "sword." Despite the continuing uncertainty, the general meaning of the verse is clear.

Additional Notes §119

33:16 / The verb **terrify** (Heb. *khtm*) ordinarily means "seal/close up" (NASB "seals their instruction"). Most translators take the form from the similar verb *khtt*, "terrify," with a third-person masculine plural pronominal suffix (-*am*) added as the object.

§120 Rebuttal: God Chastens with Pain
(Job 33:19–22)

33:19 / **Or ... chastened on a bed of pain.** Elihu's second rejection of Job's claim that God is silent seeks to turn Job's own suffering into an illustration of divine communication and instruction. God employs the constant "pain" and **distress** that he is experiencing as a means to apprise Job of divine displeasure.

33:20–21 / These verses accurately sketch the consequences of the enduring pain of terminal disease. Even the **choicest meal** becomes **repulsive.** His **flesh wastes away** so that his **bones ... stick out.** This is, of course, what Job has been experiencing personally (2:5; 3:24; 6:6; 19:18; 30:17).

33:22 / **His soul draws near to the pit.** Death is near, although it is Job's animated self (*nepesh*), and not an eternal, immaterial soul, that is at risk here. The translation, "**messengers of death,**" softens the Hebrew a bit, which reads more literally "those who cause to die," or, perhaps, "executioners." Whether these are demons from *Sheol* or members of the "sons of God" (Job 1:6; 2:1) who do God's bidding is not entirely clear. Elsewhere the Hiphil verb from which this participle comes means "carry out a sentence of death; execute" (2 Sam. 14:7; 2 Kgs. 14:6; Esth. 4:11). Proverbs 16:14 mentions an "angel/messenger of death" (Heb. *malʾak mawet*) that more directly compares to the NIV translation here. The mention of a mediating "angel" in the next verse may suggest that the author has in mind a sort of opposition between heavenly forces here: those who would execute the divine decree of judgment communicated through Job's suffering and wasting away, and one who stands at Job's side to plead his cause. However, Elihu's point is clear: in his suffering Job has already received clear divine communication that he stands judged guilty and deserving of death!

§121 Restoration through Repentance
(Job 33:23–30)

Elihu now begins to describe the appropriate response for one who accepts divine discipline as he has described it in the preceding verses and who desires restoration. Such restoration requires an intercessor to mediate between God and sinner.

33:23–24 / Over against God and the "executioner" of verse 22, stands an **angel** (Heb. *mal'ak*) who serves as a **mediator** (*melits;* see the discussion on 16:20 in §58) to secure a stay of execution and pardon. Job himself envisions such a champion standing up for him in the heavens in 16:19–21. Such a mediator is rare in Elihu's estimation: **one out of a thousand.** It may be that Elihu considers himself to be this kind of "angel" seeking Job's restoration—especially if the alternate translation of *mal'ak* as "messenger" is employed. Some translations take the phrase **to tell a man what is right for him** as a statement of the accused party's upright character (NRSV; NLT) rather than corrective guidance. If Elihu himself is this mediator, this phrase would characterize his speeches to Job and would suggest that correction is intended. **Spare him.** The mediator speaks up on behalf of the accused and demands a pardon. The **pit** is a reference to *Sheol,* the abode of the dead. In verse 22, the one who is besieged by God "draws near to the pit." The mediator secures his deliverance—the commutation of a death sentence. **I have found a ransom for him.** The term "ransom" (Heb. *koper*) can also mean "bribe" (1 Sam. 12:3; Amos 5:12; Prov. 6:35), but it most often indicates the price for a life, or a payment to avoid punishment (Exod. 21:30; 30:12; Num. 35:31; Ps. 49:8; Prov. 13:8; 21:18; Isa. 43:3). The related Hebrew word *kippur* takes on the connotation "atonement for sin," as in the common designation of *yom hakkippurim,* "day of atonement."

33:25–26 / Delivered from the brink of death, the afflicted (v. 21) is now restored to full, youthful health: **his flesh is**

renewed like a child's. He prays to God. The Hebrew translated "prays" (*ʿtr*) means to supplicate with sacrificial offerings. It seems that this sacrifice is not the means by which the sufferer is restored to God, but it serves here as *evidence* that restoration has taken place. Before, the supplicant's sacrifices went unheeded and unanswered. Now that the mediating angel has brought about restoration, God meets sacrifices of supplication with **favor.** Verse 26 provides a list of the benefits of restoration. Prayer is met with divine favor. The supplicant **sees God's face** (previously hidden) with **shouts for joy.** The ultimate consequence is to be **restored by God to his righteous state.**

33:27–28 / Restoration leads to confession and testimony before the community of faith. **I sinned, and perverted what was right.** These imagined words of confession make it clear that Elihu considers Job to be a sinner in need of confession. Job's words are not right, but "perverted." This stands in contrast with God's ultimate judgment in 42:7. There, it is the three friends who have not spoken rightly. **I did not get what I deserved.** What an ironic statement! Elihu counsels Job to admit sin and confess that his punishment is not fitting (Heb. *shwh*) to his sin. Elihu means that Job's suffering is *less* than he deserves: a sign of God's mercy. Job has also claimed inequity of punishment but, since Job maintains his innocence, his charge is that his suffering is *heavier* than is fitting.

Execution has been stayed, he has been **redeemed . . . from going down to the pit.** In light of the preceding verse, this perhaps indicates that Elihu assumes that any punishment short of death is less than Job "deserved." **I will live to enjoy the light.** The Hebrew actually says "my life will see the light"—another way to say that the death penalty has been overturned.

33:29–30 / **God does all these things.** Elihu clearly understands Job's suffering as divinely sent, not as a natural disaster or accident. Extended or repeated suffering **twice . . . three times**— such as Job's loss of family, wealth, and personal health—are divinely-given *opportunities* for repentance and change before the final judgment (death) comes. In the phrase **to turn back his soul from the pit,** again "soul" translates the Hebrew *nepesh*, the animated physical being, and *not* the immaterial soul distinct from the material body. Elihu gives a particularly disciplinary cast to suffering. Suffering is intended to bring recognition of sin, repentance, and, ultimately, restoration.

§122 Remain Silent, Learn Wisdom
(Job 33:31–33)

Elihu concludes the chapter and his first attack on Job by addressing Job directly. While he seems to offer Job an opportunity to reply and refute his claims, there is little to indicate that he sincerely desires a reply. Job's silence is not unexpected, since we have already encountered the postscript in 31:40 announcing, "The words of Job are ended."

33:31 / **Pay attention . . . listen . . . be silent.** Elihu is not really interested in hearing Job but wants his full attention. **I will speak.** Clearly Elihu is not done yet, but has more to say. This verse, along with verse 33, forms a bracket around this conclusion. Note the similarity of structure and vocabulary in these two verses.

> Pay attention, Job, and listen to me; be silent, and I will speak.
> . . . listen to me; be silent, and I will teach
> you wisdom.

This envelope pattern consolidates these three verses into a unified conclusion.

33:32 / **If you have anything to say.** The clear assumption is that Job can have no effective response to Elihu's declarations. Elihu is convinced of the truth of his claims and expects no rebuttal. The imperatives **answer me** and **speak up** remind me of an angry parent confronting an offending child with their wrongdoing. There can be no response to the parent's assumption of wrong and the demand for an answer emphasizes that there is no possible response. The Hebrew which the NIV renders, "**for I want you to be cleared,**" is literally translated, "I would delight in a declaration of your righteousness." The declaration is not Job's, but that of the judge who declares *mishpat* in Job's case. Elihu's claim rings hollow to me, as does his earlier demand that Job speak up in refutation. If God declared Job righteous, that would nullify entirely the case Elihu has developed to this point. Elihu does not expect anything of the sort to be possible, and so he feels safe to invite Job's response.

33:33 / **But if not.** Elihu clearly expects no response from Job. There is more to come in Elihu's attack: **then listen to me; be silent, and I will teach you wisdom.** Elihu intends Job's continued silence to be understood as his acquiescence to the truth of Elihu's words and his submission to the "wisdom" that is forthcoming. It does *not* follow, however, that the author/editor of the book accords the same authority to Elihu's words. The claim to **teach** "wisdom" prepares the reader for the extended discussion in chapter 34 that is directed throughout to "wise men [*khakamim*] and men of understanding [*yodʿim*]," who are called to judge the truth of Elihu's claims against Job (34:1, 10, 16, 34).

§123 Introduction: Advice to Sages (Job 34:1–4)

Elihu begins his second attack on Job by calling a consultation of sages to render judgment on Job's claims. It is likely that he has the three friends in mind—Eliphaz, Bildad, and Zophar—although they never speak and so remain anonymous in this context. It is possible that Elihu is referring to any or all sages, in an attempt to appeal to more universal wisdom to buttress his claims.

34:1 / Then Elihu said. The Hebrew actually employs the normal formula for *responding* to another's words (*wayyaᶜan* [X] *ᵓiyyob wayyoᵓmar,* "and [X] answered and he said"), although Elihu speech here continues uninterrupted.

34:2 / Hear my words . . . listen to me. The imperative call to hear also entails an expectation of response and acceptance, as when Yahweh calls Israel to a response of obedience in Deuteronomy 6:4 ("Hear, O Israel: The LORD our God, the LORD is one"). Elihu addresses the three silent friends as **you wise men . . . men of learning,** seeking to establish a common front against Job.

34:3 / For the ear tests words as the tongue tastes food. Elihu ironically quotes an aphorism spoken earlier by Job (12:11) as he began a long discourse (12:11–25) affirming that God is the effective power behind the disturbing patterns of a world where the righteous suffer and the wicked prosper. And that true wisdom is ultimately the possession of God, and not the result of the gradual accretions of human observation and experience. Here Elihu, by adopting this adage without qualification, subjects himself to the criticism of Job's earlier discourse and undermines his own argument. Like those who are deceived by thinking that their human wisdom can capture the fullness of divine purposes, Elihu offers his own comments for inspection, confident that they cannot be refuted but must be accepted.

34:4 / Let us discern for ourselves. Employing the cohortative verbal form ("Let us . . ."), Elihu seeks to enlist the friends in his cause against Job. The verb "discern" (*bakhar*) can also mean "choose." The Hebrew for **what is right** is *mishpat,* the formal decree of a judge concerning what ought to have occurred in a case. This leaves the friends in the position of "choosing" the standard of righteousness against which to measure Job. The co-alition of friends is clear (**let us learn together**) and they exclude Job, who is the object of investigation. This appears more like an official enquiry into Job's affairs than the reciprocal discussion of the earlier chapters.

In these verses, Elihu sets out for a second time what he perceives to be Job's complaint. His loose summary draws on some of
Job's previous statements, but his interpretations do not always
reflect the original meaning and context of Job's words.

34:5 / **Job says, "I am innocent . . . "** Job uses the precise
term quoted here (*tsadaqti*, "I have been declared righteous") on
only one occasion (9:15), where he is describing the hypothetical
possibility of his confrontation as an innocent person with God,
who is both defendant and judge. His statement is more along the
lines of, "Even if I had been declared innocent beforehand, how
could I defend myself in such a situation?" While this cannot be
taken as an exact quote, it does seem to capture the essence of one
aspect of Job's ongoing complaint. Elihu's words, **but God denies
me justice,** quote Job in 27:2 exactly. The translation is, perhaps, a
bit stronger than the original allows. The phrase more literally
means, "he [God] has caused my declaration of righteousness to
turn aside." It is not that God has declared Job guilty in any sense,
but Job is saying that God has, for whatever divine purpose, prevented Job from experiencing the anticipated result of having been
declared legally innocent. Similarly Job has declared in 19:6–7 that
God has misled (NIV "wronged") him and trapped him like an animal in a net so that, when Job cries out for redress from violence,
"there is no justice."

34:6 / **Although I am right, I am considered a liar.** This
is an expansive translation of a somewhat difficult passage. More
literally the Hebrew says: "Concerning my declaration of righteousness I will lie." This is most likely to be taken as a question,
rather than a simple declaration: "Should I lie concerning my
right?" (NASB). The word for **his arrow** is difficult in this context,
especially since the Hebrew is actually "my arrow" (*khitsi*). Others
modify the word to create "my wound" (*makhtsi*, e.g., NASB; NRSV;
NJB), which makes more sense in this context.

34:7–8 / **What man is like Job . . . ?** Elihu intends his opening question to unite his hearers—the sages—in opposition to Job. His negative evaluation of Job's complaint is clear as three parallel statements deride Job's words and associations. Job **drinks scorn like water; keeps company with evildoers;** and **associates with wicked men.**

34:9 / **For he says, "It profits a man nothing . . ."** Although NIV follows the path of most translations with this Hebrew phrase (*lo' yiskon geber*), it is unclear why. Elsewhere in Job this verb (*skn*) is translated "be of benefit" (15:3; 22:2; 35:3). If rendered in this usual fashion, Job would be accused here of claiming that a human is not of benefit *to God* when trying to please him. The nearest parallel to these words is found in Eliphaz's rebuke of Job in 22:2–3: "Can a man be of benefit to God? Can even a wise man benefit him? What pleasure would it give the Almighty if you were righteous? What would he gain if your ways were blameless?" The verb normally used in Job to mean "receive profit" is *y'l*, and the verb *skn* is never found on Job's lips, so this is not a direct quote. The closest Job comes to these sentiments is his imaginative quote of the wicked, who cry out in 21:14–15: "Leave us alone! We have no desire to know your ways. Who is the Almighty, that we should serve him? What would we gain by praying to him?" Perhaps Elihu reveals his assumption of Job's guilt here by attempting to connect Job with this attitude of the wicked.

Additional Notes §124

34:6 / **Although I am right, I am considered a liar.** Others suggest changing the verb to third masculine singular, "Concerning my right he [God] will lie."

§125 Rebuttal: God Does No Wrong (Job 34:10–12)

Having set him up a second time, Elihu proceeds to counter Job's claims. His attack is no reasoned argument, but a restatement of an established tenet of faith: since God is incapable of wrong, whatever Job experiences from the hand of God is just.

34:10 / **So listen to me, you men of understanding.** Again, Elihu directs his comments not to Job, but to the council of Job's friends (or some large group of sages), united in judgment against him. In a sense Job is experiencing his day in court and the human judges arrayed before him are no less implacable in their opposition to his case than Job had imagined God to be (9:14–21). The "men of understanding" are literally "men of heart," since the heart is the place of moral decision-making and commitment. Perhaps the emphasis here is more on commitment to a cause—God's justice—than on intellectual prowess.

Far be it from God. This is a rather harsh oath: "Accursed; profaned!" The idea is that should God be proven to be connected with evil, the speaker will be under a curse (compare 27:5). The oath attempts to separate God decisively from **evil** and wrongdoing. The word for **wrong** (*ʿawel*) has more the sense of "dishonesty" or "injustice." If God had perverted justice and allowed Job to suffer wrongly, that would have undermined the very structures of faith on which Elihu and the friends depend.

34:11–12 / **He repays a man for what he has done.** The verse confirms the principle of retribution as the operative pattern in Elihu's worldview. The phrase **what his conduct deserves** is a rather loose translation of the Hebrew, which is literally: "according to the way of a man, so he [God] causes him to find." Elihu leads the judging council in an attempt to uphold the propositions of retribution (one reaps what one sows) by affirming that what Job suffers confirms his guilt—precisely the conclusion Job disputes.

It is unthinkable . . . Elihu is certain of his reading of the structures of life. It is impossible that God would act in evil ways. The Hiphil of *rsh^c*, **do wrong,** does not mean "be evil" but "commit evil acts; do wrong." Consequently it is equally inconceivable that God would **pervert justice** by punishing the innocent. Obviously the *permissive* will of God is not on the radar screen here, as God is understood actively to be behind all that humans experience.

§126 Who Appoints the Judge on Whom All Depend? (Job 34:13–15)

Not only is God incapable of doing evil, he is also the irresistible creator and ruler of the universe upon whom all humans depend for their very existence. How dare the creature rise up to question the creator?

34:13 / **Who appointed him ... Who put him in charge ... ?** The answer is clear: God is responsible to *no one* for his authority. This statement is tantamount to a claim that God defines the nature of justice and injustice, and thus approaches the rather pessimistic conclusion that there is no good or evil, only what is. If everything comes directly from the hand of God, and if all that God does is only good by definition, then everything that humans experience in this life—regardless of *their* perception of it—must be considered good. The book of Job cautions us against falling into this simplistic trap. When Job is affirmed in 42:7 as having said "what is right" concerning God, then the reader learns once and for all that it is possible in this world for the righteous to suffer without undermining the goodness of God.

34:14–15 / **If it were his intention.** The phrase describes a hypothetical situation, not a reality. The point is to stress the absolute dependence of all humans on God for their very breath and life. If God were to gather the animating **breath** (Gen. 2:7) that gives life to all humans, then all would die. In Hebrew thought, a human is a *nepesh khayyah,* "a living being," because the animating breath of God resides within. Without the divine breath to sustain them all humankind **would perish together and ... return to the dust.**

§127 The Judge of Kings and Princes
(Job 34:16–20)

34:16 / **If you have understanding.** Shifting to singular imperatives, Elihu calls rather sarcastically for Job to affirm his teaching. Job claimed earlier to have understanding equal to or superior to that of the friends, yet he has consistently denied what seems so patently obvious to Elihu: whatever God does is just. Elihu demands acquiescence to his claims, not just consideration and reflection: **hear this . . . listen!**

34:17 / **Can he who hates justice govern?** The meaning of this question is less than certain since the Hebrew verb translated "govern" (*khbsh*) is used with this sense only here. Elsewhere the term has the sense of "bind" or even "imprison." Most translators read it as NIV does and consider the phrase a rhetorical validation of the justice of divine rule. In this case, **he who hates justice** would be a restatement of Job's complaint against God. That an unjust God should rule is unthinkable to Elihu, but Job's experience of unjust suffering dictates that he must consider the question. A few interpreters take "he who hates justice" as Elihu's condemnation of Job and understand the verb to mean something like "conduct the inquiry" (see M. Dahood, *Psalms II*, p. xxiv), assuming that Job has mounted an investigation into the justice of God. The minority translation has the benefit of supporting the second half of this verse more nearly.

Will you condemn . . . ? The verb has a more formal, legal sense—as a judge may "pronounce/declare guilty" a party in a legal case. The **just and mighty One** is an unusual combination of two titles for God which have the effect of binding together the two halves of Job's complaint: either God is not righteous or he lacks power to institute justice in the world. Elihu, of course, affirms both divine power and justice—so Job's suffering can only be his justly deserved punishment for sin.

34:18–20 / God's power is such that he calls even the most powerful of human rulers to account. He is **the One who says to kings . . . and to nobles.** This illustrates the principle that verse 17 established: justice and power must go hand in hand. If the powerful fail in their administration of justice, God is quick to declare them **worthless** or **wicked.** (Of course, this also suggests that the unjust abuse of power by human rulers is a reality that must be remedied by divine judgment!) God further displays his justice in his fair treatment of the **poor** (with an emphasis on their powerlessness) as well as the powerful elite (**princes** and **the rich**). Regardless of social status, **they are all** equally **the work of his hands.**

They die in an instant. Sudden death and disappearance of the powerful is terrifying evidence of divine control and judgment intended to testify to humanity that God remains both mighty and righteous. No revolt or coup is necessary to overturn corrupt rulers, because they are **removed without human hand.** God does this quickly so that these seemingly invincible humans **are shaken.**

§128 God Sees What All Humans Do (Job 34:21–30)

As Job has claimed elsewhere, God is constantly watching over what humans do. Nothing escapes his awareness. For Job, this was, at certain points, a cause of sorrow (10:14; 13:27; 14:16), since he felt God scrutinizing every detail in order to punish harshly any imagined failing, no matter how small. In his final monologue, however, Job sees God's constant attention to the details of his life as grounds for certainty that God must admit his innocence (31:4, 37). Here, Elihu sees God's constant scrutiny of human affairs as evidence of his alert concern to rule justly by freeing the weak from the wicked abuses of the powerful.

34:21–22 / **His eyes are on the ways of men.** The Hebrew is actually in the singular ("a man"), so that the words speak directly to Job rather than making sweeping generalities. Elihu's intent is to convict Job with this description of divine scrutiny. It is Job whom God watches constantly, Elihu claims, and Job is the evildoer unable to discover a **dark place** or **deep shadow** in which to **hide** himself.

34:23–24 / **God has no need.** This translation is quite interpretive, as the Hebrew does not mention "God" as the subject here, nor does it say anything about "need" or necessity. The text actually says something like: "He [presumably God, but not certainly] will continue to appoint" (see also Hartley, *Job,* pp. 455, 458: "For it is not for a man to set a time . . ."). The awkwardness of the phrase has led NIV (and others) to its interpretive translation. The reference to God in **come before him for judgment** is explicit in the original text. The point remains clear: Job ought not to seek any future meeting with God to establish justice in his case. God has already seen all and will shatter **the mighty** without warning and replace them. Elihu intends the warning to convince Job that God's judgment is already determined and that the sudden destruction of Job's easy life is evidence of God's decision against him.

34:25–26 / God **takes note** and is alert to the evil **deeds** of the wicked and acts suddenly **in the night, he overthrows them** so that they **are crushed** in judgment. The punishment of the wicked takes place—like Job's suffering—in a very public place **where everyone can see them.**

34:27–28 / The wicked **turned from following him.** The evil for which the wicked are punished is twofold. First they cease to follow God's **ways.** This in turn leads them to abuse their power by oppressing **the poor** and **the needy** (see the discussion on 22:7–9 in §79 with regard to the poor). This abuse causes the **cry** of the weak and defenseless to come to the attention of God.

34:29–30 / **But if he remains silent.** God always hears the complaint of the suffering, but he cannot be expected always to respond. Elihu attempts here to draw in Job's own experience of divine silence in the face of his suffering and complaint. Elihu intends to undermine Job's complaint by defusing any expectation of divine response. God's failure to respond to Job is no indication of divine weakness or inattention. God hears and **hides his face**—an indication of divine judgment. Yet God remains in power over individuals and nations alike and continues to keep the powerful wicked in check.

§129 Confession Required for Restoration (Job 34:31–33)

Elihu now imagines a hypothetical situation in which a guilty person acknowledges his sin and vows to return to God and sin no more. Such an act of repentance is diametrically opposed, in Elihu's view, to Job's continued arrogant refusal to acknowledge his sin and repent of it.

34:31–32 / **Suppose a man says to God.** This sets up the hypothetical nature of the scene Elihu is about to describe. **I am guilty.** The translations differ in their treatment of this verb (*nasʾati,* "I have lifted up"). Some take it as an admission of having borne punishment (NRSV) or chastisement (NASB) and some take it as a claim of being misled (NJB). The words **no more** do not occur in the Hebrew, which simply states: "I will not act corruptly." The verb in the phrase, **"teach me,"** is the same one behind the noun *torah,* "guidelines; instruction." The sinner seeks (as does Job!) instruction as to the reason for the punishment he experiences. Like Job, the hypothetical penitent desires to know what he **cannot see,** what he has **done wrong** (6:24; 10:4–7; 13:23). Unlike Job, however, the repentant sinner of Elihu's imagination expects to learn of his sin and is prepared to turn from it once it is revealed: **if I have done wrong, I will not do so again.** By contrast, Job (6:24; 13:23; 31:35–37) expects to be completely exonerated by divine scrutiny and so anticipates no reason to change his blameless behavior.

34:33 / **Should God then reward you on your terms?** Elihu concludes his imaginary case by turning directly to Job once again. If such a hypothetical person acknowledges his sin and vows to turn from it, why would God consent to give Job what he wants when Job refuses to even acknowledge the presence of sin in his life? The presence of sin is, of course, an established *fact* in Elihu's mind because of the airtight case he assumes he has presented in this chapter. God defines the essence of justice. God remains in control of all aspects of human affairs. Punishment is evidence of divine judgment for sin. Job's experience of punishment means that he *has sinned.* He tells Job that **when you refuse** to acknowledge sin or **to repent,** this prevents any hope of divine grace. **You must decide, not I.** Elihu thrusts the case into Job's hands with a rather false claim of modesty. What he really means is that the case he has established is so irrefutable that Job can only submit in defeat. In a similarly sarcastic vein, Elihu, convinced of the invincibility of his argument, invites Job to respond: **so tell me what you know.** There is no real indication that Elihu expects any response, since he rushes on to judgment.

§130 Conclusion: Job's Sin of Rebellion (Job 34:34–37)

34:34 / **Men of understanding . . . wise men.** Like a prosecuting attorney making his final summation before a jury, Elihu lays out his accusation against Job before the gathered sages he called at the beginning of the chapter (34:2–4, 10) to render judgment.

34:35 / **Job speaks without knowledge: his words lack insight.** This is a general rejection of all of Job's speeches. He has been measured and found wanting.

34:36 / **Oh, that Job might be tested.** Elihu expresses the desire that Job be examined or tried. This is, of course, exactly what Job has been seeking all along. The difference is that Elihu has already tried Job and found him guilty, while Job anticipates complete exoneration in a divine court of law. Elihu's human court convicts Job because it examines external evidence only and operates within the closed system of retribution. On the other hand, Job knows that God sees the inward truth of Job's blameless character and would have to declare him innocent. Elihu desires the most extreme examination possible, **to the utmost,** to remove any doubt. Elihu wishes this for Job's **answering like a wicked man.** Job's answers are only evil if one has determined his guilt beforehand, as Elihu certainly has. I am rather sadly reminded of justifications offered in recent years for the use of torture to extract information from captives judged to be in league with the evil enemy. Is this perhaps what Elihu's desire for an extreme testing of Job amounts to?

34:37 / **To his sin he adds rebellion.** Having concluded that Job is guilty of "sin" (Heb. *khatta'␣t*, "error"), Elihu is now in the position to interpret Job's continued refusal to repent as an indication of his "rebellion." The phrase **he claps his hands** is difficult, and the commentators offer a number of emendations or rearrangements of words (see Hartley, *Job,* p. 461, n. 5, for a description of the options). Clapping the hands can be a sign of joy (2 Kgs. 11:12; Pss. 47:1; 98:8; Isa. 55:12; Ezek. 25:6) or derision and scorn (Job 27:23; Nah. 3:19). In the final analysis, Elihu considers that Job **multiplies his words against God,** that he has accused God of wrong and undermined confidence in his justice and power. For Elihu, this is unforgivable. It is interesting that the preposition "against" is not the usual *ʿal,* but *le,* which usually means "to, toward." This leaves open the possibility that while Job certainly "multiplies words" in his many statements, these may be read as addresses *to* God, seeking understanding, rather than hostile attacks *against* God.

§131 What Profit for God? (Job 35:1–3)

Elihu's third attack against Job picks up on Job's earlier statements about human sin affecting God so little that it should not be harshly punished (7:17–21). Eliphaz expressed similar sentiments in 22:1–3, questioning whether Job's claimed righteousness could be of any benefit to God or give him any pleasure.

35:1–2 / **Do you think this is just?** Elihu states what he believes Job seeks as a just settlement. Unfortunately the Hebrew of the next phrase (*tsideqi me'el*, "my righteousness is from God") is less than clear, as variations in the different translations indicate. The NIV understands that Job expects to **be cleared by God.** Other translations consider the words to be a claim that Job's "righteousness is more than God's" (NASB; see also NRSV).

35:3 / The difficulties in translation continue into this verse. The question is who is speaking and to whom. **Yet you ask him.** The NIV assumes that Job is addressing God here, although "him" is not in the Hebrew text, which only says "because/when you say." **What profit is it to me . . . what do I gain?** NIV alters the Hebrew text, which says "to you" in the first phrase, to read "to me." This change makes this first line a closer parallel to the second line, "what do I gain." If Job is indeed the speaker (as is likely), then he would be addressing God here. As the Hebrew stands, however, Elihu is suggesting that Job claims that his blameless character turns no profit for *either* God or Job. As in his earlier accusation in 34:9, Elihu misrepresents what Job has said. Job only uses this verb (*y'l*, "gain profit") to characterize the claims of the wicked (21:15), not himself. The wicked reject God when they say: "Who is the Almighty, that we should serve him? What would we gain (*y'l*) by praying to him?" Once again Elihu betrays his presumption of Job's wickedness by putting this statement in the mouth of Job.

§132 Rebuttal: An Unaffected God (Job 35:4–8)

The God Elihu describes in these verses is removed from, and seemingly unaffected by, what humans do. Neither human sin nor righteousness can sway God from his set and determined sovereignty over the universe. Humans can only observe, understand, and respond to what God is doing in the world. They have no hope of persuading God or influencing his plans or judgments.

35:4 / In his response to Job Elihu implies that his wisdom is greater than that of Job *and* **your friends with you.** As a result, Elihu hopes to succeed where the friends have failed.

35:5–7 / As the **heavens** and **clouds** are **so high above** Job and the friends, so God is far removed from the influence of humans and the world they inhabit. God makes his judgments from the vantage point of the heavens and without becoming involved in the heat of human argument. As we have already seen, Elihu assumes that Job sins. The hypothetical statement, **if you sin,** is merely formal. Even if Job's **sins are many,** they have no effect on this distant, transcendent deity.. The opposite is also true, Elihu contends (**if you are righteous**). Human righteousness is no bargaining chip with which to manipulate the actions of God. It is no bribe for God to **receive from** Job's **hand.**

35:8 / **Your wickedness affects only a man like yourself.** Human "wickedness" and **righteousness** are only concerns for the human world. God is removed and his judgments already determined. It is humans who suffer in the face of oppression and who benefit from acts of human kindness.

§133 The Cries of the Wicked Go Unanswered (Job 35:9–16)

Having described a hermetically sealed environment in which human actions affect no one but themselves, Elihu moves on to convince his audience that any attempts to influence and move God are futile.

35:9–11 / **Men cry out.** It is no secret that humans in trouble call out for deliverance from their **load of oppression** and **for relief from the arm of the powerful.** But, says Elihu, it is senseless to call out to **God my Maker** for redress. If humans wish to effect change with regard to human oppression, they must appeal to the source of the human action they desire to change, or act themselves to end it.

With the words, **who teaches more to us than to the beasts . . . and . . . the birds,** Elihu seems to be responding to Job's claim in 12:7 that the friends should look to the "animals" and "birds of the air" for instruction in the failure of retributive theology. Elihu assumes a human knowledge of wisdom that exceeds that of the animals and concludes rather ironically that humans endowed with such wisdom ought to know better than to try to influence God.

35:12–13 / **He does not answer when men cry out.** Elihu does not mean to say that God has no interest or concern in human affairs. Nor does he intend to suggest that God does not act to judge **the arrogance of the wicked** or to prosper the righteous. Such statements would completely undermine his argument. What Elihu *is* trying to do at this point is to stifle any attempt on Job's part to call God into conversation. Any such attempt is ridiculous, according to Elihu, because while God is aware and active in establishing justice, human pleas, no matter how justified, never influence his decisions and actions. Such a cry to God would be, in effect, an **empty plea,** and God **pays no attention to it** because he has already determined the appropriate course of action.

35:14–15 / **How much less?** If the cries of the righteous under oppression do not influence God, why should he care about the pleas of Job? For Elihu clearly relegates Job to the company of the oppressors suffering just punishment for their deeds. Elihu now recounts what he assumes to be the empty words of Job: **when you say that you do not see him.** Job ought not to expect to see God, since God does not respond to the righteous or the wicked. Nevertheless, Elihu would understand that Job in his suffering is experiencing the decision and punishment of God. Job's **case is before him.** His final affidavit in effect subpoenaed God for a court appearance to decide Job's case. Job **must wait for him** to come in response to the summons. Such hopes, however, are futile according to Elihu, because God does not come at the whim of humans, and Job's case is already decided.

God's **anger never punishes.** Elihu considers Job's claim that the wicked prosper unpunished to be nonsense. In his view, Job's suffering is clear evidence that God does act to punish wickedness. He is, of course, omitting the evidence of Job's own experience of innocence, and instead he makes his decision on the basis of the closed system of retributive theology. God does take **notice of wickedness,** but not by responding to human pleas for deliverance. Rather, God acts in his own deliberate time to reward all as they deserve.

35:16 / **So Job opens his mouth with empty talk.** As a consequence of his theology, Elihu evaluates Job's desire to see God and to press God for acknowledgment of his blameless character as senseless and "empty." The term for "empty" here is the same employed by Ecclesiastes for worthless vanity (*hebel*). Job's words are like vapor, having no substance or reality. Since he does not agree with Elihu's theology, Elihu considers Job's views to be ignorant and foolish, **without knowledge.** That Job **multiplies words** means he is the epitome of foolishness (Prov. 10:19; Eccl. 10:13–14; see also Elihu's accusation in 34:7), rather than the well-spoken sage he claims to be.

§134 True Words from Elihu (Job 36:1–4)

Once again an introductory phrase signals a new speech from Elihu. In 32:6 and 34:1, the formula of response (used in the dialogue section to introduce the reply of each speaker to his predecessor: *wayyaʿan ʾelihuʾ* ... *wayyoʾmar*, "and Elihu ... answered and said ...") rather inappropriately introduced Elihu's speeches. The formula of response in 32:6 is unexpected because Job's words were clearly completed in 31:40 with a postscript that anticipates no further response (*tammu dibre ʾiyyob*, "completed are the words of Job"). Similarly, the introduction of Elihu's second monologue in 34:1 also employs the formula of response when Elihu is simply continuing his monologue without a break. Here in 36:1, the opening formula does indicate continuation by the same speaker (*wayyosep ʾelihuʾ wayyoʾmar*) "and Elihu continued and said" (as in the continuation of Job's speeches in 27:1 and 29:1). The rather awkward and inappropriate use of these formulas may be evidence of an editorial attempt to bind the secondary material associated with Elihu into the previously existing dialogue cycle.

In chapter 36, Elihu is primarily concerned with affirming the power and control of God in support of retribution. Along the way he cautions Job against resisting God's punishment for his wickedness. There is no question here. In Elihu's mind, Job is wicked and receives what he deserves. The only course left open to Job is to confess, repent, and submit to the sovereign will of God. Toward the end of the chapter, Elihu describes the power of God in terms reminiscent of the storm (36:29–31). This description continues into chapter 37 and, in effect, prepares the reader for the eventual coming of God in the theophanic whirlwind. While Elihu's theology denies the possibility of God coming in response to Job's pleas, his words actually prepare for that very divine appearance.

36:1–2 / **Bear with me a little longer.** Elihu acknowledges that his argument is winding down, although **there is more**

to be said. Although Elihu continues for another two chapters, he adds little that is new to what he has already said. Mostly he reaffirms the truth of retributive theology and the sovereign power and control of God.

36:3–4 / Elihu seeks to legitimate his argument one more time. That he gets his **knowledge from afar** means that his wisdom is not his own creation but the result of divine prompting. **I will ascribe justice to my Maker.** Elihu makes sure his intent is plain. He has, from the beginning, been certain that God is in the right and Job's argument has no standing (33:8–12; 34:10–12). His claim that **my words are not false** is, of course, the issue under discussion. If Job's claims are true, then Elihu's words would indeed be proven false—as they are by the end of the book. Not only does Elihu deny falsehood, he also claims that he is **perfect in knowledge.** The word "perfect" here (*temim*) is from the same root (*tmm*) that describes Job's own character in chapters 1 through 2 (see the discussion on 1:1 in §1 and on 31:40 in §111). This verbal link pits these two characters and their conflicting words against each other. The term *temim* suggests completeness of knowledge.

In his final thrust, Elihu turns once again to affirm God's power displayed in retribution. In what follows, Elihu offers no argument to refute Job's experience. Instead, he simply seeks to overwhelm Job with impassioned rhetoric. God *always* acts to punish the wicked and prosper the righteous, he says. This can leave little doubt that Elihu ranks Job among the sinners who falsely proclaim their innocence.

36:5–7 / Elihu begins by denying three accusations that God fails to uphold retribution. Each accusation, as Elihu styles it, has roots in Job's complaints, but none can be called a direct quote. For each, Elihu offers a counter affirmation. **God is mighty, but does not despise.** First, Elihu claims that God never abuses his power by acting out of disdain for humans (NIV's **men** does not appear in the Heb.). By contrast, Elihu affirms that in his might God is also **firm in his purpose,** he is not swayed by human attempts at persuasion. In 8:20, Bildad essentially agrees with Elihu. Job, on the other hand, questions whether God despises him in 10:3. The Hebrew verb in all of these instances is *m's,* "reject, despise."

He does not keep the wicked alive. In response to the second accusation—perhaps derived from Job's bitter reflection on the prosperous and extended lives of the wicked in 21:7–16—Elihu denies that God allows the wicked to continue to live unpunished. However, he offers no evidence to back up this claim. On a more positive note Elihu counters that God **gives the afflicted their rights.**

He does not take his eyes off the righteous. In countering the third accusation, Elihu has in mind God's *protective* watch over the righteous. Job would agree, but he has experienced God's constant gaze in a much different light. In 7:17–21, Job offers extended descriptions of the painful scrutiny of the "watcher of men," who waits to pounce on any failing, no matter how insignificant. There, and again in 14:1–6, Job desires that God "look away" even for a moment (7:19; 14:6). For Elihu, however, divine watchfulness over the righteous results ultimately in their exaltation to the thrones of **kings.**

36:8–10 / With **if men are bound in chains . . . cords** Elihu moves to consider the meaning of human suffering. In his view, such distress can only be God's disciplinary punishment that is intended to bring the sinner to repentance. Through the discipline of pain God **tells them what they have done.** By such punishment God **makes them listen** and **commands them to repent.** Job, however, looks within and sees no misdeed for which to repent. And the reader knows that God concurs with Job's assessment. If Job is blameless, as the narrator and God both affirm, then his suffering cannot be explained away, as Elihu attempts to do, by recourse to a traditional theology of retribution. Of course, the reason for Job's suffering is not really at issue here. There has been no mystery since the opening scenes between God and *the* Satan why Job suffers—it is an extreme test of his willingness to fear God *for nothing.* We are now in the final throes of that examination, as Elihu denies Job's claims of righteousness and hammers him again and again with an inflexible view of a retributive world.

36:11–12 / **If they obey and serve him.** Grounded in his unyielding belief in retributive theology, Elihu can admit only two possibilities for the future. Those who **obey and serve**—by confessing their sin and repenting of it—will experience blessing: a life of **prosperity** and **contentment** awaits them. **But if they do not listen,** on the other hand, refusing to respond to divine discipline with repentance, they will suffer the opposite result: **they will perish . . . and die.** Not only do they "die," but they do so **without knowledge.** This is Elihu's last call for Job to acknowledge the wisdom of his words.

36:13–15 / The **godless** (*khanepim*) are those who despise God. To be "godless" **in heart** is to make a conscious decision to reject the way of God, rather than to be simply ignorant of God's expectations. Such persons actively resist the claims of faithful living. Those who knowingly reject God often do so and **harbor resentment** out of anger. Clearly Elihu is trying to indict Job here for his lack of submission to God's disciplinary suffering. Even when suffering, the wicked refuse to **cry for help.** Job similarly characterizes the attitude of the prosperous wicked in 21:14–15: "Yet they say to God, 'Leave us alone! We have no desire to know your ways. Who is the Almighty, that we should serve him? What would we gain by praying to him?'" Yet the wicked Job knows suffer little (21:7–13).

They die in their youth. Untimely death was considered evidence of divine judgment on the deceased. Job's case, however, is the opposite. He desires to die in order to escape unremitting pain, but God prolongs his suffering interminably. Some have tried to reduce the offense in the phrase **among male prostitutes of the shrines** by translating, rather periphrastically, "youthful shame" (Hartley, *Job,* p. 470) or some other parallel to "youth" in the first line of the verse. Pope, however, is certainly correct when he says, "there is no other evidence to support this view" (Pope, *Job,* p. 233; see also the discussions in Hartley, *Job,* p. 470; Gordis, *Job,* p. 415). The "male prostitutes" (*qedeshim*) were personnel in the Canaanite fertility cult who engaged worshipers in sexual activity that was considered particularly shameful to Israelites. While the exact significance of the reference here is uncertain, the overwhelming shame associated with this group is clearly transferred to the rebellious wicked (and Job!) Elihu is condemning.

But those who suffer he delivers in their suffering. Elihu wishes to affirm the redemptive nature of suffering when it leads to repentance. Only those who refuse to acknowledge divine discipline experience the early death described in the preceding verse. Elihu understands pain and suffering to be tools of divine communication: **he speaks to them in their affliction.** Unlike Job, who experiences undeserved pain as unclear and confusing, Elihu reads suffering as a clear message of divine displeasure and punishment.

§136 Wooing and Warning Job (Job 36:16–21)

Elihu now speaks directly to Job in a last attempt both to woo him from a path of wickedness and to warn him of the consequences of his resistance.

36:16–17 / **He is wooing you.** The Hebrew of verse 16 is notoriously difficult, and many have attempted to emend and reinterpret it. The general sense seems to be that God employs suffering in Job's life to persuade him to flee from distress to the unrestricted **spacious place** and the well-laden **table** set by divine hospitality. Job is **laden** with suffering which, again, is understood to be just punishment for his sin. Job is one of the **wicked** who has been **taken hold of** by God's judgment.

36:18 / These verses are even more difficult to render, as the various translations indicate. **Be careful** is based on an emendation suggested by Pope (*Job*, p. 234). Other translations read "lest anger," the more natural rendering of the Hebrew *khemah*. Without "anger" as the subject of the following verb, NIV must supply **no one**. The verb **entices** is the same Hebrew word translated "wooing" in verse 16. Those who read "anger" also understand the Hebrew word translated **riches** to mean "scoffing" (NASB; NRSV), thus the translation is: "*Beware* lest wrath entice you into scoffing" (emphasis added; NASB; see also NRSV). Behind **bribe** stands the Hebrew *koper*, "price of a life; ransom." The significance of a ransom, or how this can be interpreted as a "bribe," is not clear. At least the danger that Job is to avoid is clear. Job is not to be distracted from repentance and restoration by anger, or "riches," or a "large bribe"—whichever is understood here.

36:19 / **Would your wealth . . . sustain you?** Here is yet another difficult verse. Some take the Hebrew that NIV translates "wealth" (*shuaᶜ*, see NASB "riches") to mean "nobles; powerful persons" (NJB), "cry of distress" (NRSV), or even "deliverance; salvation" (Hartley, *Job*, pp. 472–73). The verb ᶜ*rk*, "prepare; lay in order" is interpretively rendered "sustain; keep" (NIV; NASB) or "take to law" (NJB). Depending how one takes the key terms, the translation can be something like "take the powerful [nobles] to law" (NJB), "Would your wealth . . . sustain you" (NIV), or "Will your cry avail" (NRSV). The common assumption of most translations is that Elihu is denying that wealth or power would be sufficient to enable Job to avoid distress or suffering. Of course, in Job's circumstance, neither wealth nor power is any longer an issue since he has lost every vestige of both.

36:20 / **Do not long for the night.** The "night" is either the time for accomplishing evil under the cover of darkness, or the time of divine judgment. The NIV understands the latter interpretation and assumes that the "going up of peoples" described in the literal Hebrew is the act of the wicked to **drag** powerless **people away from their homes.** God will judge such evil harshly.

36:21 / **Beware of turning to evil.** This is the clearest statement Elihu has made for some time. He warns Job that, contrary to his claims, evil will not go unpunished. Elihu caustically accuses Job of preferring evil **to affliction.** This does not make much sense in light of Elihu's constant claims that God punishes the wicked for their evil.

Additional Notes §136

36:19 / **Sustain.** Hartley's suggestion, "arrange (your deliverance)," while appropriate to the basic meaning of the verb, does not seem to fit the context well. How does one "lay in order" deliverance?

§137 Exalting God (Job 36:22–25)

Similar phrases indicating a new beginning introduce both this section and the next (vv. 26–33). In verse 22 we find *hen-ʾel yasgib bekokho*, "God is exalted in his power." Compare the beginning of verse 26: *hen-ʾel saggiʾ weloʾ nedaʿ*, "God is great and we do not know him." This repetition helps structure the remaining verses of chapter 36.

36:22–23 / **God is exalted in his power.** Elihu now turns from warning Job to praising God. The key praiseworthy feature of God in these verses is his "power" that separates him from human weakness and establishes his sovereignty. Elihu's praise of divine power is also an oblique warning to Job to lay down his demands and submit. **Who is a teacher like him?** The obvious answer to this rhetorical question is "No one." This is another subtle slap at Job who, in Elihu's view, has the audacity to teach God. Yet Job has expressed similar sentiments—that God is beyond human instruction—in 21:22: "Can anyone teach knowledge to God, since he judges even the highest?"
Who has prescribed his ways? Again the presumed answer is "No one!" God's "power" is so overwhelming that he is beyond any humanly imposed limits. Of course, the irony in this statement is that it is Elihu (who intends to accuse Job with these words) and Job's three friends who have "prescribed" God's "ways" by their inflexible application of retribution theology! Job, on the other hand, has consistently pressed against those narrow boundaries while agonizing over the mysterious freedom of God to act in new and unanticipated ways.
It is unthinkable to Elihu and the three friends that someone would say to God, **"You have done wrong."** Because God *defines* right, he cannot be accused of "wrong." Again, Elihu has Job in mind here. However, as close as Job may come to accusing God of "wrong," his assertions always need to be understood in the context of his desire to see God and come to understanding. To

seek to understand the conflicts between one's understanding of God and the realities of experience is a valid form of faith seeking understanding. Elihu and friends, on the other hand, are unwilling to admit any question for fear that their whole carefully constructed worldview will collapse.

36:24–25 / **Remember to extol his work.** Here is yet another subtle critique of Job! Elihu assumes, rather one-sidedly, that all that one experiences in life is from the hand of God and, consequently, one ought to praise God for all "his work." Job seeks to understand what it is that God does in this world but also to understand the painful consequence of sinful humans living in a broken world. The phrase **which men have praised in song** (and, I might add, *women* as well!) reminds us of the praise psalms and their frequent exaltation of God. The assertion that **all mankind has seen it** seems to assume a sort of natural theology akin to that of Psalms 8 and 104. But it may also refer to God's deeds of salvation and judgment that are equally awesome (Pss. 105–107). God's power, as displayed in his deeds of creation and salvation, is so overwhelming that humans are most comfortable when they can **gaze on it from afar.** Similarly, the Israelites distanced themselves from the fearful presence of God at Sinai and set Moses as their mediator (Exod. 20:18–21).

As does the preceding section, the final segment of chapter 36 begins with an exclamation acknowledging the greatness of God in the form "Behold, God . . ." (Heb. *hen ʾel* . . .). The feature of divine greatness that these verses extol is not "power" (as in v. 22), but the *otherness*, or transcendence, of God.

36:26 / God is **beyond our understanding.** The statement in verse 25, that "men gaze at" God's mighty acts and deeds "from afar," prepares the reader for this transition. Here we also learn that God's distance from humanity is not just a matter of size or magnitude of power, but that it is further complicated by humanity's lack of comprehension of God's purposes. **The number of his years.** While stopping short of a concept of eternality, this statement clearly communicates the OT belief that God surrounds all human history before and behind. This enduring quality of God undergirds his sovereignty. All others—including the world itself—will wear out like a garment (Ps. 102:25–28), but God is from everlasting to everlasting (Ps. 90:2–4). The term behind the expression **is past finding out,** *kheqer,* has the root meaning "searching by digging up" the earth.

36:27–28 / **He draws up the drops of water.** The imagery shifts now to portray the approach of God as a thunderstorm. Just how much this description reflects an understanding of the science of evaporation and condensation associated with rainfall is not clear. It does seem that the ancients understood a cycle of water purification in which God is at work, drawing water from the earth and distributing it in the form of **rain to the streams.** Some difficulty attends the translation of the final phrase of verse 28: **abundant showers fall on mankind.** The problem lies in the final two words (*ʾadam rab*), since *ʾadam,* "humankind," is a collective and unlikely to be modified by the adjective *rab,* "many." On the basis of Ugaritic, Pope (and NIV) takes *rab* as related to *rebibim,* "showers" (*Job,* p. 274). Others understand the term as an adverb modifying the preceding verb *yir'apu*, "trickle, drip," with the translation "drip abundantly" (NASB; NRSV).

36:29–30 / **Who can understand how.** God's actions in the storm are beyond human understanding. Psalms 68:4 and 104:3 picture God riding on **the clouds.** The Psalms frequently employ storm imagery to describe theophany (e.g., Pss. 29; 18:9–12; 77:17; 97:2). This imagery emphasizes the unknowable *otherness* of God. The **pavilion** (Heb. *sukkah*) refers to the surrounding clouds over-arching the presence of God like a tent or temporary dwelling (Ps. 18:11 = 2 Sam. 22:12).

The Hebrew word for **lightning** here is not the common *baraq*, but the more general term for light (*'or*). Rather than the de-structive force of a lightning strike, the emphasis here seems to be on the blinding flashes associated with lightning—flashes that il-luminate the entire landscape. The translations offer a variety of interpretations of the phrase **bathing the depths of the sea,** which literally means "covers the roots of the sea." The most popular op-tions are to read the verb *kissah* as meaning the opposite, "un-cover" (Gordis, *Job,* pp. 421–22; Hartley, *Job,* p. 476), or to render *kissah* as the noun *kisso,* "his throne," yielding the translation: "the roots of the sea are his throne" (Pope, *Job,* p. 237). The NIV has cho-sen to consider "lightning" as the subject of *kissah,* "cover," and to understand the illuminating effect over the surface of the "sea." It remains difficult, however, to understand how the flash of light would illuminate the "roots" of the sea, which is commonly a ref-erence to the bottoms of suboceanic trenches or mountains.

36:31–32 / **This is the way.** This phrase extends the storm metaphor to the sovereignty of divine rule on the earth: **he gov-erns the nations.** It is not immediately clear how the storm illus-trates divine rulership. As we will come to see in the following verse, however, it is most likely the display of divine power in "lightning" that brings the nations into submission. Along with di-vine power, the storm also demonstrates divine providence, with fertility resulting from rain producing **food in abundance** for ani-mal and human alike (Ps. 104).

He fills his hands with lightning and commands it to strike its mark. Scholars have suggested numerous small emen-dations for this verse. Hartley (*Job,* p. 476) offers a convenient summary of the options. While the grammar and syntax are diffi-cult, the basic meaning remains: God, the powerful deity, sends forth his lightning bolts bringing the earth and its inhabitants under his sovereignty.

36:33 / This is another difficult verse which has been subject to many emendations and interpretations. **His thunder announces the coming storm** is an interpretive translation of the Hebrew, literally, "His thunder announces/makes known concerning it/him." It may be that this verse is announcing *God's coming,* since the word "storm" does not appear in the Hebrew. The phrase **even the cattle** makes sense if we understand it to refer to cattle sensing the approaching storm before humans. While this may be the case, other interpreters suggest emendations in light of parallelism with the first line. One of the more promising suggestions is to understand *miqneh,* "cattle," as from the root *qn',* "be jealous; indignant." The term then refers to thunder as an indication of God's "indignant wrath." The translation **make known its approach** has little connection with the underlying Hebrew (*ʿal ʿoleh,* "concerning the one going up"). Others suggest reading the Hebrew as a single word known in later Rabbinic Hebrew (*ʿilʿolah*) and meaning "storm, whirlwind" (Gordis, *Job,* p. 424; Hartley, *Job,* p. 477).

This last chapter of Elihu's monologues continues to associate God with the power of the storm (imagery that began in 36:26). The storm produces thunder and lightning as indicators of God's mysterious and unknowable power. At the same time, the rain that falls on the earth is a sign of God's loving providence for the world and its creatures (v. 13).

37:1 / **At this.** This phrase connects the description in chapter 37 with the preceding storm passage at the end of chapter 36. The approach of God provides an adrenaline rush: **my heart pounds and leaps from its place.** God's appearance provokes a strong reaction.

37:2–3 / **Listen! Listen!** The imperative is a plural form. Elihu is calling his larger audience, including Job and the friends, to attention. The Hebrew construction (imperfect followed by an infinitive construct of the same root and stem) is emphatic, demanding close attention to what is to come. Here it is **the roar of** God's **voice** to which they are to attend. The parallel **rumbling** in the next line confirms that it is the distinctive growl of thunder (NASB; NRSV) the author has in mind. **He unleashes his lightning.** The storm arrives with a vengeance, with lightning flashing **beneath the whole heaven** and **to the ends of the earth,** meaning a storm stretching from horizon to horizon.

37:4–5 / **After that comes the sound of his roar.** After the flash of lightning comes the grumble and shake of thunder, which this verse depicts as the roaring of a lion. These verses repeat the Hebrew noun *qol,* "voice, sound," three times, mimicking the peals of thunder in the storm (see also Ps. 29). Again, these natural weather phenomena are metaphors pointing to the power of God displayed in his theophany. The graphic storm imagery describing God's glorious approach in Psalm 29 provides a clear parallel. God's power and presence are unrestrained—**he holds**

nothing back—unlike his impressive but guarded appearance to Moses in Exodus 33:18–23. As the Exodus passage suggests, the full revelation of God in his very essence has potentially destructive consequences for sinful humans. Thus Elihu employs this description of divine power not with any real hope that God will respond to Job's pleas, but to dissuade Job from pursuing a destructive course.

God's voice thunders in marvelous ways. The term for "marvelous" commonly describes divine actions or characteristics that stretch the capacity of human comprehension. Here the "marvelous" actions of God include his awesome appearance in the storm and, in parallel to the second half of the verse, the **great things** God accomplishes that are **beyond our understanding.**

37:6–8 / **He says to the snow.** Elihu now depicts God doing the great and marvelous wonders he alluded to previously. **"Fall on the earth."** I have seen snow blanketing Jerusalem and the surrounding countryside and it is, indeed, an unusual marvel in such a consistently temperate and desert location. Equally wonderful in such an arid climate is the unusual downpour of rain that replenishes water sources and makes agricultural productivity possible. God directs this marvelously unexpected natural phenomena by imperative demands that they "Fall on the earth" and **be . . . mighty.**

The translation, **"he stops every man from his labor,"** is an interpretation of the Hebrew text, which actually reads: "he seals the hand of every man." The sealing that God accomplishes by these extraordinary phenomena *may* prevent action—as the seal on a message prevents unauthorized access. But it may also represent a *reminder* of God's great power displayed in nature (NRSV translates "serves as a sign on everyone's hand"). **So that all men he has made may know his work.** The NIV performs another bit of creative translation here by rendering the single phrase *maʿasehu,* "his work," twice. The phrase first modifies "men," emphasizing their creaturely dependence on their creator. Second, the phrase is the object of the verb "know" that explains just what these marvelous experiences reveal to the humans: God at work in the world. The first of these uses is less likely, since it is probably the result of the accidental omission in textual transmission. **The animals take cover . . . remain in their dens.** Animals, too, are forced to refrain from their usual activity and to take note of this divine intrusion into habitual routine.

37:9–11 / **The tempest comes out from its chamber.** The description takes on a wintry tone with stormy skies and **cold** brought on by **driving winds.** Metaphorically, the winds are said to originate from a **chamber,** or storehouse, from which they come at God's call. **The breath of God.** Elsewhere **the breath** (Heb. *nishmah*) **of God** creates and sustains life (Gen. 2:7; 7:22), but it can also breathe fire and destruction (Isa. 30:33). The result here is **ice** and **frozen** waters. **He loads the clouds . . . scatters his lightning.** Again, the natural phenomena of the storm reveal God's power and control.

37:12–13 / **At his direction.** The noun "direction" implies navigational skill (Hartley, *Job,* p. 481), as if God controls the "rudder" of the wind. Winds, clouds, and lightning flashes **swirl around** in the winter storm that stretches from horizon to horizon covering the **whole earth.** God's control is evident since these swirling storm masses come **to do whatever he commands them.**

He brings the clouds. This phrase is an interpretive addition by the NIV that does not stand in the Hebrew text, but it intends to clarify a difficult verse. For **to punish men** the Hebrew literally says "whether for a rod," meaning a rod employed for discipline. The NIV's **or to water his earth** is a very expansive rendering of the literal Hebrew: "or for his earth." Some emend this phrase (*lʾrts*) by dividing the letters differently (*lʾ rtsw*) to mean "if they [humans] are unwilling" (see Hartley, *Job,* p. 479). Others posit the existence of an otherwise unknown word with the meaning "grace" (Pope, *Job,* p. 243). The phrase **show his love** is a third speculative reading in the same verse. This translation ignores the balanced structure of the three Hebrew phrases, each of which begins with the particle *ʾim,* "if, or." The three balanced phrases seem to express possible purposes for the coming of the storm and all conclude with the summation, "he [God] causes to find it." This probably means that God causes the purpose to be accomplished, or to "find its mark" (Pope, *Job,* p. 240).

Additional Notes §139

37:2 / The term **roar** is the Heb. *rogez,* that emphasizes attendant excitement and turmoil (3:17, 26; 14:1; 39:24).

37:3 / For **unleashes,** Hartley (*Job,* p. 477) and others read "flashes" on the basis of a reading in Ugaritic.

37:4 / His **roar** is probably better translated "a roaring noise/ sound." The verb *sh'g* describes the roaring of a lion. Contrast the "sound of sheer silence" (NRSV), translated as "gentle whisper" in the NIV, that comes to Elijah after wind, earthquake, and fire in 1 Kgs. 19:11–12.

37:6 / As Pope (*Job,* p. 241) indicates, the translation **shower** does not do the context justice, and "downpour of rain" is a better translation of *geshem matar / geshem mitrot* in this verse.

37:7 / **Men.** The final *mem* on the word "men" was omitted so that *'anshe,* "men of [his work]," should be *'anashim,* "men." The error is one of haplography, in which one of two adjacent and identical letters is omitted. In this case, the original consonantal text *'nshym m'shw* became *'nshy m'shw* through the accidental omission of the first of two consecutive *mem*s in the middle of the phrase.

37:10 / **The breath of God.** Pope (*Job,* p. 242) cites several passages with a similar phrase, but employing the Heb. *ruakh* instead of *nishmah.*

§140 God's Wonders, Job's Ignorance (Job 37:14–20)

Having established, through the imagery of the storm, that God is powerfully active in the world to accomplish his will and purpose, Elihu returns to confront what he considers Job's rebellious ignorance. He does so by tossing a series of perplexing questions at Job to demonstrate his lack of understanding. These questions are similar to, and prepare the reader for, the barrage of divine questions that constitute the heart of the divine theophany in chapters 38–41. So once again, while Elihu firmly denies that God will come in response to Job, he nevertheless subtly prepares us for that appearance.

37:14 / **Listen to this, Job.** Besides God and the narrator, as we have seen, Elihu is the only voice in the book to speak the name of Job directly (he does so six times: 33:1, 31; 34:5, 35, 36; 37:14). Here, in Elihu's final address to Job, he relates back to his initial invocation of Job's name in 33:1 by using the imperative *haʾazinah*, "listen," to again direct Job's attention to his words. These similar imperative phrases at the beginning and the end bracket Elihu's monologue as a unified set of speeches. The imperative **stop** is probably better taken as "stand; stand up; take (your) stand," since Job is not actively engaged in the dialogue at this point. The idea is that now is the time for Job to take stock of all that Elihu has said. In particular, Job should **consider God's wonders**—that Elihu has just been describing—as evidence in support of Elihu's claims.

37:15–18 / **Do you know?** The same interrogative verbal form (*hatedaᶜ*) begins this verse and the next, binding these rhetorical questions together. The fact that God **controls the clouds** and **lightning,** causing them to **hang poised** in the sky, is beyond human understanding. These are **wonders** known only to God **who is perfect in knowledge.** While God is able to move the clouds about by means of the wind and bring rain to cool the earth, Job is helpless to cool himself **when the land lies hushed under the south wind.**

The next question is **can you join him?** The comparison continues with the creation imagery of God **spreading out the skies** like a mass of molten **bronze,** poured out onto a flat surface to be burnished into a highly polished **mirror.** The image takes the relatively common human task of mirror making to an impossible scale to emphasize the futility of Job in trying to understand the wondrous works of God.

37:19 / **Tell us what we should say to him.** Elihu ridicules Job's determination to bring God to court to hear his case. If Job is unable to match God in the realm of nature, how can he hope to stand against him in a contest of words? There is no way for humans to set out an effective **case** against the master of the universe. The **darkness** here symbolizes the lack of knowledge that prevents Job from understanding (and accepting) what God is doing in the suffering he is experiencing.

37:20 / **Should he be told that I want to speak?** Elihu mockingly assumes Job's position of desiring an opportunity to present his case before God. Such a desire, according to Elihu, is equivalent to asking **to be swallowed up.** Job expresses similar sentiments in 10:16–20. Humans are powerless before the might of God, and even the blameless will condemn themselves when face to face with God in a court of law. Job's desire to take his case before God is doomed to failure from the start. No reasonable person would set out knowingly on a course that leads to certain destruction.

§141 The Splendor of God's Coming
(Job 37:21–24)

The chapter—and the Elihu speeches—ends here with a description of the approach of God likened to the blinding light of the sun. While Elihu employs this description metaphorically for the absolute justice of God, he does not expect an actual appearance of God in response to Job's demands because, in his opinion, God has already made his judgment known through Job's suffering and loss. Nevertheless, the passage prepares the way for the advent of God in the whirlwind to begin his response to Job (38:1).

37:21–22 / **Now no one can look at the sun.** Elihu changes from storm to sun metaphors to describe God's appearance to humans. Here it is the brightness of the "sun" in a sky **swept . . . clean** of clouds *after* a storm that Elihu portrays. As we are told never to look directly at the sun during an eclipse, so the ancients knew the power of direct sunlight to blind the incautious observer. The glory of God's appearing, then, can have destructive consequences on those drawn to experience it—a caution to Job that he may get more than he asks for!

Out of the north he comes. Although Elihu intends this description as a metaphorical caution to Job not to seek the appearance of God, who will certainly (in Elihu's opinion) judge Job with destruction, the words have the literary effect of preparing the reader for the advent of God's whirlwind theophany at the beginning of chapter 38 **in golden splendor . . . awesome majesty.** The emphasis is on the powerful essence of God and its destructive potential for sinful humans. The word translated "awesome" (*nora'*) means "fear producing," which further underlines the threatening nature of God's approach.

37:23–24 / **The Almighty is beyond our reach.** What the preceding verses expressed implicitly, this verse now makes explicit. God's awesome majesty and sovereign power are "beyond" humans for two reasons. First, they are unable to comprehend God's purposes. Second, they cannot influence or manipulate him. The Hebrew actually says "we do not find him," rather than he "is beyond our reach." The point is that God is transcendent other—outside our world of experience. God's commitment to **justice** and the fulfillment of **righteousness** balance his great **power,** in Elihu's view. Thus humans can rely on him because **he does not oppress.** This should be the basis of great confidence in humans. Job's personal experience, however, has raised the question of whether the intense suffering he has known justly rewards his righteous character. If Job is indeed blameless (as the reader knows he is) and yet he suffers (as we know he has), is it correct to describe God as both **exalted in** "power" and defender of "justice" as Elihu does?

Therefore. Elihu reaches the conclusion of his argument. Because God is both sovereign and just, **men revere him.** The term translated "revere" is the verb *yr*ʾ, "fear," and implies much more than simply reverence. The "fear of God/Yahweh" describes the essential relationship of righteousness with Israel's God. In Exodus 20:20 and throughout the OT, we learn that to "fear God" is *not* to be afraid of him, but to acknowledge one's absolute dependence on him for all life and goodness. The psalmist expressed this attitude in Psalm 73:25–26: "Whom have I in heaven but you? And earth has nothing I desire besides you. My flesh and my heart may fail, but God is the strength of my heart and my portion forever." The NIV turns the phrase **for does he not have regard** into a question in order to create a more positive divine response to the **wise in heart.** The Hebrew is actually a negative declaration: "He does not see/regard" (NASB; NRSV). The phrase "all the wise in heart" appears only here and in Exodus 28:3, where it describes "skilled persons" responsible for producing the priestly garments of Aaron and his sons. Some translators take this to mean those who trust in their own wisdom (NRSV "wise in their own conceit"). Others assume God shows no "regard" even for those who evidence great wisdom (NASB).

Elihu's extended monologues conclude, then, with a warning to Job not to press for an audience with God, since God is sovereign and just, and even those who are wise are not able to influence his just decisions by persuasion.

§142 Excursus: God's Appearance and Examination of Job

It should be clear from the outset that the fact God that appears in response to Job's plea for a meeting immediately puts the lie to any claims to the contrary that Elihu and the other friends have made. God *does* appear in response to Job. His very appearance, therefore, proves Elihu's earlier claim false—that God will not respond to Job because he has already spoken his final word of judgment in Job's suffering.

Deciding how to characterize this divine appearance is a difficult matter that has occupied interpreters of the book since the beginning. Most interpreters consider God's rather bombastic confrontation of Job to be, in some way, a rebuke of Job's inappropriate stance over against God—a position or attitude from which Job must "repent" in order to accomplish resolution. According to such a reading, God's questions ridicule Job's lack of understanding and power and *force* him to recant. Job has been presumptuous, it seems, and now needs to be put in his place. God's appearance to Job is therefore a sort of rebuke of Job and of his position throughout the book—a position from which he must ultimately withdraw.

I am less than fully persuaded by this common view of the purpose of the divine theophany in Job. I am troubled mostly because such an understanding flies in the face of two very important structural aspects of the book—one before and one after the theophany section. The first is that the structurally important prose prologue consistently affirms Job to be blameless and upright, innocent of any charges that might justify the suffering he experiences as a result of the test of his faithfulness. It is important that the reader know from the outset that Job is blameless, and the reader must evaluate the dialogue conversations on the basis of this knowledge. The second aspect that stands against this common view of the theophany is God's commendation of Job *and his*

words in the prose epilogue. After all is said and done, God rebukes not Job but the three friends, and this by saying that they
have not spoken rightly of God (the only place they speak is in the
dialogue!) as God's servant Job has. This strongly indicates that
God is *commending* Job's counter speeches in the dialogue as having spoken rightly about God. If this is indeed the case (as I am
convinced it is), then there is nothing that Job has said in his
speeches that calls for divine rebuke or which Job needs to recant.

If the rather caustic questions of the theophany are not intended as ridicule and rebuke of Job's inappropriate stance, then
what *is* their purpose? I have increasingly come to accept that
there is simply no more effective way for the poet-author to depict
a God who is so powerfully other than humans, who exceeds the
bounds of complete human comprehension, whose ways are not
our ways and whose thoughts are not our thoughts (Isa. 55:8–9),
than to bombard Job with an overwhelming array of unanswer-
able questions that threaten to submerge him. This is not rebuke
or even ridicule, but it is simply the author's attempt to demonstrate experientially what it is like for humans—even blameless
and upright humans of great wisdom like Job—to enter into the
presence of the sovereign God of the universe and of all time! To
do so is to take the wondering stance of the author of Psalm 8 and
marvel at the insignificance of humanity compared to the mani-
fest works of the creator God. Or, in the face of the clear failure of
retribution theology, to acknowledge along with the poet in Psalm
73, "Whom have I in heaven but you? And earth has nothing I desire besides you" (v. 25). The theophany is God coming into the
world and shaking the very foundations of human understanding and existence!

It is important for the reader to understand this point, for to
read the theophany as God's rebuke of Job is to send the reader
back into the dialogue section to discover what it is that Job has
done wrong to "deserve" this rebuke. And to embark on this
search for Job's "error" is, in a sense, to fall into the role of Job's
friends all over again. Once we accept that the depiction of God in
the theophany is not a description of divine anger and rebuke, but
simply the ineffable otherness that separates God from human
understanding, then we will be free to understand the final and
important interaction between God and Job in chapter 41 in a different light.

§143 Introduction (Job 38:1–3)

38:1 / **Then the LORD.** With one exception (12:9), the appearance of God in response to Job's plea occasions the first use of the divine name Yahweh since the prose prologue. Some speculate that the omission of the divine name from the dialogues and Elihu speeches reflects the non-Israelite character of Job and his interlocutors—who all instead have links with the region of Edom (Whybray, *Job*, p. 157). In Exodus the divine name Yahweh was part of a particularly intimate and personal revelation of God to Israel.

Unlike the other occurrences of the formula of response (**[he] answered**) in the dialogue section and in the speeches of Elihu, "[he] answered" here includes an object, **Job,** indicating the recipient of the divine response (*wayyaʿan yhwh ʾet ʾiyyob wayyoʾmar*). It is necessary to clarify the recipient at this point to indicate that God is responding to Job and not to Elihu, whose speech has just ended (or was interrupted). The use of this new formula would only be necessary if the Elihu speeches—regardless of their origin—already stood sandwiched between the final speech of Job (chs. 27–31) and God's response (chs. 38–41).

This particular style of formula, which includes the object, appears only in the theophany section (38:1; 40:1, 3; 42:1) and in the conversations between God and *the* Satan in chapters 1 and 2 of the prose prologue. There, however, only *the* Satan is said to "answer" God (*wayyaʿan hassatan ʾet yhwh*), while God always "speaks to" *the* Satan (*wayyoʾmar yhwh ʾel hassatan*). This sort of arrangement maintains God's authority over *the* Satan—a relationship in which God "speaks" and *the* Satan must "reply." It is also significant that in these two conversations between God and *the* Satan, God's statements bracket the answers of *the* Satan before, in the middle, and after, so that God always has the first and last word (1:7–12; 2:2–6) and remains the authority that initiates and concludes these interactions.

In his conversations with Job, however, God employs the normal formula of response with the addition of the object. This indicates that God does not seek to maintain his position of authority in the conversation, a position that would disadvantage Job and inhibit real interaction. Rather, God condescends, so to speak, and enters the conversations on a level of intimacy that offers Job a real opportunity for participation. It is also of interest that, in these conversations with Job, God allows Job's words to bracket his own, so that God comes in response to Job's earlier words in the dialogue (concluding in 31:40) and gives Job the final word (42:1–6).

This evidence of condescension and accommodation on the part of God gives the interaction between God and Job a different character than is commonly assumed. God is not the caustic, confrontational deity who seeks to rebuke Job and to ridicule him with sarcasm. Instead, God comes in his fullness and brings to Job an overwhelming experience of the reality of God that at once emphasizes the inadequacy of the human, Job, and the utter adequacy of the sovereign God. Thus Job (and the reader!) is put in his place—not by a rebuke, nor by a warning against questioning God, but by the gracious advent of God who allows himself to be seen inasmuch as that is humanly possible. As a result, the theophany—overwhelming as it *must* be—can only be understood as an act of grace.

The definite article on *hasseʿarah*, **the storm**, would normally indicate reference to an element that had been previously introduced in the narration. This particular term, *seʿarah*, does not appear earlier in Job, and it occurs again only in 40:6, which is a reprise of the statement in 38:1. This suggests that the author of the theophany section has in mind that the divine storm imagery in the concluding portions of the Elihu speeches is the precedent for "the storm" here, and that the description in chapter 37 serves as preparation for the theophany. The grammar, therefore, supports a theory of a unified editorial structure for the book in which the Elihu speeches immediately precede the theophany and prepare for it.

The term *seʿarah* commonly means a "storm wind" rather than a cyclone or tornado as we might associate with the translation "whirlwind" (NRSV). Some sort of whirlwind may be in mind, however, in the description of Elijah being taken up into heaven by means of a *seʿarah* (2 Kgs. 2:1, 11). Elsewhere in the OT *seʿarah* describes a destructive "storm wind" that carries off stubble and chaff and is a metaphor of divine judgment (Isa. 40:24; 41:15; Jonah 1:13). In Job 9:17, Job uses the related word *se'arah* (beginning with the letter *sin* rather than *samek*) to describe his fear that, should he gain an audience with God, "He would crush me with a storm." Thus Job (and the reader) cannot know at first what God's intentions are in appearing as he does. The "storm" cannot be taken universally as a sign of judgment, however, since fierce storm imagery describes the presence of God in a variety of circumstances (Exod. 19:16–24; 2 Kgs. 2:1, 11; Ps. 29). At the most, one can say that the "storm" cloaks the fierce otherness of the presence of God in his fullness in the midst of the world of human experience—a presence that causes all who see it to tremble and to cry with the psalmist: "Glory!" (Ps. 29:9).

38:2–3 / **Who is this that darkens my counsel?** It is clear from Job's restatement of this question in 42:3 that God is addressing Job here. Here Job replaces the word "darkens" (*makhshik*) with "obscures" (*ma'lim*). The word "counsel" (*'etsah*) can also mean "design; plan," and this nuance seems most appropriate here. God's choice of terms suggests that the problem is one of muddling the divine plan by speaking **without** full **knowledge.**

Brace yourself. The literal translation ("gird your loins") describes preparation for a difficult task by drawing up one's flowing robes into a girdle to free the legs for action. The task of knowing God is not easy labor and requires preparation and perseverance. The Hebrew here for **man** (*geber*) is an alternate word that can mean "fighter, warrior" (NJB), but it is usually translated with the more general term "man." God calls Job to prepare himself for the difficult task of answering the divine cross examination.

I will question you. God styles the conversation from the beginning as a divine examination of Job, not a dialogue or debate as those between Job and his friends. The examination proceeds through a series of questions that have two emphases: knowledge and power. Many questions ask Job to supply information or knowledge about the intricate details of creation and the ongoing affairs of the world. God clearly makes the point that, as creator, God has full knowledge of the intimate details of the world about which humans have only hazy understanding. In the other questions God asks Job to exercise power and control over some aspect of the creation. These questions emphasize the sovereign power of God over against the futility of human power to order the world. While God says, **and you shall answer me,** it quickly becomes clear that Job has no answers for the kinds of questions God asks. The Hebrew translated "answer" is not the same verb as the one that describes God's response to Job (*ʿnh*), but it is an imperative form of the verb *ydʿ* ("know"), meaning "cause me to know," or perhaps "declare" or "instruct me." The verb emphasizes that God is calling Job to supply knowledge or information rather than a response or retort.

Additional Notes §143

38:1 / **The storm.** The related cognate term *saʿar*, "storm; horror" occurs in 18:20, but there it seems to have the secondary nuance, "horror," rather than any meaning associated with "storm."

§144 Foundations of the Earth (Job 38:4–7)

God begins the questioning by probing Job's understanding of the foundational events of creation. The main emphasis here is on God's sovereign power and control rather than Job's ignorance. Humans (including Job) were not present at creation and can have no firsthand knowledge of it. Nor do they, unlike God, exercise any control over it. Isaiah 40:12–14 presents a comparable series of questions drawing on creation imagery to establish the sovereignty of God. Note how the movement from "where were you?" (v. 4) to "Who marked . . . stretched?" (v. 5) shifts focus from Job's lack of knowledge to the power of God. Later questions ask "Can you . . . ?" (e.g., v. 20).

38:4–5 / Where were you . . . ? Job is forced to admit his complete lack of any firsthand knowledge of God's creative acts (**when I laid the earth's foundation**) to establish the earth in which humans find themselves living. The ancient cosmology understood the earth as a flat, circular plate over which an inverted bowl (the firmament) stood, sealed at the farthest horizon to hold off the chaotic waters above and below the earth. This protective "envelope" provided a secure environment for plant, animal, and human life and was thought to be founded on pillars that extended down into the waters under the earth. **Tell me, if you understand.** It is not so much Job as *all* humans (including the friends and Elihu) that must adopt this attitude of humility in relation to the inferences they make based on observations of nature. Wisdom, of course, believed that observation and experience of nature and life would lead to better and better understanding of God's world and his purposes in it. Humans with such understanding would be able to live rightly and so prosper. While Job has maintained his certainty regarding his own blamelessness, he has tended to adopt a position of uncertainty regarding God's activity in and through creation. The friends and Elihu, on the other hand, have constantly spoken with certainty about the operation of retribution in God's world and their own abilities to discern truth based on their observations of life.

Who marked off its dimensions . . . stretched a measuring line? The change from "Where were you?" to "Who?" shifts the focus from the ignorance of Job to the sovereign power of God displayed in creation. God is the obvious answer to these "Who?" questions. Therefore, not only must Job admit his own lack of knowledge, but he must also affirm God's power and control in creation. These images depict God as a master carpenter, marking and measuring, stretching out lines to guide construction of his world. **Surely you know!** God does not allow Job to forget that his knowledge is incomplete and therefore lacking. Are the friends also present during this theophanic display? If so, ought we to assume that they experienced a similar critique of their knowledge and understanding?

38:6–7 / **On what were its footings set?** The verb "set" (*tbᶜ*) describes a drowning person "sinking" into the water (30:24), fallen gates sinking into the earth (Lam. 2:9), and feet sinking into the mud (Jer. 38:22). The imagery drawn from ancient cosmology describes the "footings" of the earth as pillars or pilings driven into the waters or mud to provide a stable foundation for the building (1 Sam. 2:8; Pss. 18:15; 24:2; 75:3; 104:5; Prov. 8:29). The question **who laid its cornerstone?** is another metaphorical reference taken from building technique that helps to explain God's creation activity, of which Job can have no personal knowledge.

God is not following the order of the creation narrative in Genesis 1 in which he created sun, moon, and **stars** *after* the earth/dry land. The Genesis narratives do not mention **angels** (lit., "sons of God") in relation to creation, although other texts describe them as creatures of God who do his will and join in the praise of divine creation (e.g., Pss. 103:20; 148:1–6). Laying the foundation of an important building was the occasion for celebration and joyous singing: **sang together . . . shouted for joy** (see also Ezra 3:10–11). The picture here understands creation as a great construction project under God's direction.

The creation imagery continues in this section as God describes the boundaries he provides to contain the chaotic primeval waters (Gen. 1:6–7; 9–10; see also Gen. 8:2; Job 12:15; Pss. 33:7; 104:7–9; Prov. 8:27–29).

38:8–11 / **Who shut up the sea behind doors?** The sea is confined "behind doors" as if in a prison or a storehouse. Other texts refer to God placing the seas in a jar (Ps. 33:7) or in the hollow of his hand (Isa. 40:12). The chaotic waters were a threat to creation and made the world a formless and empty place (Gen. 1:2) where nothing could live. Only God was able to restrict these waters in an orderly way and harness them to beneficial purposes for humankind. God acts as a midwife at the birth of the chaotic waters of the seas as they **burst forth from the womb.** The "womb" refers metaphorically to the origins of the seas as part of God's creation. But even the power with which they "burst forth" could not overwhelm God's control. In the Mesopotamian narrative of the flood (found in both the Gilgamesh and Atrahasis Epics), once the gods unleash the chaotic waters, the waters threaten to overwhelm them. The Mesopotamian gods then cower behind the walls of their abode, screaming like dogs because of their powerlessness to control what they started (see S. Dalley, ed. *Myths from Mesopotamia: Creation, the Flood, Gilgamesh, and Others.* Trans. S. Dalley. Oxford: Oxford University Press, 1989). Not so Yahweh! The mighty roaring of the ancient waters is no match for Israel's God, who remains unafraid and unchallenged (Ps. 93).

God makes his claim of creation power explicit: **When I made.** The "who" is no longer an issue, so the questions become less about Job's lack of knowledge and focus instead on the recognition of God's power. The translation **the clouds its garment** obscures the parallel between this phrase and the next which means, literally, "and [I made] deep darkness its swaddling band." God displays his power through his ability to clothe the tempestuous seas in a "garment" of "clouds." The parallel description of these garments as a "swaddling band," the cloth used to wrap up a baby, intensifies the image of his power. The mighty sea is a helpless baby, bundled up in a blanket of clouds by the midwife God, who attended its birth!

The Hebrew for **when I fixed limits for it** is difficult, primarily because the verb translated "fixed" (*shbr*) normally means "shatter, break," and the word translated "limits" commonly means "statute; thing decreed." Suggested emendations usually end with a reading similar to NIV. Drawing on the second half of the verse, it seems reasonable to assume that God is placing restrictions on the seas. City gates were **doors** fastened with **bars** often made of iron (Neh. 3:8) to prevent them from being broken easily. Here the image is of a storehouse with secure "doors."

God expresses his power in word as well as deed: **when I said.** His words articulate the meaning of his actions. Perhaps the author has in mind here the creative power of the divine word in Genesis 1. **"This far you may come and no farther."** These are the "fixed limits" mentioned in verse 10. A recent tsunami that inundated the coastal regions of Southeast Asia further proved the inability of human power to predict or control the devastation of the **proud waves** of the seas. The power of God to **halt,** or prescribe limits to, the chaotic waters is clearly beyond human understanding.

§146 A Purified Earth (Job 38:12–15)

The questions in this section illumine the weakness of Job (and all humans) in comparison with the sustaining power of God over creation.

38:12–14 / **Have you ever . . . ?** The Hebrew adds "in all your days," ironically suggesting that even in a long life of great wisdom Job is unable to approach the power of God to direct and order nature. God gives **orders to the morning** and positions **dawn** in the correct **place,** like a military commander or a stage choreographer.

God's power does not extend only over the physical features of the earth; he also establishes justice where he reigns. "Morning" and "dawn," like two children assigned to shake out the dirt from a rug or a tablecloth, **take the earth by the edges and shake the wicked out of it** (lit., "and the wicked are shaken out of it"). The **garment** of the earth flaps, and the cleansing shake creates ripples in the cloth, likened here to the ripples in **clay** under the pressure of a cylinder **seal** used for signing clay tablets. These seals were small cylinders of stone, clay, or other materials, carved with a unique set of characters and symbols to identify the owner. People wore these seals on cords around their necks so that they were readily available when they needed to sign necessary legal documents. Seal patterns were carved in reverse so that, when pressed into the damp clay and rolled, they produced an impression in the proper order.

38:15 / **The wicked are denied their light.** Shaken from the earth like crumbs or dirt, the wicked are no longer able to experience the light of "morning" and "dawn." The breaking of the **upraised arm** of the wicked nullifies any oppressive power they might wield. Thus, the imagery depicts God purifying the earth of wickedness and restricting its power. By providing the sun to bathe the earth in light, God has brought the evil perpetrated in the dark to the light, exposing the oppression of the wicked. Like God's restriction of the chaotic seas, light places limits and restraints on evil.

38:16 / **Have you journeyed . . . walked?** There are places humans cannot go, and parts of the earth they cannot see—this was especially true in the ancient world. The chief unexplored region of the earth, even with the present advances of technology, is beneath the oceans. Without submarines or remote submersibles with video links, Job and all the people of his day had no way to experience the floor of the oceans and the deep marine trenches. As lakes and rivers flow from springs, here the sea is imagined to find its source in **springs** that are **deep** beneath the surface and cut off from human experience.

38:17–18 / Equally deep and removed from human experience are the **gates** of *Sheol,* the abode of the dead (see Job 17:16; Pss. 9:13; 107:13; Isa. 38:10). *Sheol* was understood to lie under the earth. Entrance was through a series of gates that prevented the shades of the dead from departing and the living from entering. The **shadow of death** translates the Hebrew *tsalmawet,* which is taken to combine the words *tselem,* "shadow," and *mawet,* "death." Often translations of this construction express a superlative on the order of "darkest shadow." The term occurs most often in Job (10:22; 12:22; 16:16; 24:17 twice; 34:22; 38:17; also Ps. 23:4; Isa. 9:2; Amos 5:8). On some occasions, as here, it is clearly the abode of the dead, *Sheol,* that is in view.

The depths of the seas, *Sheol* under the earth, and now **the vast expanses of the earth** (perhaps better "the most distant reaches of the earth"), are all beyond the experience and knowledge of human exploration. Even today, while much of the earth's surface has been explored, there remains unexplored territory, and the floors of the ocean and its deep trenches, which cover more than seventy percent of the face of the earth, are largely unknown. **Have you comprehended?** In the Hitpolel, as here, this verb means to examine something carefully, or pay close attention to it. **Tell me, if you know.** Once again the ironical question drives home Job's lack of knowledge and understanding of the physical world that God created—much less the divine creator himself.

Additional Notes §147

38:17 / For a description of the gates to the netherworld in Mesopotamian myth, see "The Descent of Ishtar to the Netherworld," *ANET,* pp. 106–9.

38:18 / Hartley, *Job,* pp. 498–99, takes **earth** to be a reference to the vast underground world of *Sheol.* He also understands the "gates" of *Sheol* to stand at the "springs of the sea," so that there would be a progression downward in these verses: the seas and their springs, the gates of *Sheol,* and then the expanses of *Sheol.*

§148 Above the Earth (Job 38:19–30)

38:19–21 / The inquiry at this point begins to consider God's work above the earth. The question about the **abode of light** parallels the following query concerning **where does darkness reside,** recalling the separation of "light" and "darkness" in Genesis 1:3–5. The knowledge of such events eludes humans—and even if they were able to discover it, they have no power to **take them to their places** or travel along the **paths to their dwellings. Surely you know, for you were already born!** These words once again display Job's lack of knowledge and power. More irony dwarfs Job before the eternality of the creator God, before whom Job's **many years** dwindle to nothingness.

38:22–24 / **Have you entered the storehouses of the snow . . . hail?** As God has shut the chaotic waters of the seas behind doors or in containers, so the picture here is of "snow" and "hail" shut up in heavenly "storehouses" awaiting deployment as God's weapons in **days of war and battle.** Psalm 18 gives a good description of the divine warrior God striking out with the weapons of the storm: wind, rain, lightning, and hail. As if dispatching military troops into battle, the commanding God sends forth **lightning** and **the east winds** into the world. Like Job, no human is able to find the **place** where God gives the orders, let alone have any control over the process.

38:25–27 / **Who cuts a channel?** Like a farmer irrigating his fields, the picture here is of God digging an irrigation "channel" to deliver **torrents of rain** and **the thunderstorm** to the spot he wishes to enliven with water. "Torrents" and "thunderstorm" suggest an abundance of rain **to water a land where no man lives.** In God's world, even the uninhabited wilderness receives his providential care *in abundance.* I am reminded how in California, following the wettest season in almost 100 years, lakes formed in Death Valley where none had been seen before and a profusion of grass and flowers bloomed, including species never before observed. God knows the thirst of the **desolate wasteland** for water and satisfies it in abundance, even showering it with unseen beauty. His attention to such details of beauty in an isolated wilderness proclaims his interest and concern with the *whole* world—not just its human inhabitants. "The earth is the LORD's," contends the Psalmist, "and everything in it, the world, and all who live in it; for he founded it upon the seas and established it upon the waters" (Ps. 24:1–2).

38:28–30 / **Does the rain have a father?** The question strikes metaphorically at the mystery of the origin of "rain" and **dew.** For the ancients, rain and dew came at the will and whim of God (or the gods). Clearly the question of origins in both of these cases goes back to God, emphasizing his control and mastery over the whole universe. These verses also communicate once again the lack of human control and knowledge. **From whose womb comes the ice?** God is both father and mother of the phenomena of this world, for it is certainly his "womb" that the poet envisions giving **birth** to "the ice" and **the frost.** Only through divine power can the waters of rivers and even the **surface of the deep** be **frozen.** The verb translated frozen (*lkd*) normally describes capturing the enemy and emphasizes the power of God that wrestles even the great chaotic seas into icy submission.

§149 Authority in the Heavens (Job 38:31–33)

Thus far the divine examination of Job has focused on questions probing human understanding and knowledge. God has asked, "Where were you when . . . ?" and "Have you seen . . . ?" and "What is the way to . . . ?" He punctuates these questions with ironical statements driving home the paucity of human knowledge: "Surely you know!" and "Tell me, if you know!"

Now the examination shifts to focus on the powerlessness of Job, and all humans, to shape their world. A new style of questioning, involving verbs of action such as "Can you . . . ?" and "Do you . . . ?" indicates this shift. The purpose is to establish clearly that humans have no power to order creation, and that God remains the sovereign in control of his creation. In addition, these questions explore aspects of creation that are far removed from the world of human affairs and reveal God's concern with creatures and matters unrelated to human life. God's concern, it seems, is far from being myopically focused on humans and their way in the world. God exercises his creative and sustaining power for the benefit of *all creation,* of which humans are but one part. By these questions God calls Job (and all humans) to acknowledge their utter dependence on his power and care. God further calls human beings to a new and humble perspective on their place and role within the divine economy. The world does not revolve around humans and their wants and needs. God has other creatures to care for, other opportunities to create beauty and to pour out his grace on rock, plant, and animal alike.

38:31–32 / **Can you bind . . . Can you loose . . . ?** The focus on human powerlessness is immediately clear. The ability to "bind" and "loose" is evidence of power to control. **Pleiades** and **Orion** are two constellations of stars that are beyond the reach of human control and manipulation. The NIV's translation **beautiful** is against the norm. Most translations understand the Hebrew *ma'adannot* to mean "chains" or some other means of binding. This fits with the parallel term **cords** (*moshkot*) in the second half of the verse and is probably the better reading. God treats the stars like domesticated animals, binding them together like oxen into constellations, or loosing them to wander alone as he wishes. Humans can only look on with amazement as God works in the distant heavens (Ps. 8). **Can you bring forth . . . lead out?** The probing of the limits of human power continues with reference to the manipulation of additional **constellations** of the night sky including **the Bear with its cubs.**

38:33 / **Do you know the laws of the heavens?** The rules and order that govern the movement of the stars through their seasonal rotations are beyond Job's knowledge. Even the best of today's scientists must admit to only a partial understanding of the laws governing celestial bodies. And even should they be able to describe these rules perfectly, they still have no power to **set up** (or establish) **dominion over the earth.**

Additional Notes §149

38:32 / The Heb. *mazzarot* occurs only here and its meaning is thus uncertain. However, most speculations center around particular stars, **constellations,** or groups of constellations.

38:34–35 / Can you raise your voice to the clouds? From the human vantage point of the earth, one would have to bellow very loudly to be heard by "the clouds" far above the earth. The shout is intended to stir the clouds to action to produce **a flood of water.** Clearly it is God who commands the clouds, and not humans. Humans have no power over the rain clouds. Nor do they dispatch the **lightning bolts** on their way, or receive the obedient response due to the sovereign lord: "Here we are!"

38:36–38 / Who endowed the heart with wisdom? There is considerable debate about this difficult verse. The problem centers on the meaning of the rare words translated "heart" (*tuhot*) and **mind** (*sekwi*). These words could refer to the inner recesses of the human body and the heart as the deliberative center. While this choice—followed by NIV—is in keeping with the references to wisdom in this verse, the links in terms of meaning are tenuous at best. Another suggestion is to understand the terms as references to the Egyptian god of wisdom, Thoth, and his Roman counterpart, Mercury. Gordis (*Job,* p. 452) questions whether pagan gods would be so invoked in a context considering God's wisdom in the created world. Others relate the terms to different types of cloud formations (RSV), but the reference to wisdom, then, does not make as much sense. The final option is to understand these words as describing two birds, the ibis and the cock. Both birds are associated with wisdom (the ibis is also linked with Thoth in Egypt), and both are thought to have the ability to predict the coming of the rain (NJB). Regardless of the interpretation of these words, God is the one who "endowed" wisdom.

Who has the wisdom to count the clouds? The assault on human understanding continues. Humans are unable to "count the clouds." Neither are they able to release the rain on the earth by overturning the heavenly **water jars** (or skins) in which the rain is collected before being dispersed. With the addition of water, **dust becomes hard,** forming mud (lit., "pours out like a casting") and lumps of clay **stick together.**

Additional Notes §150

38:35 / The Heb. is *hinnenu,* "Here I am!" The phrase is a response to the call to duty by a superior and evidences readiness to obey.

§151 Languishing Lions and Ravenous Ravens (Job 38:39–41)

Not only does God's control of the world reach to realms beyond the possibility of human power, but it also declares sovereignty in matters that do not concern humans at all. The series of animal portraits that follow have been related to the genre of the onomasticon, developing lists of items that embody a particular category. As Hartley (*Job*, p. 504) notes: "With these portraits Yahweh asserts his lordship over the entire earth—the cultivated land and the wilderness, the domesticated animals and the wild beasts. No part of the world lies outside his rule. No hostile forces exist beyond his authority."

38:39–41 / **Do you hunt the prey for the lioness?** God's providence includes the animal world with which humans have little contact and for which they have less concern. Here, like a heavenly zookeeper, God sees to the needs of "the lioness" and satisfies **the hunger of the lions.** Because lions are a threat, tearing cattle and humans alike, humans avoid or destroy them. Humans must defend themselves from "the hunger of the lions" that threatens to decimate the herd and end human life. But God cares for these animals and provides for them. The lions hide **in their dens** or seek security **in a thicket.** This is not the proud, hunting lion or lioness, but the fearful, shrinking beast, in need of the nourishment that God provides.

Who provides food for the raven? God demonstrated his care for humans when he used the ravens to feed the prophet Elijah who was hiding from Jezebel in the wilderness (1 Kgs. 17:1–6). Now it is "the raven" that is in need—its young **cry out to God** in desperation because of their **lack of food.** Humans demonstrate little concern for the plight of such birds and do even less to relieve their hunger.

§152 The Mountain Goats and Birthing Deer (Job 39:1–4)

39:1–4 / **Do you know . . . ?** The interrogation continues, stressing human ignorance of the animal world over which God exercises providential and protective care. Notoriously isolated animals, **the mountain goats** hide away in inaccessible hideouts to **give birth.** It is unlikely that humans would be able to find these hideouts and observe the birthing process. **Do you watch . . . ?** The Hebrew verb more accurately expresses protective care, in the sense of "watch over," than mere observation. It is the same verb (*shmr*) used to command the first human to "keep; care protectively" for the garden in Genesis 2:15. God is asking Job whether he has ever watched protectively while **the doe bears her fawn.** The implication, then, is that God has done so.

Do you count the months . . . know the time . . . ? A protective herdsman is constantly aware of the condition of his flock. He knows when they conceive and is able to project when they will **give birth.** My cattleman brother-in-law keeps careful records on the breeding of his cows so he can be prepared to assist when the time of delivery comes. God is claiming to be such a protective herdsman, unlike Job, watching over the flocks and herds of wild animals beyond human knowledge and involvement. **They crouch down . . . their labor pains are ended.** The whole process comes to completion far removed from human concern and control.

Their young thrive and grow strong. Without human assistance, the wild goats and deer "grow strong" under the protective providence of a caring God. At maturity, **they leave** their mother's care **and do not return,** asserting their independence and freedom.

§153 The Freedom of the Wild Donkey (Job 39:5–8)

39:5–8 / Unlike his domesticated counterpart, the **wild donkey** remains free from human domination. Never having submitted to the **ropes** of bondage, to slavery, the donkey lives in a remote and barren **wasteland** characterized as **salt flats.** Far removed from the **commotion** produced by humans and their working animals concentrated in villages, the donkey **laughs** defiantly at the efforts of humans to bring his world under their control. Yet God affirms his dominion even in "the wasteland" when he states directly: "**I gave him the** wasteland **as his home.**"

The donkey in the wild is free to pursue his own course without having to heed the coercive **driver's shout.** This verse describes what may seem a desperate task of eking out a meager existence in a foreboding landscape as an image of freedom from human control as the donkey **ranges the hills** in search of **any green thing.** The wild donkey depends only on the providential care of God, who establishes the donkey's habitat and provides its necessary fodder. Humans are not part of this equation.

§154 The Wild Ox (Job 39:9–12)

39:9–12 / Neither does the **wild ox consent** to a human's domination and control and will not **serve** him. Even the offer of free fodder in a **manger** is no temptation for this free beast. This wild creature possesses all the power of the domesticated ox, but it expends all of this **great strength** with no benefit for the human. The "wild ox" cannot be forced to **till** the ground or transport the harvested **grain** to the **threshing floor.** This untapped resource for agricultural **heavy work** must have seemed a tremendous waste to those for whom humanity occupied the center of creation. The almost frivolous expenditure of energy in the wild, created and sustained by God, indicates that in God's view the creation is about far more than the welfare of humans. We have here a window into the divine pleasure in his creation and its many distinctive creatures—a pleasure that calls us as humans to the task of environmental concern and protection.

§155 The Ostrich (Job 39:13–18)

This section, on what is traditionally understood to be the ostrich, does not follow the question format established in the previous verses. Instead we have a colorful description of the habits of this animal based on human observations from afar. The emphasis is on the bird's lack of utility to humans and lack of wise behavior in relation to its own offspring. And yet, the animal remains a free and sustained part of God's creation outside the control of humans.

39:13 / **The wings of the ostrich flap joyfully.** The Hebrew word translated "ostrich" literally means "bird of piercing cries." Varied translations indicate the difficulty in the second half of this verse. The Hebrew as it currently stands (lit., "if wing stork and plumage") makes little sense, but most scholars understand it to indicate a comparison between the wings of "the ostrich" and "the stork." Pope (*Job*, p. 260) and Hartley (*Job*, p. 509) accept an emendation of "stork" to a word meaning "lacks" so that the verse means "the wings (of the ostrich) lack feathers" (NRSV).

39:14–15 / **She lays her eggs on the ground.** This statement questions the maternal instincts of the ostrich. The term "lays" is actually the verb for "abandons." Unlike many species of birds that lay their eggs in nests elevated for protection in trees and shrubs, the ostrich, being a heavy bird, must build its nest on the ground. The observations of modern ornithologists do not confirm this assumed disregard the ostrich displays towards her eggs, although it is a common misunderstanding reflected broadly in ancient literature (see Pope, *Job*, p. 261; Gordis, *Job*, p. 459). When the ostrich hen leaves the nest in search of food, she normally covers the eggs with **sand** to protect them from the sun and predators, yet it seems to the poet that she is **unmindful that a foot may crush . . . trample them.**

39:16–17 / **She treats her young harshly.** The parental aloofness and lack of concern attributed to the ostrich must have puzzled humans, who tend to provide extended protective care to their offspring. Yet God has created these unusual creatures with the characteristics they possess and continues to sustain them in all their apparent foolishness. The ostrich hen is actually a fierce protector of her eggs, using her strong legs and hardened toenails to pummel or slash predators. This presumed abandonment of offspring suggests that the hen has little concern that they might perish and her reproductive endeavors would be **in vain.**

Verse 17 traces the ostrich's lack of parental protection and concern for her offspring to the action of God in creation, who **did not endow her with wisdom . . . good sense.** God is the one who chose to shape the ostrich with these particular characteristics—a decision that is beyond human understanding and control. The ostrich has huge eyes and only a walnut-sized brain, which may explain traditional references to the bird's lack of "wisdom" and "good sense."

39:18 / The passage concludes with a description of the great speed of the ostrich. This is the bird's chief glory. The phrase **when she spreads her feathers to run** is difficult because the verb occurs only here. Some take it to mean "lift herself on high" (NASB; see also NRSV), but this is inappropriate because the ostrich does not fly. Others understand the meaning to be "urge oneself on," or think that it describes a peculiar spreading of the tail feathers as the ostrich accelerates (see Gordis, *Job,* pp. 460–61; Pope, *Job,* p. 262). In a chase or race, the ostrich leaves the **horse and rider** behind and **laughs** in derision at all attempts to run faster. Ostriches have been clocked at peak speeds approaching 80 kph (50 mph) and, since they can turn sharp corners at top speed, the bird can easily outstrip most horses and outmaneuver pursuers. The reference to "horse and rider" provides a nice transition to the next vignette, which considers the domesticated warhorse.

Additional Notes §155

39:13 / For more information on the ostrich, search the website of the National Wildlife Federation: www.nwf.org, or the site run by the American Ostrich Association: http://www.ostriches.org.

§156 The Horse (Job 39:19–25)

39:19–25 / This section is distinct from the rest of the vignettes collected here in that it does not describe a *wild* animal, but the domesticated war stallion. While their riders could control these animals, these horses must have seemed terrifyingly ferocious to infantry soldiers who were in danger of being bitten or crushed under their hooves. **Do you give . . . ?** Returning to the questioning mode of earlier vignettes, God questions Job's ability to manipulate and control the animal order represented by the **horse.** God takes pleasure in both the power (**strength**) and aesthetics (**flowing mane**) of the horse—he has made the creation beautiful as well as useful. Thus humans are not only to use the resources of the earth (see Gen. 1:26), but to appreciate and preserve its artistic wonders. Since they did not make any aspect of the creation, humans ought to follow the pattern of protective care and enjoyment modeled by the creator in his loving response to the world.

Do you make him leap? While most translators render the Hebrew verb (r'sh) "leap" because of the connection with the horse, the common meaning is "quake," or "shake." Some have suggested that the picture is of the quivering tension in the war stallion just before the charge, compared with the rippling effect of a field covered with millions of **locusts.** As the warhorse, barely held in check, anticipates the dash into battle, he prances about nervously **snorting** in loud gusts and **paws** the ground **fiercely** before charging **into the fray** (Heb. "goes forth to meet weapons"). In the charge the war stallion seems fearless and unafraid, willing to plunge among the enemy with no regard for **the sword.** The picture is finely drawn, with attention to the weapons of the rider—**quiver** (arrows), **spear,** and **lance**—rattling **against his side.** The horse rushes toward the enemy in **frenzied excitement** and at such speed that it seems he **eats up the ground.** As the **trumpet sounds** announcing battle, the stallion is unable to **stand still** but **snorts,** excited by the **scent** and sound of the distant **battle.**

This well-drawn portrait suggests some firsthand experience with horses in battle. The emphasis is upon the strength and ferocity of the powerful animal barely kept under control. Such a creature can perhaps be exploited by riders, but only God can create such a marvel of strength and excitement.

Additional Notes §156

39:19 / The Heb. translated **flowing mane** is, lit., "quivering" (*raʿmah*), although the Arabic reference to the hyena as "mother of the mane" uses a cognate term (*riʿim*). The poet may have intended a play on words here to evoke the idea of a mane quivering in the wind.

39:26–30 / This long series of animal vignettes concludes with a description of the **hawk** and **eagle,** birds that soar on high, employing thermal uplifts to prolong their flight in search of prey. The term translated "hawk" (*nets*) is less common than "eagle" (*nesher*), and the latter term is often translated "vulture" since the bird is frequently described as eating carrion or the bodies of fallen soldiers. The corpses of the dead left exposed after the battle may explain the literary connection between this concluding vignette and the preceding one concerning the warhorse.

Verse 26 begins, as usual, with a question regarding Job's "wisdom" to create such marvels of the natural world. "Wisdom" here indicates both the knowledge to understand and the ability to create the flight skills associated with these high-flying birds of prey. The descriptive term **spread his wings** captures the sight of hawk or eagle soaring on rising currents of air with open wings. The Hebrew for **toward the south** can also mean "south wind," on which the birds soar, or "toward Teman," a location associated with the south of Edom to the east of the Dead Sea. It is from this place that God is said to come in Habakkuk 3:3. Some connect this movement southwards with a seasonal migration pattern that is evidence of the "wisdom" that the creator implanted in these creatures.

Does the eagle soar at your command? Job is no more capable of commanding the eagle than he is of creating the bird and implanting the "wisdom" of flight within it. These are the sole prerogatives of the creator God who expends his efforts on unimaginable details of the animal world far beyond human comprehension or control. **He dwells on a cliff.** These birds remain aloof from humans and thus offer little immediate benefit for them. Nesting in a **rocky crag,** the eagle remains safe as if in a military **stronghold.** Soaring high above on the air currents the bird has such acute eyesight that it can see **from afar** the movement of small mice and other creatures of prey upon which it plummets in a deadly swoop. **His young ones feast on blood.** The adult bird carries bits of flesh back to the young in the aerie. The references to feasting on "blood," and the presence of this bird **where the slain are,** seem to imply a carrion bird or vulture instead of the more traditional translation referring to a "noble" bird of prey.

Additional Notes §157

39:26 / The terms for **hawk** and **eagle** are variously translated. Gordis (*Job,* p. 463) suggests "eagle" would be better translated "vulture" because of the connection with battle (and, by extension, corpses) in the preceding verses.

Toward the south. Interestingly, the term for God in Hab. 3:3 is *ʾeloah,* the same term used throughout the poetical portions of Job. Teman is also associated with the sons of Esau—the progenitor of the Edomites—in Gen. 36:11, 15, 42; 1 Chr. 1:36, 53. See also Jer. 49:7, 20; Ezek. 25:13; Amos 1:12; Obad. 9.

§158 Job's Non-response (Job 40:1–5)

Growing up in southeast Texas, I sat through a number of devastating hurricanes. I remember well the rushing winds, the deafening downpour of rain, watching the creeping floodwaters rising to submerge the landscape. But perhaps the most eerie experience of all was sitting in the dark after the electricity had been cut off and hearing the raging winds still to an equally deafening *silence* as the eye of the storm passed over us. The first few verses of chapter 40 are a similar kind of lull in the storm of divine interrogation. They constitute a sort of *intermezzo* pause in the midst of the torrent of divine words. The pause allows Job, and the reader, an opportunity to catch their breath (we find we have been holding our collective breaths ever since God began!) and to reflect briefly on what has gone before. Experience taught me as a child, however, that the eye of the hurricane was not the end of the storm—more was yet to come.

40:1 / The LORD said to Job. The NIV translation obscures the fact that the formula introducing God's speech here is the same as the one found at the beginning of chapter 38. Here only the location of God within the whirlwind, or "storm," is missing. The more literal translation is: "And the LORD answered Job and said." As we mentioned in the discussion on 38:1, this particular introduction shows that God is still responding to Job's earlier words with intimacy and condescension and invites a response in return.

40:2–5 / Will the one who contends with the Almighty correct him? This sentence is somewhat difficult and scholars have suggested various translations. Some take the word translated "correct" as a noun meaning "faultfinder" and render the question as, "Will a faultfinder contend with the Almighty?" (NASB; NRSV; NJB). To contend in this sense is to confront another in court over a breach of covenant obligations. Job has been asking God to render account in court, explaining how his treatment of Job fulfills the assumed covenant of retribution. The translation "correct" assumes that Job has accused God of error. The actual meaning is closer to "instruct" or "reprove." The point seems to be that God is asking Job—in light of his newfound experience of the power and wisdom of God—if he is in a position to instruct God on the workings of the creation and the creatures within it. What Job actually seeks, as we considered earlier, is a public affirmation of his integrity and righteousness, not a full explanation of God's purposes and activities in the world.

Let him who accuses God. The term "accuses" here (Heb. *ykkh*) assumes a legal setting and means something like "seeks a legal determination." It can mean "reprove" or "rebuke," but it may also mean "establish the truth" in a particular situation. Job certainly believes he is innocent and undeserving of the suffering he experiences. Job's certainty, along with his desire to have God acknowledge his righteousness, runs the risk of putting God in the wrong. In response, God has begun to display to Job the essential nature of his power and character in relation to the world. At this *intermezzo* Job is given an opportunity to reflect on what he has learned and to balance it against his desire for vindication.

God provides space within the overwhelming onslaught of the theophany for Job to **answer him.** As we saw in 38:1, the formulae introducing the divine speeches in this section downplay the divine authority and place Job on a more equal footing with God. These indicate that God pursues real interaction with Job (and humans in general). Here is the opportunity Job has been seeking all along: a chance to state his case before God.

Then Job answered the LORD. Job has the opportunity to respond, and he does. But in reality his reply constitutes a non-answer, since he refuses to press his case or to withdraw. **I am unworthy.** The Hebrew means something like "I am a lightweight." The theophany has brought home to Job the reality of what he knew all along in the abstract: the essential power of God overwhelms any human who attempts to stand before it! It is like a featherweight boxer in the ring with the heavyweight champion—a complete mismatch. God's very presence prevents Job from pressing his case, and so he asks, **how can I reply?** Perhaps because he feels anything he might say would ultimately condemn him (as he predicted in 9:14–21), Job refuses to speak at all. This may be the biblical equivalent of "taking the fifth" (invoking the Fifth Amendment to the U.S. Constitution in an attempt to avoid self-incrimination). **I put my hand over my mouth.** Even today this gesture indicates an attempt to control one's speech.

I spoke once . . . twice . . . Job does not revoke his claims but stands by them. This first opportunity for a reply shows Job as shaken, but still steadfast. If he had collapsed and recanted immediately, then his arguments would have less power to persuade. **I have no answer . . . will say no more.** Job refuses to take up the offer to confront God, but not because he has recanted his claims. Having seen the power of God, Job is unwilling to carry out his confrontation in the legal setting. Yet he does not withdraw his claims, even if he has nothing new to add.

The eye of the storm has passed and the winds pick up again, battering Job as strongly as before. After a renewed challenge in 40:6–8, God makes it clear in verses 9–14 that humans have no power to stand on their own in the world. The remainder of the examination consists of two extended animal portraits—behemoth in 40:15–24 and leviathan in 41:1–34—that drive home the inability of humans to control these amazing creatures in God's world. If humans have no power to control these animals, then how could they ever hope to bend the creator to their will? In the Hebrew text, chapters 40 and 41 are differently divided so that the initial description of leviathan in 41:1–8 becomes 40:25–32. This links the description of these two beasts even more closely together as parts of the same final examination.

40:6–8 / **Then the LORD spoke to Job out of the storm.** This is exactly the same phrase found at the beginning of chapter 38, signifying that this is a continuation of the original storm of words after a brief pause. **Brace yourself.** Again, as in 38:3, God challenges Job to face head-on into the torrent of divine words. The difficult task for which Job is to prepare himself by girding his loins is not over yet. The use of the term *geber,* **man,** emphasizes the inequity between God and his human creations, who can only prepare themselves like human beings and not as God. **I will question . . . you shall answer.** The second interrogation begins.

Would you discredit my justice? With this question, God brings to the fore the crux of Job's focus on vindication for his own righteousness. It is impossible to understand the import of this statement without realizing that the question asks whether Job's desire for personal vindication is grounded in the same retribution theology that his friends have used to convict him. If so, then Job desires *what is his due* as a righteous man. And his claim to be righteous while suffering would "discredit" God's "justice." If Job is seeking the restoration of retributive cause and effect, then *the*

Satan's claim is true and humans do serve God for the benefits they receive. The subtlety of the question often goes unnoticed.

Would you condemn me? Job has nowhere questioned the right of God to allow the righteous to suffer. Job has come even to accept his own righteous suffering as inevitable. What Job seeks in this meeting is a public acknowledgement that he suffers as a righteous man, not as the just consequences of his sin. The claims of Job have little to do with the justice of God, but everything to do with the failure of retribution to accurately describe the world which God has made and over which he rules as sovereign. The justice of God fails only if one accepts retributive theology as defining the nature of the world. Job's own situation strongly establishes that this is *not* the case!

Would you do this, God asks, **to justify yourself?** Vindication is what Job seeks. He knows he is righteous and yet suffers. The implication of Job's desire for vindication in a world where retribution theology dominates is that for Job to be vindicated as right, God must be declared wrong. But is this what the narrator wishes to get across? Does he wish to say that Job is wrong and must repent? Have Job's words about God distorted the divine purposes and threatened to undermine divine justice? The answer is no clearer here than Job's own non-response was in the preceding verses. We will have to wait until the epilogue for the final resolution of this question.

Following the renewed challenge, the final examination continues with a rather sarcastic offer to allow Job to assume the responsibility for establishing justice in the world.

40:9–10 / **Do you have an arm like God's?** God's mighty "arm" is the means of unleashing his power into the world (Exod. 15:16; Deut. 4:34; 9:29; Job 35:9; Ps. 44:3). If Job had such power, then he might presume to judge the wicked and establish righteousness. The question, **can your voice thunder like his?**, reminds Job (and the reader) of the powerful demonstration of God's power in the storm theophany of the preceding chapters.

Then adorn yourself with glory and splendor. The two terms "glory and splendor" have more to do with exaltation and rising to the heights, perhaps suggesting that Job rise into the heavens while taking on storm attributes. Clearly God is calling Job to assume God's own role in the cosmos. The second half of the verse tells Job to put on the garments of **honor and majesty** reserved for God the king. These words remind Job that only God has the power and position to rule the world and those that live in it.

40:11–13 / **Unleash the fury of your wrath.** God's sarcasm is effective here. If Job had the power to act like God, surely it would be an easy matter for him to set things right in the world. From his vantage point in the heavens he could **look at every proud man** and easily render judgment. The verbs are imperatives, challenging Job to accomplish what God ought to have done. The subtler implication of these verses comes through. If the creation of justice in the world was a simple matter of knowledge and power, God has both in infinite abundance. The existence of innocent suffering in the world cannot be solely a matter of divine knowledge and power; God both knows and is able to respond. Thus any attempt at a resolution of this conundrum can only determine that the world in which God rules as the knowing and powerful sovereign is not just about justice; it is also—and perhaps primarily—about human freedom and undeserved grace.

The world that Job inhabits—the fallen world in which we also live today—is a world we are unable to manipulate to our advantage. Where would divine grace be if we were able to earn reward through our righteous behavior? Rather than a closed system of retribution, however, we face a world in which the wicked may prosper unpunished while the righteous suffer. In such a world, *the* Satan's question is of utmost importance: Can, or will, humans remain righteous for no profit? We are sometimes tempted to think we could do a better job than God in ruling the universe. We would know how and when to **humble** and **crush the wicked where they stand.** We could **bury them all in the dust together.** The fact is that we *cannot*, and God *does not*. This forces us to acknowledge the failure of a simple theology of retribution as an adequate explanation of the real world. It also forces us to rely on divine grace rather than trade on our own righteousness. The righteousness in which we *do* trust is the "righteousness of God" accomplished through the redeeming work of Jesus the Christ, who was willing to live the life of Job to its ultimate conclusion. He was willing to die while considered by friend and foe alike to be a fool, a blasphemer, even a criminal, powerless to save himself.

40:14 / **Then I myself will admit to you.** If humans could administer justice in the world by delivering to the wicked their just desserts, they would be praiseworthy indeed. The verb rendered "admit to you" (Heb. *ydh*) would be more accurately translated "praise." Here the subtle implication is ironic, since the God-human roles would be reversed with the divine praising the human. Even subtler still, the expression of divine praise suggests that the human desire to rule the universe is a way of making ourselves God. When our **own right hand can save** us, what need do we have for God?

§161 Beastly Behemoth (Job 40:15–24)

The examination by God concludes with extended consideration of two more of the larger, untamed beasts of God's creation: behemoth and leviathan. There is, perhaps, an attempt to be representative and inclusive with the choice of these two animals since one (behemoth, hippopotamus) is a land creature while the other (leviathan, the whale) inhabits the oceans. Some (see in particular Pope, *Job*, p. 339) suggest that these animals are mythological references to beasts of chaos, as the primeval seas in the Mesopotamian mythology. While God is able to rule over chaos, what hope does Job or any human have of doing so?

40:15 / The word for **behemoth** is the plural for the general Hebrew term *behemah*, beast—either wild or domesticated. This is the only place in the whole OT where the plural indicates a *single* beast. Some interpreters have identified the "behemoth" as the crocodile, primarily because of the water imagery in the verses. Currently, the term is most often understood to designate the hippopotamus, known to have populated the area of Palestine in the Iron Age. God reminds Job that humans are only one part of the creative work and concern of God—he made this creature **along with you.** Divine care extends to the animal world as well. The description of "behemoth" as an herbivore who **feeds on grass like an ox** would seem to fit the hippopotamus better than the crocodile.

40:16–18 / **What strength . . . what power!** These verses marvel over the strength of behemoth. While the **loins** may be the center of reproduction, here the reference seems to be to the physical strength of the beast the poet is considering. The hippopotamus is quite powerful, able to propel itself underwater by kicking its legs and even to run along the bottom of rivers or lakes! **His tail sways like a cedar.** The tail of the hippo is relatively small, leading some to suggest behemoth must be the elephant or water buffalo. Others interpret the word "sways" to mean "stiffen" instead, and claim that the tail of the hippopotamus stiffens when it runs or is frightened. The description **the sinews of his thighs are close-knit** suggests a stocky, compact animal more like the hippo than the elephant or water buffalo.

His bones are tubes of bronze. Again the metaphorical reference is to the strength of limb associated with behemoth. "Bronze" and **iron** are the two most common metals prized for their strength. Israel came into existence as a people at the transition point between the Bronze Age (3400–1200 B.C.) and the Iron Age (1200–500 B.C.), so both metals would have been known and used to make tools and weapons that needed to be strong.

40:19 / He ranks first among the works of God. This is perhaps a reference to the list of land beasts God created in Genesis 1:24, where cattle (*behemah*) is the first category to be mentioned. It is very difficult to make good sense of the second half of the verse, **yet his Maker can approach him with his sword.** The literal meaning is "and his maker will approach him his sword." Is God threatening behemoth with a "sword" for some reason, perhaps to prevent him from inhabiting the mountain regions in verse 20 (NJB)? Or is the sword a reference to the defensive tusks of the hippo and the meaning that God is able to approach the beast, while humans are too fearful?

40:20–23 / These verses depict the habitat and habit of behemoth. **The hills bring him their produce.** The hippo leaves the river at night and ranges up to six miles in search of vegetation. The verb rendered "bring" more literally means "raise up," so that NRSV reads "the mountains yield food." Since behemoth is an herbivore, **the wild animals play nearby** and have no reason to fear him as predator.

Under the lotus plants he lies. During the day the hippo populates the pools of the rivers, keeping moist and out of the sun since his skin easily dries out and cracks. If this were the crocodile, it seems the animals would have more to fear as he lurks in wait for his prey. The hippopotamus lies almost completely submerged, **hidden among the reeds** with his protuberant eyes above water. **The lotuses** and **poplars** provide shade from the sun.

When the river rages. The hippopotamus is very buoyant and quite a strong swimmer, so **he is not alarmed** by swift river currents but remains **secure.** The poet has **the Jordan** in mind as the location, although the abundant water and the "lotus" lead many to think of the River Nile instead.

40:24 / **Can anyone capture him?** The question returns to Job, regarding his power to control God's creation. Almost the only part of the hippo visible above water is **his eyes.** Placing a ring in the **nose** of a wild ox provides a means of controlling him. In some ways the hippopotamus looks like a heavy, aquatic ox. The question infers the impossibility of bringing such a unique and powerful wild beast under human control. In the larger, more metaphorical sense, Job (and the reader) is forced to admit that only God is able to bring order to the chaos that otherwise reigns in his creation.

Additional Notes §161

40:19 / **He ranks first among the works of God.** Some take the meaning of this to be one of prestige and use the term "masterpiece." See Murphy, p. 97.

Having returned to the question mode in 40:24, God now leaps rather unexpectedly to consider a second chaotic super beast—in this case the great sea creature, leviathan. This final examination occupies all of chapter 41—although in the Hebrew text (MT) these first eight verses are included at the end of the preceding chapter and numbered 40:25–32. While there is no obvious reason for this division of the text in the middle of the portrait of leviathan, the Greek LXX concurs with the Hebrew division.

41:1–2 / Various attempts to identify **leviathan** have been inconclusive. Both the whale and crocodile have been considered from the world of common animals, but the latter lacks the necessary association with the seas and oceans, while the description of ferocious teeth and armored scales (vv. 13–17) does not seem to fit the former. Certain aspects of the portrait of "leviathan"—both here and elsewhere in Scripture—point in the direction of a monstrous sea serpent associated with the defeat of chaotic waters and the institution of creation order. In Isaiah, "leviathan" is called "the gliding serpent (*nakhash beriakh*) . . . the coiling serpent (*nakhash ʿaqallaton*) . . . the monster of the sea (*tannin*)" (27:1). The Psalms associate "leviathan" with the sea (Ps. 104:26) and depict the sea monster (*tannim*), whose multiple heads God crushes in primordial battle (Ps. 74:13–14). The description in verses 18–21, of smoke and fire going forth from the beast's mouth, recalls images of fire-breathing dragons from the mythological lore of many nations.

Regardless of the identity of the beast, the purpose of the description is clear. This is a creature so powerful and fearsome that humans have no hope of destroying it or bringing it under their control. God, on the other hand, created this sea monster to frolic (Ps. 104:26) before him in the remote regions of the oceans rarely penetrated by humans. This description of "leviathan" continues the themes set forth in the earlier descriptions of the natural order. First, God's concern extends far beyond his *human* creation to unique, untamed creatures that inhabit the farthest reaches of the world, and that offer no utilitarian benefit for humans to exploit even if they could. Second, it is as impossible for humans to bind "leviathan" to fulfill human will as it is to capture and control God himself. Ultimately, "leviathan" is a powerful symbol to Job (and the reader) of a world (and a God!) outside human control.

Can you pull in . . . with a fishhook? The humor here is unmistakable, regardless of what animal is envisioned. The impotence of "a fishhook" against a whale or sea serpent is obvious. The poet vacillates between hunting and fishing imagery of capture and killing on the one hand, and domestication imagery of binding and exploitation of the beast's power on the other. The imagery depicted with the words **tie down his tongue with a rope** seems to suggest haltering an animal or bridling a horse to force compliance by pain applied to the tongue. As in 40:24, a ring or **cord** through a hole in the sensitive **nose** is a well-known way of controlling bulls and other bovines. The term for **hook** here is not the same as in verse 1. The term can mean a "thorn," or perhaps some prod used to control animals.

41:3–4 / The idea of such a fearsome creature submitting passively to human control and **begging . . . for mercy** is ludicrous. Stating the ridiculous opposite, **speak to you with gentle words,** ironically evokes the loud outrage that would erupt at such feeble attempts to capture and control "leviathan." **Will he make an agreement with you?** Here the Hebrew evokes covenant-making language to envision a mutual agreement between beast and human master. The Hebrew is *yikrot berit* [MT 40:28], "cut a covenant," which is standard terminology for "make a covenant." While a certain mutuality may develop between humans and the animals they put to labor, it should always be remembered that the animal's willingness to serve is no voluntary pact, but the result of coercive training and discipline (**your slave for life**). Even skilled trainers of elephants and large cats can find themselves dangerously vulnerable if the animal turns on them. The author is demonstrating the futility of humans exercising such coercive control over leviathan.

41:5–6 / The verb translated **make a pet of him** means to "make sport" or "laugh; amuse oneself." This term (Heb. *skhq* [MT 40:29]) describes the demeaning abuse of the blinded and (supposedly) weakened Samson by his Philistine enemies (Judg. 16:25). The word implies power on the part of the one who is amused to exploit the other for his or her amusement. A small animal **like a bird** that humans can hope to control stands in direct contrast to the untamed power of leviathan. To **put him on a leash** is to limit and control the activities of the animal. The phrase **for your girls** probably indicates the docility of the leashed animal.

Will traders barter . . . divide? To "divide" the beast suggests a different form of exploitation for gain: selling it as food, or perhaps using various valued portions of the beasts. Parts of powerful beasts are often sought-after commodities. Elephant tusks are prized for carving and the rhinoceros horn for its association with virility. The likelihood of turning a profit by subduing, dividing, and selling off parts of leviathan is remote!

41:7–8 / The usual implements for spearing sea creatures, **harpoons** and **fishing spears,** have no effect on the immense and well-armored leviathan. To engage this beast is to enter into a battle (Heb. *milkhamah* [MT 40:32]) one will never forget (**you will remember the struggle**) and will never repeat—possibly because one will not survive the first attempt!

41:9–11 / There is no **hope of subduing** this beast since the mere sight of it is **overpowering.** There may be an intentional parallel here with God and his theophanic appearance. Job has no more hope of "subduing" God, whose presence is far more overwhelming, than he does of "subduing" leviathan. In the face of such power, who would dare to **arouse** such a beast? In Job 3:8, Job refers to "those who are ready to arouse Leviathan" as those who are willing to pronounce curses that unleash chaos to destroy the order of creation. At that point, Job is ready to invoke such curses to end the suffering he experiences. Here, however, the poet realizes that such an act borders on nihilism that would uncreate the cosmos and all of human existence. **No one is fierce enough** (or *foolish* enough?) to take such a step.

Who then is able to stand against me? This half-verse and the next make the metaphorical connection with God explicit. If no human is fierce enough or foolish enough to take on leviathan, then why would anyone (like Job) take an even more futile stand against God? Is it possible for humans to encumber God with a debt, **a claim . . . that I must pay?** This seems to cast doubt on the idea of retribution that grounds the friends' theology. If human actions entail a particular response from God, then God would

seem to be under obligation to humans. Job, however, is not seeking repayment of a debt for his righteous actions; he desires public
vindication as a righteous man. Is this public declaration itself an
obligation that God "must pay"? These verses lead Job and the
reader to understand that God is free from such a cause and effect
relationship between human action and divine response. **Everything under heaven belongs to me.** Since everything in creation—
including humans and their actions—belongs to the creator, how
could God be obligated by any claims humans might make?

41:12 / This verse is difficult and has been taken two
ways: most often as a return to the description of leviathan or, less
frequently, as a condemnation of the one, from verses 10–11, who
would "stand against" God (see the discussion in Pope, *Job,* pp.
283–84). The crux of the problem is the term *bad* [MT 41:4] here
translated **his limbs** or "parts." Pope (and others) derives his interpretation from a cognate form that means "loose talk; boasting"
and assumes divine rejection of boastful human talk. As it is clear
by verse 13 that the description has returned to leviathan, it seems
preferable to follow the common view as in NIV. As Hartley mentions, God's creation of leviathan—no matter how fearsome—
combines a balance of power and grace.

41:13–14 / **Who can . . . Who dares?** The rhetorical questioning presumes that *no one* is able to encounter and subdue leviathan so as to **strip off his outer coat** or armored scales. The
second half of this verse is variously translated, depending on
the interpretation of the Hebrew phrase *bekepel risno* [MT 41:5],
which is here rendered **bridle.** The term *kepel,* however, means
"doubled"—a term that is less than clear coupled with "bridle."
Some take this combination to be a reference to some sort of
"double bit" or "doubled reins." Others, following the LXX, assume
a transposition of letters and read *kepel siryono,* "his double-armor."
This possibility requires more questionable reinterpretation of the
verb *yabo*ᵓ, "enter; come," to mean "penetrate; pierce" (NASB; NRSV;
NJB). Because **his fearsome teeth** are a deterrent to any who would
attack leviathan, none dare **open the doors of his mouth.**

41:15–17 / These verses describe the armored scales that
protect leviathan's **back.** The hardened scales are like **shields
tightly sealed together** so that not even **air can pass between**
them. These scales **are joined** so closely to one another that they

cannot be separated. Leviathan is thus rendered impervious to attack by sword or spear.

41:18–21 / Here we see leviathan in dragon-like terms. Fire imagery dominates, with references to **flashes of light, firebrands, sparks, smoke, coals,** and **flames.** These rush from leviathan's **mouth** and **nostrils,** fanned by **his snorting** and **his breath.** The picture is clearly of an incredible, raging beast, beyond human comprehension or control. Yet this is a creature that God created— for purposes only he can imagine!

41:22–25 / **Strength** associated with the **neck** would seem more characteristic of the ox or bull than a crocodile or whale. A coiled serpent or dragon, however, might fit this description. There is some question whether it is **dismay** or "vigor" that precedes (lit., "dances") before leviathan. A sort of balance between verses 22 and 25, where the opponents of leviathan **are terrified** and **retreat,** suggests that "dismay" may be the correct reading.

The folds of his flesh. This once again emphasizes the impenetrable nature of leviathan's skin. There is no weak spot to allow access to vulnerable spots. The **chest** is hardly a concern for the low-slung crocodile, but the chest of a coiled serpent preparing to strike is exposed to attack. There is no vulnerability here, however, because leviathan's chest is **hard as a lower millstone.** As a result **the mighty** (lit., "gods") "are terrified," since their weapons have no effect. Their only recourse is to "retreat."

41:26–29 / These verses list various weapons that are useless against leviathan's impregnable defenses—**sword, spear, dart, javelin, arrows, slingstones, club,** and **lance.** The strongest metals used to make weapons—**iron** and **bronze**—are like **straw** or **rotten wood** to leviathan. "Slingstones" create as much damage as lightweight, airborne **chaff.** Confronted by all these pretensions of human power, leviathan is unconcerned and **laughs.** Leviathan's lack of concern reminds us of God's own derision in response to the grumbling conspiracy of the nations in Psalm 2:4.

41:30–32 / The rough armor of leviathan is like **jagged potsherds** and gouges a deep **trail in the mud** as he slides along. The motion of leviathan through the sea causes the water to **churn like a boiling caldron** and leaves a **glistening wake** that resembles the **white hair** of the elderly.

41:33–34 / **Nothing on earth is his equal.** No animal or human in God's creation is able to match leviathan's invulnerable strength. As a result, he is **without fear.** When he surveys **all that are haughty** (or "those who are exalted") he finds none to compare, because **he is king** by virtue of his invincible power. Similarly, **all that are proud**—including Job and all humans—shrink before leviathan. Certainly this description turns Psalm 8, with its awed reverie on the divine gift of power over the created order to humans, on its head. Any such pride as might develop from an uncritical reading of Psalm 8 must come to grips with the clear message of Job 38–41. Humans are able to exercise little control over the world in which they live.

The theophany concludes rather abruptly, without any attempt at summation. There is only the brief intrusion in 41:10b–11 referring directly to the issue that Job's claims raises before Job's final reply in chapter 42. The theophany has clearly made the point, however, that God remains fully in control of the universe he created. His purposes and concerns are often beyond human knowing, and they certainly are not exclusively focused on humans and their benefit. The world is larger than Job and his friends ever imagined, but this realization emphasizes God's immensity and power even more. The book turns now to consider how Job responds to this experience of God.

Additional Notes §162

41:30 / The **mud** here can be the mire left behind in a well (Jer. 38:6), or the wet clay trod upon by the potter to mix it (Isa. 41:25).

§163 Job's Final Concession (42:1–6)

Job's final words provide a more satisfying response to the theophany than his earlier *non*-speech in 40:3–5. There Job essentially refused to say anything more than he had uttered in the dialogue section. We were left with no clue as to how the appearance of God had affected or changed him. Job is now apparently ready to say his piece in response to God, suggesting that the poetic discourses are reaching their conclusion.

42:1 / **Then Job replied to the LORD.** The introduction to Job's response employs the formula characteristic of the theophany section and relates back to the conversation between God and *the* Satan in the prose prologue. The fact that in this case there is no divine query inviting Job's response (as there was in 40:1–2) is probably significant. On the one hand, Job supplies a sort of recollection of the earlier divine questions to which he now responds (verses 3a, 4). On the other, the absence of the divine interrogation at this point suggests that Job's words in both chapters are actually part of a single, unified response to God's appearance. The first *non*-response serves as a literary delay to break the ceaseless flow of divine words and provides a reflective pause for both Job and the reader. Further, Job's reticence perhaps suggests a subtle change in the normally pugnacious and vociferous Job. Also, as we have seen in the discussion of the new formulas of response this section employs (see the discussion in §142), the positioning of Job's responses in chapters 40 and 42 allows Job's words to bracket the speech of God before, in the middle, and after the divine has spoken. God has come in response to Job and graciously allows Job to have the final word in their conversation.

42:2 / **I know that you can do all things.** This is not a departure from Job's previous attitude. Job has assumed all along that God is capable of acting to end his undeserved suffering (and injustice in general!). It is the fact that the Almighty *allows* a righteous man to suffer without public acknowledgment of his righteousness that exercises Job. So this is a *reaffirmation* of faith in God's sovereign power. Job acknowledges that God has a **plan** that he actively pursues. The world is not a place of happenstance or willy-nilly chance. Humans may not understand God's purposes, but that does not mean he does not have any. God remains sovereign and cannot be **thwarted.** But this statement is so much more than an admission of defeat and failure to sway God. The true implication of these words is that the suffering that Job has experienced must fall within the divine purposes of God. Of course, we already know the purpose that lies behind Job's innocent suffering. It has been a test in response to *the* Satan's question regarding the willingness of any human to fear God without profit. We are about to learn—as Job himself must already have learned—that it is indeed possible to do just that. Job (and other humans) can continue to fear God for no profit, even when the profit is no more than public recognition of the righteous character of the one who suffers.

42:3 / *You asked.* The italics (added) indicate that these words are not in the original Hebrew but have been supplied interpretively to clarify who originally spoke these words. **"Who is this that obscures my counsel without knowledge?"** The question is a near quote of God's opening question at the beginning of the theophany (38:2), differing only in the substitution of the participle *ma'lim* for the earlier participle *makhshik* and the omission of the phrase "with words" toward the end of the sentence. Both participles are usually understood as synonyms, meaning "make dark; obscure," although the replacement here in verse 3 may be a bit stronger: "conceal; hide." The recollection of the divine question links Job's second response to the first so that the two are not separate but unified.

I spoke of things I did not understand. Job acknowledges that a lack of understanding hampered his ability to speak of God and his relation to the world *before* the theophany. The implication is that the appearance of God in chapters 38–41 has supplied the knowledge necessary for a new and deeper understanding. Yet Job's new appreciation of God does *not* constitute *complete* understanding. What God is about in the world is **too wonderful** for any human to **know,** even by direct experience.

42:4 / *You said.* Once again the italics (added) indicate that this phrase is not in the original Hebrew but is interpretively supplied to suggest this is a quote from God, parallel to that just above in verse 3a. **Listen now, and I will speak.** The problem is that nowhere in the book does God speak these words to Job. When God confronts Job in 38:3b he speaks the words in the second half of the verse, **I will question you, and you shall answer me,** but this first phrase is not found on God's lips. The words are similar to Job's statement in 13:22 that God should "summon me and I will answer, or let me speak, and you [God!] reply." It may be that, rather than quoting God in this initial phrase, Job is recalling his earlier certainty that God would have to respond in words that would confirm Job's expectations—expectations based on what has now proved to be severely limited knowledge.

"I will question you, and you shall answer me" does repeat the essence of God's initial confrontation with Job in 38:3b. There this statement ironically anticipates Job's utter inability to "instruct" God (a better translation of the Hebrew *hodiʿeni,* "cause me to know") concerning the operation of the creation. Now, having had direct experience of God and of "things too wonderful" for Job to know (v. 3), Job is ready to admit his limited understanding and the futility of his demand that God reply to his complaint (13:22). God has replied, but even so, the answer so far exceeds Job's expectations that it remains beyond human understanding.

42:5 / **My ears had heard of you.** Having now seen God face-to-face, so to speak, Job realizes how all his former knowledge of God approached unsubstantiated hearsay. Job knew *about* God previously, **but now my eyes have seen you.** He now has direct experience of the creator. That knowledge, as set forth in chapters 38–41, is entirely overwhelming and has demonstrated once and for all that God is beyond complete human knowing. We must be careful not to assume, however, that God remains a complete mystery to Job. From his experience Job now knows a number of things about God: God is sovereign and just. God is concerned with all of creation, not just humanity. God's purposes and plans for humanity and the world are often mysterious and beyond human knowing. Nowhere has God attempted to refute Job's claims that the world as God maintains it does not correspond neatly to the closed, cause and effect theology of retribution.

42:6 / **Therefore.** Job grounds his response in this verse on the face-to-face experience of God he has just described. **I despise myself.** The meaning of the Hebrew here is much debated and variously translated. First, "myself" is not in the Hebrew text but reflects the interpretive conclusion of the NIV translators. The Hebrew verb (*m' s*) means "refuse" or "reject," and translators have typically gone one of two ways in rendering it. One way is to assume, with NIV, that Job is rejecting *himself*—possibly because of some wrong he now perceives in himself as a result of the divine encounter (NIV; NRSV). The other approach is to translate the verb as "retract" (NASB; NJB), understanding that Job is now withdrawing some earlier statement or understanding that he wants to correct in light of his new experience.

The interpretation of the phrase **repent in dust and ashes** depends largely on how one has translated the first part of the verse. If Job is taken to "despise himself," then usually he is said to "repent." The verb *nkhm* can mean this, and it often does. But it can also mean to "change one's mind." Such a rendering does not require that Job has committed some sin of which he needs to repent. Rather, he needs to understand God in a new way because his old perceptions have changed. Those who take the repentance route must come up with some sin that Job has committed. Often this sin is pride, or at least the danger of pride (Hartley, *Job*, p. 536). It seems to me that what Job changes his mind about is his desire for personal vindication. His new understanding of God practically obliterates any need for a public declaration of his innocence. It is enough for him to stand in right relationship with this sovereign God, who is so far beyond human knowing. If *the* Satan's question whether it is possible to fear God for no profit is the driving concern behind the book, as I have suggested, then it would seem that Job's change here provides the definitive answer. Job is willing to fear God even if he is never publicly vindicated as a righteous man. He has given up all claims to any profit at all in his relationship with God.

Additional Notes §163

42:3 / Some recommend removing the phrase in 42:3a, **"Who is this ... knowledge?"** altogether as a scribal addition (e.g., Gordis, *Job*, p. 492).

§164 Excursus: The Epilogue: Resetting the Clock (Job 42:7–17)

Once Job withdraws his demand for vindication at the end of 42:6 we have come, in a very real sense, to the end of the book. The text shifts from poetry back to the prose of the prologue. The prose narrative continues to the end of the chapter and the book. The concluding epilogue exhibits elements that tie it back both to the prologue and to the poetic dialogues. Both prologue and epilogue discuss Job's blessings in very similar terms: reputation, money, herds, and progeny (42:10–15). As the poetic dialogue, the epilogue also refers to Job's *three* friends (it nowhere mentions or even alludes to Elihu) and to their conflict of words about God (42:7–9).

At the end of the epilogue, Job receives from God twice the possessions he lost in the prologue. This turn of events has led many to note the apparent conflict between the rejection of retribution in the poetic section and its affirmation in the concluding events of the epilogue. There are three important issues we need to recognize in regard to this apparent conflict that are essential for understanding the message of the book as a whole. First, we need to realize that Job definitively answers the foundational question of *the* Satan—whether humans can fear God without profit—when he retracts his desire for vindication at the end of 42:6. Remember, Job has no way of knowing that God will restore his fortunes and family when he makes that retraction. His decision is unadulterated submission without any expectation of profit. What happens in the epilogue cannot undermine Job's free decision here.

Second, we need to recognize that God's decision to restore the fortunes of Job need *not* be related in a cause and effect way with Job's retraction. What the poetic section—and in particular the theophany chapters (38–41)—has demonstrated about God is that he is a *free agent* whose activities are beyond human control and influence. Thus, Job's statement in response to his initial loss of wealth, property, and family—"The LORD gave and the LORD has taken away" (1:21)—is equally true in reverse. If God chooses to restore Job, it is certainly within his sovereign power to do so.

Finally, it is important to note that the restoration of Job's circumstances relates closely to the nature of Job's loss and suffering as a *test*. When God tests Abraham by commanding him to sacrifice his only son, Isaac, God restores that son to Abraham once he passes the test (Gen. 22:1–18). So here the restoration of Job's family and possessions are part of the test story formula. In a sense, the epilogue simply sets the clock back to the pre-test circumstances. Thus, in my opinion, the epilogue events have *nothing* to say about retribution theology. The author has already set forth full commentary on retribution in the poetic sections of the book.

§165 Intercession for the Three Friends (Job 42:7–9)

42:7 / **After the LORD had said these things to Job.** This phrase connects back to the formula that introduced the theophany in 38:1. As there, this phrase makes clear to the reader that the divine interrogation in chapters 38–41 addresses Job—and not Elihu, whose speeches immediately precede God's appearance. This editorial comment also links the prose epilogue to the theophany and demonstrates a purposeful movement to unify the various segments of the book. Stating the obvious in this way—"After the LORD had said"—has the effect of emphasizing the disjuncture between the final statement of Job in verse 6 and the subsequent events of the epilogue. The restoration of Job, therefore, cannot undermine the critique of retribution that is so fundamental to the poetic core of the book. Since this rebuke of the friends took place *after* Job's submission, he could not have known God's evaluation of him before he changed. Thus the disinterested nature of his decision is preserved.

The words **he said to Eliphaz the Temanite** make the explicit link between the epilogue and the dialogue cycle. God singles out Eliphaz, the first of the three friends to speak there, as the representative of the group. **I am angry with you.** The initial reference to "you" is masculine singular, reflecting God's address to Eliphaz. But God's anger extends to the other friends as well: **and your two friends.** Note here that they are called "friends" of Eliphaz and not Job, perhaps revealing the author's evaluation of the hostility of their comments towards Job. Note further that God does not include Elihu in this divine rebuke, a fact that leads many to assume his monologues are a late addition to the poetic portion of the book. Whether this absence of reference means that God intentionally excludes Elihu from this critique is not clear. But we need to remember that the actual appearance of God in the theophany has already nullified Elihu's primary claim: that God would not respond to Job because he had already revealed his judgment through the suffering Job was experiencing.

The **because** here introduces the reason for the divine expression of displeasure with Job's three friends. God says, **you have not spoken of me what is right.** Here the subject "you" is masculine plural, clearly implicating all three friends. Where have the three friends "spoken" of God other than in the dialogue? The obvious inference is that God now declares what the friends claimed in opposition to Job to be "not right." The term "right" is the Hebrew *nekonah*, "established as correct" and not *tsaddiq*, "righteous." This rebuke of the friends over against **my servant Job** *does not* amount to a subtle reverse declaration of Job's righteousness. It is not the public vindication of his innocent suffering Job sought, but a confirmation that the view of God Job articulated during the dialogue is an accurate portrayal of divine reality, while the friends' words lead astray. Thus we must always be careful how we use the friends' words to inform our worldview, since they have been declared inaccurate representations of God. As much as we might be tempted to pull nuggets out of the verbal mother lode of the friends' speeches, this verse cautions us that God himself has weighed these words and found them wanting.

God affirms Job's words, but he never validates Job's claims of righteousness. Thus, even after surrendering his hope in his retraction, Job never receives vindication. Despite all of the restoration that *does* take place in the end for Job, the epilogue does not return to the prologue's oft-repeated evaluation of Job as *tam weyashar*, "blameless and upright" (1:1, 8; 2:3).

42:8 / The **sacrifice** of **seven bulls and seven rams** is an incredibly expensive one that only the wealthiest could afford to offer. The number "seven" indicates completeness and efficacy (see Num. 23:1, 4, 29, where Balaam three times offers up an equivalent sacrifice in his attempt to curse Israel). **My servant Job.** Elsewhere, the book only describes Job as God's "servant" in God's conversation with *the* Satan in the prologue. Here, verses 7–8 repeat the phrase four times to emphasize Job's status and his acceptance by God. Despite his complaint, Job remains the "servant" of God. The primary purpose of the ʿolah, **burnt offering,** described here is to remove the sin of the offerer. Thus, not only were the friends' words wrong, but they also need to be restored to God.

My servant Job will pray for you. This is, of course, the ultimate irony—the friends' restoration to God is dependent on the intercession of the one they had condemned as a sinner! **I will accept his prayer.** Job's prayer will be efficacious in removing the friends' sin and restoring their relationship to God. God designates the friends' misleading speech as **folly.** This is not simply thoughtless, uninformed, or frivolous speech. "Folly" in the OT always has a willful edge to it, rejecting the purposes of God—thus the fool is culpable for failure to fear God rightly and follow his path. It seems here, therefore, that the friends fall under the judgment of sin because they promulgate a distorted worldview and use that view to condemn innocent sufferers as sinful persons. This is an instructive warning for us all! **You have not spoken . . . what is right.** The rebuke of the friends in verse 7 opened with this same phrase. Its reappearance here emphasizes the failing of the friends, while God reaffirms Job's words as **right** and Job as his **servant.**

42:9 / **Eliphaz the Temanite, Bildad the Shuhite and Zophar the Naamathite.** The reference to all three friends (but *not* Elihu!) makes it clear that each of them is the recipient of the divine word of rebuke. The friends respond in repentance, **did what the LORD told them,** and God restores them because **the LORD accepted Job's prayer.** These are important steps, both to clarify the misleading nature of the friends' arguments about God and also to restore the essential state of things before the test began. Now both Job and the friends will experience restoration.

Additional Notes §165

42:8 / **Seven bulls and seven rams.** The daily sacrifices required in Ezek. 45:22–25 are the same as here, while Lev. 4 requires fewer beasts. The passage in Ezekiel is probably indicating a perfection of sacrifice and its efficacy in the restored and purified temple.

§166 The Restoration of Job (Job 42:10–15)

42:10–11 / **After Job had prayed for his friends.** "After" here (as in v. 7) does not establish a causal link between Job's prayer and the restoration of his prosperity, as if God rewards Job for his gracious intercession for his friends. Rather, this temporal conjunction again emphasizes the important fact that Job acts as intercessor without any knowledge of the ultimate restoration that he would experience. Here we see again the disinterested character of Job's submission and intercession.

With **the LORD made him prosperous again,** at last we have it—God restores Job. The Hebrew actually says something like, "God overturned the captivity of Job," with the meaning "restored his circumstances." There is no explicit reference to prosperity here, although that becomes clear in the following verses. While God **gave him twice as much,** it is important to remember that there is no tit-for-tat retribution at work here. The narrative has already removed that possibility. So the double blessing Job receives cannot be the result of some increased value God places on Job and his faithful submission to God. Nor is it some attempt to assuage divine guilt over the undeserved suffering of Job. The restoration comes not because Job earned it, but because the whole event has been a test and the test formula consistently results in the restoration of the one tested. The restoration, in a sense, resets the clock back to the pre-test situation. Since God established his freedom in the theophany and Job confirmed it in his concession, the double portion can only be the consequence of God's freedom and grace. God is not required by any sort of divine retributive mathematics to restore to Job the precise number of possessions he had at the beginning—such an act would have suggested that amount of possessions was Job's *due.* So here God's free grace allows him to bless Job with even more than he had before—twice as much indeed.

All his brothers and sisters and everyone who had known him before. We have not heard about these brothers and sisters before, and we might wonder where they were during the mourning period. But the point of the narrative is that Job's reputation is restored so that all of his former acquaintances, who had shrunk from association and avoided him, are now restored to fellowship. Job's isolation on the refuse heap is ended. In the ancient world, table fellowship indicates the deepest intimacy: they **ate with him in his house.** This is another evidence of the completeness of Job's restoration. **They comforted and consoled him.** The memory of suffering is still fresh and mourning continues, but Job now stands in the midst of a supportive family and community. It is clear from the statement **over all the trouble the LORD had brought upon him** that the narrator understands that God is the active force behind Job's suffering. *The* Satan is no opposing force acting contrary to the will of God but functions always with divine permission. The consolation of Job's friends suggests that while they attribute his suffering to God, they no longer have suspicions regarding his righteous character. Thus the restoration at the end does amount to the kind of public vindication that Job desired. But this vindication only takes place *after* Job chooses to continue to fear God regardless, whether he is vindicated or not. The restoration of Job's financial fortune begins with the acknowledgment of his restored reputation and associations: **each one gave him a piece of silver and a gold ring.**

42:12–13 / **The LORD blessed the latter part of Job's life more than the first.** God's blessing of Job is abundant *and free.* There is no causal link here other than the gracious care of God for his servant. We have learned that the servants of God may suffer horrendously (as Job has) without giving up their claim to righteousness. Job does not earn this final blessing but receives it freely—and it is freely given.

A quick comparison of the numbers of Job's livestock before and after the test reveals the doubling of his herds in every instance (e.g., **fourteen thousand sheep**). God pours out his grace in abundance. This is not simply restoration, but even greater blessing than before. **And he also had seven sons and three daughters.** The pattern of double blessing is broken when it comes to Job's children—he is given the same number of sons and daughters as before. Perhaps this is because there is an element of perfection linked to "seven sons"—how can one improve on perfection? On the other hand, the balance seems to acknowledge that no number of children could ever compensate for those lost. And so Job receives back the number of children he had before and no more.

The loss of Job's children—over the loss of his herds and servants and possessions—is certainly the harshest aspect of the narrative and raises the question of innocent suffering in its own right. While the question is certainly worth pursuing theologically, we must accept that the book of Job is never interested in the question of innocent suffering. Since we know from the outset that Job is blameless and that his suffering is a test of his faithfulness, the book never addresses the question of why the innocent suffer. Similarly, the loss of Job's children is understood as a necessary part of testing Job's faith to the utmost.

42:14–15 / **The first daughter he named Jemimah.** The naming of the daughters (and not the sons!) is unusual, as is the extended discussion of their beauty and inheritance. "Jemimah" means "dove," or "turtledove," a bird known for its grace and beauty (Song 2:14). **Keziah** refers to the perfume derived from *kassia,* a variety of cinnamon. **Keren-Happuch,** "horn of kohl," is a container of eye makeup used to highlight the eyes. As Pope (*Job,* p. 292) puts it, "The names of Job's daughters represent natural feminine physical and spiritual charms enhanced by perfumer's and beautician's art." The reference to these daughters' unparalleled beauty and their unusual inheritance indicates that Job's prosperity was so great that he had sufficient wealth to ease the lives of his daughters as well as his sons. Thus Job's beautiful and prosperous daughters would be attractive partners with an assured future.

Additional Notes §166

42:13 / Gordis (*Job,* pp. 496–98) and Pope (*Job,* p. 291) take the unusual form of the numeral "seven (sons)" as a possible dual form meaning "twice seven" and suggest that Job does receive back fourteen sons. The Aramaic Targum agrees.

42:14–15 / See the narrative in Num. 27 of the five daughters of Zelophehad who inherited because their father had no sons.

§167 The Death of Job, Full of Years
(Job 42:16–17)

42:16–17 / After this, Job lived a hundred and forty years.
There is some discussion regarding the total years of Job's life. The
LXX states that Job lived 170 years "after the affliction" and totals his
life at 240 years, meaning that he was seventy years old at the beginning of his suffering. Pope (*Job*, p. 293) theorizes that seventy
years *before* the suffering were increased by seventy years afterwards, as part of the doubling pattern employed in the final blessing of his possessions. Gordis (*Job*, p. 499) believes that Job was "in
the prime of life" when he began suffering but sees no reason to limit
Job's total life to 140 years. Regardless, Job's long life serves as an additional confirmation of his righteousness (Deut. 6:2; 22:7; Ps. 91:16).

Job **saw his children . . . to the fourth generation.** Job's lin-
eage was insured—and not cut off, as the destruction of his family
at the beginning of the book had threatened. His long life enabled
him to experience the blessing of his progeny.

And so he died, old and full of years. Job did die—he was
only mortal after all. But his death came not only after a *long* life,
but after a satisfied one as well. The term translated "full" is the
Hebrew verb *sbᶜ*, "sated; satisfied." The narrative of Job comes to
an end not in suffering, but in satisfaction. In the free will and purpose of God, such blessings can—and often do—come to the righteous. The world is, after all, a broken place beset with evil and
pain. The righteous cannot hope to avoid all suffering and pain in
this life, but they can rest assured, on the testimony of Job, that
God is sovereign over all that he has made. His concern extends to
the ends of the earth—even beyond humans to the unique and
unknown creatures he has made. And for Job there is satisfaction
in seeing this God, satisfaction that is more important than any
wealth, pleasure, and personal vindication that this world can
contain. This God, says Job, is even worth dying for, penniless,
bereft of friends and family, and reviled as a sinner! Aren't we glad
that the incarnate Word of God felt the same about us?

For Further Reading

Commentaries on Job

Clines, D. J. A. *Job 1–20*. Word Biblical Commentary. Nashville: Nelson, 1990.
———. *Job 21–37*. Word Biblical Commentary. Nashville: Nelson, 2006.
Gordis, R. *The Book of Job*. New York: Jewish Theological Seminary, 1978.
Habel, N. C. *The Book of Job: A Commentary*. Old Testament Library. Philadelphia: Westminster John Knox, 1985.
Hartley, J. *Job*. New International Commentary on the Old Testament. Grand Rapids: Eerdmans, 1988.
Holladay, W. L. *A Concise Hebrew and Aramaic Lexicon of the Old Testament*. Grand Rapids: Eerdmans, 1971.
Murphy, R. E. *The Book of Job: A Short Reading*. New York: Paulist, 1999.
Pope, M. H. *Job*. Anchor Bible. Garden City: Doubleday, 1965.
Rowley, H. H. *Job*. New Century Bible. New Series. Greenwood, S.C.: Attic, 1970.
Terrien, S. "Job: Introduction and Exegesis." Pages 877–905 in vol. 3 of *Interpreter's Bible*. Edited by G. A. Buttrick. 12 vols. Nashville: Abingdon, 1954.
Tur-Sinai, N. H. *The Book of Job: A New Commentary*. Rev. ed. Jerusalem: Kiryat Sepher, 1967.
Whybray, N. *Job*. Readings: A New Biblical Commentary. Sheffield: Sheffield Academic Press, 1998.

Other Works

Albright, W. F. "The Names Shaddai and Abram." *Journal of Biblical Literature* 54 (1935), pp. 173–93.
Dahood, M. *Psalms II: 51–100*. Anchor Bible. New York: Random House, 1968.
Magallanes, S. A. "The Hymn to Wisdom as an Utterance of Job." M.A.R. thesis, Azusa Pacific University, 2004.
Pritchard, J. B., ed. *The Ancient Near East: An Anthology of Texts and Pictures*. Princeton: Princeton University Press, 1958.
Wilson, G. H. "Orientation." Page 615 in vol. 3 of *International Standard Bible Encyclopedia*. Edited by G. W. Bromiley. 4 vols. Grand Rapids: Eerdmans, 1986.
———. "The Structure of the Psalter: Theological Implications of Shape and Shaping." Pages 229–46 in *Interpreting the Psalms: Issues and Approaches*. Edited by D. G. Firth and P. S. Johnston. Downers Grove, Ill.: InterVarsity, 2005.

Subject Index

Scripture Index

Old Testament

Genesis **1**, 253, 306, 429; **1:2**, 132, 285, 286, 306, 428; **1:4**, 286; **1:21**, 70; **1:24**, 457; **1:25–30**, 57; **1:26**, 445; **2**, 57; **2:2**, 360; **2:7**, 68, 106, 108, 271, 364, 370, 387, 414; **2:15**, 440; **2:19**, 57; **2:21**, 374; **3:1**, 57, 111; **3:14**, 57; **3:17–19**, 355; **3:19**, 106, 271; **4:10**, 182, 356; **6–8**, 57; **6–9**, 86, 88; **6:3**, 108, 149, 151; **6:10–13**, 182; **6:11–13**, 204, 238; **7:22**, 414; **8:2**, 428; **9**, 57; **9:2**, 57; **10:23**, 20; **11:10–26**, 151; **14:8**, 142; **16:2**, 37; **18:11**, 147; **19:24**, 199; **20:18**, 37; **22**, 19; **22:1–18**, 470; **22:21**, 20; **24:16**, 335; **29:31**, 37; **30:22**, 37; **31:36**, 145; **36:10–11**, 33; **36:11**, 448; **36:15**, 448; **36:22**, 448; **36:28**, 20; **37**, 374; **38**, 199, 242; **38:9**, 179; **40–41**, 374; **41**, 17, 161; **42:23**, 182; **46:4**, 97; **49:10**, 98; **50:10**, 34

Exodus **1:14**, 370; **3:2**, 247; **3:20**, 24; **5:2**, 227; **6:2–3**, 57; **7:3**, 186; **9:9–11**, 31; **9:15**, 24; **12:26**, 228; **13:21**, 247; **15:16**, 454; **16:20**, 281; **16:24**, 281; **16:28**, 195; **19:16–24**, 424; **19:18**, 247; **20:5**, 228; **20:10**, 206; **20:12**, 206; **20:18–21**, 408; **20:20**, 19, 311, 419; **21:20**, 98; **21:30**, 377; **22:2**, 274; **22:25–27**, 242, 269; **23:1**, 97; **23:10–11**, 354; **24:17**, 247; **25:4**, 281; **26:34–35**, 354; **27:20**, 114; **28:3**, 419; **30:12**, 377; **30:34**, 114; **33:18–33**, 14, 413; **34:6–7**, 231; **34:7**, 228, 231

Leviticus **4**, 473; **18:17**, 340; **19:19**, 356; **19:27–28**, 28; **19:29**, 340; **20:14**, 340; **24:3**, 142; **25:25**, 210; **26:30**, 349

Numbers **1:3**, 66; **6:24–26**, 322; **6:25**, 104; **11:1–3**, 247; **12:14**, 327; **14:11**, 195; **14:18**, 228, 231; **15:39–40**, 79; **16:35**, 247; **16:48**, 133; **22–24**, 36; **23:1**, 472; **23:4**, 472; **23:29**, 472; **24:17**,

98; **27**, 476; **29:36**, 20; **31:14**, 66; **35:31**, 377

Deuteronomy **2:34**, 270; **4:9–10**, 228; **4:10**, 106; **4:11–15**, 247; **4:23**, 79; **4:24**, 247; **4:31**, 79; **4:34**, 454; **5:1**, 79; **5:9**, 228; **5:14**, 206; **5:15**, 79; **6:2**, 477; **6:3–12**, 79; **6:4**, 381; **6:10–11**, 218; **6:12**, 79; **7:5**, 247; **7:18**, 79; **7:25**, 247; **8:2**, 79; **8:11**, 79; **8:18**, 79; **8:19**, 79; **9:7**, 79; **9:29**, 454; **11:17**, 133; **11:19**, 228; **14:1**, 28; **14:28–29**, 243; **16:11**, 206; **16:14**, 206; **17:2–7**, 349; **22:7**, 477; **24:6**, 242; **24:16**, 228; **24:17**, 65, 243; **24:19–21**, 65; **25:4**, 270; **25:5–10**, 199; **25:9**, 329; **26:12–13**, 243; **27:19**, 65, 243; **28**, 276; **28:27–28**, 31; **28:29**, 281; **29:9**, 356; **29:23**, 199; **31:17**, 145; **32:20**, 145; **32:33**, 331; **32:39**, 103; **33:2**, 102

Joshua **2:1**, 89; **2:3**, 89; **6:17**, 89; **6:23**, 89; **6:25**, 89; **17:16–18**, 302; **18:3**, 195; **22:12**, 66; **22:23**, 66; **24:13**, 218

Judges **1:19**, 302; **2:20**, 88; **4:3**, 302; **4:13**, 302; **5:14**, 98; **5:16**, 117; **7:9–15**, 374; **12:3**, 140; **16:25**, 461; **18:2**, 117; **20:6**, 340; **21:22**, 336

Ruth **2:2**, 343; **2:7**, 343; **2:15–16**, 343

1 Samuel **2:1**, 180; **2:8**, 427; **2:10**, 180; **4:2**, 142; **6:5**, 28; **12:3**, 377; **13:19–22**, 302; **15:24**, 88; **17:7**, 302; **18–31**, 269; **19:5**, 140; **20:12**, 117; **26:12**, 374; **28:1**, 66; **28:21**, 140; **31:13**, 34

2 Samuel **1:11**, 28; **6:8**, 179; **7:14**, 98; **10:3**, 117; **12:1**, 20; **14:7**, 376; **17:29**, 218; **18:33**, 149; **22:12**, 410; **22:28**, 278; **22:29**, 312; **23:21**, 98; **24:1**, 25; **24:25**, 133